THE GOALKEEPER

\> \> \> \> \> \>

THE GOALKEEPER

THE NABOKOV ALMANAC

Edited by Yuri Leving

Boston
2010

Publication was made possible through the generous support of the Department of Russian Studies, Faculty of Arts and Social Sciences, Dalhousie University

Excerpts from the works of Vladimir Nabokov by special arrangement with the Estate of Vladimir Nabokov.
All rights reserved.

Library of Congress Cataloging-in-Publication Data

The goalkeeper : the Nabokov almanac / edited by Yuri Leving.
    p. cm.
Includes bibliographical references.
ISBN 978-1-61811-830-1
1. Nabokov, Vladimir Vladimirovich, 1899-1977—Criticism and interpretation. I. Leving, IUrii.
PS3527.A15Z715 2010
813'.54—dc22
                    2010038364

Copyright © 2010 Academic Studies Press
All rights reserved

Book design by Ivan Grave

Published by Academic Studies Press in 2010
28 Montfern Avenue
Brighton, MA 02135, USA
press@academicstudiespress.com
www.academicstudiespress.com

EDITORIAL BOARD

Editor
Yuri Leving (*Dalhousie University*)

Associate Editor
Nassim W. Balestrini
    (*University of Regensburg*)

Associate Editor for Reviews
Andrei Rogatchevski (*University of Glasgow*)

Editorial Assistant
Olga Gurin (*Independent Scholar*)

Editorial Board
John Barnstead (*Dalhousie University*)
Stephen Blackwell (*University of Tennessee*)
Brian Boyd (*The University of Auckland, New Zealand*)
Alexander Dolinin (*University of Wisconsin-Madison*)
Donald Barton Johnson
    (*University of California*, Santa Barbara)
Georgy Levinton (*European University, St. Petersburg*)
Maria Malikova (*Institute of Russian Literature (Pushkinskii Dom)*, St. Petersburg)
Eric Naiman (*University of California, Berkeley*)
Akiko Nakata (*Nanzan Junior College*, Japan)
Tatiana Ponomareva
    (*Vladimir Nabokov Museum*, St. Petersburg)
David Rampton (*University of Ottawa*)
Thomas Seifrid (*University of Southern California*)
Savely Senderovich (*Cornell University*)
Tadashi Wakashima (*Kyoto University*)

The goalkeeper is the lone eagle, the man of mystery, the last defender...
— Vladimir Nabokov, *Speak, Memory*

Not that we know a fool thing about football.
— Truman Capote, "A Christmas Memory"

CONTENTS

SLIDE TACKLE
From the Editor IX
TEAM
About the Contributors XIII

FIELD   > > > > > > > > > > >
Forum
   Brian Boyd, Jeff Edmunds, Maria Malikova, Leona Toker
   Nabokov Studies: Strategic Development of the Field
   and Scholarly Cooperation 1

FIRST TIME BALL   > > > > > > > > > > >
Russian Nabokov
   Neil Cornwell
   Orhan Pamuk and Vladimir Nabokov on Dostoevsky 15
   Franklin Sciacca
   Sacrificing the Maiden('s)Head: Decoding Nabokov's Burlesque of Sex
   and Violence in *Invitation to a Beheading* 28
   Yelizaveta Goldfarb
   Irony Behind the Iron Curtain: Internal Escape from Totalitarianism
   in Nabokov's *Invitation to a Beheading* 48
   Alexander Moudrov
   Nabokov's Invitation to Plato's Beheading 60

CENTER CIRCLE   > > > > > > > > > > >
Forum
   Alice Lotvin Birney, Isaac Gewirtz, Tatiana Ponomareva, Katherine Reagan
   Institutionalizing Nabokov: Museum, Archive, Exhibition 74

NARROWING THE ANGLE   > > > > > > > > > > >
Memoir
   Irwin Weil
   A Neophyte's Collision with Vladimir Vladimirovich 96

CONTENTS

CORNER ARC
English Nabokov

> Gerard de Vries
> Nabokov's *Pale Fire* and Alexander Pope 102
>
> Conall Cash
> Picturing Memory, Puncturing Vision: Vladimir Nabokov's *Pale Fire* 124
>
> John A. Barnstead
> Two Notes on *Pale Fire* 152
>
> Juan Martinez
> A Fold of the Marquisette: Nabokov's Lepidoptery in Visual Media 158

GOAL BOX
Interview

> An Interview with Dmitri Nabokov by Suellen Stringer-Hye
> "*Laura* is Not Even the Original's Name" 177

ONE TOUCH PASS
Nabokov Across the Lines

> Samuel Schuman
> "Which is Sebastian?" What's in a (Shakespearean and Nabokovian) Name? 193
>
> Marta Pellerdi
> Aesthetics and Sin: The Nymph and the Faun in Hawthorne's
> *The Marble Faun* and Nabokov's *Lolita* 201
>
> Mikhail Efimov
> Nabokov and Prince D. S. Mirsky 218

CORNER FLAG
Interview

> An Interview with Alvin Toffler by Yuri Leving
> "Lost in Transit" 230

MIDFIELD LINE
Forum

> Priscilla Meyer, Christine Raguet, David Rampton, Corinne Scheiner
> Teaching Nabokov 239

RED CARD
Archive

> Yuri Leving
> "The book is dazzlingly brilliant...But"
> Two early internal reviews of Nabokov's *The Gift* 251

CONTENTS

DANGEROUS PLAY
Conference

> Marie Bouchet
> "Revising Nabokov Revising" Nabokov Conference in Kyoto 261

PENALTY AREA
Book Reviews

> Zoe Aiano
> Graham Vickers, *Chasing Lolita: How Popular Culture Corrupted Nabokov's Little Girl All Over Again* 273
>
> Joseph Lynch
> *Approaches to Teaching Nabokov's* Lolita, edited by Zoran Kuzmanovich and Galya Diment 277
>
> Rose France
> *Verses and Versions: Three Centuries of Russian Poetry,* selected and translated by Vladimir Nabokov, edited by Brian Boyd and Stanislav Shvabrin 281
>
> Siggy Frank
> Vladimir Nabokov, *Tragediia gospodina Morna: P'esy, lektsii o drame,* introduced and edited by Andrei Babikov 286
>
> Jan F. Zeschky
> Pekka Tammi, *Russian Subtexts in Nabokov's Fiction: Four Essays* 291

END LINE
Bibliography 297

Index of Names 311

SLIDE TACKLE
From the Editor

> Am I so round with you, as you with me,
> That, like a football, you do spurn me thus?
> You spurn me hence, and he will spurn
> me hither:
> If I last in this service, you must case
> me in leather.
> —William Shakespeare,
> *The Comedy of Errors* (II, 1)

Evgeni Nabokov, a goaltender for the Russian national ice hockey team, was about to lose his temper. Fierce Canadians did not leave any chance for Russians to win the game this time. Russia bitterly lost a quarterfinal match at the 2010 Winter Olympics held in Vancouver—7:3. As the dramatic game continued, one hoped that Evgeni remembered his celebrated namesake who stated: "I was less the keeper of a soccer goal than the keeper of a secret."[1] What breathtaking eternal truths was Vladimir Nabokov pondering as he stood at the goal? Did they have any relation to the worlds of his fiction? What was the riddle behind his creative success? Who invents the rules of literary games based on the structures and strictures of language? The questions are manifold; the contributors to the present collection of articles are trying to tackle some of them.

---

[1] Vladimir Nabokov, *Speak, Memory* (New York: G. P. Putnam's Sons), 268.

SLIDE TACKLE

With the launch of the *Nabokov Online Journal* (www.nabokovonline.com) almost four years ago, it was clear that the times were changing and that the era of electronic press had overstepped the threshold at which some colleagues could frown upon the suspicious Internet and its murky webs. In order for scholarship to remain dynamic we have to keep abreast with the times and employ cutting-edge technology—all this without compromising scholarly quality. Bringing Nabokov studies to a virtual portal has allowed us to offer operative responses to the growing demands of modern academia and to stay in touch with our readership.

On average, *Nabokov Online Journal* enjoys 600 to 1000 hits each month, from fifty countries and territories, ranging from Estonia to Hungary and South Korea. Thanks to the help of Google tools (a detailed breakdown and maps, overview of traffic sources, keyword searches, average time spent on site, and other useful data), we are able to monitor our readers' preferences and strive to provide general public and refined experts alike with intellectually rewarding material. One cannot help but imagine and appreciate those few loyal visitors who browse our site still using frail dial-up connections from remote Ukraine.

In 2009 we introduced the new look of the journal. I am particularly grateful to the members of the editorial board, friends, and colleagues for their creative input when we tried to conceptualize the main page. Only one question was posed then: what specific verbal images from Nabokov's prose evoke your acute and memorable visual perceptions? The results can be seen online; they are accompanied by unattributed quotes which appear and vanish on the main page along with playful animation (hopefully, the Nabokovians will derive pleasure from recognizing the sources of these quotes). The design work was done by a talented Israeli art guru, Andrey Bashkin, who transformed mere chaotic ideas into a functional and aesthetically appealing website. The background soundtrack is by Sergei Rachmaninoff, a great Russian composer and an avid reader of Nabokov, and is performed by Sergei Prokofiev.

Himself an ardent goalkeeper, the author of *Lolita* viewed soccer as more than a game. The goalkeeper "is the lone eagle, the man of mystery, the last defender," he writes in his memoirs.[2] Mysteries shroud Nabokov's image and also those who study him.

Every major Nabokov conference traditionally features some twist that reminds the participants of the omnipotent presence of our master. The first

---

[2] Ibid., 267.

FROM THE EDITOR

Nabokov conference in Nice, organized by Maurice Couturier, was notable, among other things, for a huge butterfly that suddenly flew into a densely packed audience amidst a public lecture. A few years later, at the closing banquet of the centennial Nabokovian festivities in Pushkinskii Dom, on the bank of the Neva River in St. Petersburg, an abrupt blast of wind gusted into a pillared hall and overturned the champagne tray. A powerful thunder followed: greetings from the Otherworld. The 2010 Nabokov conference in Kyoto was no exception.

Scene one: outside of the conference rooms, two people stand next to the coffee table: a lady, who must be a participant (judging by a nametag hanging from her neck), and an aged Japanese gentleman who has stumbled across the lobby. The man looks perplexed as he studies Nabokov's portrait on a huge poster adorned with Japanese hieroglyphs. He then turns around, and inquires with a heavy (one is tempted to say, Pninian) accent:

'What is it?'
'This is a conference...'
'A CAN-fe-ren-ce?'
'Yes, it's like a meeting!'
'Ah, the man acknowledges with a slight sense of relief, a meeting! What about?'
'It is about Nabokov, the woman patiently explains, you know, an author...'
The Japanese gentleman still does not understand.
'A writer,' the lady continues. 'Fiction, non-fiction, NA-BO-KOV!'
Suddenly the man's face lights up: 'So... is he *famous*?'
'Very famous,' reassures the lady.
'Is *he* there? I wanna see 'im right after the meeting!' The man smiles, now obviously satisfied with the answer, and cheerfully strolls away.

Scene two: a tourist bus is taking more than three dozen of the conference participants for a tour at Shisendo castle and Philosopher's Walk. After one of the stops in Kyoto's picturesque suburbs, the prominent scholars and their family members return to the parked vehicle. Everyone is already comfortably seated, but Professor Maxim D. Shrayer realizes that he is missing his grey jacket that he had left in the top luggage area prior to leaving the bus. At first people joke that the jacket is probably behind someone's bum, but as time goes by, all realize the gravity of the situation. Finally, someone plucks out a long grey coat. But Maxim rejects it: "Mine was the very same color indeed, but shorter; this one has buttons and it's old, while mine had a zipper and was brand new!"

Invisible tensions rise. Joseph, the young American guide, solemnly announces into his mike: "Okay, gentlemen, here we are, all sealed in one bus and there is a coat missing." Is it a coincidence that Professor Catharine Nepomnyashchy entitled her paper on Nabokov and Agatha Christie, "Revising the Detective Story and the Terms of Engagement"? And, really, why is there an extra coat that seems to have increased in size in its owner's absence, to paraphrase Samuel Marshak's celebrated Russian poem "Baggage"? Another dreadful possibility: what if someone never came back from the Buddhist shrine above the hill? Shoko Miura, the current President of the Nabokov Society of Japan, frantically starts counting the people on the bus. Everyone is in. "Now, I really want to find my coat," exclaims the coatless victim. Another moment and the final day of the conference will be on the brink of an inevitable catastrophe...

Suddenly a fragile pause is broken by simultaneous and indistinct chatter. The short coat is being delivered from the front of the bus...The French *psychoanalyst* (yes!) had mistakenly put on Maxim's coat and, as it turns out, has been peacefully contemplating the landscape out of his side window during the entire search.

True to its playful title, *The Goalkeeper* combines innovative scholarly strategies and different academic styles while pursuing a single common goal: a greater understanding of Vladimir Nabokov's art and his genius. This inaugural collection of the Nabokov Almanac features contributions from two dozen leading Nabokov specialists worldwide, including academic articles, roundtable discussions, interviews, archival materials, the Kyoto Nabokov conference report, and book reviews. I am grateful to our keen peer-reviewers, members of the editorial board, and to Theresa Heath for her invaluable editorial assistance in preparation of this volume.

Let the game begin!

TEAM
About the Contributors

John A. Barnstead is Associate Professor at Dalhousie University's Department of Russian Studies, and President of the Elizabeth Bishop Society of Nova Scotia. He was recently made a minor character in Robert Heinlein's posthumous collaboration with Spider Robinson, *Variable Star* (New York: TOR Books, 2006, pp. 213-216).

Alice L. Birney earned a doctorate in literature from the University of California, San Diego, in 1968. After teaching at several universities, she joined the Library of Congress in 1973 and has been the literary and cultural historian in the Manuscript Division since 1990. She administers the major Nabokov and Whitman collections as well as over 2,000 others in the arts. She has published a variety of essays on Whitman, Roth, Malamud, Zora Neale Hurston, Ayn Rand, Joshua Logan and Johnny Carson, as well as a book on Shakespeare as satirist (University of California Press), a Garland bibliography on literary biographies of Jesus, and an Arcadia local history volume.

TEAM

Marie Bouchet is Associate Professor of American Literature at the University of Toulouse, France. One of the founding members of the Société Vladimir Nabokov France, she defended her Ph.D. in 2005, under the supervision of Christine Raguet-Bouvart. It dealt with the representation of figures of desire in Nabokov's fiction. Her publications on Nabokov's writings include: *Lolita* (Paris: Atlande, 2009), "From Dolores on the Dotted Line to Dotted Dolores" (*Nabokov Studies* 9, 2005), "Lolita, the Secret of/in *Lolita*: 'Poerotics' of Secrecy" (*American Secrets*. Ed. J. Liste. Madison, NJ: Fairleigh Dickinson University Press, 2010).

Brian Boyd is Distinguished Professor of English at The University of Auckland, the author of the definitive biography of Nabokov, published by Princeton University Press in two volumes (*Vladimir Nabokov: The Russian Years*, 1990; *Vladimir Nabokov: The American Years*, 1991), as well as of *Nabokov's Ada* (Ardis, 1985), *Pale Fire: The Magic of Artistic Discovery* (Princeton University Press, 1999), and most recently, *On the Origin of Stories: Evolution, Cognition, and Fiction* (Belknap Press, 2009). Boyd's continuing series of annotations to *Ada* appear in *The Nabokovian* and are now available as ADAonline.

Conall Cash holds an honours degree in English from Haverford College (USA), and is currently a graduate student in Film Studies at Monash University (Australia). He also works as a film critic for several online publications.

Neil Cornwell is Professor Emeritus of Russian and Comparative Literature at the University of Bristol. He is the author of *Vladimir Nabokov* (in the series "Writers and Their Work," Northcote House, 1999) and has written several essays on Nabokov (in *The Nabokovian*; on Zembla; and in collections of Nabokov conference proceedings). He is also an editor of the online *Literary Encyclopedia* (www.litencyc.com) with responsibility for Nabokov (as well as for Russian literature, and for Henry James). He is author of two studies of Vladimir Odoevsky (1986 and 1998); *The Literary Fantastic* (1990); *James Joyce and the Russians* (1992); and *The absurd in literature* (Manchester University Press, 2006). His *Odoevsky's Four Pathways into Modern Fiction: A Comparative Study* is forthcoming with Manchester University Press in 2010. He has also translated works by Odoevsky, Lermontov and Kharms, as well as Mayakovsky's *My Discovery of America* (2005). His edited books include *Reference Guide to Russian Literature* (1998) and *The Routledge Companion to Russian Literature* (2001).

Jeff Edmunds, creator and editor of *Zembla*, a website devoted to Nabokov studies. He is a cataloging specialist at the University Libraries of

Pennsylvania State University, whose server is home to *Zembla*. His texts have appeared in *Nabokov Studies*, *The Slavic and East European Journal*, *McSweeney's*, and *Formules* (Paris, France), among others. Translated into Russian, his work has appeared in *Nezavisimaia gazeta*, *Novaia Iunost'*, and *Inostrannaia literatura*. In 2003, his tale *La feintise* was published with Jean Lahougue's *La ressemblance* (a rewriting of Nabokov's *Despair*) by Les Impressions Nouvelles. In addition to designing and overseeing the *Zembla* site, Edmunds has contributed an annotated bibliography of French Nabokov criticism; regular updates to Dieter E. Zimmer's bibliographies of Nabokov criticism; and translations of critical articles from French, Russian, and Japanese.

Mikhail Efimov is an historian and a graduate of the Murmansk State Pedagogical Institute. Currently he serves as the Deputy Director (Research) of the State Historical-Architectural and Natural Museum and Preserve "Park Monrepos" (Vyborg, Russia). Efimov's articles are published in the journals *Neprikosnovennyi zapas* and *Istorik i khudozhnik*, and he is mainly interested in the history of Russian liberal ideology as well as Russian-European cultural relations in the eighteenth and nineteenth centuries.

Isaac Gewirtz has served as Curator of the New York Public Library's Henry W. and Albert A. Berg Collection of English and American Literature since September 2000. After studying in the University of Virginia's doctoral program in English, he received his Master's of Library Service degree from Columbia University in 1984, with a specialization in rare books and, in 2003, a Ph.D. in Early Modern History, also from Columbia, focusing on early Renaissance France (The Prefaces of Badius Ascensius: The Humanist Printer as Arbiter of French Humanism and the Medieval Tradition in France). He served as Curator of Special Collections at Southern Methodist University's Bridwell Library from 1990 to 1996, and as Director of Special Collections at the St. Mark's Library of the General Theological Seminary, in Manhattan, from 1996 to 2000. Dr. Gewirtz has curated numerous exhibitions including, at the New York Public Library, *Victorians, Moderns, and Beats; Passion's Discipline: A History of the Sonnet in the British Isles and America*; "I am With You": Walt Whitman's *Leaves of Grass*, 1855-2005, with an accompanying volume of the same title; and *Beatific Souls: Jack Kerouac's On the Road*, 1957-2007, also with a volume of the same title.

Yelizaveta Goldfarb is a graduate student at New York University researching émigré literary cultures. She is currently exploring subversive humor and games/rhetorical play in the works of Vladimir Nabokov and Milan Kundera.

TEAM

Yuri Leving is Associate Professor and Chair of Dalhousie University's Department of Russian Studies. He is the author of three books: *Train Station — Garage — Hangar. Vladimir Nabokov and the Poetics of Russian Urbanism* (2004), *Keys to* The Gift. *A Guide to V. Nabokov's Novel* (2010), *Upbringing by Optics: Book Illustration, Animation, and Text* (2010), and has also co-edited two volumes of articles: *Eglantine: A Collection of Philological Essays to Honour the Sixtieth Anniversary of Roman Timenchik* (2005) and *Empire: N. Nabokov and His Heirs* (2006). Leving has published over sixty scholarly articles on various aspects of Russian and comparative literature. He served as a commentator on the first authorized Russian edition of *The Collected Works of Vladimir Nabokov* in five volumes (1999-2001), and was the curator for the exhibition "Nabokov's *Lolita*: 1955-2005" in Washington, D.C., which celebrated the 50th anniversary of the publication of *Lolita*.

Maria Malikova is a literary scholar and translator. She graduated from Leningrad State University with a degree in English language and literature in 1990. In the late 1990s she began graduate studies at the Institute of Russian Literature (Pushkinskii Dom) in St. Petersburg and at the Department of Literature and Arts at the University of Tampere (Finland), and received "kandidatskaia" and PhD degrees. Since 2002 she has been working as a researcher at the Department of Comparative Literature at Pushkinskii Dom. Dr. Malikova is the author of *Nabokov: Auto-bio-grafia* (2002, in Russian). She also edited a volume of Nabokov's collected poetry and translations for the academic series *The Poet's Library* (2002) and wrote commentaries for some of his work included in the five-volume *Collected Russian Works* (St. Petersburg: Symposium, 1999-2000). In 2004-2005 Malikova held the post of Fulbright scholar at Stanford University. Recently she became interested in Soviet literature of the New Economic Policy (NEP) period and the writings of Walter Benjamin. She lives and works in St. Petersburg.

Juan Martinez is a doctoral candidate in literature at the University of Nevada, Las Vegas. He runs Waxwing, a Nabokov appreciation website at http://fulmerford.com. His fiction has appeared in *Glimmer Train, Conjunctions, McSweeney's, The Santa Monica Review*, and elsewhere.

Priscilla Meyer is Professor of Russian at Wesleyan University, and author of *Find What the Sailor Has Hidden: Vladimir Nabokov's Pale Fire* (Middletown, CT: Wesleyan University Press, 1988); Russian translation by Maria Malikova (Moscow: *Novoe Literaturnoe Obozrenie*, 2006) and *How the Russians Read the French: Lermontov, Dostoevsky and Tolstoy*

ABOUT THE CONTRIBUTORS

(Madison: University of Wisconsin Press, 2009), as well as editions, including *Essays on Nikolai Gogol: Logos and the Russian Word*, ed. with Susanne Fusso (Evanston, Illinois: Northwestern University Press, 1994), *Nabokov's World*, ed. with Jane Grayson and Arnold McMillin, 2 vols. (London and New York: Macmillan, 2001), numerous translations, articles, and reviews. Meyer is editor of the *Notes and Commentaries* section of *The Nabokovian*.

Alexander Moudrov is a lecturer in Comparative Literature at Queens College (The City University of New York). He teaches courses in global literatures, intercultural relations, as well as interdisciplinary courses that bridge literary studies with other disciplines, particularly philosophy, religion, and history. His recent essays include "Wilde Rereads the Myth of Orpheus and Dies," "The Scourge of Foreign Vagabonds: George Thompson and the Influence of European Sensationalism in Popular Antebellum Literature," and "Early American Crime Fiction: Origins to Urban Gothic."

Marta Pellerdi teaches English and American Literature at Pazmany Peter Catholic University in Hungary. She has published several articles on Nabokov and is currently working on a book on the Anglo-American literary tradition in the Russian-American writer's English novels.

Tatiana Ponomareva is Director of the St. Petersburg State University Vladimir Nabokov Museum located in the former Nabokov mansion. A graduate of St. Petersburg State University, she was a teacher and translator before joining the Nabokov Museum as a part-time guide in 1999. She became Director in 2002 and was busy developing and securing the future of the then unfunded Museum. This work resulted in the Museum becoming a branch of St. Petersburg State University in 2008. Dr. Ponomareva is the author of many articles on Nabokov in the Russian media and the organizer of several international Nabokov conferences. She also teaches at St. Petersburg State University. More information on the Museum is at www.nabokovmuseum.org.

Christine Raguet is Professor at the Université Paris 3-Sorbonne Nouvelle, director of a research center in translation studies (TRACT) at the same institution, and director of a journal of translation studies, *Palimpsestes*. She has published more than two dozen articles, in both French and English, on Nabokov, as well as Henry James, other American and English authors and on translation studies. She is editor of a special issue of *Europe* (no. 791, 1995) devoted entirely to Nabokov, and author of *Lolita, un royaume au-delà des mers* (Talence: Presses Universitaires de Bordeaux, 1996). She has translated two volumes of Nabokov's correspondence, and his novel

Laughter in the Dark, into French. She currently serves on the editorial board of the Pléiade edition of Nabokov's collected works, where she is responsible for the annotation, commentary and revision of the translations of *Laughter in the Dark, Invitation to a Beheading, Bend Sinister, The Enchanter, Pale Fire, Ada*, and *Transparent Things*.

David Rampton is Professor of English at the University of Ottawa where he teaches and works on twentieth-century American literature, with a special emphasis on fiction since 1950. His books include *William Faulkner: A Literary Life* (Palgrave Macmillan, 2007), *Vladimir Nabokov* (New York: St. Martin's; London: Macmillan, 1993), and *Vladimir Nabokov: A Critical Study of the Novels* (Cambridge: Cambridge University Press, 1984). Rampton also is co-editor of *Short Fiction* (Toronto: HBJ, 2004) and *Prose Models* (Toronto: HBJ, 1997).

Katherine Reagan is Assistant Director of Collections and Ernest L. Stern Curator of Rare Books and Manuscripts in Cornell University's Library Division of Rare and Manuscript Collections. Prior to her arrival at Cornell in 1996, she worked at the Morgan Library & Museum in New York. She is a past president of the Rare Books and Manuscripts Section of the American Library Association and she teaches book history in Cornell's English Department and for Rare Book School at the University of Virginia.

Franklin Sciacca is Associate Professor of Russian at Hamilton College. He has lectured extensively on Orthodox iconography and monasticism. His ongoing research interests include the Pochaev Monastery and the cultural politics of Right Bank Ukraine, as well as topics in Russian and Ukrainian folklore.

Corinne Scheiner teaches at Colorado College where she is Maytag Associate Professor of Comparative Literature. Her publications include "In Search of the 'Real' Smurov: Doubling and Dialogic Construction of Identity in Nabokov's *Sogladatay* (*The Eye*)" in *Poetics, Self, Place: Essays in Honor of Lisa Crone* (Bloomington, IN: Slavica, 2007), and "Teaching Lolita with Lepidoptera" in *Approaches to Teaching* Lolita, ed. Zoran Kuzmanovich and Galya Diment (New York: The Modern Language Association of America, 2008).

Samuel Schuman's books include *Vladimir Nabokov, A Reference Guide* (G. K. Hall, 1979), a guide to secondary studies of Nabokov, and his contributions are included in *The Garland Companion to Vladimir Nabokov* (Garland, 1995). He has published more than two dozen articles on Nabokovian subjects and made several presentations at professional meetings. Twice he has organized the Nabokov session at the Modern Language Association (MLA). During Schuman's term as President of the Nabokov Society, it succeeded in becoming an affiliated organization of the MLA. He directed the Honors Program at the University of Maine, and later served as Vice President for Academic Affairs and Professor of English at Guilford College, Greensboro, North Carolina, and as Acting Chancellor and Vice Chancellor for Academic Affairs at the University of Minnesota, Morris.

Suellen Stringer-Hye is the Web Coordinator at the Vanderbilt University Libraries. She has written on "Nabokov and Popular Culture," "Nabokov and Melville," and *Ada*. From 1994-2004, she was the creator and compiler of "VN Collations," a regular column of references to Nabokov from the online and print popular presses, posted on NABOKV-L. In 1996, she conducted an online interview with Stephen Schiff, screenwriter for Adrian Lyne's film interpretation of Lolita, also published in *Zembla*. She also interviewed Stacy Schiff, author of the Pulitzer Prize winning biography of Véra Nabokov; and Azar Nafisi, author of the bestselling *Reading* Lolita *in Tehran*. Other interests include Pierre Bernard and the history of the Clarkstown Country Club of South Nyack, New York. Some of her research on this topic will contribute to a forthcoming biography of Bernard by Robert Love called *The Great Oom*.

Leona Toker is a Professor in the English Department of the Hebrew University of Jerusalem. She is the author of *Nabokov: The Mystery of Literary Structures* (1989); *Eloquent Reticence: Withholding Information in Fictional Narrative* (1993); *Return from the Archipelago: Narratives of Gulag Survivors* (2000); *Towards the Ethics of Form in Fiction: Narratives of Cultural Remission* (2010); and many other articles on English, American, and Russian writers. She is the editor of *Commitment in Reflection: Essays in Literature and Moral Philosophy* (1994) and co-editor of *Rereading Texts / Rethinking Critical Presuppositions: Essays in Honour of H.M. Daleski* (1996). At present she is the editor of *Partial Answers: A Journal of Literature and the History of Ideas*, a semi-annual periodical published by the Johns Hopkins University Press.

Gerard de Vries has been a reader of Nabokov's works for several decades. In addition to essays published in Dutch magazines on art and literature, he has published articles on Nabokov in English-language academic journals. He is co-author of *Vladimir Nabokov and the Art of Painting* (Amsterdam University Press, 2006) with D. Barton Johnson, and with an essay by Liana Ashenden.

TEAM

Irwin Weil is Professor Emeritus in the Department of Slavic Languages and Literature at Northwestern University. He is noted for his work in promoting cultural exchange and mutual understanding between the USA and the USSR/Russia. He recorded a popular series of lectures *Classics of Russian Literature* for The Teaching Company in 2005. Weil is the author of *Gorky: His Literary Development and Influence on Soviet Intellectual Life* (New York: Random House, 1966).

> > > > > >

THE GOALKEEPER

*THE NABOKOV
ALMANAC*

FIELD

< < < < < <

FORUM

Brian Boyd
 (*University of Auckland*)
Jeff Edmunds
 (*Editor of Zembla*)
Maria Malikova
 (*Institute of Russian Literature, St. Petersburg*)
Leona Toker
 (*Hebrew University of Jerusalem*)

NABOKOV STUDIES: STRATEGIC DEVELOPMENT OF THE FIELD AND SCHOLARLY COOPERATION[1]

INTRODUCTORY REMARKS

Yuri Leving: I would like to welcome the participants of our present forum representing various academic traditions in Nabokov studies. The idea is to generate an expert discussion around the issues that can range from your own vision of the future of our area to emerging trends and potentially productive venues of research within Nabokov scholarship. What are our major challenges, accomplishments and weaknesses? What multilingual and multicultural approaches in the Nabokov community can we recognize? How can we improve the quality of research? How do we sustain traditional scholarly values

---

[1] First appeared in *Nabokov Online Journal*, Vol. I (2007).

vis-à-vis technological advancement and growing information resources, as well as guide their impact on the development of Nabokov studies?

Jeff Edmunds: In framing the topics to be discussed, Yuri Leving uses the phrases "our major challenges" and "the Nabokov community." Who is the "we" implied by the "our"? Who is "the Nabokov community"? Does this (hypothetical?) group share a common aim? Should it? If so, what is that aim, or what should it be?

THE FUTURE (I.E. THE PRESENT) OF NABOKOV STUDIES

Brian Boyd: Nabokov was wary of prophecy and so am I. Late in 1997 I had no idea I was about to write a book on *Pale Fire* over the next couple of months. If I couldn't foresee my own imminent future then, what hope do I have now of predicting a whole field over a longer span of time?

Nabokov remains not particularly fashionable but exhilarating to good readers. He seizes hold of some imaginations but is ignored by others in academe who prefer what fits easily into periods or places or worthy causes. Fortunately he also inspires writers from John Updike, Andrei Bitov, and Edmund White through Martin Amis and Orhan Pamuk to Zadie Smith. One legitimate measure of writers' deep creativity is the extent of their influence, as demonstrated through Nabokov's inspiration from Pushkin and Shakespeare, which saturate *The Gift* and *Pale Fire*. In this respect Pamuk's debt to Nabokov seems a particularly fecund field to explore.

Maria Malikova: My experience in the sphere of Nabokov studies is limited to research and editing rather than teaching. Considering that I no longer study Nabokov, my experience tends to be negative, but this cynical view should be regarded as just my personal opinion. Furthermore, I am most likely unaware of the latest developments in the field. Since the people invited to participate in this forum all represent different national traditions, I assume that we are meant to speak about our individual national experiences in Nabokov studies. Therefore, I will concentrate on my Russian experience.

In Russia, Nabokov is no longer considered to be in academic vogue — yet, the provincial universities have developed programs of study to rival those of metropolitan. This can be taken as a sign that Nabokov studies will eventually become a standard scholarly subject in Russia. However, while this might cause overall interest in the field to increase, it simultaneously causes a decrease in specialized study at more accredited institutions in Moscow and St. Petersburg.

There have been two major peaks of interest in Nabokov studies. The first occurred in the early 1990s with the first republications of Nabokov in post-Soviet Russia, and the second occurred around 1999 with Nabokov's centennial jubilee. However, we are currently witnessing a dramatic decrease of interest in Nabokov studies. From the perspective of the general reading public this is probably caused in part by the overall social devaluation of literature, as well as the growing prevalence of popular fiction. In terms of scholarship, I believe that the initial reception of Nabokov as a "missing link" between nineteenth century Russian classics, Russian émigré literature, European modernism and early Soviet postmodernism (e.g., Andrei Bitov) clashes with Nabokov's easy appropriation as a commercial brand. This branding was, of course, facilitated by his highly pragmatic self-positioning on the literary market.[2]

There might still be some potential for the promotion of Nabokov as a popular figure — from new film versions of *Lolita* to parodies and literary mystifications. Another reason might be that Nabokov's declaration of extraterritoriality to his contemporaneous Russian literary field appears to be true. The idea was first enthusiastically disapproved by Russian scholars as a retrospective stance adopted by the writer in accordance with his late, American literary politics (in the process they uncovered a number of interesting subtexts from Russian and émigré literature). The fact remains that Nabokov is loosely, and for the most part anachronistically, embedded in a Russian literary context. In times of high modernism he was described as a belated heir of the Russian classical tradition; then as an émigré writer working within a very limited and highly specific émigré literary field; and finally as an American writer of Russian origin living in voluntary isolation in a deluxe Swiss hotel. To a large extent, understanding Nabokov can do without literary context and does not add much to the understanding of any wider literary movements, which means that Nabokov scholars either have to remain independent, or risk treading the swampy terrain of typological comparisons. However, I think that Nabokov's aesthetic project of total literary autonomy is still worth studying. As far as I can see, in Russia Nabokov is now most often explored as an exponent of wider literary and

---

[2] Cf. Yuri Leving and Evgeny Soshkin, ed., *Imperia N. Nabokov and Heirs* (Moscow: New Literary Observer, 2006).

historical trends and devices (romanticism, urbanism, poetics of memory, narrative structures), and the future of Nabokov studies depends solely on the talents of individual researchers.

Brian Boyd: The direction of Nabokov scholarship will continue to depend mostly on unpredictable individual energies (like Dieter E. Zimmer's work on Nabokov's butterflies and Nabokov's Central Asia) and unpredictable cultural and critical trends. The imaginations captured by Nabokov often become Nabokov specialists. He does need hard work and, ideally, knowledge of three languages and their literatures.

Nevertheless I would like to see more non-specialists encouraged to write on Nabokov; people like Michael Wood and Robert Alter, whose independence of mind and range of reading outside Nabokov and his personal literary canon more than make up for their non-specialization.

Jeff Edmunds: In rereading the comments by Maria Malikova and Brian Boyd, I found myself mentally nodding in agreement to Malikova's statement "the future of Nabokov studies depends solely on the talent of individual researchers," and Boyd's "Where Nabokov scholarship will move will continue to depend mostly on unpredictable individual energies." If a Nabokov community can be said to exist, it can only benefit, I think, from encouraging and supporting such talents and energies, wherever and in whatever form they happen to arise.

NABOKOV STUDIES AND TECHNOLOGICAL ADVANCEMENT

Jeff Edmunds: At least two of the presentations at last year's Nabokov conference in Nice included digital audio and video. Given the bandwidth now available on the Internet, it seems inevitable, and desirable, that future critical responses to Nabokov's work will be multimedial rather than purely textual or texto-pictorial. When it came to gathering material for his art, Nabokov was a magpie. Sound and moving pictures were no less worthy of his attention than images or the printed word.

Multimedial criticism allows a more polydimensional appreciation of Nabokov's work. Conference presentations are as likely to be made available as audio or video as they are as text. Students and specialists can listen to podcasts of presentations or lectures "on the go" as they walk to class, drive to work, or prepare dinner.

Scholar, record thyself!

FORUM

Brian Boyd: Regrettably NABOKV-L, once an invaluable venue for scholarly and readerly exchange, and still an occasional route to discovery, has become mostly incessant chatter and uncontrolled speculation. Perhaps a more tightly moderated forum associated with the *Nabokov Online Journal* could serve the function that NABOKV-L once fulfilled?

Jeff Edmunds: I agree with Brian Boyd. As the Internet passes its infancy as a form of what is sometimes referred to as "scholarly communication" (a hot topic in American academic libraries and at universities in general) and enters adolescence, I think we will see the ground rules shift, just as parenting a baby is different from parenting a teenager. Babies don't talk much and are utterly guileless. Teenagers talk nonstop and, as the joke has it, one can tell if they are lying by looking to see whether their lips are moving. The Internet is now a teenager—but hang on. Either forums for scholarly discourse will need to evolve away from the LISTSERV model (e.g. NABOKV-L), or the very notion of scholarly discourse will have to be redefined to accommodate what undoubtedly strikes many veteran researchers as "elephant talk" (in the Belewian sense of the phrase). Better tools will have to be deployed for data mining—so we can effectively pick the nutritious bits of grain from enormous mounds of logorrheic excess.

Jeff Edmunds: As evidenced by Brian Boyd's *ADAonline*, a website built by volunteers from five countries, the Internet is an ideal forum for collaborative work.

Nabokov studies would benefit immeasurably from an online, free, multilingual, comprehensive, annotated, and up-to-date bibliography of Nabokov criticism, preferably one that can be built and maintained collaboratively and which will allow scholars themselves to add and edit entries. The logical next step would be to link each entry to the full text of the article itself, thereby producing an online repository of Nabokov scholarship. Volunteers?

Brian Boyd: We also need specialist scholarship: annotated editions of the published works (in book or web formats), and editions of the still uncollected or unpublished material (translations, interviews and articles, letters and lectures). We very much need a primary bibliography to update Michael Juliar's and an annotated secondary bibliography of material in all languages. Clearly this would have to be an international project, preferably in book form but also perhaps in a readily updatable CD or web version.

Jeff Edmunds: Again, I concur with Brian Boyd about the needs he identifies, especially for editions and translations of unpublished material. Translation is especially important. To cite two examples: can any serious Anglophone scholar of Nabokov appreciate *Invitation to a Beheading* without having read Alexander Dolinin's article "Pushkinskie podteksty v romane Nabokova *Priglashenie na kazn'*,"³ currently only available in Russian? Or the early lecture on Pushkin by Nabokov, held in the Berg Collection, to which Dolinin refers in the same article, and which is unavailable in print?

Such lacunae in the literature are partially the result of what Maria Malikova discusses below in her response to the concept of challenges faced by Nabokov scholars: "permission to use and quote materials from the Vladimir Nabokov archive is granted either on commercial or on purely subjective grounds." Certainly the translation and presentation of Nabokov's unpublished writings requires extreme care, but the need for such care should not and cannot be taken as an insurmountable obstacle.

POTENTIAL WEAKNESSES

Jeff Edmunds: Three potential weaknesses come to mind when considering the future of Nabokov scholarship: mediocrity, academic faddishness, and parochialism. Nabokov abhorred mediocrity; his commentators should follow suit. Specialists should reject the mediocre, whether it is a poorly written thesis or a poorly researched article. The academic industry, at least in the US, churns out vast quantities of drivel every year simply because professors are required to "publish or perish." Disdain the perfunctory. Maintaining high standards for Nabokov scholarship becomes ever more important as the field of discourse (e.g. the Internet) expands and the possibilities for cross-contamination by what Brian Boyd referred to above as "incessant chatter and uncontrolled speculation" increase.

Academic faddishness could be defined as shoe-horning Nabokov into this or that currently fashionable *ism*. (I am reminded of Alain Robbe-Grillet's reference to Roland Barthes' comparison of such systems of thought to boiling oil: "vous pouvez y plonger n'importe quoi, il en ressortira toujours une frite.")⁴ Parochialism in the context of Nabokov studies can be defined as monolingualism, ethnocentrism, and temporal chauvinism. Teachers of Nabokov should encourage the sustained study of Russian and French, the translation of key critical texts, and an understanding of how critical appraisals of Nabokov have changed over time.

---

[3] http://www.libraries.psu.edu/nabokov/dolininpush.htm
[4] Alain Robbé-Grillet, *Contemporains*, vol. 21 (Paris: Editions du Seuil, 1997), 98. "You can throw in whatever you like, but it will always emerge a French fry." — *Ed. note*.

Maria Malikova: A repertoire of ready-made undergraduate research papers covering a whole range of topics in Nabokov studies is available on the Russian web for only 600 rubles (25 US dollars). These topics include synaesthesia, literary bilingualism and enantiomorphism as literary devices, and classical tradition (Pushkin and Gogol) in Nabokov's art, e.g. narrative structures of short stories; word games. Another symptom of the latest trivialization of Nabokov studies is the fact that the overwhelming majority of dissertations devoted solely to Nabokov in the last five or six years have been defended in universities outside of Moscow and St. Petersburg — including Rostov, Omsk, Saratov, Voronezh, Stavropol, Bashkiria et al. In Russia, unlike in the States, geographical provincialism with very few exceptions means scientific provincialism (due to meagre libraries, limited funds for travel and inviting renowned scholars, etc.).

Jeff Edmunds: Maria Malikova's observation on the "trivialization of Vladimir Nabokov studies" is interesting and at least partially a result, in a broader sense, of the ever expanding virtual space in which scholarly discourse occurs, i.e. the Internet. It seems indisputable to me that the signal-to-noise ratio has diminished logarithmically as the Internet has matured and scholarly communication has begun to cohabit the same virtual space as the elephant talk I mentioned above.

CHALLENGES

Jeff Edmunds: Much of what can be done to benefit the field (dissemination of lectures in digital format, translation of secondary texts) falls outside the traditional equation for academic success (publish or perish). In my experience, there is scant support, almost zero funding, and precious little glory in trailblazing. Securing funding and support for initiatives will be a significant challenge. The traditional scholarly carrots (tenure and impressive job titles) may not be enough, especially for members of the hypothetical community who are not academics.

Maria Malikova: In Russian scholarly tradition there are a number of key approaches to the legacy of a major writer (apart from interpretative research) that culminate in definitive "academic" editions, including archival, biographical and textual research, as well as informed commentary. Even in the case of writers whose heritage was scattered in the mishaps of the twentieth century — Leonid Dobychin, Konstantin Vaginov, Andrei Nikolev (Egunov), the "Chinary" (OBERIU) authors and many others — attempts have been made to provide as definitive editions as possible. By "definitive" I mean that these editions have been prepared with the presumption of maximum completeness by thorough archival/textological work and exhaustive commentary.

Although all of Nabokov's Russian works are available in numerous post-Soviet editions, the quality of key editions (not to mention their popular versions) falls far behind the level of academic editions and is inadequate for a writer such as Nabokov, who has been accepted to the highest rank of the Russian literary canon. However, it should be mentioned that Russian editions surpass European and American ones as they compile *all* of the scattered critical essays by Nabokov.

The obvious objective reason is that the Nabokov archives in Montreux, the Library of Congress in Washington, and the Berg Collection of the New York Public Library are not easily accessible to Russian scholars. This is due not only to the fact that most of us cannot afford prolonged archival research overseas, but also because the Nabokov archives have areas of limited access, lacunae in the catalogue and, in the case of the private Montreux repository, is, as rumours say, in a state of chaos. To the detriment of Nabokov studies, it is not likely to ever be fully opened to visiting researchers.

Furthermore, permission to use and quote materials from the archives is granted either on commercial or purely subjective grounds. As a consequence, textological work and commentary simply cannot be carried out according to the demands of Russian academic editions. The necessity to view Nabokov's archived manuscripts is reinforced by the fact that close scrutiny of Russian émigré and *Ardis* editions generates many questions, not to mention that it is always desirable to reconstruct text evolution. Due to these restrictions, Russian scholars unsurpassed in archival study tend to shy away from Nabokov. This is my understanding of the situation — it would be interesting to hear the opinions of such scholars as, for example, Roman Timenchik.

The Poems of V. V. Nabokov in the *Poet's Library* series[5] that I edited is a compromised product handicapped by limited access to the archives and the publisher's inability to pay the Vladimir Nabokov Estate for the right to republish poems first printed in the *Ardis* 1979 *Stikhi* [Poems] collection. I agree that the publisher could have displayed greediness; however, I still think that it would have been symbolically profitable for the Nabokov legacy to have his *complete* poems published in this highly respected series. While working on this edition I had some access to Nabokov material in the Berg Collection

---

[5] Considered the most authoritative and definitive series for publication of classical Russian poets, *Poet's Library* [Biblioteka poeta] was initiated by Maxim Gorky in 1931. — *Ed. note.*

and to periodicals unavailable in Russian libraries. As a consequence, it became possible to publish dozens of Nabokov's poems and translations that had *never* been reprinted before, to correct numerous mistakes in Nabokov's own notes to his 1979 *Stikhi* and *Poems and Problems*—this alone proves how fruitful unlimited access to Nabokov archives and their proper cataloguing would prove for Nabokov studies. For example, Nabokov's *Dar* (*The Gift*) could be edited and published in a single volume according to the principles of the *Literaturnie pamjatniki* series,[6] including all of its unpublished sequences as well as the reconstruction of its complex history (the scholar ideally suited to carry out this task would, of course, be Alexander Dolinin). Some ten years ago I enthusiastically began to prepare Nabokov's editions, armed with a "bird in the hand is worth two in the bush" attitude. Now, however, inaccessibility to the archival materials required to produce the elusive definitive edition discourages me from participating in those projects.

Yuri Leving: This is a rather pessimistic picture. Can you describe the shape of Nabokoviana in present day Russia?

Maria Malikova: Logically, the result of the previously described situation is that, legally, Nabokov's works in Russian are now published either by the Symposium publishing house or in the popular classics series *Azbooka*. The five-volume *Symposium* edition of "Russian" Nabokov (1999-2001), in which I took part, is unfortunately a broth spoiled by too many cooks. For health reasons, the collection's editor-in-chief could not closely supervise the work on the project. It was also terribly prolonged for financial reasons, and therefore became a playground for dilettante experimentation by numerous commentators and publishing house editors. In the end, Nabokov's works were published according to an idiosyncratic "chronological" principle. The idea was to present his evolution as a writer but, in the final run, his authorized collections of stories and poems were disjointed; texts were not published according to the author's latest will but based on earlier editions; and commentaries were drastically discordant in tone, scope and adequacy. The greatest stroke of luck for this five-volume collection was Alexander Dolinin's introductory essays that would later comprise the major part of his monograph.[7] *Azbooka* paperbacks, while cheap, popular and laudatory

---

[6] The Literary Monuments [Literaturnye pamiatniki] is a prestigious series with extensive commentary and textological analysis, published in the USSR / Russia in accordance with academic standards since 1949. — *Ed. note*.

[7] A. Dolinin, *Istinnaia zhizn' pisatelia Sirina: Raboty o Nabokove* [The Real Life of the Writer Sirin: Works on Nabokov] (St. Petersburg: Akademicheskii proekt, 2004). — *Ed. note*.

as an enlightenment project, were never intended to provide extended commentaries and introductory essays (these were limited either to popular brief introductions or to Russian translations of Nabokov's own introductions to English translations of his Russian works—which themselves require clarification).

Therefore, although all of Nabokov's texts are now easily available in Russia, their textology and commentary are not satisfactory. Considering that the general public is quite happy with the existing editions, regularly replenished with *Azbooka* paperbacks, and that the archives are not readily accessible (preventing responsible scholars from approaching the task), definitive editions of Nabokov's works are not likely to appear in the near future.

To sum up, I think that the brief heyday of Nabokov studies in Russia is over. I do not see where new inspiration could come from, so within the Russian literary canon Nabokov will be (and already is) dethroned from his place next to Pushkin and moved to the more appropriate company of Ivan Bunin and Mark Aldanov. Nabokov strove for that lofty literary status and he very nearly reached it in 1999, with his centennial anniversary and Pushkin's bicentennial.

Jeff Edmunds: To this I would add only that, if Maria Malikova's characterization of the "chaos" of the Nabokov collection in Montreux is accurate, organizing and cataloguing the collection is imperative. Digitizing the collection would merit whatever resources were required. Digital versions of the holdings, accompanied by a searchable catalogue, should be made available online.

MULTILINGUALISM

Brian Boyd: One pressing need is for the burgeoning field of Nabokov scholarship in Russian to be better assimilated outside of Russia. Surveys, reviews, abstracts and digests in English would all be useful. For those who read Russian but do not travel there, finding out about, let alone purchasing, important annotated editions of the Russian works or collections of scholarship can be difficult. Russian scholars need to build bridges to the West—and the Internet, and the *Nabokov Online Journal*, should be among the sturdiest.

Jeff Edmunds: I would add only that Western scholars need to build bridges to Russia as well.

Maria Malikova: The same can be said of the status of English-language Nabokov scholarship in Russia today. Even the cultivated Russian public still generally tends to read foreign books in Russian translations. Scholarly articles written in the local tradition still supply all quotations from foreign texts in Russian. There are many translations of Nabokov by Gennady Barabtarlo, Mikhail Meilah, and Dmitri Chekalin (as well as others that are not widely acknowledged or available). However, the majority of translations have been monopolized by Sergei Il'in, who almost single-handedly translated all of Nabokov's major works for the five-volume *Symposium* edition of Nabokov's "American years." Il'in, being an indigenous translator, does not possess the specific translator's virtue of effacing himself. More importantly, it is well known that translating the complex texture of Nabokov's later works, written in an idiosyncratic interweaving of languages, is next to impossible and in many ways violates the author's intention. As a result, Russian readers do not possess adequate knowledge of Nabokov's later works (though they are aware of their subject matter). I have only utopian visions of solving the problem of publishing English-language paperbacks in Russia, or English texts with parallel Russian translations; this, of course, will never be done. However, the very exercise of translating Nabokov's highly idiosyncratic and artificial English prose into Russian is often a great challenge to translators. Another point here is that as a bilingual writer celebrated in Russia, America and Europe, Nabokov created for himself an international field of studies that far surpasses anything available either to far greater Russian writers or to far lesser bilingual ones. Nabokov studies probably have more potential for development through the enrichment of different national traditions.

Leona Toker: Though Nabokov was practically always recognized as a great prose stylist, and though for some time it was necessary to argue that he was considerably more than that, critical accounts of what makes Nabokov's style so finely artistic are still insufficient. One of the important directions that Nabokov studies can still take is a philological analysis of Nabokov's style.

This analysis should concentrate on both the "translatable" and lapidary features of his style. The former are common to his English and Russian works and include defamiliarization of the familiar / deautomatization of perception and imagination, semantic collocation (with the inevitable differences in the semantics of Russian and English vocabulary items), relationships between abstract and image-bearing vocabulary, lexical recurrence/reprise, heteroglossia, the use or withholding of adjectival and adverbial modifiers, and transitions between different stylistic registers within the same chapters, paragraphs and even sentences. The latter, the lapidary features of his style, are associated with his exploration of linguistic effects particular to English and Russian.

Lapidary characteristics include prosodic effects (such as following and avoiding the metrical undersongs favored by each language) or the use of words of different etymological origins. In Nabokov's English, for instance, pitting the vocabulary of Anglo-Saxon origin against that of Romance or Latinate origin produces a wealth of effects; one may ask whether similar effects of etymological heterogeneity (e.g., the deployment of Slavic, Western-European, Tatar and other variously blended lexes) are also explored in his Russian texts. In English, specific effects are also produced by Nabokov's handling of monosyllabic and bi- or polysyllabic words (it makes a considerable difference, for instance, to describe Pnin's love affair with Mira as "banal and brief" rather than "brief and banal"). An additional feature of Nabokov's Russian texts is their existence in a linguistic universe contemporaneous with and parallel to the language of the Revolutionary and post-Revolutionary era in Russia—existing studies of the lexical changes that took place in the Russian language after 1917 may be helpful in pointing out the trap areas which Nabokov instinctively or deliberately avoided.

A special field of interest in terms of style is the compensations that Vladimir and Dmitri Nabokov have found in English for what is untranslatable in the Russian texts. This may be compared and contrasted to the modifications that the author devises in moving from Russian to English (in translating *Lolita* and *Conclusive Evidence*)—modifications that lie only within the prerogative of the author. In fact, some of the most interesting work on Nabokov's style (for instance, G. Barabtarlo's study of Nabokov's Russian *Lolita*) has been done on precisely these issues.

Jeff Edmunds: I agree with Leona Toker's statement that "critical accounts of what makes Nabokov's style so finely artistic are still insufficient." To her mention of Gennady Barabtarlo's study of the Russian *Lolita*, I would add a reference to Peter Lubin's magnificent essay "Kickshaws and Motley," in which Nabokov's use of language is brilliantly (and playfully) analyzed.

POTENTIALLY PRODUCTIVE AVENUES OF RESEARCH

Jeff Edmunds: Rework resulting from ignorance is a bugbear in every field of scholarly endeavour. In a perfect world, Nabokov specialists would be able to search a single source to quickly discover whether a given line of argumentation has been previously pursued and, if so, when and by whom.

One possible solution is a comprehensive online bibliography mentioned at least twice above.

A related issue is the availability of Nabokov criticism in translation, which too has already been mentioned. Much good work remains unknown to the scholar unfamiliar with the language of his colleagues in other countries. Translation of core Nabokov criticism strikes me as an invaluable avenue for future work. Unfortunately, academia tends not to support or reward such work.

Brian Boyd: I happen to have become interested in linking literature and evolution. I think a cognitive and evolutionary understanding of human nature offers insights into literature unavailable in other ways, although it does not invalidate old insights. The fact that Nabokov might have been wary of this approach — he was guarded about evolution and skeptical of the possibility of understanding thought — makes it more, rather than less, appealing. Those of us who *are* Nabokov specialists perhaps have come under his spell and taken his directions more than we should. His directions have long seemed to me more promising, more reasonable and more imaginative than others that have been current in academe, yet keen readers of Nabokov should not hesitate to show the independence of mind he so valued and exemplified.

But how my interest in literature, evolution and cognition will impact on my future work on Nabokov I do not yet know. Research has to make its own trail to discoveries that it can't predict in advance.

Jeff Edmunds: Brian Boyd's statement that some Nabokov specialists, among whom he may count himself, "have come under his spell and taken his directions more than we should," is revealing. As a non-academic, I have formed, rightly or wrongly, a very clear sense that there are Orthodox and Heterodox approaches to Nabokov's work, and that the current climate remains much more hospitable to the former than to the latter.

Leona Toker: Though the study of [various] stylistic phenomena cannot be entirely divorced from the interpretive analysis of Nabokov's text, it would nevertheless concentrate on what, to borrow the concepts of Hans Ulrich Gumbrecht's *Production of Presence*,[8] one can call "the effects of presence" as distinct from "the effects of meaning." The effects of presence are more massively characteristic of visual arts and of music, but style is the area where the sense of the "author's" presence is conjured up for the reader

---

[8] Hans Ulrich Gumbrecht, *Production of Presence: What Meaning Cannot Convey* (Stanford: Stanford University Press, 2004), 108.

of literature, enhancing the sense of dialogue; of interactive communication in that "other state of being" in which the aesthetic, ethical, and intellectual heighten one another through competition and mutual support.

Maria Malikova: I have practically no experience teaching Nabokov. However, the few attempts I have made proved that his prose offers an ideal forum to train and refine students' skills of close reading (especially as the subject matter does not yet seem as antiquated as that of Russian classics), teaching them how to savour literary artifice.

Jeff Edmunds: I second Maria Malikova's opinion. Although, like her, I have no experience teaching Nabokov in the traditional sense, I think his work as a translator would be excellent source material for teaching not only the appreciation of literary artifice but also the translation of literary texts.

FIRST TIME BALL

RUSSIAN NABOKOV

Neil Cornwell

ORHAN PAMUK AND VLADIMIR NABOKOV ON DOSTOEVSKY

Orhan Pamuk's writing, his fiction and non-fiction, is not by any means short of references, allusions, and often tributes to other writers. Both Dostoevsky and Nabokov are prominent among such literary foils or mentors.[1] This essay will survey Dostoevsky's role in this respect, before proceeding to a discussion of Nabokov, in order to make comparisons between the attitudes of Pamuk and Nabokov towards Dostoevsky.[2]

---

[1] On Pamuk and Nabokov, see Neil Cornwell, "Secrets, Memories and Lives: Nabokov and Pamuk," in *Transitional Nabokov*, ed. Will Norman and Duncan White (Oxford: Peter Lang, 2009), 115-33.

[2] For a summary of Nabokov's dealings with Dostoevsky, see Georges Nivat, "Nabokov and Dostoevsky," in *The Garland Companion to Vladimir Nabokov*, ed. Vladimir E. Alexandrov (New York and London: Garland, 1995), 398-402. More specialised essays include: Sergej Davydov, "Dostoevsky and Nabokov: The Morality of Structure in *Crime and Punishment* and

PAMUK AND DOSTOEVSKY

Pamuk's activities as a collector of books and other objects "in the early days" (referring to his formative period around 1972), he told himself (and much later us, in his memoir), would eventually "all form part of a great enterprise—a painting or a series of paintings or a novel like those I was then reading by Tolstoy, Dostoyevsky and Mann."[3] And, indeed, we are also told: "[Pamuk's] early untranslated novels, *Cevdet Bey and His Sons* (1982) and *The Quiet House* (1983), were family sagas, modelled on Dostoevsky, Tolstoy and Thomas Mann."[4] Mann is another author (along with Dostoevsky) to whom Pamuk, unlike Vladimir Nabokov, wants to return "again and again."[5] In addition to Tolstoy, both Pamuk and Nabokov much admired Flaubert. Other Russian writers make appearances in Pamuk's works; for instance Turgenev and Pushkin in the novel *Snow*.[6]

Demons (or *The Devils*) [*Besy*] is referred to as *The Possessed* in *The Black Book* (probably Pamuk's major novel), in which its plot is said to be "replicated...down to the last detail" in the carrying out of a political murder.[7] This, no doubt, stemmed too from the fact that "a similar crime" (to that of

---

Despair," *Dostoevsky Studies* 3 (1982): 157-70; Katherine Tiernan O'Connor, "Rereading *Lolita*, Reconsidering Nabokov's Relationship with Dostoevsky," *Slavic and East European Journal* 33.1 (1989): 64-77; plus four essays by Julian W. Connolly: "Dostoevski and Vladimir Nabokov: The Case of *Despair*," in *Dostoevski and the Human Condition after a Century*, ed. Alexej Ugrinsky et al. (New York: Greenwood Press, 1986), 155-62; "Madness and Doubling: From Dostoevsky's *The Double* to Nabokov's *The Eye*," *Russian Literature Triquarterly* 24 (1991): 129-39; "Nabokov's Dialogue with Dostoevsky: *Lolita* and 'The Gentle Creature,'" *Nabokov Studies* 4 (1997): 15-36; and "Nabokov's (re)visions of Dostoevsky," in *Nabokov and his Fiction: New Perspectives*, ed. Julian W. Connolly (Cambridge: Cambridge University Press, 1999), 141-57. For more recent treatments, see: Dale E. Peterson, "White [K]nights: Dostoevskian Dreamers in Nabokov's Early Stories," in *Nabokov's World. Vol.2: Reading Nabokov*, ed. Jane Grayson, Arnold McMillin and Priscilla Meyer (Houndmills, Basingstoke: Palgrave, 2002), 59-72; and Alexey Sklyarenko, "'Grattez le Tartare...' or Who Were the Parents of *Ada's* Kim Beauharnais?" *The Nabokovian* 59 (2007): 40-9; 60 (2008): 8-17.

[3] Orhan Pamuk, *Istanbul: Memories of a City*, trans. Maureen Freely (London: Faber, 2006 [original 2005]), 319.

[4] Interview by Maya Jaggi, "Between two worlds," *The Guardian*, Saturday, December 8, 2007, 11, Features and reviews.

[5] Orhan Pamuk, *Other Colours: Essays and a Story*, trans. Maureen Freely (London: Faber, 2007 [originals 1999-2006]), 3.

[6] Orhan Pamuk, *Snow*, trans. Maureen Freely (London: Faber, 2005 [original 2002]), 31, 244, 435 (Turgenev: one character has translated *First Love*, "from the French," and in prison, 435; Pushkin, 325).

[7] Orhan Pamuk, *The Black Book*, trans. Maureen Freely (London: Faber, 2006 [original 1990]), 244.

Nechaev, and as re-presented in Dostoevsky's novel) "was perpetrated [albeit "unwittingly imitated"] in Turkey [by a] revolutionary cell to which a number of my classmates belonged."[8] Asked much later about his "first literary throbs," Pamuk replied: "*The Possessed* and *Anna Karenina*. I realized I loved them a thousand times more than any of my architecture books, and even more than my books on painting."[9] Yet, Pamuk still considers *Demons* "the greatest political novel of all time," to which he had been able to affix something of a Turkish understanding, in its own way adding to Dostoevsky's Russian-Slavic brand of non-Westernism.[10]

Pamuk was first "engrossed in" and overwhelmed by *The Brothers Karamazov* [*Brat'ia Karamazovy*] (a novel which his father's library contained in both English and Turkish) at the age of eighteen.[11] Twenty years later, in his own novelistic work, an apparently fictional "source" for The Grand Inquisitor purports to be a certain *Le grand pasha*, by one Dr. Ferit Kemal, a Turkish author writing in French, supposedly published in Paris in 1870, and "our only writer to present the Almighty in all His glory."[12] This work "does not — to the regret of many — feature in our [that is, evidently, the Turkish] literary canon" and indeed it appears to have been mischievously proposed by Pamuk in *The Black Book*:

> To exclude the only work that shows the Almighty in His true colours, simply because it was written in French, is as grievous as to allege that the Russian author Dostoyevsky stole the model for the Grand Inquisitor in *The Brothers Karamazov* from the same slim treatise — though it must be said that those who made this charge in the eastward-looking journals *Fountain* and *The Great East* did so with trepidation.[13]

"The Grand Inquisitor" returns later in the novel, referred to as someone's "copycat *nazire*," amid a controversy of smokescreen, translation or plagiarism.[14] For that matter, a quotation attributed to "Fyodor Dostoevsky, *Notebooks for The Brothers Karamazov*" serves as one of the epigraphs in

---

[8] Pamuk, *Other Colours*, 145.
[9] "Interview With Orhan Pamuk" by Lila Azam Zanganeh, trans. Sara Sugihara and Lila Azam Zanganeh, from "Orhan Pamuk: Être un artiste libre," *Le Monde*, May 12, 2006: htttp://www.lazangeneh.com/inside/pamuk.html (citation posted on NABOKV-L, September 25, 2007).
[10] Pamuk, *Other Colours*, 143; 144-5.
[11] Ibid., 147.
[12] Pamuk, *Black Book*, 153.
[13] Ibid.
[14] Ibid., 351.

Neil Cornwell

Snow: "Well, then, eliminate the people, curtail them, force them to be silent. Because the European Enlightenment is more important than people."[15] An intriguing, though frustratingly brief, paragraph in Pamuk's essay "Cruelty, Beauty and Time" (discussing *Ada* and *Lolita*) notes "Nabokov's quarrels with Freud," with guilt felt from "the golden age of his childhood," and Nabokov's own attempted "sorcery of a Freudian sort."[16]

Dostoevsky is the subject of three short essays by Pamuk; he also makes occasional appearances in his novels.[17] The Dostoevsky works mainly featured here are *Notes from Underground* [*Zapiski iz podpol'ia*], *Demons*, and *The Brothers Karamazov*. The two areas commented on that are perhaps of greatest potential interest for present purposes are Dostoevsky's talent for dramatisation, and his treatment of European ideas and of those who hold them.

The "experiment," as Dostoevsky terms it, singled out by Pamuk from *Notes from Underground*, is the scenario and events arising from the tavern fight around the billiard table. Commenting on this episode of "unexpected humiliation," Pamuk writes, "I see all the elements that characterize Dostoyevsky's later novels in this small scene."[18] With *Demons* particularly in mind, Pamuk affirms: "There are very few writers who can personify or dramatize beliefs, abstract thoughts, and philosophical contradictions as well as Dostoyevsky."[19] According to Pamuk, "Dostoyevsky is a consummate satirist, especially on crowded sets."[20] The dramatic effect is also implicit (as is the unmentioned concept of polyphony) in the "awe" expressed "for Dostoyevsky's ability to create so many characters who are so distinct from one another and to bring them to life in the reader's mind in such detail, color, and convincing depth."[21]

On the European front, Pamuk writes of the "true subject and wellspring" of *Notes from Underground* being "the jealousy, anger and pride of a man who cannot make himself into a European," rather than (as he himself had earlier thought) "his personal sense of alienation."[22] In his reaction to Chernyshevsky:

---

[15] Pamuk, *Snow*, np.
[16] Pamuk, *Other Colours*, 156.
[17] Chernyshevsky even gets into one of these, too: see *Black Book*, 69. "Dostoyevsky's *Notes from Underground*: The Joys of Degradation;" "Dostoyevsky's Fearsome Demons;" "The Brothers Karamazov": *Other Colours*, pp. 136-142; 143-146; 147-52.
[18] Pamuk, *Other Colours*, 141.
[19] Ibid., 144.
[20] Ibid., 145.
[21] Ibid., 150.
[22] Ibid., 137.

> [Dostoevsky's] anger was not a simple expression of anti-Westernism or hostility to European thinking. [...] What Dostoyevsky resented was that European thought came to his country at second hand. What angered him was not its brilliance, its originality, or its utopian leanings but the facile pleasure it afforded those who embraced it. He hated seeing Russian intellectuals seize upon an idea just arrived from Europe and believe themselves privy to all the secrets of the world and — more important — of their own country. He could not bear the happiness this grand illusion gave them.[23]

Dostoevsky's "gloomy, damning ambivalence" is what strikes Pamuk: "his familiarity with European thought and his anger against it, his equal and opposite desires to belong to Europe and to shun it."[24] Dostoevsky (rather like Pamuk himself, in his, and our, modern era) feels himself caught between the two worlds. As a young leftist reading *Demons*, Pamuk felt that Dostoevsky was being pulled into

> a society of radicals who, though inflamed by dreams of changing the world, were also locked into secret organizations and taken with the pleasure of deceiving others in the name of revolution, damning and degrading those who did not speak their language or share their vision.[25]

Ignored in leftist circles in Pamuk's Turkey, Dostoevsky, it might be said, was not so much against the ideas themselves, but the people who held them — deceiving not only others, but each other (and themselves) as well. In any event, Pamuk would no doubt strongly agree with A. N. Wilson's comment that "it is essential to read the novels [as opposed to the same author's journalism] as narratives in which ideas repellent to Dostoevsky are given freedom to breathe."[26] In a later piece, Pamuk perhaps puts his argument even more cogently:

> I am in sympathy with Dostoevsky, who was so infuriated by Russian intellectuals who knew Europe better than they did Russia. At the same time, I don't see this anger as particularly justified. From my own experience, I know that behind Dostoevsky's dutiful defences of Russian culture and Orthodox mysticism was a rage not just against the west, but against those who did not know their own culture.[27]

---

[23] Ibid., 138.
[24] Ibid., 142.
[25] Pamuk, *Other Colours*, 144-5.
[26] A.N. Wilson, "Shot at the altar," review of *Dostoevsky: Language Faith and Fiction*, by Rowan Williams, *TLS*, October 10, 2008, 3-5 (5).
[27] Orhan Pamuk, "The collector," trans. Maureen Freely, *The Guardian Review*, October 18, 2008, 19.

One reviewer of *Other Colours*, Christopher de Bellaigue, stated that

> Pamuk is a better novelist than essayist;...[i]n a ponderous description of the effect that the *Brothers Karamazov* had on him as a boy, for instance, he takes a page to say what the arresting first line of his novel, *The New Life*, says in a sentence: "I read a book one day and my whole life was changed."[28]

There are weak points in Pamuk's views on Dostoevsky. He appears to believe, for instance, that Dostoevsky reached "the age of seventy,"[29] and one would certainly hesitate to go all the way with Pamuk's conclusion that "Dostoyevsky, who wrote one of the greatest novels ever, hated the West, and Europe, as much as today's provincial Islamists."[30] Nevertheless, de Bellaigue may be somewhat discordant, as well as unfair, in asserting that "[Pamuk] situating himself so close to the likes of Dostoevsky and Nabokov strikes a discordant note, at once aspirational and unadventurous."[31]

NABOKOV AND DOSTOEVSKY

Dostoevsky is undoubtedly one of the writers lurking behind Nabokov's much-quoted fulmination to his students at Cornell: "Style and structure are the essence of a book; great ideas are hogwash."[32] Similarly, in Nabokov's lecture on Dickens: "The effect of style is the key to literature, a magic key to Dickens, Gogol, Flaubert, Tolstoy, to all great masters."[33] Another student reports on Nabokov's grading of Russian writers, with Dostoevsky rating just C- ("Or was he D-plus?"), Tolstoy getting the sole A+, while Pushkin and Chekhov each manage to achieve an A.[34] In a 1946 letter to Edmund Wilson, Nabokov referred to Dostoevsky as "a third rate writer and his fame

---

[28] Christopher de Bellaigue, "Portrait in black-and-white," *TLS*, March 21, 2008, 19. Cf. Orhan Pamuk, *The New Life*, trans. Güneli Gün (London: Faber, 1998 [original 1994]).
[29] Pamuk, *Other Colours*, 151.
[30] Ibid., 152.
[31] de Bellaigue, "Portrait," 19.
[32] This is reported by a student (Updike's "own wife," her name not here given) of Nabokov's "last classes" in 1958, in Vladimir Nabokov, *Lectures on Literature*, introduction by John Updike, ed. Fredson Bowers (London: Weidenfeld and Nicolson, 1980), xxiii.
[33] Ibid., 113.
[34] Turgenev was allegedly as high as A-, and Gogol merely a B-. Hannah Green, "Mr Nabokov," in *Vladimir Nabokov: A Tribute*, ed. Peter Quennell (London: Weidenfeld and Nicolson, 1979), 37.

is incomprehensible."³⁵ Occasionally, though, Nabokov's somewhat extreme deprecations are accompanied with a qualification. In a 1964 *Playboy* interview, Nabokov, carefully prepared, as always, interposes the sentence "I admit that some of his scenes, some of his tremendous, farcical rows are extraordinarily amusing" between the two statements: "He was a prophet, a claptrap journalist and a slapdash comedian. [...] But his sensitive murderers and soulful prostitutes are not to be endured for one moment — by this reader anyway."³⁶ In a similar manner, even with a modicum of consistency one might say, not even the A+ Tolstoy escapes Nabokov's criticism: "The mystical didacticism of Gogol or the utilitarian moralism of Tolstoy, or the reactionary journalism of Dostoevski, are of their own poor making and in the long run nobody really takes them seriously."³⁷

The mightier the (in particular, American) reputation of a Dostoevsky work, from among "his worst novels," the stronger the (at least purported) ire it inspired in Nabokov:

> I dislike intensely *The Karamazov Brothers* and the ghastly *Crime and Punishment* rigmarole. No, I do not object to soul-searching and self-revelation, but in those books the soul, and the sins, and the sentimentality, and the journalese, hardly warrant the tedious and muddled search.³⁸

Yet in February 1950, between his comments to Wilson in 1946, and his interview with the BBC in 1968, Nabokov was proposing to translate the intensely disliked Karamazovs for Viking, presumably due largely from despair at existing translations; but we are told that the project was "relinquished" "in April after he was hospitalized."³⁹ Apparently he had considered translating Dostoevsky much earlier, in 1923, for Orbis in Berlin; an imprint set up by the father of Véra Slonim (Nabokov's future wife) to produce Russian classics for the American market.⁴⁰ This was despite his

---

35 Vladimir Nabokov, *Dear Bunny, Dear Volodya: The Nabokov-Wilson Letters, 1940-1971*, Revised and Expanded Edition, ed. Simon Karlinsky (Berkeley: University of California Press, 2001), 197.
36 Vladimir Nabokov, *Strong Opinions* (London: Weidenfeld and Nicolson, 1974), 42.
37 Ibid., 65.
38 Ibid., 148.
39 Vladimir Nabokov, *Selected Letters 1940-1977*, ed. Dmitri Nabokov and Matthew J. Bruccoli (London: Vintage, 1991), 97. See also Brian Boyd, *Vladimir Nabokov: The American Years* (London: Chatto and Windus, 1992), 146-7. Boyd calls this "a surprising project," agreed to when Nabokov was "still short of money" (146).
40 Brian Boyd, *Vladimir Nabokov: The Russian Years* (London: Chatto and Windus, 1990), 212.

negative assessment of *Crime and Punishment* on rereading it at the age of nineteen: "long-winded, terribly sentimental, and badly written," as opposed to having earlier declared it "a wonderfully powerful and exciting book," admittedly at the age of twelve.[41]

Nabokov's one sustained piece of discourse on Dostoevsky is, of course, the lecture in his posthumously published volume *Lectures on Russian Literature*, which first appeared in 1981.[42] At the outset, Nabokov acknowledges: "My position in regard to Dostoevski is a curious and difficult one." Nabokov approaches literature as "enduring art and individual genius." He continues: "From this point of view Dostoevski is not a great writer, but a rather mediocre one — with flashes of excellent humor, but, alas, with wastelands of literary platitudes in between." He admits (or perhaps even boasts): "I am very eager to debunk Dostoevski."[43]

The discredit comes thick and fast in the form of general exposition, followed by five mini-analyses, much of which are taken up with synopsis and quotation (on *Crime and Punishment*; "Memoirs from a Mousehole," as he insists on calling *Notes from Underground*; *The Idiot*; *The Possessed*; and *The Brothers Karamazov*).[44] Many of the comments are the sort of thing that we might now expect. Dostoevsky found "a neurotic Christianism," so as not to go "completely mad" in his penal servitude years; his characters have "this trick [...] of 'sinning their way to Jesus.'"[45]

Dostoevsky is credited with being "an intricate plotter" who "keeps up his suspenses with consummate mastery"; however, he does not bear rereading.[46] The real "flaw" in *Crime and Punishment*, causing "the whole edifice to crumble ethically and esthetically" is epitomised in one sentence from part ten, chapter four:

> ...sheer stupidity has hardly the equal in world-famous literature [...] The candle was flickering out, dimly lighting up in the poverty-stricken room the murderer and the harlot who had been reading together the eternal book.[47]

---

[41] Vladimir Nabokov, *Lectures on Russian Literature*, ed. Fredson Bowers (London: Weidenfeld and Nicolson, 1982), 110. On this initial 1911 opinion, Brian Boyd comments: "That is not the Nabokov we know." Quoted in Boyd, *The Russian Years*, 150, 91.
[42] Nabokov, "Fyodor Dostoevski (1821-1881)," *Lectures on Russian Literature*, 97-135.
[43] Nabokov, *Lectures on Russian Literature*, 98.
[44] The last named work being omitted from the Contents page, at least in the 1982 edition.
[45] Nabokov, *Lectures on Russian Literature*, 100-01, 104.
[46] Ibid., 109
[47] Ibid., 110.

This dreadful "triangle" (of "murderer," "harlot," and "eternal book") is judged "a shoddy literary trick, not a masterpiece of pathos and piety."[48] Such a formulation is seen as deriving from "the conventional link of the Gothic novel and the sentimental novel,"[49] coming from the influence of "the European mystery novel"—the extraction of "the last ounce of pathos."[50] Western influence remained in Dostoevsky, to an extent that "one is tempted to say that in a way Dostoevski, who so hated the West, was the most European of Russian writers."[51] At the same time, credit is occasionally given: "In *The Possessed* there is the delightful skit on Turgenev"[52]—a detail also singled out by Pamuk, who calls it "a biting caricature."[53]

Nabokov held that Dostoevsky should have been "Russia's greatest playwright, but he took the wrong turning and wrote novels;" *The Brothers Karamazov*, for instance, seemed "a straggling play."[54] "What his novels represent is a succession of scenes, of dialogues, of scenes where all the people are brought together—and with all the tricks of the theatre."[55] Dostoevsky is "a writer of mystery stories,"[56] at times a successful exploiter of "the detective story technique," capable of writing "a riotous whodunit—in slow motion," though he is still liable to "a bad flaw" (in this case, Ivan Karamazov's failure to tell the court about Smerdiakov's admitted use of the heavy ashtray).[57]

The longest analysis goes to "Memoirs from a Mousehole," whose title, Nabokov says, should really be "Memoirs from Under the Floor" (*Notes from Underground* being a "stupidly incorrect title"). In terms of "a study in style," it is "the best picture we have of Dostoevski's themes and formulas and intonations. It is a concentration of Dostoevskiana."[58] Nabokov does not single out the scene admired by Pamuk, instead going for the "mouseman" being thrust aside by the military man; and he then hones in on the dinner scene, with Zverkov and his cronies: "one of the best scenes in Dostoevski," who did have "a wonderful flair for comedy mixed with tragedy." He even goes as far as to affirm that Dostoevsky "may be termed a very wonderful humorist,

---

48 Ibid.
49 Ibid.
50 Ibid., 103.
51 Ibid.
52 Ibid., 129.
53 Nabokov, *Other Colours*, 145.
54 Nabokov, *Lectures on Russian Literature*, 104; see also on *The Possessed*, 129.
55 Ibid., 130.
56 Ibid., 109.
57 Ibid., 133; 135.
58 Ibid., 115.

with the humor always on the verge of hysterics and people hurting each other in a wild exchange of insults."[59]

The one work by Dostoevsky which meets with Nabokov's full approval, although not accorded any full attention in his *Lectures*, is *The Double* [*Dvoinik*]. This early work is singled out by Nabokov (in 1955) as "by far the best thing Dostoevski ever wrote"; "a perfect work of art [...] and moreover its imitation of Gogol is so striking as to seem at times almost a parody."[60] Other things apart, this 1846 work was, of course, written before Dostoevsky's arrest and exile, and therefore before he succumbed to his obsessions with "great ideas" or any other such "hogwash."

In addition to what he has to say in his letters, interviews and lectures, Nabokov also made a protracted, and often a more subtle, use of Dostoevsky in his own fiction. Much of this activity has been discussed by a number of commentators (see especially those listed in footnote 2), though no doubt more will be said. Reflections of Dostoevsky in Nabokov's fiction are frequently taken as satire, or as variants, but, as stressed by Georges Nivat, parody may be the more fitting term.[61] The most frequently cited example is probably Nabokov's allusions to Dostoevsky in *Despair* (which are in fact amplified in what has to be considered the definitive English text of 1965). In this novel, Dostoevsky is included by Hermann Karlovich (not exactly a positive protagonist in Nabokovian terms with, apart from anything else, his respect for Marxism and the Soviet Union) among "the great novelists who wrote of nimble criminals" (alongside Doyle, Leblanc and Wallace).[62] More famously, he refers to "old Dusty's great book, *Crime and Slime*. Sorry: *Schuld und Sühne* (German edition)" and the "all Dusty-and-Dusky charm of hysterics."[63] Later, "a grotesque resemblance to Rascalnikov" is mentioned.[64] The literary

---

[59] Ibid., 122.
[60] Nabokov, *Selected Letters* 160; *Lectures on Russian Literature*, 100, 104. At the time of a 1967 interview, Nabokov still deemed it "his best work," with the qualification "though an obvious and shameless imitation of Gogol's 'Nose.'" He then adds: "Felix in *Despair* is really a *false* double" (Nabokov, *Strong Opinions*, 84).
[61] Nivat, *Nabokov and Dostoevsky*, 399, quoting in support of Nabokov's affirmation: "Satire is a lesson, parody is a game" (Nabokov, *Strong Opinions*, 75).
[62] Vladimir Nabokov, *Despair* (London: Penguin, 1981 [1987 reprint; revised English edition first published 1965; original published as *Otchaianie* 1934]), 106.
[63] Ibid., 148, 156.
[64] "In spite of a grotesque resemblance to Raskolnikov—No, that's wrong. Cancelled" (Nabokov, *Despair*, 158). Nivat (p. 399) quotes from an American edition (a Vintage, 1989, reprint; the original was G. P. Putnam's Sons, 1965) using "Rascalnikov." The Penguin imprint (1981, reprinted 1987) appears to have "corrected" [?] the American spelling.

phenomenon of the double is parodied in this work, and Nivat asserts that "In Dostoevsky's 'thrillers' [Nabokov] dislikes the philosophical and religious message. But he appreciates the plot."[65] While this may be largely so, the later Nabokov, in particular, is fully capable of complaining about Dostoevsky's "melodramatic muddle" together with his "phony mysticism."[66]

While later novels written (or revised) in English may see strong parodic uses of, or references to, Dostoevsky (one would probably think in particular of *Lolita*, *Ada* and *Look at the Harlequins!* in this respect, in addition to *Despair*; nor should *The Gift* be forgotten), Nabokov's early (Russian) fiction indulges in a perhaps more respectful exploitation. Julian Connolly and Dale Peterson have explored instances of Dostoevskian "dreamers" and "doubles" in the earlier fiction. Peterson sees it as "quite likely that the young Nabokov began his career in prose fiction as a fellow traveller of the young Dostoevsky."[67] According to Connolly, aside from "Nabokov's professed antipathy for Dostoevsky's excesses" in his public utterances, "the evidence of his prose fiction reveals a more complex relationship"; as already indicated to an extent here, "it is apparent that Nabokov's views on Dostoevsky underwent a complex evolution."[68] One could hardly do better than to stress Connolly's conclusion on the matter: "Seen as a whole, Nabokov's relationship to Dostoevsky forms an intricate design marked by points of striking engagement and recoil."[69]

CONCLUSION:
PAMUK, NABOKOV AND DOSTOEVSKY

We might well suspect that, in terms of "professed antipathy" for Dostoevsky, and at least some other of the writers regularly denounced by Nabokov (Henry James is another example),[70] his megaphoned distaste is at least partly attributable to a Bloomian anxiety of influence—the author in question having prematurely anticipated Nabokovian elements but without,

---

[65] Nivat, *Nabokov and Dostoevsky*, 400.
[66] Nabokov, *Strong Opinions*, 266.
[67] Peterson, *White [K]nights*, 71.
[68] Connolly, *Nabokov's (re)visions of Dostoevsky*, 141.
[69] Ibid., 154.
[70] On this subject, see Neil Cornwell, "Paintings, Governesses and 'Publishing Scoundrels': Nabokov and Henry James," in *Nabokov's World. Vol. 2: Reading Nabokov*, ed. Jane Grayson, Arnold McMillin and Priscilla Meyer (Houndmills, Basingstoke: Palgrave, 2002), 96-116.

of course, executing them to Nabokov's satisfaction. In Dostoevsky's case, one might also suggest that the shared biographical parallels between the two writers — of enforced exile (however different the circumstances) and the murder of the father — might not have been greatly relished by Nabokov.[71]

Pamuk and Nabokov approached Dostoevsky, ostensibly at least, from very different viewpoints (national, geographical, cultural and political) and apparent starting points of estimation. However, that being so, there is perhaps a surprising amount of common ground in some of the things that they have said, and in many of the details that interested them in the literary career of Dostoevsky.

Just one example may suffice, at this stage, to confirm this assertion. Nabokov's strong enthusiasm for Dostoevsky's *The Double* has been stressed already. Pamuk acknowledges his own immersion in "that most celebrated of literary themes: identical twins changing places," pointing to examples in Hoffmann, Poe, Dostoevsky and Stevenson.[72] In particular, Dostoevsky's early novel *The Double* is duly acknowledged as having been accorded "homage in the legend of the epileptic pope in the Slavic villages" of *The White Castle* (1979), Pamuk's first novel; though certainly not his last to exploit extensive double-formation, false doubles and identity-play.[73]

The Double, we have noted already, and now stress again, was singled out by Nabokov as "by far the best thing Dostoevski ever wrote."[74] Moreover, this particular Dostoevsky novella is now perceived to have Nabokovian qualities, having recently been honoured by Eric Naiman with a "preposterous" (i.e. "arsy-versy" or, in other words, anachronistic) reading ("What if Nabokov had written 'Dvoinik'?").[75] If the approaches of Nabokov and Pamuk to Dostoevsky can make a topic of some interest, as we hope has been here demonstrated, an even more fascinating project, following Naiman's lead, might be to

---

[71] These last two points have been made previously in Neil Cornwell, *Vladimir Nabokov* (Plymouth: Northcote House, 1999), 59; 20.

[72] Nabokov, *Other Colours* 249-50.

[73] Orhan Pamuk, *The White Castle*, trans. Victoria Holbrook (London: Faber, 2001 [first published 1990; original 1979]). See Nabokov, *Other Colours*, 249, where it is referred to as "Dostoyevsky's *The Other*."

[74] Nabokov, *Selected Letters*, 160.

[75] Eric Naiman, "What if Nabokov had written 'Dvoinik'? Reading Literature Preposterously," *Russian Review* 64.4 (October 2005): 575-89. Such a "phenomenon" (the alleged influence of T. S. Eliot on Shakespeare) features, of course, in David Lodge's novel *Small World* (London: Secker & Warburg, 1984). More recently, Pierre Bayard purports to investigate such suppositions in his *Le plagiat par anticipation* (Paris: Les Éditions de Minuit, 2009), 30-31; reviewed by David Coward in *TLS*, May 8, 2009, 32, who offers the term "forward plagiarism."

subject *The Eye*, *Despair*, "Ultima Thule," *The Real Life of Sebastian Knight*, *Bend Sinister* or, in particular, *Look at the Harlequins!* to a "preposterous" Pamukian reading. Ostensibly, this would require another—no doubt, full-length—study.

As an endnote, we should add that, not long before the end of his most recent novel, *The Museum of Innocence* (2008), Pamuk has his protagonist Kemal Bey, compulsive collector and manic museum visitor, place brief mentions of the St. Petersburg museums to Dostoevsky and Nabokov in successive sentences. He is here addressing "Orhan Bey" on "his [Pamuk's] favorite writers."[76] Pamuk is now emerging, we might think in eminently Nabokovian fashion, from mere mention as a minor character to promotion as the overseeing ultimate scribe of this particular, for want of a better expression, extended "collectionist" love-saga.

---

[76] Orhan Pamuk, *The Museum of Innocence: A Novel*, trans. Maureen Freely (London: Faber, 2010 [original 2008]), 512-13.

Franklin Sciacca

SACRIFICING THE MAIDEN('S)HEAD: DECODING NABOKOV'S BURLESQUE OF SEX AND VIOLENCE IN *INVITATION TO A BEHEADING*

What have I put in my works to suggest so many subtleties?
I have put in them a little door opening onto a mystery.[1]

BEHEADING

Two tales of decollations particularly resonate in the Western artistic imagination — that of Orpheus, the sublime musician, and of John the Baptist, the seer-prophet to whom the divine voice spoke in the wilderness. Ancient Greek myth identified Orpheus as the son of Apollo and Calliope (the Muse of epic poetry). He was renowned as a skilled player of the lyre (a gift from

I would like to thank the students in my Nabokov Seminar at Hamilton College for their astute comments and suggestions for this article. In particular I wish to acknowledge the contributions of Evan Adair, Julie Kruidenier and Martin Nedbal in articulating and crafting annotations.

[1] Odilon Redon, *To Myself: Notes on Life, Art and Artists*, trans. Jeanne L. Wasserman (New York: George Braziller, 1996).

his father) and his music bewitched the Sirens and Hades. "Not only his fellow-mortals but wild beasts were softened by his strains."² According to Aeschylus, the Maenads tore Orpheus to pieces, and his severed head, perched on his lyre, floated to Lesbos, where an oracle was established. The head prophesied with such renown that Apollo, in a fit of jealousy, eventually closed the Orphic oracle, because its popularity outrivaled that of his Delphic shrine. "Orphism" was revived, or rather, reinvented by nineteenth-century poets in the context of "the broader Romantic revival of poetic or imaginative man...Orpheus represented the reflexive or self-conscious activity of the imagination, the power by which man distinguishes himself as the single artificer of the world in which he sings."³ European artists of the century painted Orpheus's head with iconographic reverence and repetitiveness. For example, Gustave Moreau's earliest innovative renditions ("Thracian Girl Carrying the Head of Orpheus," 1864 and 1865) depict the head, crowned with the poet's laurel wreath, carried on his lyre by a young woman.⁴ Andre Breton wrote of this exemplary image, "[A] priestess exchang[es] with Orpheus the unutterable gaze of Hegelian 'death' and a human being to which it transmits its secret."⁵ Marcel Proust, on the same painting by Moreau: "Thus it is that the poets do not wholly die and something of their true soul is kept for us, something of that inner life in which alone they felt their true self expand and live."⁶ The Orphic head figures emblematically as the immortal repository of divine imagination, poetry, and mystical knowledge.

The severed cranium as a symbolic locus of knowledge is likewise developed in the various accounts and depictions of John the Baptist. One should recall the theological role of John as "precursor" or "forerunner" in the Gospels. He is among the first to be inspired by the *logos* to *know* that Jesus is the Christ ("The word of God came to John...in the wilderness");⁷ he possessed theological knowledge, *gnosis* in its pure sense. John's imprisonment was politically and morally motivated; the result of his open challenge to Herod, and his condemnation of Herod and Herod's wife, Herodias, for moral

---

² Thomas Bulfinch, *Myths of Greece and Rome* (New York: Penguin Books, 1981), 218.
³ R.A. Yoder, *Emerson and the Orphic Poet in America* (Berkeley: University of California Press, 1978), xii-xiii; see also Elizabeth Sewell, *The Orphic Voice: Poetry and Natural History* (New Haven: Yale University Press, 1960).
⁴ Pierre-Louis Mathieu, *Gustave Moreau: With a Catalogue of the Finished Paintings, Watercolors and Drawings* (Boston: New York Graphic Society, 1976), 15, 97.
⁵ Ibid., 98.
⁶ Ibid., 98-9.
⁷ Luke 3:2.

Franklin Sciacca

turpitude.[8] The Baptist's beheading was the caprice of the enraged and offended Herodias, carried out at the request of her daughter Salome, after the daughter's salacious dance so enthralled the phlegmatic Herod that he offered to give her anything she wished, up to half of his kingdom.[9] Traditional iconographic renditions of the event were literal in their visual presentation of the terse Gospel account.[10] For example, in the sixteenth-century fresco in Varlaam Monastery (Meteora, Greece), a soldier wielding a large unsheathed sword prepares to execute the haloed and kneeling John, while Salome bends close to John to catch his head on a gold plate. It was, again, the nineteenth-century poets and painters who perceived in the biblical event a mystical quality worthy of deeper analysis and interpretation. Modernist painters and writers and, a few decades later, film directors,[11] concentrated on the dance of Salome, often in the presence of or holding the detached head. Emblematic of the latter-day interpretation of the event is Moreau's "The Apparition"

---

[8] Matthew 14:3-4; Mark 6:17-18.

[9] Matthew 14:6-10; Mark 6:21-28. The dance, erotic by nature, thus takes the form of *danse macabre*, a dance of death. See Hellmut Rosenfeld, *Der mittelalterliche Totentanz: Entstehung-Entwicklung-Bedeutung* (Cologne: Bohlau Verlag, 1968); and Daniel Rancour-Laferriere, "All the World's a *Vertep*: The Personification/Depersonification Complex in Gogol's *Sorochinskaja jarmarka*," *Harvard Ukrainian Studies* VI.3 (September 1982): 344-7. In the Salome myth, eroticism prefigures death. Thomas Mann noted the correlation in his novel *Joseph the Provider* (New York: Alfred A. Knopf, 1944), 272-3: "There does exist a certain relation between death and marriage, a bridal chamber and a tomb, a murder and the abduction of a virgin. It is no great strain to think of a bridegroom as a god of death." Does Cincinnatus's dance early in Nabokov's text serve as a Salome-inspired prefiguration of his death by decapitation? Is the (homo)erotic overtone suggestive of the coitus=death equation? "Rodion the jailer came in and offered to dance a waltz with him. Cincinnatus agreed. They began to whirl. The keys on Rodion's leather belt jangled...The dance carried them into the corridor. Cincinnatus was much smaller than his partner. Cincinnatus was light as a leaf...his big limpid eyes looked askance, as is always the case with timorous dancers...They described a circle...and glided back into the cell, and now Cincinnatus regretted that the swoon's friendly embrace had been so brief" (Vladimir Nabokov, *Invitation to a Beheading* [New York: Paragon Books, 1959], 13-4).

[10] Two significant monographs on John the Baptist iconography are: Raoul Plus, *Saint Jean-Baptiste dans l'art* (Paris: Editions Alsatia, 1937), and Oskar Thulin, *Johannes der Taufer im geistlichen Schauspiel des Mittelalters und der Reformationszeit* (Leipzig: Dietrich, 1930).

[11] So striking was the visual potential of the dance of death that between 1902 and 1922, ten silent film versions of Salome were made (four American, two German, two Italian, one French, one British). See Derek Elley, *The Epic Film: Myth and History* (London: Routledge & Kegan Paul, 1984), 194-5. For a substantial analysis of the manipulation of the motifs from the legend of John the Baptist and Salome in the novel, see Gavriel Shapiro, "The Salome Motif in Nabokov's *Invitation to a Beheading*," in *Delicate Markers: Subtexts in Vladimir Nabokov's Invitation to a Beheading* (New York: Peter Lang, 1998).

(1876),[12] in which the revivified head of the Baptist, eyes wide open, blood dripping from his neck and surrounded by a halo-sunburst, hovers before the astonished dancer. Here the traditional norms of death have been abandoned. The resurrection of the head is presented as a mystical accomplishment, while the unvanquishable power of *gnosis* is proclaimed. The abstraction is carried further in a startling icon ("The Glorification of St. John") of the early twentieth century by J. H. Rosen, painted for the Armenian Cathedral in L'viv.[13] John's headless torso (a sunburst in place of his head) stands serenely in a row of saints. The head, with the mouth opened wide in agony, is held by an attendant saint. The rays of light forming the sunburst are an iconographic *topos* traditionally reserved for the mystical dove, the Holy Spirit, which is the divine manifestation that can confer charismatic gifts of prophecy and knowledge. In the poetic realm, then, the severed head is to be recognized as metonymic of poetic imagination and mystical knowledge.[14]

BOATING AND BLUENESS

In the literature of the Romantics and their followers, imagination and fantasy were likened to boats, more precisely to ship cabins, which were envisioned as isolated, expansive crania-wombs surrounded by the nurturing sea. The cabins, with their single portholes, symbolized the place of mental gestation and imaginistic peregrinations. Des Esseintes, the effete decadent of Huysmans' novel *Against the Grain* (1884), for example, constructs precisely such a womb-cabin as the dining room (the place of nurturing) in his hideaway: "The dining room...resembled a ship's cabin with its wooden ceiling of arched beams, its bulkheads and flooring of pitch-pine, its tiny

---

[12] Pierre-Louis Mathieu, *Gustave Moreau, The Watercolors* (New York: Hudson Hills Press, 1985), 28-29, plate 11. See also Mathieu, *Catalogue*, 131, 157-164, 176, 328-9 (Moreau's variations on the theme of Salome); and 247, plate on Jean Delville's "Dead Orpheus," 1893, in which the severed head appears to grow out of the lyre, a pure evocation of the notion of the head as the repository of the Muses (whose attribute was the lyre).

[13] Plus, *Saint*, 120.

[14] It is curious to note in passing that in the psychoanalytic realm, decapitation is interpreted as castration. Freud developed the thesis in his analysis of the mythological theme of "the horrifying decapitated head of Medusa." "To decapitate=to castrate. The terror of Medusa is thus a terror of castration that is linked to the sight of something" (Sigmund Freud, "Medusa's Head." *The Standard Edition of the Complete Psychological Works*, vol. 18 [London: Hogarth Press, 1953], 273). Is that "something" secret knowledge?

Franklin Sciacca

window-opening cut through the woodwork as a porthole in a vessel's side."[15] This is the sea-worthy room in which, often under the influence of exotic liqueurs, des Esseintes hallucinates and carries on long, thoughtful discourses with himself.

The mythology of boat-womb-cranium as a vehicle for imaginative travel is further developed in Arthur Rimbaud's "*Le Bateau ivre* [*The Drunken Boat*]." The title conjoins the boat with intoxication, itself a mental transformation and an inducement to imaginative journey.

> Ostensibly, "*Le Bateau ivre*" describes the journey of the voyant in a tipsy boat that has been freed from all constraints and launched headlong into a world of sea and sky that is heaving with the erotic rhythms of a universal dynamic force. The voyant himself is on an ecstatic search for some unnamed ideal that he seems to glimpse through the aquatic tumult.[16]

Vladimir Nabokov hinted at the link between Rimbaud's poem and his own work. In *Lolita*, the verse is conjured up with a deliberately but tellingly travestied title, "*Le Bateau bleu* [*The Blue Boat*]."[17] Nabokov employed the image of the boat in *Invitation to a Beheading* in a way quite sympathetic to the significance it had attained in earlier literature. Quite contrary to his adamant claim that he "detest[ed] symbols and allegories (which is due partly to my old feud with Freudian voodooism and partly to my loathing of generalizations devised by literary mythists and sociologists"),[18] a statement that only brings attention to those things he claimed to avoid, Nabokov made full use of a large cache of traditional symbols and metaphors. The prison cell of Cincinnatus (the hero of *Invitation*) is likened to a ship's cabin. As such, it is representative of the imaginative writing he composes there (his "criminal mind" being nurtured by it the way Raskol'nikov's mind drew peculiar strength from his tiny garret [каюта]).[19] The cell is thus Cincinnatus's hyperbolically expanded brain, the womb of imagination, the dwelling-place of the last true

---

[15] J. K. Huysmans, *Against the Grain* (New York: Dover Publications, Inc., 1969), 18.

[16] Magaret Davies-Mitchell, "Rimbaud, Arthur," *Encyclopædia Britannica* (2006). Encyclopædia Britannica Online. 10 May 2006, http://search.eb.com/eb/article-6202.

[17] "In horrible taste but basically suggestive of a cultured man—not a policeman, not a common goon, not a lewd salesman—were such assumed names as 'Arthur Rainbow'—plainly the travestied author of *Le Bateau Bleu*—let me laugh a little too, gentlemen..." (Vladimir Nabokov, *Lolita* [New York: G. P. Putnam's Sons, 1955], 252).

[18] Nabokov, "On a Book Entitled Lolita" (in *Lolita*, 316).

[19] A workman who comes to give Raskol'nikov money called the garret "a ship's cabin; *ekaia morskaia kaiuta*"—this the room in which Raskol'nikov ruminates and hallucinates (F. M. Dostoevskii, *Prestuplenie i nakazanie* [Moscow: Nauka, 1970], 94).

gnostic ("I knew what it is impossible to know").[20] The cell, "with its peephole like a leak in a boat," is where Cincinnatus becomes seasick, or alternately, nearly drowns.[21] From this "port" he sets off on an imagined journey by tub-canoe in the spirit of des Esseintes. The mental journey is induced by Cincinnatus's *writing* a journal entry on Day five.[22] Thus accomplished though art, the journey is reminiscent of the symbolist painter Odilon Redon's variation of the Orphic head. In his *"Tete d'Orphee flottant sur les eaux"* (c. 1881), the upright head floats, its neck rooted in and drawing sustenance from the water. Here is a vision of the cranium of imagination as a boat. In a later variant (*"Tete d'Orphee sur la lyre"*), the lyre serves as vessel.[23] How eloquent and clear is the visual portrayal of the unity of symbols—head, boat, water—the sources and nourishers of creativity and imagination!

Nabokov reveals in *Lolita* that blue is the color of the boat inspired by Rimbaud's poem. Blue thus becomes the synonym for intoxication-fantasy. Those critical colorists who have exhaustively analyzed the symbolic values of various colors in various poetries and literatures report with great consistency that

> the blue sky...is a symbol employed throughout post-romantic literature of the nineteenth and twentieth centuries to reveal man's isolation, the indifference of everything beyond the human sphere to the sufferings within him, to the hardships and catastrophes of his existence.[24]

Further, as the critical psychoanalyst Jung states

> We would conjecture that blue standing for the vertical means height and depth (the blue sky above, the blue sky below)...The vertical would correspond to the unconscious. But the unconscious in a man has feminine characteristics, and blue is the traditional colour of the Virgin's cloak.[25]

---

[20] Ibid., 95.
[21] Nabokov, *Invitation*, 12-13, 57.
[22] Ibid., 64-5.
[23] Robert Coustet, *L'Univers d'Odilon Redon* (Paris: Henri Screpel, 1984), 84; Roseline Bacou, *La donation Ari et Suzanne Redon* (Paris: Editions de la Reunion des musees nationaux, 1984), 13.
[24] W. J. Lillymans, "The Blue Sky: A Recurrent Symbol," *Comparative Literature* 21 (1969): 118. See also the discussions of the significance of the color blue in Allan H. Pasco, The Color-keys to *"A la recherche du temps perdu"* (Geneva: Librairie Droz, 1976), 85-100, 211; William Gass, *On Being Blue: A Philosophical Inquiry* (Boston: David R. Godine, 1975).
[25] Carl G. Jung, *Psychology and Alchemy*, vol. 12 of *The Collected Works*, trans. R. F. C. Hull (London: Routledge & Kegan Paul, 1953), 203-4.

Thus blue possesses two symbolic referents, the intellect and femininity. The bilingual punster has yet another trick he can play: *Goluboi (goluben'kii)*, the "blue" of blue skies, of Nabokov's blue porthole ("*goluboi glazok*"), blue temples ("*golubizna viskov*"), and "bluest blue" pulsating veins ("*golubye, kak samoe goluboe, pul'sirovali zhilki*"), are all slang for gay/homosexual, the Russian equivalent of *l'amour bleu*, linking Cincinnatus's imagination to his ambiguous gender role.²⁶

Nabokov accepts and employs both the normative significance of blue as intellect, and its secondary significance as femininity in his novel *Invitation to a Beheading*. The reader is *invited* to the *beheading* of a "blue" character, one who stands out from the others in the text because of his intellectual capacities and his uncertain sexuality. But the text is also an invitation to intellectual search and creative thinking on the part of the reader; the text is riddled with allusions to boating and to the color blue. These hints underlie the entirety of the novel, forming its hidden structure of signification in a multi-layered, bilingual, shifting, and expansive verbal game. Let us attempt to trace these underlying meanings; to enter Nabokov's game to unravel its significance. To do so requires the reader to become a player and match the moves of the well-known chess master.

NABOKOV'S CEREBRAL WEDDING GAME IN *INVITATION TO A BEHEADING*

> The Queen turned crimson with fury, and...began screaming. "Off with her head! Off with—" *Koroleva pobagrovela ot iarosti...i riavknula: "Otrubit' ei golovu! Otrub..."*²⁷

The traditional Russian village wedding as recorded by nineteenth-century ethnographers was a protracted ceremony which, in folk parlance, was termed *igra*, a ritualized "game," a community-wide performance with formalized acts and scenes. The celebration was an elaborately orchestrated

---

[26] Nabokov, *Invitation*, 26, 36, 121, 124.

[27] Lewis Carroll, *Alice's Adventures in Wonderland: and, Through the Looking-glass and what Alice found there* (London: Penguin Classics, 2003), 281; Vladimir Nabokov, trans., *Ania v strane chudes*, Sobranie sochinenii russkogo perioda v 5 tt. vol. 1 (St. Petersburg: Symposium, 1999), 405.

affair, highly theatrical, that is, artificial, in nature. Mid- and late- twentieth century American weddings, those "once-in-a-lifetime" staged extravaganzas, share much of the spirit of their Russian counterparts.[28] The bride and groom become king and queen for a day, the central characters in an often overly staged drama of union which climaxes, at least ideally, in the annihilation of the bride's virginity on the wedding night. One expansive subtext of Nabokov's *Invitation to a Beheading* [*Priglashenie na kazn'*][29] is a broad burlesque of this wedding "game," which is intensified by delightful inversions and perversions. Nabokov's will be in essence a gay wedding—the mock union of two men, an executioner and the executionee, Pierre and Cincinnatus, whose nuptial bed is an execution block on Thriller Square.

The crux of Nabokov's wedding game is the linking of balls and berries, the folkloric images of ripe female fecundity, with Cincinnatus's head. The berry is frequently encountered in East Slavic wedding songs, particularly in *velichaniia*, songs of praise, often deliberately profane,[30] sung to the bridal couple during the wedding feast. In a song addressed to the bride, for example, we hear: "*Zemlianika-iagodka / Otchego-zhe ty krasna? / Oi, liuli, oi liuli, / Otchego-zhe ty krasna?*; O little berry, little strawberry/ Why are you so red? / O la-dee-da, / Why are you so red?"; and in a typical expanded couplet addressed to the bride and groom: "*Vinograd v sadu tsvetet, / A iagoda, a iagoda sozrevaet. / Vinograd-to—Ivan-sudar', / A iagoda, a iagoda—svet Praskov'ia ego, / A iagoda, a iagoda—svet Ivanovna ego*; A vine blossoms in the garden, / A berry, a berry is ripening. / Now the vine is Master Ivan, / And the berry, the berry is his beloved Praskov'ia, / And the

---

[28] For an evocative collection of photos of American weddings, quite in keeping with the spirit of Nabokov's commentary on the "glossy fictionalization" of life (*Invitation*, 50-1), see Barbara Norfleet, *Wedding* (New York: Simon and Schuster, 1979). This was the catalogue for an exhibition of photographs at the Carpenter Center for Visual Arts, Harvard University (1976). Note in particular a 1944 photo of a chubby fellow in a bridesmaid's veil holding a bouquet of pansies and the photos of guests admiring gifts.

[29] Russian text written in 1934 and first serialized in the Paris émigré journal *Sovremennye zapiski* June 1934-March 1936. *Invitation to a Beheading*, English translation (New York: Paragon Books, 1959).

[30] A universal tendency corroborated in Mann's recounting of Joseph's wedding feast: "More and more as the evening wore on, the laughter and rejoicing rather coarsely betrayed the real idea at the bottom of a wedding feast, the thought of what was naturally to follow. One might put it that the idea of abduction and murder and the idea of fertility came together and flowed into license; so that the air was full of offensive innuendo, of winking, obscene allusions, and roars of laughter" (*Joseph*, 276). Compare with Nabokov's description of the "informal supper," at which "the guests roared" at Pierre's telling of a bawdy anecdote (*Invitation*, 183-4).

berry, the berry is his beloved Ivanovna."[31] In *Evgenii Onegin*, Pushkin plays with this folkloric connotation: "When we've lured a fellow, / when afar we see him, / we shall scatter, dear ones, / pelter him with berries, / with cherries, with raspberries, / with red currants."[32] "The snowball tree, the raspberry, the red currant," the folklorist Sokolov modestly observed in his discussion of the imagery of wedding songs, "are the symbols of a girl just entering into marriage. The latter symbols, like many others, are based upon frankly sexual, erotic factors."[33] Clinically speaking, the berry makes reference to the *virgo intacta*, the symbol of the state of maidenhead. Balls (and melons) are hyperbolic inflations of that symbol of intact virginity, a grotesque gigantism of the *petite flora* "cherry" that, in English slang too, connotes virginity and the intact hymen.

Nabokov's *Invitation* is cluttered with berries, red fruits and balls—a cornucopia of feminine sexuality: "ruddy and glossy" cherries, apples, "rosy kisses tasting of wild strawberries," "a dozen yellow plums," "a piece of brilliant barberry-red hard candy" on Emmie's tongue, "a spurting peach," "apricot moon."[34] Even Pierre identifies himself as "an Elderburian; *Vyshnegradets*" ("Call on me, I shall treat you to some of our elderburies" [rendered as *vyshni* in the Russian text]) jubilates Pierre a la Rudy Panko.[35] The ball appears as

---

[31] N. P. Kolpakova, *Lirika russkoj svad'by* (Leningrad: Nauka, 1973), 144, 157-8.

[32] This is Nabokov's translation from the Russian, from Aleksandr Pushkin, *Eugene Onegin*, trans. with a commentary Vladimir Nabokov (Princeton: Princeton University Press, 1975), 172.

[33] Y. M. Sokolov, *Russian Folklore* (Hatboro, Pa.: Folklore Associates, 1966), 522. See also the folkloric examples culled from Propp and Dal' in Daniel Rancour-Laferriere, "Pushkin's Still Unravished Bride: A Psychoanalysis of Tat'jana's Dream," in *Russian Literature and Psychoanalysis*, ed. Daniel Rancour-Laferriere (Amsterdam and Philadelphia: J. Benjamins Publishing Co., 1989). In Russian literature, particularly among the "village-prose" writers and those influenced by them, the motif is prolific. See for example Yevgeny Yevtushenko, *Iagodnye mesta* (Moskva: Sovetskii pisatel', 1982) [Wild Berries (NY: W. Morrow, 1984)], and Vasilii Shukshin, *Snowball Berry Red* [*Kalina krasnaia*] (Ann Arbor, Mich.: Ardis, 1979). Updike, undoubtedly unaware of the rich folkloric associations, laments the repetition of the symbol in Yevtushenko's novel ("as if repeating things rendered them profound"). "*Wild Berries* begins...with a hail of berries, as symbols of succulence, Siberian freedom, and female charms. A seduced and spurned woman ponders, 'He's picked all my berries, and now he's looking for new berry patches;' another, also seduced and spurned woman sports 'red bilberry nipples' and 'dark, berrylike birthmarks' 'sprinkled' on her 'soft but blinding white' skin; and still another, while being seduced preliminary to being abandoned, has a full basket of berries spilled over her (of course) 'naked breasts'" (John Updike, "Books. Back in the U. S. S. R," *New Yorker*, April 15, 1985, 115).

[34] Nabokov, *Invitation*, 12, 83, 185, 28, 33, 76, 141, 181.

[35] Ibid., 110; Vladimir Nabokov, *Priglashenie na kazn'* (Ann Arbor: Ardis, 1979) 114.

the extended symbol of that ripe, but as yet innocent, female sexuality. The ball is Emmie's—that Ur-Lolita's—plaything, her object of temptation.

> Emmie, the director's daughter...a mere child, but with the marble calves of a little ballerina was bouncing a ball, rhythmically against the wall...Emmie was gazing after them, while she lightly plopped the glossy red and blue ball in her hands.[36]

Now the colors red and blue take over and forge the link to Cincinnatus. Red is the color of blood, streaming from the decapitated head/deflowered maidenhead, as well as the color of the place of execution, "the vermillion platform of the scaffold"[37]—a perfect anthropomorphic touch, Cincinnatus's world mirroring his condition. The pain of execution itself will be "red and loud," "*bol' rasstavaniia budet krasnaia, gromkaia,*" Cincinnatus wrote in his diary.[38] Cincinnatus's head is blue, the Romantics' color for divine inspiration, as well as an indication of homosexual proclivity. Nabokov speaks first of "the azure of [Cincinnatus's] temples," and later of "the *other* Cincinnatus...all curled up in a ball."[39] In his poetic reverie on Day eight, Cincinnatus espies his "dream world": "Dreamy, round, and blue, it turns slowly toward me; *Sonnyi, vypukhlyi, sinii, on medlenno obrashchaetsia ko mne.*"[40]

Presaging the decapitation, Cincinnatus's head, the repository of artistry, becomes Emmie's red and blue ball. Nabokov approaches his most grotesque in the playfulness of Emmie's vague offer of escape in the form of her rolling ball.

> Just then, silently and not very fast, a red-and-blue ball rolled in through the door [of the cell], followed one leg of a right triangle straight under the cot, disappeared for an instant, thumped against the chamber pot, and rolled out along the other cathetus—that is, toward Rodion, who without noticing it, happened to kick it as he took a step; then, following the hypotenuse, the ball departed into the same chink through which it had entered.[41]

The kicking of Cincinnatus's head repulses the attentive reader.

---

[36] Ibid., 41.
[37] Ibid., 218. It is of curious note that an arcane secondary meaning of "maiden" is "a former Scottish beheading device resembling the guillotine," Merriam-Webster's Collegiate Dictionary Tenth Edition (Springfield, Mass.: Merriam-Webster, Inc., 1993), 699.
[38] Ibid., 194, 190.
[39] Ibid., 69.
[40] Ibid., 93, 99.
[41] Ibid., 66.

Nabokov expands and reinforces the motif during the pre-execution feast: the table is loaded "with heaps of apples each as big as a child's head, [shining] among dusty-blue bunches of grapes." The boys who run after the carriage carrying Cincinnatus to the execution block are sympathetically identified as "red and blue."[42] The berry is hyperbolically expanded into succulent melons and watermelons, the objects of sexual teasing and play.

> Emmie sat down at the table...[and] began spreading sugar...on her shaggy slice of melon; thereupon she bit into it busily, holding it by the ends, which reached her ears, and brushing her neighbor [Pierre] with her elbow. Her neighbor continued to sip his tea, holding the spoon protruding from it between second and third fingers, but inconspicuously, reached under the table with his left hand. "Eek!" cried Emmie as she gave a ticklish start, without, however, taking her mouth from the melon.[43]

Here again is the delightfully vulgar Nabokov at work.

The imagery suggests, in the end, that Cincinnatus's head is at once toy, plaything, and maidenhead, a female sex organ. Nabokov is toying with the classical and Romantic notion that art, inspiration, the Muse are to be allegorized as feminine. Cincinnatus's head is for many reasons the object of Pierre's desire. This sense of longing is reinforced by the incessant attention Pierre pays to Cincinnatus's neck.[44] In the cache of Nabokov's recurrent motifs, the "female neck seems to focus [on]...desire...Throughout Nabokov's world, the attraction of female necks ranges from a delicate, melancholy beauty to intense desire,...attended by a specific seeking of relief."[45]

The verbal and visual attention Pierre lavishes on Cincinnatus's neck again serves to highlight the artificially and symbolically sexual nature of the relationship, including the casting of Cincinnatus in the role of undefiled maiden, "preparing for those involuntary bodily movements that directly follow severance of the head."[46] In his pretentious boasting of his attraction to women Pierre declares that he is particularly attracted to necks as the focus of sexual longing.

---

[42] Ibid., 185, 215.
[43] Ibid., 166-167.
[44] Ibid., e.g., 89, 109.
[45] W. W. Rowe, "A Note on Nabokov's Erotic Necks," *Russian Literature Triquarterly* 16 (1979): 50, 52. Rowe makes no attempt to comment on the significance of Pierre's attraction to Cincinnatus's neck. Material from *Invitation* is cited in such a way that Pierre fits the category of Nabokov's precocious experts on women!
[46] Nabokov, *Invitation*, 17.

"I caught just a glimpse of your spouse—a juicy little piece, no two ways about it—what a neck, that's what I like"; "*sheia bol'no khorosha*". "I don't know about you, but when it comes to caresses I love what we French wrestlers call '*macarons*': You give her a nice slap on the neck, and, the firmer the meat..."⁴⁷

Pierre's eyes consistently focus on Cincinnatus's neck with unambiguous sexual desire.

> "The vein on our neck is throbbing..." [...]
> "Excuse me, what is that you have on your neck—right here, here—yes, here."
> "Where?" Cincinnatus asked mechanically, feeling his neck vertebrae.
> M'sieur Pierre went over to him and sat down on the edge of the cot. "Right here," he said, "but I see now that it was only a shadow. I thought I saw...a little swelling of some kind. You seem uncomfortable when you move your head. Does its hurt? Did you catch a chill?"
> "Oh, stop pestering me, please," Cincinnatus said, sorrowfully.
> "No, just a minute. My hands are clean—allow me to feel here. It seems, after all...Does it hurt here? How about here?"
> With his small but muscular hand he was rapidly touching Cincinnatus's neck and examining it carefully, breathing through the nose with a slight wheeze.
> "No, nothing. Everything is in order," he said at last, moving away and slapping the patient on the nape—"Only you do have an awfully thin one—otherwise everything is normal, it's just that sometimes, you know..."⁴⁸

We can understand the reference to the "shadow" as the "shadow of an ax," introduced in the preceding chapter; while the "slap" is precisely the *macaron* of the "French wrestler," the indication of virile sexual arousal, the symbol of which is the ax.⁴⁹ Finally, Pierre recounts how he maneuvered to get to know Cincinnatus.

> The results are before you. We grew to love each other, and the structure of Cincinnatus's soul is as well known to me as the structure of his neck. Thus it will

---

⁴⁷ Ibid., 144-145. Here Nabokov is certainly paying tribute to Tolstoy, and Pierre's namesake in *War and Peace*. In Book Eleven of Tolstoy's novel, Pierre Bezukhov drinks with Ramballe, who, impressed by Pierre's presence on the field of battle at Borodino, extols him, "'So you are one of us soldiers!...So much the better, so much the better, Monsieur Pierre! Terrible in battle...gallant...with the fair' (he winked and smiled), 'that's what the French are, Monsieur Pierre, aren't they?'" Leo Tolstoy, *War and Peace*, Norton Critical Edition, Second Edition (New York: W. W. Norton, 1996), 805.
⁴⁸ Nabokov, *Invitation*, 85, 109.
⁴⁹ Ibid., 92.

be not an unfamiliar, terrible somebody but a tender friend that will help him mount the crimson steps, and he will surrender himself to me without fear...[50]

It is now abundantly clear that the "crimson steps" lead to the platform-bed where the "surrender" will occur, in the position Pierre calls "chop-chop."[51]

If there are other significant male organs in the text, they are frail indeed. Aside from "the Priapus who had nourished [Marthe]" and Quercus, the giant oak of the "famous" novel,[52] the most persistent phallus in the chronicle is Cincinnatus's pencil, a penile motif that Nabokov no doubt extrapolated from Andrei Bely's *Petersburg* and employs in *Invitation* as an homage to the Symbolist writer. Bely's pencil is the attribute of the father-statesman, Apollon Apollonovich, and is introduced very early in the novel. While the Freudian significance of such scenes as "Apollon Apollonovich was wont to express his agony by breaking packets of pencils which were kept for just such an occasion,"[53] is tangential to our argument here, its psycho-symbolic function in betraying the perverse sexual tension between father and child is not. The following passage was a ripe field for Nabokov, from which he seems to have harvested fruit, pencils, throbbing necks, convulsing heads and red faces—the stuff of his little game in *Invitation to a Beheading*. Would it in fact be too absurd to suggest that this very passage inspired much of the essence of *Invitation*?

> Apollon Apollonovich stood chewing his lips ironically. His skin gathered in tiny wrinkles. It stretched taut on his skull. A serious talk was in the air: the fruit had ripened; it would fall; it fell and—suddenly:
> Apollon Apollonovich dropped a pencil [*karandashik*] (by the staircase). From ingrained habit, Nikolai Apollonovich rushed to pick it up. Apollon Apollonovich rushed to forestall him, but he stumbled and fell, his hands touching the bottom steps. His head fell forward and down and unexpectedly landed under the fingers of his son's hand. Nikolai Apollonovich caught sight of his father's neck (an artery was throbbing on one side). The neck's warm pulsation frightened him. He snatched his hand away, but he snatched it too late: at the touch of the cold hand the senator's head convulsed in a spasm. His ears twitched slightly. Like a jumpy Japanese ju-jitsu teacher, he threw himself to the side and straightened up on cracking knees.

---

[50] Ibid., 175.
[51] Ibid., 178.
[52] Ibid., 141, 122-3.
[53] Andrei Bely, *Petersburg*, trans. Robert A. Maguire and John E. Malmstad (Bloomington: Indiana University Press, 1978), 160.

All this lasted but a moment. Nikolai Apollonovich handed his father the tiny little pencil.

"Here!"

A trifle had knocked them one against the other, and had produced in both an explosion of thoughts and feelings. Apollon Apollonovich got completely flustered by the fear he felt in response to politeness (this male in red [domino] was the flesh of his flesh, and to be frightened by one's own flesh was disgraceful). He had been sitting *under* his son, on his haunches. Apollon Apollonovich felt annoyance as well. He assumed a dignified manner, bowed from the waist, and compressed his lips primly:

"Thank you. I wish you pleasant dreams."

Nikolai Apollonovich felt a rush of blood to his cheeks, and when he thought he was beginning to blush, he had actually turned crimson. Apollon Apollonovich, seeing that his son was turning crimson, himself began to blush. In order to hide the blush, he flew up the staircase, with coquettish grace.[54]

In Bely's text the pencil is a key motif in exposing a disturbing sexual tension between father and son, which frightens them both. Moreover, because it is the instigator of this strange encounter between father and son, who are also victim and would-be murderer, the pencil, clearly linked here to Apollon Apollonovich's neck, draws from Nikolai Apollonovich the realization that his father is human and vulnerable. Nikolai Apollonovich's power over his father as the old man tumbles down the stairs to his feet is a mixture of sexual domination (focused, as in *Invitation*, around the neck and its pulsating veins) and control over life and death. The Nabokov pencil is similarly symbolic of these themes of mortality and sexuality; it measures the time to Cincinnatus's execution/wedding day, growing shorter and shorter as his diary lengthens.

The pencil is first introduced on Day one: "On the table glistened a clean sheet of paper and, distinctly outlined against this whiteness, lay a beautifully sharpened pencil, as long as the life of any man except Cincinnatus..." By the eighth day it "has lost more than a third of its length" — a hint of the execution day to the careful reader, who now is privy to that piece of information so sought by Cincinnatus, "the exact execution date."[55] The narrator opens Chapter eight, which, by the way, is almost entirely excerpted from Cincinnatus's diary, with a parenthetic notice, perhaps a comment on some technique of intercourse or masturbation:

---

[54] Ibid., 152 (1922 text).
[55] Nabokov, *Invitation*, 12, 89, 36.

> There are some who sharpen a pencil toward themselves, as if they were peeling a potato, and there are others who slice away from themselves, as though whittling a stick...Rodion was of the latter number. He had an old penknife with several blades and a corkscrew. The corkscrew slept on the outside.[56]

Such intimate details about the life of the pencil independent from Cincinnatus add to its phallic shape to decisively establish the pencil as a male character intruding into the text. It provides a means of eternalizing Cincinnatus's imagination in the form of his diary; the union of the female intellect with the male pencil produces a text, an independent entity. The (hetero)sexual intercourse of mind and pencil is an act of reproduction creating art.

The interaction, however, is not equal. While the execution that follows the completion of the journal fulfills Cincinnatus's imagination and propels it into eternity, into a new world "where, to judge by the voices, [stand] beings akin to him,"[57] the conclusion of Cincinnatus's work represents absolute death for the pencil, which returns to the oblivion and meaninglessness of the other props around Cincinnatus once its task is accomplished. Indeed, the shortening of the pencil corresponding to Cincinnatus's diminishing life span is underscored by its gradual disappearance from the text; on the day before the execution, Cincinnatus's writing implement is no more than a "stunted pencil,"[58] and once Cincinnatus has completed his text with the word "death" (which is "immediately crossed out"), the pencil vanishes from the text. He is now, in effect, castrated.

By dropping and losing any further contact with his pencil, Cincinnatus is left with only his intellect, his blue and red feminized head, his berry, ripe for the picking. Cincinnatus is ready to become Pierre's bride, his maiden fair, as Pierre had pronounced to him, "To me you are as transparent as—excuse the sophisticated simile—a blushing bride is transparent to the gaze of an experienced bridegroom."[59] It is established early in the text that both Cincinnatus and Pierre shun sexual relations with women. Cincinnatus rejects his wife and Emmie, the former with the imperious exclamation, "Oh, don't—what nonsense," in response to her offer, "If you need it badly, Cin-Cin, go ahead, only do it quickly."[60] As for Pierre, he is impotent with women. In spite of his declarations of sexual prowess, he is unable to "perform" with Marthe:

---

[56] Ibid., 89.
[57] Ibid., 223.
[58] Ibid., 206.
[59] Ibid., 162.
[60] Ibid., 197.

> [Marthe] returned only in three quarters of an hour, snorting contemptuously. She put one foot on the chair, snapped her garter, and, angrily readjusting the pleats below her waist, sat down at the table,... "All for nothing," she said with a sneer... "Shouldn't try if you can't manage it..."[61]

We learn that Pierre was the object of her scorn from the impotent himself: "'Outrageous! Intolerable!' M'sieur Pierre was shouting... 'I am not well... They serve me with spoiled fish they offer me a disgusting whore...'"[62] In Cincinnatus's presence, on the contrary, Pierre is sexually aroused. Having just referred to Cincinnatus as a blushing bride, Pierre exposes to him the "broad shining ax," the instrument of execution, and then quickly is unnerved, saying, "We are both young—you must not remain here any longer... I too am excited, I too am not in complete control of myself, you must understand this."[63] The reader fully grasps that the execution will indeed mime the sexual act, while at the same time it functions in imitation of the beheadings of Orpheus and John the Baptist—decapitations that mystically liberate artistry and spirituality. Pierre will brandish his ax (the object of "anxiety" in Nabokov's word play in the English text);[64] Cincinnatus will sacrifice his innocent maiden-like head, his berry.

But what of the wedding ritual preceding intercourse, required by tradition and law? Pierre is too decorous to permit sex without marriage, hence the nuptial rituals, starting with the formal introduction of Cincinnatus and Pierre, the bride and groom. This is, in the Russian folk tradition, an arranged match. The carefully monitored meetings of the betrothed couple are to permit their getting acquainted before the ceremony. They are first introduced on Day seven. This is the *svatanie*, complete with the Director's (he plays the role of the *svat*) admonition to Pierre not to "find fault" with Cincinnatus.

> "Allow me to present to you M'sieur Pierre," said the director to Cincinnatus in jubilant tones. "Come in, come in, M'sieur Pierre. You can't imagine how you have been awaited here—Get acquainted gentlemen—The long-awaited meeting—An instructive spectacle... Do bear with us, M'sieur Pierre, do not find fault..."[65]

---

[61] Ibid., 199.
[62] Ibid., 208.
[63] Ibid., 163.
[64] Ibid., 103.
[65] Ibid., 81.

The groom accepts Cincinnatus as his fiancée and pronounces formulaically, "I make bold to hope that we may get to know each other more closely." Pierre proceeds to court and charm Cincinnatus, in part with comic demonstrations of physical feats and with jokes, while Rodrig's eyes "[grow] moist from all these joyous titters and ejaculations."[66] Pierre judges his efforts to be successful. On Day sixteen he gives clear voice to the notion of ceremonial sacrament, the union of the two:

> [Pierre] went on, batting his eyelashes: "I need not explain how precious to the success of our common undertaking is that atmosphere of warm camaraderie which, with the help of patience and kindness, is gradually created between the sentenced and the executor of the sentence. It is difficult or even impossible to recall without a shudder the barbarity of long-bygone days, when these two, not knowing each other at all, strangers to each other, but bound together by implacable law, met face to face only at the last instant before the sacrament itself. This has all been changed just as the ancient, barbaric wedding ceremony, more closely resembling a human sacrifice—when the submissive virgin was hurled by her parents into the tent of a stranger—has changed with the passing of time."[67]

The proclamation asserts that the union, a mystical bond, has been achieved. The feast to celebrate the marriage takes the form of an "informal supper," which is a cinematically inspired perversion of a traditional wedding feast. The inverted sexual undertone is emphasized by the identification of all guests as men, save for a lone physiologically stereotyped lesbian:

> There were no ladies present, unless one counted the district superintendent of schools, a very stout, elderly woman in a gray frock coat cut like a man's, with large flat cheeks and a smooth hairdo as shiny as steel...[and a] husky voice...[68]

The waiters were "adroit dandies—the best representatives of its purple youth"; "*luchshie predstaviteli ego malinovoi molodezhi.*" Thus, an all-male cast celebrates the union of Pierre and Cincinnatus, who sat "side by side at the head of a dazzling table...identically clad in Elsinore jackets" and "everyone began to glance, with restraint at first, then with benevolent curiosity—which in some began to turn into surreptitious tenderness—at the pair..." The nuptial nature of the event is further emphasized by the traditional chanting of "Bitter, bitter, sweeten it with a kiss," "*Gor'ko!*"[69]

[66] Ibid., 82, 84.
[67] Ibid., 173.
[68] Ibid., 182, 188.
[69] Ibid., 180, 182, 185.

The final ritual is the consummation, the deflowering-decapitation to which, in the Russian folk tradition, the gathered guests were eager witnesses of a sort. This is attested to in the less prudish ethnographic accounts of the peasant wedding-game—the public examination of the marriage night bed sheet. Only the red stain of blood on the sheet (sympathetically anticipated in the text by the "red platform")[70] would prove the virginity of the bride, the mark of the "red" wedding. In his memoirs, Damon Orlow recounts just such a moment in the wedding drama:

> We are approaching the most important, the most delicate, yet essential act of the wedding. Its very nature compels your narrator to seek refuge, if possible at all, in euphemistic phraseology...
> Behind a door locked from the outside, the couple was closeted, to spend the night...The supervisory committee, holding the keys to the chamber, stood on guard the whole night...[In the morning] the committee, having duly examined the marks and signs of the memorable night, came out and officially reported the glorious findings, positively and unquestionably certifying to the unimpeachable purity of [the bride's] virtue, of her integrity, of her virginity.[71]

Nabokov is less discreet. Assembled guests (with the reader as an implied observer) watch Pierre and Cincinnatus engage in disrobing and preparation for intercourse, the beheading to which all had been invited in the title of the novel—ax to neck, the sacrifice of head-cherry, with which the game, Nabokov's text, climaxes:

> "No excitement, no fuss, please," said M'sieur Pierre. "We shall first of all remove our little shirt." "By myself," said Cincinnatus. "That's the boy. Take the little shirt away, men. Now I shall show you how to lie down." M'sieur Pierre dropped onto the block. The audience buzzed. "Is this clear?" asked M'sieur Pierre, springing up and straightening his apron (it had come apart at the back, Rodrig helped tie it). "Good. Let's begin. The light is a bit harsh...Perhaps you could...There, that's fine. Thank you. Perhaps just a wee bit more...Excellent! Now I shall ask you to lie down." "By myself, by myself," said Cincinnatus and lay face down as he had been shown, but at once he covered the back of his neck with his hands. "What a silly boy," said M'sieur Pierre from above. "If you do that how can I...(yes, give it here; then, immediately after, the bucket). And anyway why all this contraction of muscles? There must be no tension at all. Perfectly at ease. Remove your hands, please...(give it to me now). Be quite at ease..."[72]

---

[70] Ibid., 202.
[71] Damon Orlow, *Red Wedding* (Chicago: Henry Regnery Co., 1952), 33-4.
[72] Nabokov, *Invitation*, 221-2.

Franklin Sciacca

FIRST TIME BALL

These final words of M'sieur Pierre ring out beyond the stage-set world of the town and the prison, beyond Cincinnatus's world of imagination, directly to the reader, who is seeing and caressing the last page of the *Invitation*. We also must soon "remove [our] hands" from the book. Nabokov's voice, through Pierre, is commanding us to be "quite at ease," to let go of Cincinnatus's life and of our anxiety for him. Now indeed

> ...we are nearing the end. The right-hand, still untasted part of the novel, which, during our delectable reading, we would lightly feel, mechanically testing whether there were still plenty left...has suddenly, for no reason at all, become quite meager: a few minutes of quick reading already downhill...[73]

We readers had been watching Cincinnatus's twenty-day progress to the execution block along with the other invitees, the vomiting librarian, the transparent spectators, the dog-masked guards, M'sieur Pierre the executioner; but now we are about to part with them and with their quickly disintegrating world. The references to Russian and American marriage traditions, which had been hovering around the sexually charged execution, emerge in our understanding as an allegorical parody. The verbal games and symbols Nabokov had been using begin to form coherent structures, and his hints finally surge with meaning as our comprehension of the novel clarifies.

In fact, when we begin to understand Nabokov's games with colors, boats, and berries, we are surprised to find that he applies at least some of the imagery to *our* world, to the readers' world outside the novel. He continues his description of the "still untasted part of the novel" by comparing it to a bowl of cherries, reminding us that

> The heap of cherries whose mass had seemed to us of such a ruddy and glossy black, had suddenly become discrete drupes: the one over there with the scar is a little rotten, and this one has shriveled and dried up around its stone (and the very last one is inevitably hard and unripe) O horrible![74]

What has Nabokov achieved in this giant verbal, imaginative game? It is a grotesque farce, a game invented around the humdrum vulgarity of "average reality" and its traditions. The mock wedding ceremony is one act in the vast circus-panorama of the text—a display of artifice remarkably versatile and evasive. Taken as a burlesque, a mini-comedy, it fits neatly into

---

[73] Ibid., 12.
[74] Ibid.

Nabokov's own proclaimed concept of the lack of value of ideas in art. But Nabokov is cajoling us to do more than double-think about berries, crania, allegories and marriage; his verbal games are training exercises. Since reading is an individual experience, the beheading must ultimately be ours, the readers'—we have read, we have been trained to read allegories and, with open minds, we can learn from them. Cincinnatus's beheading was allegorically an escape from the constraints of the world where "everything was falling" to a shimmering, shiny world. Nabokov is inviting us to transcend the limits of "average reality" with our imagination, to join voices with which we can communicate in created intellectual worlds. The very process of decoding Nabokov's verbal game is a signpost on the route to this liberating world of the intellect. Just as Orpheus's and John the Baptist's severed heads served as conduits to the worlds of poetry and gnosis, so should Cincinnatus's blood-letting lead to true existence. The decapitated head is a boat released from its moorings free to travel the sea of "true reality." The overall effect is that the reader, laying aside the novel, leaves the stage *with* Cincinnatus, and is now free to make "his way in that direction where, to judge by the voices, stood beings akin to him."[75]

---

[75] Ibid., 223.

Yelizaveta Goldfarb

IRONY BEHIND THE IRON CURTAIN: INTERNAL ESCAPE FROM TOTALITARIANISM IN NABOKOV'S *INVITATION TO A BEHEADING*

Although Vladimir Nabokov was a Russian émigré opposed to the communist revolution, his *Invitation to a Beheading* has little to do with the Soviet regime. Iron Curtain in this text's title is not meant literally. Instead, this iron curtain is intended to partition the political theatrical stage, the precise narrative platform upon which we will appraise the boundaries and paths between totalitarian and democratic states. *Invitation* is a special case of narrative which defies any real-life setting, and calls upon the reader to become a willing participant in the narrative's dissolution. This staging results in something similar to those systems as investigated by Jacques Derrida and Georgio Agamben. But, missing in these theorists' texts, and what *Invitation* allows by means of its structure, is a search for the internal core of democracy.[1] The question of how democracy can be instituted and developed in a political system of complete isolation cannot be explored when dealing with actual political examples. *Invitation* is able to ask questions that the theorists cannot, and it is able to posit a relevant rhetorical solution—a permanent parabasis[2] of irony, a permeating inner mood of questioning that denies totalitarian control.

The response to Nabokov's *Invitation* has been voluminous, but few critics seem to allow the novel a platform and power to question political methods themselves. As Dale E. Peterson has acknowledged, the original reviewers of Nabokov's English translation of *Invitation to a Beheading* condemned it as pure "celebrations of lexical play and imaginative artifice."[3] But subsequent critics (publishing after 1970) have constructively commented on its artistic elements, almost to the point of simplifying the novel. Leona Toker and D. Barton Johnson, in particular, have dwelt not only on the portrayal of the artist in *Invitation*, but also on the very narrative structure as allegory for the expression of the inexpressible. In "Spatial Modeling and Deixis: Nabokov's *Invitation to a Beheading*,"[4] Johnson focuses on the link between reality and "verbal art," and in his "The Alpha and Omega of *Invitation to a Beheading*,"[5] establishes a construction of "prison-house of language" based on *Invitation*—the artist is restricted both by the language he is to work with and by the philistine audience that cannot or will not understand what he is trying to express. As political readers of the novel, nearly all critics bring Nabokov's personal history into the text—his émigré status and "escape"

---

[1] Jacques Derrida, "The Other of Democracy, the 'By Turns': Alternative and Alternation," *Rogues: Two Essays on Reason,* trans. Pascale-Anne Bault and Michael Naas (Stanford, CA: Stanford University Press, 2005), 28-41; and "The Last of the Rogues States: The 'Democracy to Come,' Opening in Two Turns": Alternative and Alternation," *Rogues: Two Essays on Reason,* trans. Pascale-Anne Bault and Michael Naas (Stanford, CA: Stanford University Press, 2005), 78-94. Giorgio Agamben, *Homo Sacer: Sovereign Power and Bare Life,* trans. Daniel Heller-Roazen (Stanford, CA: Stanford University Press, 1995).

[2] Paul de Man in his "The Concept of Irony," *Aesthetic Ideology* (Minneapolis, MN: University of Minnesota Press, 1996), 179, argues for the "violent paradoxical" nature of "permanent parabasis," as described by Schlegel. Unlike an occasional "parabasis," which is a localized interruption of the narrative line, "permanent parabasis" is able to interrupt at all points of a narrative simultaneously.

[3] Dale E. Peterson, "Nabokov's Invitation: Literature as Execution," *PMLA* 96.5 (October 1981): 824-836

[4] D. Barton Johnson, "Spatial Modeling and Deixis: Nabokov's *Invitation to a Beheading*" *Poetics Today* 3.1 (Winter 1982): 81-96.

[5] Ibid., "The Alpha and Omega of *Invitation to a Beheading*," *Worlds in Regression: Some Novels of Vladimir Nabokov* (Ann Arbor, MI: Ardis Publishers, 1985), 28-46.

from Communism are an awkward beginning to most critical readings. In "*Invitation to a Beheading*: Nabokov and the Art of Politics," Robert Alter writes about *Invitation*'s totalitarian state as the "lineaments" of a fictional fantasy, and through this realizes that the inner requisite to the totalitarian state is not necessarily the "need to achieve practical ends," which allows for something like Nazism to be conceived.[6] However, Alter does not stick to these readings of the narrative as a useful construction for the examination of politics. He reverts to the popular Aristotelian critique of the novel's self-conscious art as a model of morality.

More than a critique of art, the artist, or morality, Nabokov's *Invitation* allows for narrative to problematize politics firstly by establishing itself as a political, self-sustaining system. Dale E. Peterson stresses readers' participation in *Invitation*, and describes them as "'co-creators' of the fate awaiting those enmeshed in a composition,"[7] thereby pointing to *Invitation* as a self-contained, self-referential text. The very title unabashedly invites the reader to witness the novel's unraveling and inescapable demise. Throughout *Invitation*, Nabokov points to this "system" of text: characters attempt to escape their fate,[8] Cincinnatus measures his life by the paring down of a pencil[9] — he awaits the moment at which there can be nothing more written — and he is aware of being constantly watched through a peephole by observers and, later, a "predatory eye."[10] The reader becomes the executioner who will eventually determine the time of the beheading. From the start, Nabokov calls on the reader to be aware of his physical influence over the text's narrative speed:

> So we are nearing the end. The right-hand, still untasted part of the novel, which, during our delectable reading, we would lightly feel, mechanically testing whether there were still plenty left (and our fingers were always gladdened by the placid,

---

[6] Robert Alter, "*Invitation to a Beheading*: Nabokov and the Art of Politics," *Nabokov: Criticism, Reminiscences, Translations, and Tributes*, ed. Alfred Appel, Jr. & Charles Newman (Chicago, IL: Northwestern University Press, 1970), 41-59.

[7] Peterson, Literature as Execution, 824.

[8] Vladimir Nabokov, *Invitation to a Beheading*, trans. Dmitri Nabokov and Vladimir Nabokov (New York, NY: Vintage Books, 1959). Toward the end of the novel Marthe innocently states, "They won't be coming for me for a while yet, I talked them into giving me oodles of time," to which Cincinnatus reminds her "every word we say...They will open it in a moment" (201). There is a precise awareness here of being watched, of words being opened and uncovered. Marthe has negotiated her life beyond death — perhaps in another Nabokov text.

[9] Ibid., 89, 206.

[10] Ibid., 122.

faithful thickness) has suddenly, for no reason at all, become quite meager: a few minutes of quick reading, already downhill, and–O horrible![11]

The text progresses towards its own inevitable physical and narrative death. In this movement, we see the text as a complete, exclusive, and inescapable system with its own rigid, unchangeable laws, rules, and customs.

The narrative action exists here without a history, setting, or temporality, and so it becomes, in its self-containment, a system outside specific reference. It is difficult, then, to attribute this text to a critique of the Soviet regime, as there are no Soviet markers in place. In fact, the text denies any suggestion of or orientation with reality outside the novel. It draws into itself, denying history, nationhood, even language,[12] and in doing so is able to pose and tackle questions that theorists such as Derrida and Agamben are unable to conceptualize because of their ineluctable reliance on real-life forces of history and citizenship.

Even though these theorists cannot speak to internal escape, their exploration of political systems is useful in explaining the totalitarian system in *Invitation*. The system's exclusivity reveals nothing about its political inception. Without history, we cannot see how the system was established, and this seems to be the point. We are not tempted to turn to a context; all we can do is examine this textual moment for what it is, in and of itself, and search for what a viable escape in the present moment might look like.

Derrida's discussions of democracy are useful in addressing the *aporias* in *Invitation*. Of course, the political system in the novel is by no means a democracy, but as Derrida points out, "The alternative to democracy can always be represented as a democratic alternation."[13] For Derrida, democracy has the peculiar characteristic of swallowing up exception as part of the system by its negation. This very inability to make a distinction and the need to contain alterity within the system becomes, perhaps, the most prevalent link between *Invitation*'s totalitarianism and Derrida's "democracy." We see this containment of otherness and outsider status in *Invitation*'s structure. The reader is not permitted to inhabit a passive role in his relationship with this text. He is invited by the very title to participate in the novel, and his role as executioner and voyeur, the "predatory eye," is written into the text

---

[11] Ibid., 12.
[12] *Invitation* was published in Russian in 1935-1936 and an English translation by Nabokov and his son, Dmitri, was published in 1959, essentially giving us two original texts in two original languages.
[13] Derrida, "The Other of Democracy," 30-31.

itself. There is certainly a recursiveness in Nabokov and Derrida's systems demanding that all pieces be contained and defined within its terms. There can be no externality here: every deviation from the system must be drawn back into it by re-examination of the terms or by negation—and through these *aporias* the system essentially begins to eat its own tail. It becomes an ouroboros, a "vicious circle"[14] that breeds inescapability.

Derrida rejects any true democratic ideal, and instead finds democracy to be a "concept that has no concept."[15] This continual lack points to the risk within democracy: the risk that by following democratic ideals, democracy (as an ideal) may be, and often is, eradicated. But this risk, far from being a secret, is acknowledged and prepared for by democracy. To avoid the ultimate mistake of allowing nondemocratic power to be instilled democratically, the system will shift its definitions and markers to allow for nondemocratic functions to exist temporarily *in the name* of democracy. In *Rogues*, Derrida names colonization, decolonization, and European political ideals as symptoms of democratic interruption put in place to save a democracy threatened by its sworn enemies.

The awareness and acceptance of risk, however, seems to be exclusively a democratic trait, since totalitarianism denies all threats to the system. Instead, totalitarianism avoids specificity and establishes bio-political functions that will maintain adherence to the system. All deviation is re-conceptualized as negation or exception, thereby shifting all rules and ideals to maintain the totalitarian model. Nothing can stand outside, and so there is no risk to prepare for. Democracy creates nondemocratic spaces; totalitarianism neither creates nor tolerates non-totalitarian spaces.

We see this avoidance of specificity in *Invitation*. Cincinnatus's death sentence is announced "in a whisper,"[16] almost as if there is the hope or expectation for some information to be lost along the way. The crime for which Cincinnatus will be executed is itself unnamable, and can only be referred to as "gnostical turpitude," a divertive euphemism repeated throughout the text.[17] Specific knowledge is not treated as a necessity: Cincinnatus is repeatedly denied information regarding the date and time of his execution.[18] But he is not expected to wait in a continual state of agony; instead, this

---

[14] Ibid., 32.
[15] Ibid., 32, 36.
[16] Nabokov, *Invitation*, 11.
[17] Cincinnatus's crime is referred to as simple punctuation, as a "tone," "gnostical turpitude," and "things" (Ibid., 32, 72, 96).
[18] Ibid., 15, 16, 39, 40, 47, 57, 115, 117, 176.

should be a time for play! For Cincinnatus, the knowledge of his physical (and textual) end would provide a space to fill and an ability to finalize his life in writing—"But how can I begin writing when I do not know whether I shall have time enough, and the torture comes when you say to yourself 'Yesterday there would have been enough time.'"[19] Without a specified ending, there is an expanse of uncertain temporality. Cincinnatus is suspended within the threshold of the linear past-present-future system: "There is the rare kind of time in which I live—the pause, the hiatus."[20] The anxiety of a constant uncertainty forces Cincinnatus to live within the temporal crack, a repetitive time that has a ubiquitous possibility of progressing, yet remains always between present and future.

Cincinnatus consistently evokes a further textual denotation of this threshold in the specific focus on here/there (тут/там) in the Russian version of *Invitation*, *Приглашение на казнь*.[21] Most clearly we see this in the recurring image of Tamara Gardens (Тамарины Сады), a mnemonic space that represents a place of freedom for Cincinnatus. To the Russian reader also, the "там" of "Тамарины Сады" is evident. The very notion of *там* permeates the present reality both narratively and textually, to the point where Cincinnatus can no longer distinguish between them. The Russian reader will also recognize the concept of freedom in this novel as defined not by specific ideals but by negation. There are a number of Russian words that can be used to denote "there" (туда, вон) and, as D. Barton Johnson notes in his article "Spatial Modeling and Deixis,"[22] Nabokov is deliberate in his choice and continues the тут/там polarity throughout some of his other texts, most notably his autobiography with the pseudonym Tamara. *Там* is defined as "не здесь" (not here), and this is the sense that we get from Cincinnatus's obsession with it: he is not yearning for a specific place or time of freedom, but rather his desire lies in the escape (from *here*).

Cincinnatus finds himself living within this pause between тут and там—an alternate reality. This mental and visual liberty is the "gnostical turpitude" for which he must pay. He is stuck in a space that mediates between his reality and an abstracted dream-state, a space that is unreachable to those who cannot conceive of an ability to see it: "How I wriggled out, slippery, naked! Yes,

---

[19] Ibid., 52.
[20] Ibid., 53.
[21] For more on тут/там see Johnson, "Spatial Modeling and Deixis," 85-96, and "The Alpha and Omega," 37-39.
[22] Johnson, "Spatial Modeling and Deixis," 88.

from a realm forbidden and inaccessible to others, yes."[23] More than a simple negation—an antithesis to reality or an alternate universe—this partial dream state is a space that stands beyond Cincinnatus's reality and the political system in which he lives. Following Levinas, this inconceivable capability, this "gnostical turpitude," is a crime that cannot be specified because it cannot be envisaged; it separates Cincinnatus as Other, absolutely other (*Autre*).[24]

As Other, Cincinnatus defies totality, which strives to assimilate all fragments and remainders within the system by negation. His gift allows him to go beyond categorization to a space that only he can envision, as it would not even occur to those jammed within these technologies to move beyond the absorbing system and its binaries. Pierre, the executioner, claims to know Cincinnatus, but it becomes clear that his knowledge is limited to his role as executioner: "the structure of Cincinnatus' soul is as well known to me as the structure of his neck."[25] Pierre finds kinship with his victim on the basis of their necessary relationship—there is no other option here for Pierre but to see Cincinnatus as a willing participant in this social, political, textual system.

To the executioner, Cincinnatus is "transparent as—excuse the sophisticated simile—a blushing bride is transparent to the gaze of an experienced bridegroom."[26] This relationship, far from being unpleasant in the system's logic, is the loving, albeit unbalanced, marriage between the system and the executed. Not to worry, Cincinnatus will learn so much from his friendly grim reaper! Agamben titles this sort of bond "complicity" as he discusses Marquis de Sade's "bio-political manifesto of modernity": we "find here the symmetry between *homo sacer* and sovereign in the complicity that ties the masochist to the sadist, the victim to the executioner."[27] Cincinnatus is thus to remain within the political system, even if it is through his systemically imposed relationship to death. His body is subjugated by bio-political functions that bring individual life into the care of the sovereign.

As Foucault lays out in *The History of Sexuality*, the modern body is subjugated both by the body "as machine"—its physical capabilities—and by supervision of its biological functions.[28] The body is institutionalized

---

[23] Nabokov, *Invitation*, 90.
[24] Emmanuel Levinas, "Ethics and the Face," *Totality and Infinity: An Essay on Exteriority*, trans. Alphonso Lingis (Pittsburgh, PA: Duquesne University Press, 1969), 203.
[25] Nabokov, *Invitation*, 175.
[26] Ibid., 162.
[27] Agamben, *Homo Sacer*, 135.
[28] Michel Foucault, *The History of Sexuality*, trans. Robert Hurley (New York, NY: Random House, Inc., 1990), 139.

by politics—it is contained and controlled within schools, the army, public health, and migration. Foucault's focus is on that which is classically ignored in history, in this case the body itself, and he interrogates spaces of production rather than forms of repression within central powers, which are classically examined. In this way, he attempts to move away from a sovereign power, and towards decentralization, a dispersal of government. This is perhaps closest to where *Invitation* stands, in that here we have a tight focus on the individual as he exists within his oppressive system, which allows for the search for a localized attempt to escape. Though Agamben works from Foucault's theories of bio-politics, he is either unable or unwilling to maintain the focus on the possibility of decentralization. Instead, he brings the sovereignty back into these politics, specifically by focusing on the sovereign in totalitarianism.

In *Invitation* we never see the sovereign itself, but we do have a theatrical focus on the propagation of bio-politics through a "double bind" system of individuals. These individuals are certainly seen and act as if they have an unusual devotion to the system, which is understandable in bio-political terms once they have been taken into the system and subjected to it. Foucault's "double bind" presents this phenomenon as two separate functions: political techniques, in which the state takes custody of the corporeal body of people into its center, and technologies of the self, in which individuals bind their identities and consciousness to the state by subjugation. The state thus maintains power through its people rather than exclusively through its sovereign. In *Invitation*, we see characters who represent the direct power of law enforcement—the prison director, the prison guard, the executioner—as manifestations of political techniques. But the characters who do not have this invested power—Cincinnatus's mother, wife, in-laws—also support the state by their consistent devotion and unquestioned subjugation within it.

Along with giving power to the state, the people also enforce the appearance of legal regularity, thus allowing law to act systemically. As in Agamben's totalitarian law, the law in Cincinnatus's reality creates its own space for enactment and, like the systems we have examined here, does not allow for exclusion. It swallows exception, making it regulatory, and thus maintains power through its normative value. The law rules because it creates "the sphere of its own reference in real life and make[s] that reference regular."[29] The regularity here is enforced, as with state power, by the people, and so there is always a built-in function of normativity within the political

---

[29] Agamben, *Homo Sacer*, 4-5.

systems. There is no palpable place within totalitarianism for questioning and no legal space in which to break with systemic law.

At certain moments in the narrative, Cincinnatus finds it difficult to resist this system of bio-politics, and we see him catch himself on the verge of falling into the false logic. Although he recognizes the forces of power — the prison director, the prison guard, the executioner — as extensions of the system and so avoids at all cost being taken in by their promises of friendship and escape, he cannot avoid their trickery and theatrics. The prison and the cell become stages upon which Pierre the executioner and Rodrig the guard can perform their ruses. Pierre masks himself as a fellow inmate for most of the narration before revealing his true intentions; he breaks into dance and operatic performances with the prison director, and they stage what Cincinnatus takes to be a long escape tunnel that leads him straight back to his prison cell. A spider prop is set up in the corner of the cell and Rodrig maintains the illusion of the spider's authenticity by speaking to it and feeding it until it is swept away on the morning of Cincinnatus's execution. At one point, Cincinnatus recognizes his slow subjugation to the system, which will make it easier for the system to make the final "cut": "they have succeeded in softening me...I have grown so limp and soggy that they will be able to do it with a fruit knife."[30] The theatrics and the deception are a means of wearing down resistance, but Cincinnatus, in his ability to barely withstand the technique, uses this instability as a stage that breeds a useful uncertainty.

Lacking in *Invitation*'s political system but unavoidably seen in Derrida and Agamben's political discussion is the source, the state itself, namely the sovereign, and this is the moment at which *Invitation* lends itself as a critique of these theorists. The absence of the head of state brings to light the absence of other nations, of other heads of state, of other powers at play. *Invitation*'s politics stand alone without outside influence, very much unlike the real-life systems that Derrida and Agamben point to in their texts.

In *Rogues*, Derrida uses the example of Algerian elections being halted by external European powers in order to avoid the risk of an antidemocratic Islamist Party being elected democratically.[31] Beneath this democratic intrusion lies a history of European involvement: first, of course, by the French colonization of Algeria, but also in pre-independence by allowing citizenship and voting rights to Pieds-Noir only, thus attempting to undemocratically establish a false democracy in Algeria via France.

---

[30] Nabokov, *Invitation*, 124.
[31] Derrida, "The Other of Democracy," 33.

In *Homo Sacer*, Agamben points to Western humanitarianism as a propagator of the very base functions of totalitarian sovereignty and the concentration camp. Agamben argues for *homo sacer*, bare life, whose "life cannot be sacrificed yet may, nevertheless, be killed."[32] Life is linked to the sovereign by its very inception, by the birth-nation link—citizens are created as such at birth and are immediately incepted as sovereign subjects. Agamben argues that the Nuremberg laws were the heightened principle of linking citizenship to the right to life—Jews were required to be denationalized by the Nuremberg laws before being sent to concentration camps in order for the juridical system of inalienable rights under citizenship to be preserved. The bio-political rationale of the body as sacred, bare life that allowed for Nuremberg laws and concentration camps, Agamben argues, is also used by humanitarian organizations to collect funds for starving children and refugees. Money is collected on the image of the "contemporary cipher of the bare life"[33]—refugees, limitary bodies who should be the very figures of inalienable rights, lose this basic, sacred humanity when they are outside of state sanction. Human lives are made into "the object[s] of aid and protection"[34] in the name of an external campaign for their democratization.

Both Derrida and Agamben unravel these historical *aporias* in their texts, but cannot offer a solution to escape the system of these contradictions. Here we only see democracy as soon-to-be imposed or already established, thus relying on its history to maintain its democratic ideals. There is little attempt to circumnavigate these dependent structures of democracy. *Invitation* allows us a new platform on which to discuss the nature of and the escape from totalitarianism. Here we see politics without a nation, subjects without a sovereign, citizens without a state. The system presented is simultaneously exclusive in construction and is infinitely far-reaching. We see a body politic that has a feverish loyalty to the system in this textual moment. Without a history, a setting, or a temporal location, the political landscape in *Invitation* becomes an ideal(ized) test case for political theories.

Unlike Derrida's democracy and Agamben's totalitarian state, Nabokov's body-politic does not draw from any real-life examples, and so we are able to re-conceptualize escape as an internal function rather than as a consequence of outside forces. Where can this escape come from in a nation that is *not*

---

[32] Agamben, *Homo Sacer*, 10.
[33] Ibid., 133.
[34] Ibid.

Yelizaveta Goldfarb

defined in opposition to the nations surrounding it? When hope of an escape must lie internally rather than from salvation or redemption from *elsewhere*, where is its locus, from where does it generate?

If we follow the contention that *Invitation* is a self-sustaining, self-referential system, in both a political and a narrative sense, we are able to search for cracks within the text that act as political and narrative rebellions. Cincinnatus feels as if he is being dragged into "false logic,"[35] and he recognizes the possibility of escape within this system's logic: "That is how mathematics is created; it has its fatal flaw."[36] This crack, the "fatal flaw," comes from something that Cincinnatus finds organic, something very far away from the bio-political mechanics of a system that recognizes its citizens as cogs and from a theory of narrative structure that grinds down its residents until they become transparent.[37] He discovers "the little crack in life…where it had once been soldered to something else, something genuinely alive…within this irreparable little crack decay has set in…"[38]

This little crack, as Cincinnatus discovers, is difficult to pin down. Partially this is because of its internal, self-induced nature, but also, it is because the crack permeates: once it sets in, everything is subject to its influence. Narratively, this lack of center is picked up in *Invitation*'s tone, as there is a constant turning away from direct, reliable significers.[39] Within this ghastly, dead-serious system of the dangerously unknown, of betrayal, of death, we have theater, phoniness, trickery, gimmicks, deception, parody, puns. The tone here is not of lightness, but of incertitude, of instability. Once this irony sets into the narration (as theater and deception) and the narrative structure (by means of direct reference to the reader and his participation) it does not leave the text. What we see in *Invitation*, in Schlegel's terms, is "buffo," a "disruption of narrative illusion." The reader is called upon to participate in the novel and is directly summoned in asides. With the invitation for the reader to participate, the narrative spell is broken. This break lends itself to the "permanent parabasis" of irony, a "violent paradox" in and of itself because of its permanence.[40]

---

[35] Nabokov, *Invitation*, 213.
[36] Ibid., 205.
[37] Ibid., 98. Cincinnatus says of his wife's grandparents: "one could already see through them."
[38] Ibid., 205.
[39] de Man, "The Concept of Irony," 164, identifies irony as a trope, and ties this to Northrop Frye's definition of trope: "a pattern of words that turns away from direct statement or its own obvious meaning."
[40] Quoted in Ibid., 178.

But irony here does not simply act as a rhetorical device, only meant to affect the reader through narrative. Irony introduces, much like we have seen in Derrida's discussion of democracy, the ultimate rhetorical risk. Once it figures into the equation of the system, everything is vulnerable to its trickery, and so nothing can be stable. Irony induces a general sense of unease. Classically, it hides meaning, and so there is already a sense of deception on the part of the receiver. Once this deception is introduced, paranoia sets in — suddenly everything is suspect of the ironic tone. Irony is transformed from a figure of speech to a figure of thought. It impresses its tone on the words and phrases around it, and instills unease and discomfort that give rise to questioning, criticism, and critique: the very basis of democratic thought.

With the presence of risk, there is the possibility of escape from the system. Fichte identifies a negation within the self as coextensive with the self, and de Man follows by identifying this inextricable relation as a metaphoric structure.[41] Here, irony as escape springs internally; deviation is not imposed by external forces. Unlike Derrida and Agamben, whose systems find escape only by inclusion in a larger sphere, here we have no need for a paradigm of salvation. Instead, there is something internally viral in the inception of ironic tone.

To give him due credit, Derrida does note an ironic tone in his structuring of the democratic system, but he refers to it as a necessary symptom of democracy,[42] and so in his argument it is not given the aptitude to stand alone as the sole means of escape into democracy or to spring internally as a self-induced propagator of democracy. In *Invitation* we see that if escape from the "double bind" is to be found internally rather than from an external salvation, then it must emanate from this tone of questioning. This rhetorical figure of thought is perhaps awkward for political theorists. It is difficult to pin down. In fact, the essence of this tone is that it *is* the unpinnable, constantly turning away. A trope cannot be controlled and, in fact, it resists the exacting power of the Western savior. It spreads organically by subtle, paranoid permeation, and this uncontrollable nature is perhaps the key to a wider-spread escape than even the West can catch up to.

---

[41] Ibid., 173.
[42] Derrida, "The Last of the Rogues States," 91-92.

Alexander Moudrov

NABOKOV'S INVITATION TO PLATO'S BEHEADING

I could never understand why every book of mine invariably sends reviewers scurrying in search of more or less celebrated names for the purpose of passionate comparison.[1]

Vladimir Nabokov was always reluctant to acknowledge his affinity with other writers, even though his works often betray some indebtedness to his illustrious predecessors — Gogol, Proust, Baudelaire, Poe, and Pushkin — whom he appreciated at different points in his life. A more intriguing subject, however, is his intellectual relationship with those whom he claimed to have utterly despised, particularly Freud and Plato. It took some time for scholars to look beyond Nabokov's pronounced antipathy toward Freud and to examine the complexity of his attitude toward his intellectual nemesis,

---

[1] Vladimir Nabokov, foreword to *Invitation to a Beheading*, trans. Dmitri Nabokov (New York: Vintage International, 1989), 6.

along with their shared interests.² Yet, Plato's presence in Nabokov's works is largely unexamined, in spite of the apparent affinities between the two writers and the critical interest in the metaphysical aspect of Nabokov's prose.

Nabokov gave the impression that he wanted to discourage this line of inquiry. When an interviewer mentioned that "*Pale Fire* appears to some readers to be in part a gloss of Plato's myth [and] suggests a conscious Platonism," Nabokov curtly responded that he was not "particularly fond of Plato."³ He was unmistakably clear in his letter to Edmund Wilson, stating: "I detest Plato. I loathe Lacedaemon and all Perfect States."⁴ Nabokov was referring to Plato's utopian vision of the perfect political system, which he seemed to have carelessly confused with fascism or communism. Despite such unequivocal declarations, Nabokov had a fascinating habit of standing very close to those whom he purportedly despised. In his desire to demonstrate his artistic superiority over his intellectual opponents, Nabokov often adopted and subverted their techniques, borrowed themes from their works, and even imitated their style. *Despair*, for example, appears to be at once a parody and a tribute to Dostoevsky's style. Humbert's confession in *Lolita* clearly relies on some elements of psychoanalytic literature, which Humbert, like his creator, claims to abhor. These examples demonstrate Nabokov's amazing talent for toying with other writers' techniques. In *The Gift* and *Despair* he mimics his critics so well that it becomes difficult to distinguish their views from his own. Is it possible, then, that Nabokov's admission that he was "afraid to get mixed up with Plato"⁵ was actually an invitation to explore the complexity of his attitude toward Plato—Nabokov's invitation to Plato's beheading?

The case in point is *Invitation to a Beheading*, a short novel which, in spite of Nabokov's avowed disdain for "literature of ideas" and for Plato, is laced with Platonic references and what Vladimir E. Alexandrov once called "Nabokov's 'Neoplatonic' beliefs."⁶ It recounts the last days of Cincinnatus, sentenced to death for some unmentionable crime that scandalized an entire town. Confined in a shadowy prison, Cincinnatus spends his last days

---

² There are two main works on the subject: Geoffrey Green's *Freud and Nabokov* (Lincoln: University of Nebraska Press, 1988), and Jenefer Shute's dissertation "Nabokov and Freud: The Play of Power" (Los Angeles: UCLA, 1983), a portion of which appeared in an article under the same title in *Modern Fiction Studies* 30 (1984): 637-650.
³ Vladimir Nabokov, *Strong Opinions* (New York: Vintage International, 1990), 70.
⁴ Vladimir Nabokov and Edmund Wilson, *The Nabokov-Wilson Letters: 1940-1971*, ed. Simon Karlinsky (New York: Harper Colophon, 1979), 159.
⁵ Nabokov, *Strong Opinions*, 69.
⁶ Vladimir Alexandrov, *Nabokov's Otherworld* (Princeton: Princeton University Press, 1991), 88.

contemplating a better world, which constantly escapes his imaginative efforts. In this respect, the question whether the novel's theme echoes Plato's idealism is too tempting to ignore. The atmosphere of the novel clearly evokes Plato's famous Allegory of the Cave, a vision of everyday reality as a shadowy realm whose inhabitants are barely aware of the artificiality of their existence. Only a few of them dream of the other, perfectly original world, let alone actually reach it. Those who do escape, if only in their imagination, are persecuted by their fellow cavemen, who do not share their appreciation for what is real.[7] For Plato, it was not a simple allegory. His mentor, the renowned philosopher Socrates, was put to death in 399 BC for his philosophical pursuits and impiety. Plato wrote about the trial, imprisonment, and subsequent execution of Socrates, a gripping tale about a doomed man's hopes and fears about the afterlife, in *Apology, Crito,* and *Phaedo.* It can be said that Cincinnatus's predicament was similar to that of Socrates. Numerous Platonic references in the novel reinforce the idea that Nabokov had Socrates and Plato in mind when he wrote *Invitation to a Beheading.* Pierre, Cincinnatus's executioner, repeatedly demands sympathy from Cincinnatus, which is reminiscent of Socrates' sympathy for his real-life executioner.[8] Cincinnatus's unexpected meeting with his mother, Cecilia, who arrives to reveal the mysteries of his birth, corresponds with Socrates' dream of "a beautiful, graceful woman" who tells him the day of his death.[9] Nabokov's jocular reference to "the new comic opera, *Socrates Must Decrease,*"[10] which was performed on the day of Cincinnatus's execution, is even more revealing of Nabokov's interest in Plato. Finally, as if evoking Socrates' beliefs in the afterlife, Cincinnatus apparently reaches another world after his execution.

Nabokov's persistent but notably inconsistent adaptation of Platonic references suggests that his attitude toward the philosopher was rather conflicted. At times, Nabokov very obviously satirizes Plato—often simplifying and sometimes misreading his ideas; as he also did with Freud. At other times, in this novel and elsewhere, we can discern clear signs of "a conscious Platonism," particularly in one of his essays that compares an artist to "the enchanter in his cave."[11] This inconsistency in his references to Plato

---

[7] Plato, *Republic,* trans. G.M.A. Grube (Indianapolis: Hackett Publishing, 1992), 514b-517e.
[8] Plato, *Phaedo,* trans. G.M.A. Grube (Indianapolis: Hackett Publishing, 1977), 117a-b.
[9] Plato, *Crito, The Last Days of Socrates,* trans. Hugh Tredennick (New York: Penguin, 1993), 44a-b.
[10] Nabokov, *Invitation,* 220.
[11] Vladimir Nabokov, "The Art of Literature and Commonsense," *Lectures on Literature,* ed. Fredson Bowers (New York: Harcourt Brace & Company, 1980), 372.

bespeaks some fundamental and yet unexplained tensions in Nabokov's prose, which this essay attempts to unravel. In contrast to the efforts of other commentators, who occasionally pointed out Platonic elements in Nabokov's writing,[12] my goal in this essay is to explain the Platonic theme of *Invitation to a Beheading* precisely in terms of the tension between Nabokov's artistic sensibilities and his interpretation of Plato—a great example of a modernist writer in conflict with antiquity.

Nabokov's antipathy toward Plato reflected his distinctly modernist sensibilities as well as personal experiences. We should recall that the philosopher's lasting authority in such areas as metaphysics, aesthetics, and the relation of art to politics, came under intense scrutiny during the social cataclysms of the twentieth century. The rise of totalitarianism across Europe, which Nabokov and many of his contemporaries experienced firsthand, could not help but push Plato out of favor. A refugee from Soviet Russia and Fascist Germany, Nabokov must have been quite suspicious of the kind of political ideas which one can discern, mistakenly or not, in Plato's *Republic* and some other dialogs. In his famous vision of the perfect state, Plato argued that everything, including art, should be subjugated by the state's interests. For Nabokov and other exiles from Russia, this theory was far more real than they wanted it to be. It is thus understandable that he was vehement in his denunciation of Plato.[13]

Plato's notion that art is an inferior and even dangerous intellectual endeavor must have amplified Nabokov's contempt for the philosopher. Socrates, who is generally (if naively) believed to represent Plato's own ideas, often emphasized the intellectual inferiority of art. Plato considered philosophy, which aims at the highest forms of knowledge, a much more superior intellectual endeavor than artistic pursuits.[14] As he pointed out on one occasion, an artist "produces work that is inferior with respect to truth and that appeals to a part of the soul that is similarly inferior rather than to the

---

[12] Vladimir Alexandrov explored the metaphysical and, to a lesser extent, Neoplatonic aspects of Nabokov's prose in *Nabokov's Otherworld*. Dieter E. Zimmer's notes to the German edition of *Invitation to a Beheading* (Vladimir Nabokov, *Einladung zur Enthauptung*, trans. and commentary Dieter E. Zimmer [Reinbeck be Hamburg: Rohwohlt, 1990]) briefly discuss a few Platonic references as well.

[13] Many twentieth-century readers of Plato could not ignore the totalitarian streak in his political thought. Karl Popper's *Open Society and Its Enemies* (London: Routledge, 1945) is a perfect example of a reader's dismay at Plato's notion of the ideal state. Other classics of anti-Platonism include Warner Fite's *Platonic Legend* (New York: C. Scribner's Sons, 1934) and R. H. S. Crossman's *Plato Today* (New York: Oxford University Press, 1939).

[14] Plato, *Republic*, 595a-608a.

best part."[15] This led Socrates to conclude that poets should be excluded from the perfect state. Nabokov, a refugee from two totalitarian states, could easily relate his experience to that of an exiled poet; he obviously felt no appreciation for the theories expressed in *Republic*. Neither could he appreciate Plato's apparent view of art as merely a vehicle for expressing abstract ideas and promoting the welfare of the state. Nabokov could not disagree more. Most noteworthy about Nabokov's aesthetics is that he firmly believed in "the supremacy of the detail over general,"[16] whereas for Plato details were merely meant to direct our attention to some metaphysical ideas. Furthermore, Nabokov did not share Plato's suspicion of the "irrational," instead adhering to the notion that art is a deceptive game in which "irrational standards" favorably complement "the precision of poetry and the intuition of science."[17]

Another point of contention, at once personal and philosophical, was the subject of death. Both writers had their reasons to be drawn to this topic. Plato was obviously affected by the execution of Socrates, who was his friend and mentor. Plato's preoccupation with the subject of afterlife is evident not only in his dialogs about Socrates' execution but even his writings on metaphysics, which reminds us how important this topic was for Plato. Nabokov was equally preoccupied with death, largely because of his own experiences. The assassination of his father in 1922, when the writer was just twenty-three years old, had an undeniable impact on his life and artistic development; many of his works can be read as contemplations of the mystery of death. But even though Nabokov's and Plato's personal experiences can be related, it should be acknowledged that the ways in which these writers exploited this subject reflected two strikingly different sensibilities. This is why Nabokov's conflict with Plato's lasting influence was inevitable, and it focused precisely on the subject of death.

What Nabokov must have disliked about Plato's treatment of this theme was, in part, that the philosopher turned Socrates' tragic fate into what might be perceived as a rigid tale that demands the reader's compassion for its crudely constructed heroic character. On the verge of his death, Plato's Socrates unselfishly insists on sharing his wisdom with his grieving followers. He turns down their offers to help him escape the prison, and heroically (almost histrionically) embraces death. His subsequent execution takes place amidst a serious discussion on the immortality of the soul, which he continues

---

[15] Ibid., 605a-b.
[16] Nabokov, "The Art of Literature and Commonsense," 373.
[17] Nabokov, "Good Readers and Good Writers," *Lectures on Literature*, ed. Fredson Bowers (New York: Harcourt Brace & Company, 1980), 6.

to examine even as the poison administered by his executioner takes effect. It may seem that Plato, like Jacques-Louis David's famous painting the *Death of Socrates* (1783), went too far by turning the event into what strikes some readers as a dramatic farce that turns a tragedy into a simple story of philosophical martyrdom.

Jacques-Louis David's
The Death of Socrates (1787)

Nabokov's disdain for such trite and overdramatic material is well known. It is particularly evident in his novel *The Gift* (1937-8), in which he targets Nikolai Chernyshevsky, an admired nineteenth-century Russian philosopher and a hero of the socialist movement, whose intellectual life and persecution by the authorities made him an icon of public reverence. To the dismay of his own admirers, Nabokov mercilessly turned that respectable philosopher into a symbol of intellectual and artistic failure. It was while working on *The Gift* that Nabokov suddenly decided to put that long project aside in order to write a short novel titled *Invitation to a Beheading*. It was his tribute to the subject of a dying hero and, at the same time, a stab at Plato's treatment of the same theme.

It is easy to understand Nabokov's disdain for Plato if we take a closer look at Plato's way of writing about death. In *Apology* and *Phaedo*, Plato advances his argument about the immortality of the soul. These works describe Socrates' trial, during which he expresses his faith that, if executed, his immortal soul will join the company of other remarkable people in the afterlife: "the soul that has led a pure life and moderate life finds fellow-travellers and gods to guide it, and each of them dwells in a place suited to it."[18] To the Athenian jury that has just pronounced a verdict to put him to death, Socrates convincingly declares that he is better off than any *living* being: "what would any of you not give to talk to Orpheus and Museus, Hesiod and Homer."[19] In his afterlife, a practitioner of philosophy can even expect to find himself in "the company of the gods."[20] Nabokov, for his part, has the doomed Cincinnatus imagine an equally alluring place, where "the freaks that are tortured here walk unmolested," and where he will join the company of the "beings akin to him."[21] The parallels between these passages, which suggest Nabokov's conscious use of Platonic imagery, makes even more sense when we recall that John Shade, the great poet of Nabokov's *Pale Fire*, imagines his afterlife in terms of "the talks / With Socrates and Proust in cypress walks."[22]

In spite of the apparent optimism about afterlife which pervades Plato's works, one can nonetheless perceive an undeniable lack of certainty in his discussion of death. Although Socrates often appears to be assured of his immortality, at other times his confidence is dampened by some unsettling thoughts, which many readers of his works tend to ignore. What if the afterlife is just a dream, a comforting way to cope with death? For Socrates (and, as we will see later, for Cincinnatus as well) the prospect of another existence after death is not assured at all. He has many doubts. For example, his hope of encountering Homer in afterlife starts to dissipate when he adds: "I'd be willing to die many times, *if it were truth.*"[23] "[If] it were true," he continues this thought on another occasion,

> there is *good hope* that on arriving where I am going, *if anywhere*, I shall acquire what has been our chief preoccupation in our past life, so that the journey that is now ordered for me is *full of good hope*, as it is also for any other man who *believes* that his mind has been prepared and, as it were, purified.[24]

Plato makes it unavoidably clear that Socrates' view of immortality relies merely on "good hope" and belief, which are not always convincing, even to Socrates.

---

[18] Plato, *Phaedo*, 108c.

[19] Plato, *Apology*, *The Trials of Socrates*, ed. and trans. C. D. C. Reeve (Indianapolis: Hackett Publishing, 2002), 41a.

[20] Plato, *Phaedo*, 82b.

[21] Nabokov, *Invitation*, 94, 223.

[22] Nabokov, *Pale Fire* (New York: Vintage International, 1989), 41.

[23] Plato, *Apology*, 41a, my emphasis.

[24] Plato, *Phaedo*, 67b-c, my emphasis.

On several occasions Plato gives the impression that Socrates constructs his theory of immortality simply as a way to give a special meaning to his impeding death. When Socrates is awaiting execution, Plato declares that "any man who faces death with confidence is foolish unless he can prove that the soul is altogether immortal."[25] Considering the context of this statement, the debate about immortality becomes a personal rather than a strictly philosophical endeavor. Socrates later admits: "I am in danger at this moment of not having a philosophical attitude about this [argument]." He compares himself to those who deceive themselves and

> give no thought to the truth about the subject of discussion but are only eager that those present will accept the position they have set forth. I differ from them only to this extent: I shall not be eager to get the agreement of those present that what I say is true, except incidentally, but *I shall be very eager that I should myself be thoroughly convinced that things are so.*[26]

This passage suggests that the circumstances oblige Socrates to believe in his immortality, but no matter how elaborate his argument may seem, it does not have the power to actually convince him. His interlocutors are even less convinced, but sometimes pretend to agree with Socrates only out of consideration for his situation.[27] The real tragedy of Socrates' execution, which Plato depicts with amazing literary skill, is that Socrates is ultimately facing death without a comfortable sense of certainty about his future. What is heroic about him, but painful to witness as a reader of *Phaedo*, is that he creates a reassuring theory of afterlife and immortality while remaining strong enough not to dismiss that unsettling feeling that there is no immortality at all, and resisting the natural temptation to cling to a comfortable vision of afterlife in the last days of his life.

It may well be, however, that Socrates' doubts about afterlife reflect our own uncertainties about ways of reading *Phaedo*. Plato succeeds in creating an intriguing sense of indeterminacy about Socrates' prospects of life after death, which invests the work with so many interpretive possibilities. Even a brief survey of Plato's scholarship shows how diverse our interpretations of Plato's theory of afterlife can be.

How did Nabokov read *Phaedo*? Did he recognize its literary complexity, or did he read it as a pseudo-literary philosophical work in which the death

---

[25] Ibid., 88b.
[26] Ibid., 91a, my emphasis.
[27] Ibid., 84c-e, among other places.

of Socrates is nothing more than an occasion to express Plato's seemingly simple notion of immortality? Exploring this question can help us understand whether *Invitation to a Beheading* is a parody of what its author thought was the simplicity of Plato's *Phaedo*, or an intentionally concealed tribute to its complexity.

It appears that Nabokov made his readers as conflicted about ways of reading his work as Plato made his. It is a strange coincidence (if it is a coincidence at all) that the readers of *Invitation to a Beheading* often follow the same interpretive paths as the readers of *Phaedo*. The novel can easily be read as a sterile allegory of artistic creation, in which an artist transcends the limits of his existence with his imagination. But this way of reading the novel is rather simplistic. If we take a closer look at Cincinnatus's story, we encounter a doomed man for whom the afterlife is nothing more than a comforting illusion. It is doubtful, I think, that Nabokov meant to make his novel prone to a reductive interpretation according to which Cincinnatus's hopes and imaginative powers are simply rewarded at the end. The mysterious indeterminacy of death is a recognizable trait of Nabokov's way of writing about it, a subject which Nabokov forces us to examine without any promise of certainty. It is apparent not only in *Invitation to a Beheading* but many of his other works, particularly *Pale Fire*, *Lolita*, *The Eye*, and the 1923 play *Death*. As if addressing the readers, Humbert tells Quilty at gunpoint: "I want you to concentrate. The hereafter for all we know may be an eternal state of excruciating insanity."[28] It may well be.

In what reminds us of Socrates' attempts to dispel his reservations about immortality, the central conflict in *Invitation to a Beheading* is not between Cincinnatus and the prison-world in which he is trapped, but between him and his sense of reality. His doubts, not his jailers, keep him imprisoned. His many flights of imagination, which are his way of escaping, are sooner or later undercut by doubts. In the first scene of the novel, Cincinnatus is compared to "a man who has dreamt that he is walking on water," which could be perceived as an optimistic image if it was not undercut by "a sudden doubt: but is this possible?"[29] Cincinnatus asks himself the same question throughout the novel, and the answer is not always affirmative. Even when he appears to be optimistic, his hopes still lack a convincing ring. "It exists, my dream world," Cincinnatus says in his soliloquy, "it must exist," he repeats as if in doubt. And like Socrates before him, he feels that he has to

---

[28] Nabokov, *Lolita* (New York: Vintage, 1991), 297.
[29] Nabokov, *Invitation*, 11.

prove its existence to himself: "surely there must be an original of the clumsy copy," he says, echoing Socrates' argument that our world is merely a copy of another.[30] Both Socrates and Cincinnatus are torn between their optimism about afterlife and their realization that they are mortal. This explains why there appear to be two of Cincinnatus; one is confident and hopeful while the other is complacent and fearful.[31] These polemic characteristics within the same person evoke Plato's portrayal of Socrates, who sometimes appears to be confident in his reasoning about immortality while at other times is notably ridden by doubts.[32]

Cincinnatus and Socrates, who found themselves in the same situation, are tormented by the question of how real that place is where their reasoning and imagination often take them. Strangely, most commentators do not share their doubts, discussing Cincinnatus's immortality as something certain. Brian Boyd, in his reading of the novel, comments on Cincinnatus's situation: "Only beyond death can a mind so alive find its true scope." At the execution Cincinnatus does not die, Boyd writes, but "tears a hole in his world to reach his likes beyond."[33] Cincinnatus's fate, however, is far more uncertain than

---

[30] Ibid., 93. The idea reverberates throughout Plato's works, and is exemplified by Timaeus's words: "the world has been framed in the likeness of that which is apprehended by reason and mind and is unchangeable, and must therefore of necessity, if this is admitted, be a copy of something" (Plato, *Timaeus*, *Plato: The Collected Dialogues*, trans. Benjamin Jowett, ed. Edith Hamilton and Huntington Cairns [Princeton: Princeton University Press, 1961], 27c-29d).

[31] Nabokov, *Invitation*, 15, 25, 29, 40, 69, and 222-3.

[32] We can also distinguish two distinct images of Socrates in the context of Socratic literature in general. Xenophon, in "Apology of Socrates," portrays Socrates as a philosopher who is so assured of his immortality that he defies the jury during his trial in anticipation of his death (or afterlife). Plato, in contrast, creates an image of Socrates as a less confident man.

[33] Brian Boyd, *Vladimir Nabokov: The Russian Years* (Princeton: Princeton University Press, 1990), 413, 415. Many critical responses to *Invitation* are equally optimistic about Cincinnatus's survival. Gavriel Shapiro, comparing Cincinnatus to Christ, argues that Christian allusions "enable us to interpret the novel's close as the resurrection of its hero" (*Delicate Markers: Subtexts in Vladimir Nabokov's "Invitation to a Beheading"* [New York: Peter Lang Publishing, 1998], 124). Vladimir Alexandrov, in his examination of the novel's Gnostic motives, is equally optimistic when he concludes that Cincinnatus "appears to transcend his mortal being following his decapitation" so that his soul is allowed to escape the confines of his body and "return to the spiritual homeland to which he had been attached throughout his life" (*Nabokov's Otherworld*, 86, 87). Julian W. Connolly writes that the "end of the novel depicts Cincinnatus picking himself up from the ruble of the world disintegrating around him and heading off toward a new realm of kindred spirits" (*Nabokov's Early Fiction: Patterns of Self and Other* [Cambridge: Cambridge University Press, 1992], 183). Dale Peterson, for his part, offers a completely different take with which I agree: although "critics [often] assumed that Nabokov invites his readers to believe that imagination can rise above everything and

this. Nabokov, perhaps unintentionally echoing Plato's way of writing about Socrates' wavering hopes for immortality, gave us many reasons to believe that Cincinnatus survives his execution, while at the same time hinting that he does not.

There are indeed many promising signs of Cincinnatus's prospects for immortality. The novel repeatedly emphasizes his dual nature, so that it appears that his soul can survive the destruction of his body. At one point Cincinnatus enjoys an out-of-body experience as he casts off his material self.

> [He] took off his head like a toupee, took off his collarbones like shoulder straps, took off his rib cage like a hauberk. He took off his hips and his legs, he took off his arms like gauntlets and threw them in a corner. What was left of him gradually dissolved, hardly coloring the air.[34]

Perhaps this passage is meant to suggest that if Cincinnatus can exist without his body, he can survive his beheading as well. We should also acknowledge the hints that the novel is narrated by Cincinnatus's ghost, which exists at least long enough to tell to the story of Cincinnatus's execution. This explains the mysterious exclamations of "O horrible!" which are meant to evoke the speech of King Hamlet's ghost. As the latter describes the circumstances of his death to young Hamlet, he interrupts his monologue with a chilling "O horrible! O horrible! Most horrible!"[35] The narrative of *Invitation to a Beheading*, like the monologue of King Hamlet's ghost, sounds like a bodiless voice that survived the death of its body. In yet another hopeful sign, the novel mentions that on the way to the place of the execution, Cincinnatus notices "the odor of warm nettles" and "a dozen geese."[36] This is undoubtedly a reference to Hans Christian Andersen's "The Wild Swans," a fairy tale about a princess who is condemned to death for witchcraft. As she awaits her execution, she weaves a nettle shirt for each of her twelve brothers to undo the spell of an evil witch that turned them into swans (or, as some Russian translations have it, geese). She continues her work even on the way to her execution, which she narrowly avoids by completing the shirts moments before her appointed time and thus breaking the spell. At the end of the story, twelve swans

---

anything, redeeming mundane hurts and losses," it is doubtful that Nabokov "can actually be irresponsible enough to advocate imaginative escapism as an adequate response to police states" ("Literature as Execution," *Nabokov: Modern Critical Views*, ed. Harold Bloom [New York: Chelsea House, 1987], 70).

[34] Nabokov, *Invitation*, 32.
[35] William Shakespeare, *Hamlet*, ed. T. J. B. Spencer (New York: Penguin Books, 1996), I.5.80.
[36] Nabokov, *Invitation*, 214.

turn into young men and the princess, who had grown ugly in her labors, regains her beauty.37 Nabokov's reference to this fairy tale, which ends with a triumphant transformation of the wrongly accused, encourages us to think that Cincinnatus also survives his execution.

Even more suggestive of Cincinnatus's immortality is the novel's optimistic epigraph by a certain Delalande: "Comme un fou se croit Dieu, nous nous croyons mortels" ("Like a madman who believes he is God, we are convinced that we are mortal").38 In *The Gift*, where we encounter Delalande for the first time, he says,

> the liberation of the soul from the eye-sockets of flesh and our transformation into one complete and free eye, which can simultaneously see in all directions, or to put it differently: a supersensory insight into the world accompanied by our inner participation.39

Delalande's statement echoes Socrates' argument that

> when we are dead, [we] attain that which we desire and of which we claim to be lovers, namely, wisdom [...]; for it is impossible to attain any pure knowledge with the body [...]: either we can never attain knowledge or we can do so after death. [...] In this way we shall escape the contamination of the body's folly; we shall be likely to be in the company of people of the same kind.40

But to trust Delalande, whom Nabokov invented, is as misleading as accepting fictitious John Ray Jr. as an authority on *Lolita*. No matter how attractive and captivating Delalande's epigraph may be, Cincinnatus, for his part, cannot shake off the suspicion that we might be mad to think that we are immortal. In spite of all these optimistic signs and reassurances, which all but state with certainty that Cincinnatus attains immortality at the moment of his execution, it would be erroneous to take them at their face value.

Nabokov, like Plato before him, constantly suggests that hope for immortality is a dream that, for both Cincinnatus and Socrates, always slips away. No matter how strong their faith is, their hopes are invariably mired in pessimism. Just a few moments after he arrives at a realization that his dream world must exist, Cincinnatus's hope bursts: "I think I have caught my prey...

---

37 Hans Christian Andersen, "The Wild Swans," *The Complete Fairy Tales and Stories*, trans. Erik Christian Haugaard (Garden City, N.Y.: Anchor Press, 1983), 117-131.
38 Nabokov, *Invitation*, 9, my translation.
39 Nabokov, *The Gift* (New York: Vintage International, 1991), 310.
40 Plato, *Phaedo*, 66e-67a.

but it is only a fleeting apparition of my prey!"[41] He is consequently compared to "a man grieving because he has recently lost in his dreams some thing that he had never found in reality, or hoping that tomorrow he would dream that he had found it again." It is "the dead end of this life," the narrator says, and crossing out the word "death,"[42] which some commentators interpret as a triumphant conquest of death, is in fact a confused gesture of hope and despair. It seems that the best Cincinnatus can do while contemplating his afterlife is to adopt a playful (but hardly hopeful) attitude of John Shade, Nabokov's poet in *Pale Fire*. He calls immortality the "grand potato," a pun on the *grand peut-être*, the Big If.[43] For Nabokov and Plato, the afterlife had very little to do with the orderliness of imagination and, as Nabokov's characters and Plato's Socrates know, can easily be turned into an object of wild and uncontrollable speculation.

This reminds us that *Invitation to a Beheading*, like any other novel by Nabokov, effectively dispels definitive interpretation. We should not conclude that Cincinnatus's ghost, whatever it may be, survives his execution. Strange as Nabokov's world is, we can find a ghost, but no immortality. The ghost can tell us a story of his life, but nothing about death. Nabokov's readers are habitually cheated of a chance to glimpse afterlife; just as his dead characters, no matter how imaginative they may be, are cheated of immortality altogether. As with Edmund, the hero of Nabokov's play *Death*, an imaginative person can tell us something about death only by imagining himself dead.[44] This may be as far as Nabokov and Plato could possibly take us when writing about death.

The noted affinities between Nabokov and Plato suggest that *Invitation*'s reference points are more diverse than previously elucidated. Apart from creating recognizable parallels between Cincinnatus and, for example, Jesus, John the Baptist, and the Gnostics, Nabokov's novel intentionally evokes such works of antiquity as Plato's *Phaedo*, and possibly (a subject for another essay) Boethius's *Consolation of Philosophy*.[45] This conclusion, however, does

[41] Nabokov, *Invitation*, 93, 94.
[42] Ibid., 205-6.
[43] Nabokov, *Pale Fire*, 52.
[44] Nabokov's *Smert'* is one of his earliest works, a nearly forgotten play written in Russian, in verse. It has not been translated into English, but a short summary is in Brian Boyd's *Vladimir Nabokov: The Russian Years*, 204.
[45] Boethius (480-524 AD) was a philosopher and statesmen who was unjustly prosecuted and executed for conspiracy against King Theodoric. While awaiting his execution, he wrote a work titled *Consolation of Philosophy*. In Platonic fashion, it strives to be a captivating literary work and a philosophical treatise.

not make it easy for us to understand the motive behind the Platonic theme in Nabokov's novel. If Nabokov introduced Platonic references merely as a joke, to ridicule Plato as someone who failed to grasp the mystery of death, then we can conclude that Nabokov misread Plato, whose approach to the subject of afterlife is as complex as Nabokov's. Arguably, he underestimated the literary complexity of Plato's dialogs, because he paid too much attention to Socrates' intentionally misleading comments about art. Plato has to be appreciated not only as a philosopher but also a literary figure—the way Nabokov can be admired for his artistry as well as his philosophic insight. We can recall Nabokov's words that a great novel unites "the precision of poetry and the intuition of science,"[46] as analogous to the spirit of Plato's works that merge philosophical pursuits with artistic endeavors. On the day of Socrates' execution, a friend caught him writing poetry. One cannot imagine Socrates writing in the first place, let alone writing poetry. Socrates responded:

> I tried to find out the meaning of certain dreams and to satisfy my conscience in case it was this kind of art they were frequently bidding me to practice. The dreams were something like this: the same dream often came to me in the past, now in one shape now in another, but saying the same thing: "Socrates," it said, "practice and cultivate the arts."[47]

I am guessing that if Nabokov had noticed this passage, he would have been inclined to accept it, at least privately—but would have denied it in print.

---

[46] Nabokov, "Good Readers," 6.
[47] Plato, *Phaedo*, 60d-e.

CENTER CIRCLE

FORUM

Alice Lotvin Birney
(*The Library of Congress*)
Isaac Gewirtz
(*Berg Collection,
The New York Public Library*)
Tatiana Ponomareva
(*Vladimir Nabokov Museum,
St. Petersburg*)
Katherine Reagan
(*Division of Rare and
Manuscript Collections,
Cornell University Library*)

INSTITUTIONALIZING NABOKOV: *MUSEUM, ARCHIVE, EXHIBITION*[1]

NABOKOV COLLECTIONS

Yuri Leving: Can you briefly describe the Nabokov-related holdings at your institution?

Katherine Reagan: Cornell's Nabokov collections are comprised of: a comprehensive book collection, including many copies inscribed or annotated by the author; manuscript materials in the University's Archives documenting Nabokov's years as a Cornell faculty member ca. 1948-1959; and a collection of several hundred letters and documents exchanged between Nabokov, his literary agent Doussia Ergaz, and Olympia Press publisher Maurice Girodias. Written in both French and English, this series includes correspondence and contracts related to many of Nabokov's published works from the 1950s through the 1970s.

---

[1] First appeared in *Nabokov Online Journal*, Vol. III (2009).

Tom Fecht, photograph, 2005 ©
"Lolita" models in Cornell University's historic
Andrew Dickson White Library.
Used by permission.

Nabokov's books and manuscripts form part of Cornell's Division of Rare and Manuscript Collections, which features 400,000 printed books and more than seventy million manuscripts, photographs, artifacts, and other research materials. Portions of Cornell's Nabokov collection developed organically, beginning in the 1960s when curators in the Department of Rare Books started collecting his first editions. Others have their origin in the Library's University Archives program, which preserves the papers of Cornell's colleges, departments, and faculty members. Additional materials were purchased with funds donated by Cornell alumni in the 1990s, a time when a significant amount of Nabokov material was circulating in the antiquarian market, partly in anticipation of the 1998 centennial celebration of his birth.

Tatiana Ponomareva: Our collection and library together consists of over 4000 items but we are still in the initial phase of development. We only have a limited number of items that actually belonged to Vladimir Nabokov himself but a lot of things that are related to the Nabokov family, the house and the Nabokov country estates. Basically, the museum collection was started from scratch in the early 1990s. Only the house itself was there, no things remained. Everything we have now was collected within the last ten years. Our items come from different sources — mostly from our good friends and benefactors, of whom Terry Myers deserves special gratitude. We are also proud to have a few things donated by Dmitri Nabokov. In addition, a lot of selfless and enthusiastic people in Russia donated their Nabokovian treasures to the museum. Readers of *Speak, Memory* will remember the kindness of Vladimir Nabokov's parents towards their servants. It is now being returned in the shape of many valuable household items which we have received from the grandchildren of the people who worked for the Nabokov family.

Alice Birney: The papers of Vladimir Nabokov at the Manuscript Division of the Library of Congress span 1918-1974 (mainly pertaining to 1925-1965). The collection that today comprises 7,000 items was chiefly donated directly by the author between 1959 and 1965. Additions were acquired by purchase in 1971 and 1991 and by gifts from Peter Pertzoff in 1964 and Jay Wilson in 1991. Covering Nabokov's work as a poet, novelist, literary critic, lecturer, and translator, the collection consists of the following series: Correspondence, Writings, Miscellany, an Addition, and Oversize. It includes holograph and typescript drafts, galley proofs, page proofs, and printed versions of biographies, in addition to book reviews, essays, interviews, memoirs, novellas, novels, plays, poems, short stories, translations of works by others, and related material. The bulk of the collection is written in Russian and English, with small amounts in French and German. In most instances, titles of Nabokov's works are based on English translations of Russian citations appearing in Michael Juliar's *Vladimir Nabokov: A Descriptive Bibliography*.

The Correspondence series is arranged as letters received and sent. Although small in quantity, it contains letters from prominent figures in Russian literature and culture including Iu Aikhenvald, Mark Aldanov, Nina Berberova, Ivan Bunin, Vladislav Khodasevich, and others. Various Russian-language émigré publishers and publications are also represented in the series, such as Petropolis, *Novoe russkoe slovo*, *Poslednie novosti*, *Russkie zapiski*, and *Sovremennye zapiski*. Subjects include publication deadlines, copyright issues, and author's fees, as well as Nabokov's interest in butterflies.

The Writings series constitutes the largest portion of the collection. It largely consists of material relating to non-fiction, translations of works by others, and novels in both the Russian and English language periods. Nabokov's first of several book-length autobiographies, *Conclusive Evidence: A Memoir,* is documented. He regarded the process of translation as a serious literary endeavour, quoting Pushkin, "Translators are the post horses of enlightenment."[2] After 1940, while in America, Nabokov began to translate many of his earlier writings into English and, at times, made extensive revisions to the original texts. Such is the case with *Drugie berega,* the Russian-language edition of *Conclusive Evidence.* Files related to Nabokov's English translation of Pushkin's verse novel, *Eugene Onegin,* include material in which Nabokov reflected upon the translation process. The file also includes copious explanatory notes, extensive commentaries positioning the narrative within the context of European society during Pushkin's time, comments on the work's significance in Russian literature, remarks on previous translations by others, two lengthy appendices and an index. (Additional material relating to *Eugene Onegin* is held in the separate Bollingen Foundation Records in the Manuscript Division.) The series also contains files on Nabokov's translation of the anonymous Russian epic, *The Song of Igor's Campaign.*

Nabokov's novels documented in the Writings series from his Russian period include *The Gift, Mary, Despair, Glory, Invitation to a Beheading,* and *The Defense.* Titles from his American period include *Bend Sinister, Lolita, Pale Fire,* and *The Real Life of Sebastian Knight.* The Writings series also contains material relating to a number of plays written in Russian by Nabokov during his early years. A sizeable amount of material documents the author's film adaptation of his novel *Lolita* entitled *Lolita: A Screenplay.*

Holograph and typescript drafts of numerous poems written by Nabokov throughout his career are in both Russian and English. Representative titles include "Bezumets" ("The Madman"), "K Rossii" ("To Russia"), "Probuzhdenie" ("The Awakening"), and "Rasstrel" ("The Execution"). The poetry section also contains examples of Nabokov's translations of poems written by others, including two in French. Short stories and novellas represented in the series include "The Double Monster," "Cloud, Castle, Lake," "The Aurelian," and "An Affair of Honor."

[2] Aleksandr Sergeevich Pushkin, *Eugene Onegin: A Novel in Verse,* trans. and Commentary Vladimir Nabokov (Princeton: Princeton University Press, 1975), 229.

Miscellaneous items in the Writings series include short works such as book reviews, classroom teaching material, and essays. Many of the poems and short stories in the collection are signed with the pseudonym "V. Sirin." Scattered throughout the collection are notes and drafts written on 4" x 6" cards. Files documenting the writing of *Pale Fire*, *Lolita: A Screenplay*, and "The Vane Sisters" consist entirely of these cards.

The Miscellany series includes a transcript of a radio interview with Nabokov. Oversize material consists of Nabokov's diploma from the University of Cambridge, passports and related material removed from the Miscellany series. An unrestricted addition to the collection, not donated by the author, contains letters from Nabokov to Princess Zinaida Schakovskoy and correspondence between the Nabokovs and Gleb Struve.

Isaac Gewirtz: The Vladimir Nabokov Archive, housed in New York Public Library's Henry W. and Albert A. Berg Collection of English and American Literature comprises some 15,254 items, consisting of manuscripts and typescripts in Russian and English for novels, short stories, poems, plays, essays, lectures, notes toward works, interviews, and scientific works; correspondence in Russian and English; diaries in Russian and English dating from 1941 to 1977; notebooks; legal documents; hundreds of photographic portraits of Nabokov, dating from his childhood to the end of his life, as well as of his parents, grandparents, and numerous other relatives, and of his wife, Véra; and pictorial works. Highlights of the writings include twenty-five notebooks; hundreds of poems in Russian, as well as many in English and French; scores of short stories in Russian and English; the four drafts of the English translation of *Mashen'ka* (*Mary*); three drafts for a screenplay of *Lolita*; notes on the French translation of *Lolita* by Eric H. Kahane; notes in Russian and galley notes on the Russian translation of *Lolita*; all of the drafts of *Ada*; all of the drafts of *Look at the Harlequins!*, with a photocopy of Blandenier's French translation, emended in Nabokov's hand; the emended typescript drafts of the English translation of *Dar* (*The Gift*), chapters 1-5, and the emended typescript and manuscript drafts of the French translation; the typescript of the revised version of *Invitation to a Beheading*; the emended typescript of *King, Queen, Knave*; all of the notes and drafts for the *Lectures on Russian Literature* and *Lectures on Literature*; the index card holographs of changes made to *Conclusive Evidence* and published as *Speak Memory*; and the drafts for *Strong Opinions*.

The author's outgoing correspondence, dating from 1919 to 1977, includes letters to, among others, his mother Elena Ivanovna, his wife Véra,

Mark Aldanov, Elia Kazan, Sergei Makovsky, Gleb Struve, Edmund Wilson, the Bollingen Foundation, the Chekhov Publishing House, the Bureau Littéraire D. Clairouin, Cornell University, Doubleday & Co. Publishers, the Librarie Gallimard, Harper & Bros. Publishers, Henry Holt & Co. Publishers, McGraw-Hill Inc., New Directions Publishers, The New Yorker Magazine, G.P. Putnam's Sons Publishers, the Viking Press, George Weidenfeld & Nicholson, Ltd., and others. Many of these letters are accompanied by reply letters *to* the author and by letters between the correspondents and the author's wife. Other communiqué consists of letters relating to the author, dating from 1944 to 1980, between various correspondents including Véra Nabokov, Matthew Bruccoli, Edmund Wilson, George Plimpton, and Prins & Prins Literary Agents and others.

The bulk of Nabokov's working literary library was acquired with the papers, descriptions of some of which are accessible through the Library's online catalog, and the bulk of his scientific (mostly lepidoptera) working library.[3] Many of the literary volumes have been copiously annotated by him.

Yuri Leving: *According to P. Bourdieu, the role of the artist cannot be understood independently of the transformations in the field of artistic production. The constitution of an overwhelming ensemble of institutions for recording, conserving and analyzing works (reproductions, catalogues, art magazines, museums acquiring the most recent works, etc.); the growth in personnel dedicated to the celebration of the work of art; the intensification of the circulation of works and of artists, with the great international exhibitions and the multiplication of galleries with many branches in various countries, etc. — everything combines to favor the establishment of an unprecedented relationship between the interpreters and the work of art.[4] How does this discourse, designed to encourage the apprehension and appreciation of an artist, reflect the meaning and value of Nabokov's works today?*

Isaac Gewirtz: This question contains several implied assumptions, the validity of which seem dubious to me because an exhibition viewer's apprehension of a work of graphic art or sculpture differs essentially from the way in which a text, or what is said about a text, is apprehended in a literary exhibition. Though the art and literary worlds share certain features,

---

[3] A description of the Archive may be found on the Berg website at: http://www.nypl.org/research/manuscripts/berg/brgnabok.xml#IDATGOPB

[4] P. Bourdieu, *The Rules of Art: Genesis and Structure of the Literary Field* (Stanford: Stanford University Press, 1997), 170.

or at least seem to share aspects of a single interpretive vocabulary and syntax, in regard (for instance), to sources of creativity, methods of interpretation, critical categorization, the roles of academic and public reputation, commercial appeal, faddism, etc., the question posed above is more relevant to the art world than the literary.

A crucial difference between the two worlds is that though museums and galleries do record, conserve, and analyze works, the greatest expenditure of time and resources in these activities are performed in the service of exhibitions (whether "great" and "international" or not). The essential qualities of the vast majority of literary and artistic artifacts are so different from each other—as are the ways in which literary, as opposed to art, curators conceive of the reception to their artifacts, which account for the vast difference in the ways that literary and art exhibitions are presented—that placing literary exhibitions in an art exhibition frame of reference only serves to obscure the significance of literary exhibitions. For me, the more interesting question is how should literary exhibitions communicate and realize their curators' intentions, and what effect good literary exhibitions may have on scholarship, on how a reading public for an author may be increased, and on how the writer's reputation may be affected? But since the question was posed in the art world context, let us reveal the question's assumptions (including the implied second-class status thereby assigned to word as opposed to image) and examine their validity. Perhaps in this way we may understand what a literary exhibition may hope to do.

In the case of art galleries, exhibitions are intended to sell a product. A few very upscale dealers in books and manuscripts are also galleries and perform the same commodifying role, as do art galleries. But the vast majority of literary exhibitions, most of which are held in libraries, do not do this. The purpose of their exhibitions is not to sell an author, except metaphorically—in the sense that the curator wishes to bring a greater understanding of a particular author or literary subject to a wider audience. This is not to say that library and museum curators may not be impelled by selfish motives. But such motives are of an entirely different kind than the hope of receiving money for the sale of the artifacts on display.

Alice Birney: The role of the public repository is to preserve the primary materials so that future generations of biographers, critics, and other scholars might interpret them according to changing cultural contexts. To accomplish this goal, materials should be kept as open as possible. Exhibitions and celebrations are executed within the limitations of donor access restrictions, copyright law, preservation needs, competing personalities, and budget.

Isaac Gewirtz: The genres of museum and library exhibition have much more in common in regard to their goals. But even here the differences are vast. Visual and literary materials are apprehended by the mind in different ways. The markedly lower status that Western society in general (and increasingly so in the East, I suspect), and the exhibition-going public and culture elites in particular, assign to the word, compared to the image, means that drawing the attention of potential exhibition-goers to writers and poets, as opposed to painters and multi-media artists, is a considerably more formidable challenge to the library curator than to his or her museum colleague. A museum visitor can look at a work of art and believe that s/he has understood it because s/he has "seen" it. But in order to "see" a book or a poem, even on the most uninformed, disengaged level (the level at which many, maybe most, museum-goers relate to the art that they see in museums), one must read it. Reading a good literary work requires energetic attention, which must be sustained over a fair amount of time even for a short story.

Katherine Reagan: Alice and Isaac make interesting points about differences between the aims of museums, libraries, and art galleries. Some commonalities, however, are equally important to remember. As a rare book and manuscript curator in a library, I act as collector (helping to ensure future generations have access to original artifacts) and educator (helping to ensure materials are visible, accessible, and integral to my institution's mission to teach). I suspect a museum curator would say much the same thing. All three types of institutions—libraries, galleries, museums—are involved in shaping the market and cultural capital of a writer or artist in any given moment in time.

Through choices of who and what to collect or exhibit (or not), how much to pay for artifacts, and what we say about them when assembled, curators, along side the more obviously commercial interests of gallery owners, dealers and auction houses, reinforce or diminish artistic and literary reputations. While this influence is well-understood among those who operate in these fields, curators should remain responsibly conscious of this influence, and encourage consumers of exhibitions, and researchers in archives, to also cultivate this critical awareness.

Yuri Leving: *What about "reading" a work of visual art vis-à-vis a literary exhibition?*

Isaac Gewirtz: Now, it is true that it takes energetic attention and some time, perhaps only after many viewings, to properly "read" a good painting or sculpture. But this fact is much more easily ignored in the visual arts than in the literary. Everyone "sees" and reacts to the world all the time, and they don't expend much attention doing it.

It is a largely unconscious activity. For the most part, as I gather from the conversations I have overheard in the course of several decades of exhibition-going, the same semiconscious attention is brought into the museum and the art gallery. Now consider what occurs at a literary exhibition. If a manuscript of a novel is displayed, it will be represented by only a handful of pages; the rest will remain unseen in the archival box or sit in a pile in the exhibition case and bear mute testimony to the author's prodigious effort. The reasons for this display imbalance are obvious. First, no library gallery has enough cases or gallery space to show 600 or even 300 manuscript pages. Second, if such a facility existed, who would expect an exhibition-goer to read every page of that novel in the exhibition hall, even if every page were replete with passages that differed from the published text? Finally, even assuming that this monstrous feat of curatorship could be accomplished, there would be no room to display any of the writer's other works, or any of his/her journals, diaries, galleys, letters, photographs, etc., which help the viewer to interpret the author's body of work.

For similar reasons, keeping the viewer's attention is also a more formidable challenge to the curator of the literary exhibition than the artistic. Paintings can be "seen" in their entirety in a single glance, or certainly a few moments. But since literary works, as we have said, with the exception of poems, very brief short stories, and correspondence, cannot be displayed in their entirety, introductory panels and labels must fill the contextual gap. This task generally requires providing the literary exhibition viewer with much more text than is necessary in an art exhibition or gallery installation, just to make available basic contextual information. The prospect of all this reading shouts "snoozer" for most exhibition-goers, no matter how much visual enhancement is provided with photographs, artwork, realia, and the like. If anyone doubts the superior attractive power of art exhibitions compared to their poor literary cousins, let them consider that the largest number of people ever to attend a New York Public Library (NYPL) literary exhibition was 200,000 for the Dead Sea Scrolls. Even calling this exhibition "literary" or textual is somewhat disingenuous, since most of the exhibition attendees regarded the Dead Sea Scrolls more as a kind of holy relic than a text; even as a species of literary artifact the scrolls could be appreciated only by the several hundred scholars in the world who could actually read and understand the script (much less the implications of the words) in which they are written. But let us be generous and stipulate that this was a literary exhibition, or at least a textual one, which featured parts of one of the Western world's best known and iconic collection of manuscripts, at one of the world's greatest and best known libraries, situated in one of the Western world's most heavily populated and tourist-laden cities, at one of its most accessible sites. This extraordinary exhibition, indeed, drew a large crowd — no fewer than 200,000 visitors over a period of six months (October 1993-March 1994). But we are better able to place in perspective this "large" number when we learn that a Roy Lichtenstein show at the Guggenheim, which began in the same month and ran for only half the time (October 8, 1993-January 16, 1994), drew a total of 244,758 visitors.[5] I am not immune to the charms of Roy Lichtenstein, but his place in the art world cannot be compared to the place of the Dead Sea Scrolls in the world of words (if one may be forgiven so dramatic and clumsy a phrase). Yet in half the time, almost 25% more people went to the Guggenheim to be entertained by Lichtenstein's brightly colored and boldly drawn pop images than to the NYPL in order to stare at and read about(!) a collection of ancient, drab, crumbly parchment fragments. The contrast in drawing power between image and word becomes even more stark when comparing the Lichtenstein attendance figures to those of authentic literary exhibitions. For instance, NYPL's Nabokov exhibition drew just over 79,000 viewers over a period of four months in 1999, and 185,000 visitors toured our Jack Kerouac exhibition over a period of four months in 2007-08. Few will be surprised by these figures. But we need to reflect on them and on their causes before attempting to theorize about analogs between the reputations (critical and popular) of artists and writers, even of so sublimely gifted (and painterly) a writer as Nabokov.

Katherine Reagan: Yes, it is true. Curators of literary exhibitions can seldom hope to draw the blockbuster crowds that art exhibitions routinely bring. Libraries that offer exhibitions of rare books and manuscripts frequently struggle to find enough visually appealing elements to punctuate what often otherwise "read" to the casual visitor as bland-looking cases filled with ink on buff-colored paper, accompanied by interpretive text printed on buff-colored paper. No doubt in the future, literary exhibitions will incorporate reconstructed personal computer work stations of a distant decade, instead of Dickens's pen, or E. B. White's typewriter. Like it or not, most exhibition viewers lack patience and seek visual stimulation. With Nabokov, we are fortunate. Exhibitions of his material are likely to incorporate colorful butterflies.

---

[5] The Guggenheim as a whole, during this three-month period, drew 418,559 visitors. I am indebted to my Guggenheim colleagues Maria Celli and Alexandra Munroe for these figures.

Tatiana Ponomareva: Certainly, a literary exhibition or museum can neither be presented nor viewed as an art one. Unlike an art museum, a literary display requires some prior reading or at least some general knowledge of literature. In Russia, literary museums have always been abundant but most of them tend to simply preserve or recreate the material surroundings of the writer's daily life—furniture, books, etc. In our case it is impossible to recreate the material wealth of the house (by the way, Nabokov was the only Russian classic whose family actually owned rather than rented a house in St. Petersburg); therefore we have always aimed at providing the wealth of information instead.

ACCESS AND USE

Yuri Leving: What is the condition of the materials pertaining to Nabokov in your archive?

Tatiana Ponomareva: The condition of most items held in the Nabokov Museum is quite good. Some of the original early twentieth century photographs need special conservation and restoration, which we are working on.

Alice Birney: The Library of Congress holdings are in excellent shape. The collection was arranged and described in 1969, reorganized in 2000 when additional material was integrated, with further processing and description completed in 2003, at which time all VN manuscript cards were placed in custom-made Mylar sleeves. During the reorganization, Don Johnson assisted by identifying some of the Russian correspondence. The collection was prepared for microfilming in 2007.

Isaac Gewirtz: About half of the papers at the NYPL are brittle or in near-brittle condition. The rest of them are generally in good or excellent condition, and the printed materials are almost all in very good to excellent condition. As is the case in my colleagues' institutions, our Nabokov papers have been placed in acid-free folders and boxes (index cards have been placed in Mylar sleeves), and both papers and books are housed in an environmentally controlled and secure space. Also, almost all of the papers have been microfilmed.

Katherine Reagan: The condition of Cornell's collection is generally very good. Books and manuscripts are stored under secure, archival conditions in a temperature and humidity controlled vault. Cornell Library also has a conservation lab to help re-house or repair items as needed.

FORUM

Yuri Leving: What are the general procedures for handling, conserving, installing and displaying materials related to Nabokov in your institution?

Alice Birney: Scholars request access through the Manuscript Division literary specialist who transmits the request to the estate representative; if limited access is granted, the scholar presents a letter acknowledging the same in room 101 of the Madison building and then abides by posted rules in a policed reading room.[6] The rules for handling are pretty straightforward: "The national manuscript collection may be consulted by any adult engaged in serious research who presents a valid Library of Congress issued reader card, completes the Manuscript Division's registration process, and agrees to adhere to the division's rules for the use of rare materials. Student access to collections is limited to those engaged in graduate study. Undergraduates with previous experience in using manuscripts who are working on a senior thesis, advanced seminar paper, or similar research project under the direction of a faculty member will be admitted upon an introduction in person or in writing by their advisers. Minors are not admitted to the Manuscript Reading Room."[7] I should stress that restrictions on the use of certain materials have been imposed by donors of the Nabokov collection. Prospective readers should also bear in mind the restrictions on photocopying and publication imposed by the Copyright Act of 1976. It is the responsibility of the prospective users or their publishers to determine the copyright status or obtain the required permissions before publication of manuscript material from the Library's collections.

Isaac Gewirtz: In the New York Public Library, conservation treatments are executed in our conservation lab by professional conservators following the standards set by the American Institute for Conservation (AIC). Any aspect of an exhibition that has an impact on the condition of the materials displayed, including but not limited to treatments, handling, and gallery specifications, also follow AIC standards. Regarding access, anyone who has a legitimate research need for the materials may study them (with the exception of the restricted material referred to earlier), though undergraduates must bring a letter from an instructor affirming the student's need (this is required for all NYPL Special Collections). All material housed in the Berg is used in the Berg reading room, under the supervision of a Berg librarian or by the curator.

Alice Birney: Conservation is largely done by professional archivists and conservators in accordance with accepted standards and Library of

[6] See www.loc.gov/rr/mss.
[7] http://www.loc.gov/rr/mss/mss-use.html#Reading.

Congress manual instructions. As for display, it requires six months advance notice, various approvals on each item, a venue assessment, and charges for insurance and transport. This is generally governed by rules obtained from the exhibits registrar in the Interpretive Programs Office.

Tatiana Ponomareva: Many of our items are on permanent display; some are shown at special exhibitions. As for our library, students and scholars are very welcome to work in the museum, even though we don't lend books.

Katherine Reagan: Cornell's Division of Rare and Manuscript Collections is open to the public. Anyone may request to see its Nabokov materials with the guidance of curatorial staff. Cornell will also lend materials for exhibition when requested by a reputable library or museum. Nabokov's books and manuscripts are frequently used under curatorial supervision in the Library, and in classroom instruction sessions for Cornell undergraduate and graduate students.

PUBLICATION OF ARCHIVAL MATERIALS

Yuri Leving: Do you expect that a publication of The Original of Laura will give an additional impulse toward future discoveries and publications related to Nabokov's archival materials?

Katherine Reagan: Due to Vladimir Nabokov's widely acknowledged stature as one of the twentieth century's greatest writers, the availability of a previously unpublished work is bound to generate curiosity and excitement. Nabokov scholars have long known about the unfinished *Laura* manuscript, and several scholars and potential buyers have seen it over time. I was glad when I learned that the Estate decided to make it accessible.

Tatiana Ponomareva: I very much hope so. As far as I know there are still quite a few unpublished pieces (apart from letters) that are of immense interest to Nabokov readers.

Isaac Gewirtz: I doubt if new Nabokovian scholars will be engendered by the book's publication. Those who become Nabokov scholars will do so probably because they have been transfixed by any of a half dozen great novels. Those who already are Nabokovians will of course be interested in *Laura*. I have found them to be a passionate, highly educated lot. But they do not need the publication of *Laura* to spur them to "future discoveries."

Alice Birney: The projected publication of the incomplete, uneven, and very fragmentary short manuscript of *The Original of Laura* will surely awaken interest in Nabokov scholarship, but it may compromise his reputation. The evident design of the manuscript is quite remarkable, even while the order of the fragments is in question. Clearly, Vladimir Nabokov had the novel all composed in his mind, though he wrote out relatively little of it. A few of the cards illustrate his typically brilliant writing. Regardless of editors' efforts, critics are notoriously unkind to those who violate authors' wishes to leave unfinished works unpublished. In the present cultural climate, the general public is unlikely to revise its collective memory of the author as a "naughty writer" after this publication. To provide scholars with primary materials for examination of the editing, the holograph cards should be preserved in either of the major Nabokov manuscript repositories.

CURRENT POPULARITY

Yuri Leving: *Can you assess the popularity of Nabokov among students and the current generation of young scholars?*

Tatiana Ponomareva: As a teacher at St. Petersburg State University, I know that Nabokov is widely read and widely studied in Russia. It isn't the addiction Russian readers experienced in the late 1980s, early 1990s when the Russian Nabokov was first published in Russia. The situation was unique then — a new, fully accomplished and fully original Russian classic was being discovered; as if manuscripts of legendary ancient books were unearthed during a new construction.

Now that Nabokov's place in the Russian literary pantheon is firmly established, his readership is quite stable, I think. The sheer number of Nabokov scholars in Russia is quite impressive, even though their access to Nabokov-related materials published worldwide is often limited because of the lack of funding. This year, as many as five of my students chose Nabokov as the topic of their theses.

Katherine Reagan: In my role as curator, I collaborate with faculty to connect materials in the Nabokov archive with the undergraduate curriculum and with graduate and faculty research. In my experience working on a university campus, Nabokov continues to attract a devoted following among young people. Cornell Professor Gavriel Shapiro offers a popular seminar in the Russian Department called "Reading Nabokov," and Nabokov is taught by faculty in the English and Comparative Literature departments as well. Some Cornell students develop a special relationship with him, due to his long affiliation with the University.

CENTER CIRCLE

Isaac Gewirtz: I can judge only by those who come to the Berg. Comparable numbers of graduate students as more mature scholars use our Nabokov holdings. Such examples as the index cards for *Ada*, and Nabokov's heavily annotated volumes from his working library (such as his copy of the A. L. Loyd 1946 English translation of Kafka's *Metamorphosis*, of which he retranslated major portions), unfailingly intrigue undergraduate and graduate English classes.

Alice Birney: Requests for access to the Library of Congress collection have been about equal from fledgling and mature Nabokovians, but access is subject to at times uneven decisions by varying estate representatives.

COMMEMORATION AND CANONICITY

Yuri Leving: *A public monument is to space what a public holiday is to time: marked and set apart for collective remembrance.[8] Holidays and monuments create what the contemporary French historian Pierre Nora calls les lieux de mémoire, "the places of memory." The Nabokov exhibitions as a trend started in the late 1990s, whether marking the writer's centennial or the anniversary publication dates of his English and Russian novels (Lolita, The Gift), culminating in the erection of a statue next to the Montreux Palace Hotel. How do Nabokov's memorabilia and actual manuscripts contribute to the creation of such charged points of reference, where multiple individual rememberings intersect to form a shared sense of authorial legacy and canonicity?*

Alice Birney: The Library of Congress, being essentially a library rather than a museum, has very limited facilities for artifacts, even if a donor were to offer a statue. Correspondence is the chief source for multiple tie-ins. Resulting biographies, such as Schiff's biography of Véra Nabokov, spread the interest from the author to his associates.

Tatiana Ponomareva: Last year, even before the museum became a part of St. Petersburg University, the first public monument to Nabokov in Russia (a bronze bas-relief) was unveiled in the university garden. This was a joint effort of the museum and the Philology Faculty of the University. I hope this is only the beginning and new points of reference will appear in this city.

---

[8] G. Taylor, *Cultural Selection: Why Some Achievements Survive The Test Of Time And Others Don't* (New York: Basic Books, 1996), 178.

As for many other St. Petersburg locations described by Nabokov in *Speak, Memory* and other works, they are all still there and are included in the tour that we offer to our visitors. Some points of reference even made an unusual way from text to reality. For instance, the green ceiling in one of the rooms of the mansion described in detail by Vladimir Nabokov was only uncovered during a partial restoration of the room ten years ago. Before that it only existed in the text.

Isaac Gewirtz: Are you asking if exhibitions help to establish the shape of Nabokov's legacy, as well as which of his works will be regarded as canonical in the context of his oeuvre? Or, are you asking if exhibitions will help to determine if he has transmitted a legacy at all, and if any of his works will be accepted as canonical in the larger context of world literature? In either case, the very nature of a literary exhibition (as I elucidated earlier) requires that the viewer invest a significant degree of attention into the "viewing" process. So, assuming that the exhibition as a whole attempts to investigate the significance of the writer's work; that it has the raw materials to support such an investigation; that the exhibition is well designed and the manuscripts and other materials are attractively displayed; and that the labels are written in an engaging manner, there is a good chance that the exhibition-goer's view of the writer (in this instance, Nabokov) will be affected by the experience. I think that this likely happened to most of the attendees of the 1999 NYPL Nabokov exhibition, curated with great sensitivity by my predecessor, Rodney Philips.

Katherine Reagan: The question of Nabokov's memorabilia and canonicity is an interesting one, especially in the context of the commemorative role often played by archives and museums, and the legacy and legitimacy bestowed by academic institutions. Cornell has participated in this type of commemoration. The Library has mounted at least three exhibitions on Nabokov since the 1950s, the most substantial associated with a centennial conference hosted at Cornell in 1998. During the 1998 conference, which perhaps some readers of this journal remember, a plaque was ceremonially installed outside Room 238, Goldwin Smith Hall, an office that Nabokov occupied.

Local enthusiasts and journalists have documented the ten professorial homes that the Nabokovs inhabited during their ten years in Ithaca, enabling a Nabokov "pilgrim trail" experience. Visiting artists and writers want to know where he sat in the Library, or which classrooms he might have taught in. In 2005, visiting photographer Tom Fecht took a photo to commemorate the Fiftieth anniversary of the publication of *Lolita*, posing some volunteer contemporary "Lolitas" in the campus library that Nabokov was known to frequent.⁹

In the classroom, teaching Nabokov through his own artifacts can be a poignant experience. Mindful of the thematic role of memory in Nabokov's creative imagination, we watch students experience a kind of imagined remembering of their own. Students enrolled in a Nabokov course today can pour over a three-ring leather Cornell binder, filled with careful, extensive notes written by a student sitting in Nabokov's 1955 European literature course in Goldwin Smith Hall. And Cornell owns a copy of *Conclusive Evidence*, for example, that has writing on the front endpaper, asking the borrower to return the book to "Valdimir Nabokov, Goldwin Smith Hall." Some students respond emotionally, as if their experience is connected to him through the artifacts and the campus he knew. As an educator, it's always interesting to walk the line between not discouraging this kind of reaction but, at the same time, prompting students to think beyond nostalgia into what the artifacts may actually reveal about Nabokov's ideas on literature and teaching.

Nabokov is a Cornell touchstone, embedded in campus lore. Emeritus faculty who knew him still tell stories about him. Exhibitions, artifacts, memorials and monuments serve to reinforce not only Nabokov's own reputation as an important writer, but also institutional mythologies specific to colleges and universities — the tales, characters, songs, slang, and landmarks that bind a group of people together in a shared experience.

ONGOING ACQUISITIONS

Yuri Leving: Could you please touch upon the selection criteria and issues of ongoing acquisitions?

Alice Birney: Money.

Isaac Gewirtz: For both papers and printed materials, the chief criterion in my decisions to try to acquire material is research value, as opposed to merely artifactual allure. The chief issue in the purchase of any Nabokov papers which, for the most part, now means correspondence and drawings, is price. I cannot afford them — at least if I want to purchase material by other authors heavily represented in the Berg.

Katherine Reagan: Yes, like Alice and Isaac, affordability is the key issue. Cornell relies on gifts to build its Nabokov collections, and buys only

---

⁹ http://rmc.library.cornell.edu/lolita/

selectively, placing greatest emphasis on items that either position Nabokov in institutional context, or that document his continuing influence on contemporary culture. This strategy recognizes that more comprehensive Nabokov collections are held by other institutions (NYPL and the Library of Congress), and reflects a value-oriented approach to spending acquisition funds. Twentieth century literary materials remain the most expensive sector of the antiquarian market place.

Tatiana Ponomareva: As a growing museum we do not really have many selection criteria—we acquire everything related to Vladimir Nabokov, his family, his literary environment, etc. This year we received a few Nabokov household items donated by Lydia Matskevich, and acquired a large number of books—Nabokov editions in various languages and Nabokov criticism.

Yuri Leving: *Could you address the* market vs. institutional value *of the Nabokoviana?*

Isaac Gewirtz: The chief interest for a curator should be research value, whereas the vast majority of collectors, though certainly not insensitive to such attractions, are also seduced by artifactual features and are willing to pay a very high premium for them. For instance, a copy of a first edition *Lolita* signed by Nabokov (a very rare item indeed) will sell for several times the amount of an unsigned copy, even if the latter is in much better condition. Now, it is true that dated signatures and certainly inscriptions may have research value. They can sometimes tell you when a relationship or a trip began or ended, or prove the existence of a rapprochement between the author and a former friend, maybe turned enemy.

But the enormous price one must pay for them should give pause to any curator. Is what we learn from the inscription new? If not, I would say pass, unless the price is nominal. This is not to say that some institutions might not choose, with good reason, to buy a particular item for artifactual reasons alone. If your institution has a sizable printed Nabokov collection and you want to increase interest in it among students and faculty, and if a donor is willing to spend $9,000 for a first edition of *Conclusive Evidence* signed by Nabokov, I suppose a case could be made for the purchase in this exceptional instance. Otherwise, I'd ask the donor if the $9,000 can be spent on something else.

Tatiana Ponomareva: In the museum, we had no firsthand experience of Nabokov-related market issues. We rarely bought anything and never sold a thing.

Alice Birney: In good economic times, it is easy for agents to whip up a bidding frenzy on the sale of a literary manuscript. Unfortunately for scholars, such sales often result in the further fragmentation of an author's primary works, as in the past massive sale of the second part of the collection to the Berg. The future sale/donation of the posthumous novel manuscript should be separated from its publication, for which complex issues are at play. Primary materials should be collected, rather than scattered, in order to enhance their institutional and research value.

Katherine Reagan: Because Nabokov made Cornell his home for so many years, Cornell Library locates institutional value in collecting items that connect or document Nabokov as a member of the Cornell community. The specified interests of alumni donors, many of whom remember the author from their student days in the 1950s, have funded the majority of these types of acquisitions. Otherwise, when it comes to spending Cornell's acquisition funds, we focus on purchasing only those materials that advance the ability of scholars to answer research questions and that represent a reasonable cost for that research value.

CHALLENGING FORMATS

Yuri Leving: *What are the major challenges in the curatorship of Nabokov collections vis-à-vis the changing nature of archives (digitization for safe and compact storage, reproduction, audio / video recordings, limited dissemination of sample information through the Internet)?*

Isaac Gewirtz: Providing accurate online descriptions of the holdings.

Katherine Reagan: As a curator interested in making writers archives accessible, I am grateful that Nabokov was born with the archival instinct. He saved an enormous amount of material. Not all writers are so careful, especially those who moved around as frequently as the Nabokovs did. I am also grateful that his writing life was lived before the era of the personal computer, which means that his papers survive largely in physical, rather than electronic form. Since Cornell's Nabokov collections are largely limited to works on paper, they do not pose the greater preservation and access challenges inherent in other media formats such as video, audio, or digital files, which we will encounter in preserving the archives of more recent authors.

Alice Birney: (1) The danger of copyright infringement, especially on third person writings; (2) Misunderstanding of the means, difficulty, and proper use of digitized manuscripts; (3) Budgetary constraints.

Tatiana Ponomareva: The major positive challenge is making our collection available in digital form. This project is now being developed.

FORUM

Yuri Leving: *Like any writer's archive, Nabokov's collection includes sensitive personal documents. How, in your opinion, should the private and public spheres in Nabokov's collection be distinguished and protected, if necessary?*

Katherine Reagan: Cornell's Nabokov collection does not hold extremely personal letters or anything likely to cause embarrassment. In general, unless materials contain very sensitive or inflammatory information about living persons, we don't make distinctions between private and professional documentation in our literary collections. For example, Cornell's archives hold affectionate and personal letters between Véra and Vladimir Nabokov and Morris Bishop, a member of Cornell's faculty with whom the Nabokovs became close. Nabokov's letters to the Bishops contain matters of personal health, holiday plans, travels, and other family matters. But they also offer Nabokov's observations about writing, and sharp opinions on what he was reading and publishing. It can be difficult to separate the private and public spheres in an author's collection. Because there are no donor imposed restrictions on Cornell's Nabokov materials, we can make them freely available for research in our reading room.

Tatiana Ponomareva: In the Vladimir Nabokov case, I think, this issue is much less sensitive than with most artists. I don't think we should expect any sensational "X-files." No drinking bouts, no bigamy, no obscure dealings with those in power — Vladimir Nabokov lived a scientist's, not a bohemian's life. Unless, of course, the legend once popular among Russian underground Nabokov readers — of Nabokov's visit to Leningrad in disguise — turns out to be true...

Alice Birney: The Library of Congress imposes no "protections" (limitations on access) not already in place via the instrument of gift. If there are preservation issues, a collection is microfilmed and the originals are withdrawn from general use. The Nabokov Papers were recently microfilmed. For certain collections, there are occasional exceptions which require classified documents or private legal and medical reports to remain protected. Other matters merely judged sensitive by some, become desensitized with time.

Isaac Gewirtz: Unpublished Russian-language Nabokov papers in the Berg, as well as a small group of other materials, may not be seen by researchers without the permission of the estate. This was a condition of our purchase of his papers. My opinion is that the conditions expressed in legally executed documents should be obeyed, for both legal and ethical/moral reasons. In any case, copyright law dictates that for the next couple of decades anyway, intimate correspondence (or any other correspondence or writings by Nabokov that do not fall within the "fair use" category, for that matter) from Nabokov to others may not be quoted without the estate's permission. Whether or not access should be provided in cases in which access restrictions have not been legally agreed to is another question. I am not sure that public and private are the best words for distinguishing between...well, between what and what? I assume that the questioner feels that "private" is what happened privately between Nabokov and someone else. But there is good reason to believe that Nabokov felt that rough drafts of his work were equally intimate and deserving of being shielded from public eyes, and yet, I am delighted to say, they were included as part of the papers offered to the Library, and we delight in their use by researchers and in showing them to visiting groups whenever we can.

FUTURE DIRECTIONS

Yuri Leving: *What is your prognosis regarding the future of the study of the material culture surrounding Nabokov and his archival legacy? Could you delineate some strategic areas of public and scholarly interest? Which directions would you identify as potentially most stimulating?*

Tatiana Ponomareva: For obvious reasons, Vladimir Nabokov's early years in Russia and his European émigré years are much less researched than his American and Swiss years. I hope there will be many new finds here. I also hope that new studies of Nabokov as a unique cross-cultural literary phenomenon will appear.

Isaac Gewirtz: Literary textual studies will probably soon (I hope!) see a resurgence in popularity. When this happens, textual media (manuscripts, typescripts, journals, diaries, correspondence, and now e-mails and digitally-born media) will regain their fascination for academic elites, so that even theorists will see the value in tracing the evolution of an author's text. One researcher in the Berg was working on a comparison of Nabokov's scientific and literary work, beyond the mere elegiac effusions that are commonly found in literary criticism about Vladimir Nabokov. A detailed comparison of techniques and Vladimir Nabokov's writings about each will bear rich fruit.

Katherine Reagan: I hope that one day our institutions may join forces and make our collections collaboratively more accessible to global audiences through digital technology. But even if we're able to someday leap the legal and market hurdles to achieve this goal, the artifacts themselves will remain important. Scholars and students will continue to respond to and benefit from the study of physical artifacts. The digital information landscape will encourage, rather than obscure interest in material culture.

Alice Birney: I expect requests for digitization after 23 June, 2009, at which time both access restrictions and the copyrights on our Nabokov manuscript versions will have expired; however, other parts of the collection, such as incoming correspondence, will remain largely protected. Because we regard microfilm as the preferred preservation format, any digitization of selected items would have to be privately financed. There is current interest in intertextual, international, and cross-cultural studies relating to Nabokov. Digitization might facilitate more textual studies comparing manuscript drafts with published versions.

NARROWING THE ANGLE

MEMOIR

Irwin Weil

A NEOPHYTE'S COLLISION WITH VLADIMIR VLADIMIROVICH

Back in 1948, I was a student at the University of Chicago, an institution which was out to reshape American education in the image of Robert M. Hutchins. While approaching the study of Russian language and its magnificent literature, we innocent youngsters received instructions to read a book by a writer and critic whose work we had never read before. His name was Vladimir Vladimirovich Nabokov, and the daring publisher who called his firm "New Directions" had the temerity to publish an entirely new approach to the study of Gogol'. Nabokov's intent to startle, and perhaps irritate, the conventional world of literary criticism was clearly indicated by his early statement that he wanted the book accompanied not by a portrait of Gogol' but rather a picture of the Writer's nose!

We then made our way through Nabokov's clearly original and completely personal rendition of what he considered the only possible true approach to literature. This involved the carefully choreographed description of the nature of *poshlost'*—a German lover tenderly caressing the bottoms of two swans, while swimming in front of his beloved Gretchen. It also involved completely demolishing any notion which offered a sociological explication of Gogol's text, or—for that matter—of the text by any other writer. In Nabokov's universe, the human imagination was to reign supreme. And that imagination was, it must be clearly and finally understood, mapped out and circumscribed by the master himself.

The experience of reading him for the first time can only be described as heady. Never, in all of our young (and admittedly limited) experience, had we ever encountered such a self-centered, imaginative, and eloquent tribune of the literary imagination. Vladimir Vladimirovich's seemingly unlimited self-confidence could be off-putting, even at times irritating. But his fervour and fearless independence could not fail to make a lasting impression. At that time, little did I know that I would have some personal brushes with the master.

About five years later I worked on a research project at the Library of Congress which involved a close reading of many sources concerning Russian and Soviet culture and history. I was fortunate enough to meet and work under a remarkable former St. Petersburg lawyer and demographer, Evgenii Mikhailovich Kulischer (1881-1956?). He had been a protégé of the famous Karabchevsky,[1] and he illegally departed across the borders of the young revolutionary state in 1920. Subsequently, he taught in pre-Nazi Germany, then in France, ending that sojourn by a fortunate escape from Nazi Occupation through Spain and then to the USA.

I learned an enormous amount in the course of our mutual work, not only about the facts of Russian and Soviet history, but also about the nature of solid and helpful historical research. Among these topics, Evgenii Mikhailovich described direct connections with the Nabokov family in pre-revolutionary St. Petersburg. It turned out that for many years he sat at the evening table of V. D. Nabokov (the writer's father, a well known Russian liberal) every Friday night. Of course, this involved the politics of those who hoped to bring about a Russian republican government which could parallel that of England, France, or the USA.

When their hopes were frustrated by the Revolution of October/November 1917, Evgenii Mikhailovich succeeded in escaping across the border

---

[1] Nikolai Karabchevsky (1851-1925), a Russian lawyer who made his name in a number of highly publicized criminal cases in the late nineteenth and early twentieth centuries.

to Romania. He was intercepted by the Romanian border guards, whose initial intent was to force him back to Russia. He managed to save himself by telling them that he knew V. D. Nabokov's relative (I think a sister, but my memory is not firm here), who was married to a Romanian nobleman. The guards contacted her, and she vouched for Evgenii Mikhailovich's identity. This enabled him to avoid deportation, and he eventually made his way to a position as a docent at the University of Berlin.

It was my luck as a newly minted graduate of the University of Chicago to encounter and work closely with a man who breathed the liberal part of early twentieth century St. Petersburg's atmosphere, and then experienced the disruption of WWI and revolutionary Petrograd. Of course, this gave me a very different picture of the context presented in the Nabokovs' writing. V. D. Nabokov wrote about the valiant attempts to set up a truly parliamentary Russian government and, his son, V. V. Nabokov created some of the most interesting literature and criticism of the twentieth century. I also learned, of course, about the father's tragic demise, from a bullet fired by a Russian right wing extremist in Germany, while he was standing in front of Pavel Miliukov with the intention of protecting him.

In 1954, I left the Library of Congress to work toward a Harvard doctorate in Slavic languages and literatures. I had the privilege of collaborating with, among others, M. M. Karpovich, who had once served in Kerensky's Embassy in Washington, as well as with R. O. Jakobson, perhaps the most famous Slavist of the twentieth century. Both men had connections with Nabokov, not all entirely admirable. Karpovich had established a farm in New England, where émigré scholars could reside in the summer and relax in the countryside, while carrying on their discussions of everything Russian under the sun. Nabokov describes this delightfully in *Pnin*. Mikhail Mikhailovich invited the Wellesley ensconced Nabokov to lecture at Harvard in the Karpovich course on Tolstoy. With some rue, Mikhail Mikhailovich described to me the sad fact that Nabokov immediately threw out *War and Peace* and substituted *Anna Karenina*.

Later on, Karpovich recommended Nabokov for a permanent post in the Harvard Slavic department, which concerned itself with Russian literature. When Jakobson objected to the proposed appointment, Mikhail Mikhailovich offered the rejoinder that the candidate was, after all, a prominent Russian writer and novelist. Roman Osipovich replied with a Jakobsonism that has lived down through the ages with generations of Harvardniki: "If this were a Department of Zoology, would you then hire an elephant?" Evidently, for Roman Osipovich an elephant to the Zoology Department was as a famous writer to the Department of Russian Literature! Thus do we all become pachyderms of the literary trade!!

Quite a few years later, I sailed out upon the sea of Slavic pedagoguery and literary pronunciamenti. Among other epistolary sallies, I made the statement in a review of one of Nabokov's books that we indeed owe a considerable debt of gratitude to Nabokov for his exemplary service to the cause of Russian literature — if only he could control that terrible Nabokovian temper! As you might imagine, the riposte was not long in coming. The master exclaimed, "Well, for those — like Mr. Weil — who consider good manners a fine thing in a literary critic... so much for Mr. Weil!"

In 1966, when my book on Gorky came out under Random House,[2] I sent a copy to the esteemed Mr. Nabokov, together with a letter. I tried to explain to him that I well understood that he might not care for Gorky as a writer, but I would be grateful for his opinion of my book. Furthermore, I described my earlier relationship with E. M. Kulischer, at the Library of Congress, and I wondered if Nabokov remembered the connection with his Father. In his reply, Nabokov, perhaps remembering my statement about his temper, wrote, "Thank you very much for your courtesy in sending me your book with which I totally disagree." He then went on to say that he did remember Kulischer's presence at his father's table and he also remembered that his father once said, "If Kulischer says it, it's true." But he indicated that was all he remembered — it was such a long time earlier.[3]

Quite a few years later, in the late 1970s, my friends and colleagues at Moscow State University, located on what were then called Lenin Hills, gave me the privilege of presenting a two-hour lecture before an assemblage of several hundred Soviet undergraduate students. I was naturally quite excited, and I decided to talk about Pushkin in the USA. Before the lecture, I asked my Soviet colleagues if I could talk about Nabokov's translation and commentary on *Evgenii Onegin*. I didn't want to get them in trouble with Soviet authorities, but I indicated that the work and the ensuing polemics with Edmund Wilson were very important for understanding the place of

---

[2] Irwin Weil, *Gorky: His Literary Development and Influence on Soviet Intellectual Life* (New York: Random House, 1966).

[3] *Ed. note:* Nabokov commented in *Strong Opinions*: "I must... question an incomprehensible statement in Mr. Weil's article 'Odyssey of a Translator.' The Russian lawyer E. M. Kulisher may well have been 'an old acquaintance' of my father's, but he was not 'close to the Nabokov family' (I do not remember him as a person) and I have never said anywhere what Mr. Weil has me indicate in the opening paragraph of his article" (293).

NARROWING THE ANGLE

Pushkin in an American context. My friends told me to go ahead; there would be no trouble for them.

I then proceeded, in the course of a forty-five minute lecture which covered many topics, to include some remarks about Nabokov's translation and Wilson's rejoinders. When I first read, in *Partisan Review*, Nabokov's plans about translating *Evgenii Onegin* into English, I was quite excited. His hints about "S liubov'iu lech' k ee nogam" ("to lie down at her feet with love") seemed to promise a magnificent English text. While waiting several years, I kept repeating Nabokov's adaptation of Pushkin's "Devy...gde vy" ("Maidens...where are you"—Nabokov cleverly renders Byron's "Maidens— gay dens"); exactly my question about his translation. When it finally appeared, I had two separate reactions.

For those, like myself, who knew Russian well, it was extremely handy to have access to Nabokov when we ran across outdated or very special words, because we could trust him for the meaning. And his commentary was always useful and engaging, although sometimes absurdly drawn out; and his often nasty denigration of everyone else got quite tiresome. But for someone who doesn't know Russian, the text seems to reduce Pushkin terribly—all the music is gone! The literal English (or French derived, words, about which Nabokov is so insistent), simply loses Pushkin's extraordinary sense of rhythm and incredible lightness of movement. For the exclusively English speaker, Nabokov's Pushkin seems a strangely overly praised relic of some quaint early nineteenth century dictionary, with a little old French thrown in.

Nabokov stated that he firmly intended to create a pony, upon which the diligent student could ride, and I suppose I should have no quarrel with that. Bryan Boyd, in his brilliant biography of the man, makes a very strong and intelligent case for the translation. I deeply admire his insight, his sensitivity, and his knowledge. But I don't think he saves the translation. "All the King's horses and all the King's men / Couldn't put Humpty together again" [Vsia korolevskaia konnitsa, vsia korolevskaia rat' / Ne mozhet Shaltaia, ne mozhet Boltaia, ne mozhet Shaltaia sobrat'"]. Samuil Marshak could perhaps give us both a lesson here.

At the end of my lecture at Moscow State University, for which I deliberately left over an hour for questions, the Soviet students directed at me four questions obviously based on an extensive reading and knowledge of Nabokov's work. It is important to remember here that Nabokov was specifically and sternly proscribed by the Soviet regime; it was totally illegal for a Soviet citizen to possess, much less read, any of his works. I was of course deeply impressed by the knowledge and understanding displayed by those students.

When I returned home to the USA, I wrote to Nabokov's widow, and in my letter I described what had happened in Moscow. To my surprise, she replied that my epistle was the fourth such description she had received. Clearly, many different people in the USSR had read the forbidden work of the twentieth century master writer and critic. Nabokov's work represented a force which was more powerful than a regime superbly armed with tanks and guns and a widespread literary police force.

Since I have worked at Northwestern University for close to five decades, I have had the privilege of working with many fine and productive colleagues. Among them was the late Professor Alfred Appel, Jr. (1934-2009), a former student of Professor Nabokov at Cornell University, and a subsequent eminent critic and admirer of the master's writing. My colleague also had a close and friendly personal association with the writer. Alfred had a sharp and wonderful sense of humour, which he often used on your obedient servant, as well as upon many people around him in the academic world. He was also a wide ranging and perceptive literary scholar, whose explications of *Lolita* won him international fame. To listen to him talk, with his wonderful rendition and interpretation of many American dialects, was to take a delightful trip through the most colorful regions of American speech, both academic and popular. So, with the help of my colleague, and based on my own memories of more than six decades of academic work, I have some fascinating, and reasonably complex, memories of Vladimir Vladimirovich Nabokov and his world of literature and Russian and American history.

CORNER ARC

ENGLISH NABOKOV

Gerard de Vries

NABOKOV'S *PALE FIRE* AND ALEXANDER POPE[1]

SHADE'S "PALE FIRE" AND POPE'S POETRY

Although *Pale Fire* has been described as "a book saturated with Pope," Alexander Pope's poetry has received little attention among the readers and critics of one of Vladimir Nabokov's most intriguing and most discussed novels.[2] While there are clear references to Pope's *Essay on Criticism*, *Essay on Man*, *Temple of Fame*, and *Dunciad*,[3] the widely admired *Rape of the Lock*

---

[1] I would like to thank Brian Boyd and an anonymous reader for their most helpful comments on earlier versions of this paper.

[2] Brian Boyd, Posting to NABOKV-L, December 14, 2000. Lisa Zunshine refers to "a lacunae in contemporary Nabokov criticism" in "Alexander Pope's *The Rape of the Lock* and Vladimir Nabokov's *Pale Fire*," *Nabokov at the Limits,* ed. Lisa Zunshine (New York: Garland Publishing, 1999), 179.

[3] Gerard de Vries, "'Fanning the Poet's Fire,' Some Remarks on Nabokov's *Pale Fire*," *Russian Literature Triquarterly* 24 (1991): 255-6.

has drawn the most attention, no doubt because Belinda, its heroine, stands out in female beauty; the very quality that Hazel Shade fatally lacks. In this paper, I will attempt to demonstrate that Hazel's disposition and the social guidance she receives explain her and Belinda's different reactions to the afflictions caused by male acquaintances who were supposed to brighten their lives. I will then show that the ideas that fostered Shade's spirited breakthrough during his musings on the mountain-fountain misprint have many parallels with those expressed in Pope's *Essay on Man*. First, the affinities between Shade's poem and the poetics of Pope's verses will be discussed.

While Shade published a book on Pope and appears to talk about Pope with a frequency that makes Kinbote decide that the Augustan poet is Shade's favorite topic of discussion,[4] Pope has left only a few explicit traces in Shade's poem. There is an obvious allusion to *The Rape of the Lock* in lines 413-16, insofar as the description of Belinda's cosmetic sanctum is the most quoted and anthologized passage from Pope's oeuvre, as well as a quotation from the *Essay on Man* in line 419. One might also conclude that the mention of "Zembla" in line 937 is suggested by Pope's writings, given the marginal note that Shade added to the manuscript of this passage. Considering the fact that Shade, as a scholar, is immersed in Pope and likes to talk about his favorite poet for entertainment, the number of references to Pope in the poem seems so scanty that one is inclined to suspect that there are less overt allusions in the text that may have been missed upon first glance.

Prima facie, it is Kinbote rather than Shade who seems to be well-versed in Pope. He easily recognizes the title of Shade's book on Pope, *Supremely Blest*, as a Popean phrase, and unfailingly identifies two borrowings from the *Essay on Man*.[5] Even more surprising is the introduction of Paul Hentzner with a quotation from Pope's "Phryne," as if he belonged to that poem's "curious Germans"; the subtle allusions to *The Rape of the Lock*, such as the phrase "star ghost"; and in the final line of the novel, the longingly "distant northern land."[6] There are, however, some statements made by Kinbote that are rather puzzling: he calls Shade's poem a "narrative in the neo-Popian prosodic style" and, in the beginning of his work, he declares that *Pale Fire* is "a poem in heroic couplets."[7] The heroic couplet, popularized by Dryden and perfected by

---

[4] Vladimir Nabokov, *Pale Fire* (New York: Vintage International, 1989), 250.

[5] Ibid., 195; 203; 272.

[6] Ibid., 185; 82; 315. The allusions concern canto IV, line 154 and the final line of Pope's *The Rape of the Lock*, *The Poems of Alexander Pope*, ed. John Butt (New Haven: Yale University Press, 1963).

[7] Nabokov, *Pale Fire*, 296; 13.

Pope, consists of a pair of rhymed lines in iambic pentameter. Pope's couplets are mainly "closed"; which means that two lines in Pope, paired by rhyme, have a meaning or a felicity even when one disregards the lines that precede or follow them. For example, the lines "True Ease in Writing comes from Art, not Chance, / As those move easiest who have learn'd to dance,"[8] from Pope's *Essay on Criticism*, not only jocularly illustrate the poet's argument, but can also be enjoyed separately from the rest of the poem for their epigrammatic content. By contrast, most of the rhymed pairs of the lines of *Pale Fire* are "open" and can only be savored in connection with the lines that precede or follow them. The self-sufficiency of closed couplets might detract the reader's attention from the entirety of the composition, but this seems unlikely. A beautiful building does not suffer from being made of perfectly fabricated bricks. In Dryden and Pope, the use of closed couplets means order, not confinement. Pope formulated many rules to reach the degree of perfection to which he aspired[9] as, for example, the consideration he gives in the *Essay on Criticism*: "For *Wit* and *Judgment* often are at strife, / Tho' meant each other's Aid, like *Man* and *Wife*."[10]

Within its bounds, the heroic couplet gives room for endless modulations like antithesis, chiasmus and inversion, as well as the use of the caesura and hiatus, verse techniques intensively employed by Pope. M. H. Abrams, Nabokov's colleague and friend at Cornell, writes

> [Pope's] frequent use of a strong medial cesura, or pause, was a way of breaking the lines into smaller units in order to maximize the internal relations among the rhetorical and sonantal parts — relations of parallelism, repetition with variation, contrast, or antithesis, and between couplet and couplet, line and line, half line and half line.[11]

Two lines from *The Dunciad* may serve as an illustration: "We ply the Memory, we load the brain, / Bind rebel Wit, and double chain on chain..." With these

---

[8] Alexander Pope, *Essay on Criticism*, *The Poems of Alexander Pope*, ed. John Butt (New Haven: Yale University Press, 1963), lines 362-3.

[9] See, for example, the letters from Pope reprinted in *Alexander Pope. A Critical Anthology*, ed. F. W. Bateson and N. A. Joukovsky (Harmondsworth: Penguin Books, 1971), 39-42, and Pope, *Essay on Criticism*, lines 70-99.

[10] Pope, *Essay on Criticism*, lines 82-3.

[11] M. H. Abrams, ed., "Introduction," Alexander Pope, *The Poetry of Pope. A Selection* (New York: Appleton-Century, 1954). A. D. Nuttall (*Pope's "Essay on Man"* [London: Allen and Unwin, 1984], 27-28) shows how Pope creates no less than seven opportunities for antithesis within two lines (of ten syllables each).

lines Pope satirizes the dunces, the less gifted poets who earned a living by writing doggerels, especially those congregated on Grub Street.[12] He presents four actions which he connects with three intellectual faculties. A clear difference is made between the capacity of all individuals to use their memory and their brain, on the one hand, and the rare quality of wit or originality on the other. In the dunces' eyes, wit threatens the dullness that secures their lives, and therefore should be doubly bound.

If we compare Pope's lines with lines 159-160 of "Pale Fire," an identical subdivision into four half lines can be observed: "And then it ceased. Its memory grew dim. / My health improved. I even learned to swim." But Shade's lines cannot be fully understood without knowing what "it" represents in line 159. And only after realizing that "it" refers to "fits," one notices that the second half of line 160 is not a specified reiteration of the first half, as swimming is notably dangerous for someone liable to fainting. Pope's lines strike the reader with vigorous verbs suggesting manual labor but applied to functions of the mind, through their staccato-like pertinence. However, phrases like "whipped by the bough, / Tripped by the stump" may remind the reader of the compact style of Pope, who scarcely explicates the subjects of his sentences.[13] However, "Pale Fire" is, apart from its meter, not at all reminiscent of Pope's compressed closed couplets.[14] Clearly, the main merit of "Pale Fire" is not its allegedly neo-Popean style, as it has an inner coherence of such intricacy that depths not equaled in Pope's argumentative poems resonate within it.

Despite Pope's great concern for the correctness of his verses, his poetry has been accused of having some serious flaws.[15] George Saintsbury

---

[12] Alexander Pope, *The Dunciad*, *The Poems of Alexander Pope*, ed. John Butt (New Haven: Yale University Press, 1963), IV 157-8. Writing chiefly to earn money as the dunces did may not look very blameworthy, but in Pope's circle it was regarded as symptomatic of a greater ill, the degeneration and corruption of the cultural and political climate.

[13] Nabokov, "Pale Fire," lines 128-9. The same is true of the catalogue in lines 924-30. For a discussion of catalogues in Pope see Dennis Davidson, *Dryden* (London: Evans Brothers, 1968), esp. Chapter 4: "Verse Technique: the Heroic Couplet."

[14] Cf. Jonathan Swift, "Verses on the Death of Dr. Swift," *Selected Poems of Jonathan Swift*, ed. James Reeves (London: Heinemann, 1967), 87 who commented that Pope "can in one Couplet fix / More Sense than I can do in Six." See also Michael Wood, *The Magician's Doubts: Nabokov and the Risks of Fiction* (London: Chatto & Windus, 1994), 187, who, quoting the *Essay on Man* (II 222-226), favorably compares Pope with Nabokov: "[t]he brilliant, multiplying jokes take the breath away; even Nabokov looks a very modest magician alongside this performance."

[15] The correctness certainly does not apply to syntactical details. "I could never get the blockhead to study his grammar," said Swift, quoted in A. R. Weekes, ed., *Johnson: Life of Pope* (London: W.B. Clive, 1917), 151.

is a particularly severe critic who, although he admires Pope's versification, denies him any originality, and complains about Pope's ample use of the gradus-epithet (adjectives that qualify in non-essential ways).[16] Pope also suffered heavy contempt from the Romantics (with the exception of Byron, his staunchest supporter), who especially despised the mechanical monotony they heard in his meter. When Nabokov wrote *Pale Fire*, the revival of Pope which started in the second quarter of the previous century was still gaining momentum. Though Nabokov's novels abound in references and allusions to English poetry, Pope was hardly ever among the poets referred to therein. In *Pnin*, Nabokov calls the poetry of the eighteenth century (as a field of literary interest) "an overgrazed pasture, with a trickle of a brook and a clump of initialed trees."[17] In his Commentary to Pushkin's *Eugene Onegin*, Nabokov mentions Pope more than twenty times, which strikes the reader as more than necessary to discuss the English influences (filtered through French translations, as was Nabokov's conviction) on Pushkin. He praises Pope's description of Belinda's boudoir in *The Rape of the Lock*, which follows but transcends French models "thanks to English richness of imagery and originality of diction," as well as Pope's "charming eclogue *The Basset-table*."[18] The number of entries for Pope in the index of Nabokov's edition of *Eugene Onegin* exceeds those for all other English poets, including Browning, Marvell and Milton, with the exception of Byron and Shakespeare.

The process of sorting out Nabokov's appreciation for Pope is not greatly helped by Nabokov's hostility towards the Age of Reason, as Pope was the foremost English poet of this age. Among the "insipid products" this age produced, according to Nabokov, were "flat classical backdrop colonnades" and "flat mythological scenes with a pseudo classical slant." In addition, this age had a "pathological dislike...for the specific 'unpoetical detail' and [a] passion for the generic term." The inartistic and antipoetic verse composed by English poets in the wake of Butler's *Hudibras* could be savored only because "its enjoyment presupposes that Reason is somehow, in the long run, superior to Imagination, and that both are less important than a man's religious or political beliefs."[19]

---

[16] George Saintsbury, "Pope and the Later Couplet," 1908. Rpt. Bateson and Joukovsky, *A Short History of English Literature* (London: MacMillan and Co., 1908); *The Peace of the Augustans* (Oxford: Oxford University Press, 1951).

[17] Nabokov, *Pnin* (New York: Vintage International, 1989), 156.

[18] Vladimir Nabokov, "Commentary," Alexandr Pushkin, *Eugene Onegin. A Novel in Verse*, 4 vols., trans. Vladimir Nabokov (Princeton: Princeton University Press, 1975), II 101, 260.

[19] Ibid., II 393, 255, 541; III 290, 498.

The poetry thus lamented is in tetrameters while all of Pope's significant poetry is written in iambic pentameters. But, as *The Dunciad* so obviously shows, it cannot be denied that Pope's main concerns were strongly connected with his awareness of the cultural and moral decay and the corruption that pervaded the politics of his day. Although he was preoccupied to some degree with the Whig government, Pope composed works which are primarily the product of his imagination and poetic proficiency, especially during the first half of his career. *The Pastorals, Windsor-Forest, Essay on Criticism, The Rape of the Lock, Eloisa to Abelard,* and many of his shorter poems, are not written primarily to air or to aid any philosophical, moral or political idea.

It seems that one should be careful not to too hastily transfer to Pope the objections Nabokov raised to the Age of Reason, especially as both authors shared some literary ambitions. In his answer to the question of what literary virtues he sought to attain and how, Nabokov said: "[m]ustering the best words, with every available lexical, associative, and rhythmic assistance, to express as closely as possible what one wants to express."[20] This can be compared to Pope's objective to pursue an utter correctness in the selection of words, in terms of sound and thought, and to this end "weigh[ing] every letter of his verse."[21] Coleridge, like his fellow Romantics, is highly censorious of Pope's poetry, but nonetheless praises his "almost faultless position and choice of words."[22]

Another interest Nabokov and Pope shared is the assimilation of felicitous phrases, images or themes from other writers. Nabokov's unique allusiveness is well known. About Pope, Dr. Johnson said that "there is scarcely a happy combination of words, or a phrase poetically elegant in the English language, which Pope has not inserted..."[23] There is, however, a striking difference in the way such borrowings were employed. Pope appropriated phrases and ideas when they fit his verses and, for this reason, selected only those which he fully approved.[24] Nabokov, on the other hand, at times rephrased his borrowings or gave them an entirely new setting (which makes them so difficult to recognize). This enabled him to make his selections not only from first-rate authors, but also from second-rate and even trivial ones.

[20] Nabokov, *Strong Opinions* (New York: Vintage International, 1990), 181.
[21] Geoffrey Tillotson, *On the Poetry of Pope* (Oxford: Clarendon Press, 1950), 130.
[22] S. T. Coleridge, *Biographia Literaria* (London: J. M. Dent & Sons, 1962), 22.
[23] Samuel Johnson, *Lives of the English Poets*, vol. 2 (London: J. M. Dent & Sons, 1954), 230.
[24] Cf. Reuben A. Brower, *Alexander Pope. The Poetry of Allusion* (Oxford: Oxford University Press, 1986), 1.

Pope and Nabokov also shared a partiality for details. Hazlitt said that reading Pope's poetry "is like looking at the world through a microscope."[25] This can be read within the context of Pope's observation of insects.[26] In *Pale Fire*, we watch Nabokov magnifying small things into grand and even grotesque ones.[27]

PALE FIRE AND THE RAPE OF THE LOCK

The Rape of the Lock is probably Pope's most admired poem; its popularity has not diminished since its final form was published in 1714. It is a mock heroic poem that treats a slight offence, the clipping of some curls from a girl's head, as an epic conflict which stirs not only mortal beings but heavenly creatures as well. Pope took the notion of snipping the tress from a real-life incident that befell a certain Miss Fermor—"Belinda" in the poem. Miss Fermor was so handsome that she was celebrated as a fashionable beauty, a circumstance which probably added greatly to the attraction of the stolen lock.[28] Pope's famous poem on beauty is thus mirrored in John Shade's "favorite" canto II, about the fatal impact of a girl's unattractiveness. It seems not at all an easy task to reflect the heartrending story of Hazel's short life in the frivolity of *The Rape of the Lock*. Johnson called Pope's poem "the most exquisite example of ludicrous poetry," and Hazlitt said that "it is made of nothing." But Hazlitt also wrote that "[y]ou hardly know whether to laugh or weep."[29] The actual incident that inspired the poem was of enough brutishness to embitter the victim and her family for a long time. Miss Fermor was exceedingly angry and her family felt severely offended.[30] In the poem,

---

[25] William Hazlitt, *Lectures on the English Poets* (London: OUP, 1952), 109.
[26] Tillotson, *On the Poetry of Pope*, 96; Nuttall, *Pope's "Essay on Man,"* 110; Clive T. Probyn, "Pope's Bestiary: The Iconography of Defiance," *The Art of Alexander Pope*, ed. Howard Erskine-Hill and Anne Smith (London: Vision Press, 1979).
[27] Nabokov, "Pale Fire," lines 185-95, and also line 937 which, surprisingly, is the line in which the Popean "Zembla" is mentioned.
[28] Peter Quennell, *Alexander Pope* (London: Weidenfeld and Nicolson, 1968), 68.
[29] Nabokov, *Pale Fire*, Foreward; Johnson, *Lives*, 154; Hazlitt, *Lectures*, 110.
[30] Edith Sitwell, *Alexander Pope* (Harmondsworth: Penguin Books, 1948), 78. Quennell, *Pope*, 67. Two matching tresses were a striking feature of fashionable hairdos. In Maynard Mack's biography, one can admire the locks of Teresa Blount and Miss Fermor in the reproductions of their portraits (*Alexander Pope, A Life* [New Haven: Yale University Press, 1985], 246, 249), and in Hogarth's painting of Garrick and his wife (Royal Collection, Windsor) one can enjoy

Pope dwells at great length on the beauty of his heroine, and on all the efforts that she and her maid dedicated to enhancing the glory of her looks. This helps the reader to understand that the loss of the lock was nothing less than a social disaster for Belinda. At the same time, it invites the reader to reflect on her vanity. Whether Belinda's fury resulted from injured dignity or hurt pride, it led to feelings of distrust and hostility towards her more eager suitors. And this is not without risk, as "she who scorns a Man, must die a Maid."[31] To scorn, or to be scorned — as happened so very callously in Hazel's case — differs widely, especially when it is caused by an excess (or a lack) of beauty. But both cases may lead to the same end, the unmarried state. Remaining unmarried was a problem because Pope's age had "no employment and very little respect for spinsters."[32] Apart from this practical advice, Pope offers some sagacious considerations as well, as the poem is also "a lament for the transience of youth and the vanity of human wishes."[33] Indeed, Clarissa's lengthy speech in canto V centers on the idea that beauty dies and virtue alone survives:

> ...frail Beauty must decay,
> ...since Locks will turn to grey
> [...]
> Beauties in vain their pretty Eyes may roll;
> Charms strike the Sight, but Merit wins the Soul.[34]

However, such deliberations are not found in the second canto of Shade's poem. It focuses, instead, on the ideal of female beauty:

> A nymph came pirouetting, under white
> Rotating petals, in a vernal rite
> To kneel before an altar in the wood
> Where various articles of toilet stood.[35]

As has often been observed, these lines refer to the famous passage in *The Rape of the Lock*, lines 121-138 of canto I. Shade's lines have the taste of

---

Mrs. Garrick's carefully composed curlicue. See also lines 20-23 of *The Rape*'s second canto. The disappearance of one of the twin curls destroys the beauty of the remaining one as well, as Belinda says in canto IV, line 171. For this reason, it is highly unlikely that a *double entendre* (with a scabrous undertone) could be discovered in canto IV, line 176, as has been suggested too often.

[31] Pope, *Rape*, V 8.
[32] Mack, *Pope, A Life*, 252.
[33] Quennell, *Pope*, 77.
[34] Pope, *Rape*, V 25-26, 33-34.
[35] Nabokov, "Pale Fire," lines 413-416.

mild ridicule, while Pope's delightful lines are downright satirical. Hogarth, Pope's contemporary for half a century, parodied (like Pope) "the vices, the follies and the frivolity of the fashionable manners of his time."[36] Hazlitt, who persuasively links Hogarth's paintings with *The Rape of the Lock*, compares the bride in the first picture of the highly moralizing *Marriage à la Mode* paintings with the precise "look and air" that Pope gave his Belinda at the moment when her lock was taken.[37] Considered in this way, beauty seems to have no merits at all. It does not last, it awakens vanity at the expense of virtuous conduct, and it exposes the fair to harmful attention.[38] If beauty is such a hazardous attribute, can its absence be fatal as well? This question should be addressed because it is doubtful that "Hazel's death makes sense because of her irredeemable lack of sex appeal."[39]

Belinda's and Hazel's doomed days are marked by rays, a bright one for Belinda and an ominous one for Hazel. Dreaming about a boy, Belinda is awakened by the sun: "*Sol* thro' white Curtains shot a tim'rous Ray." A ray finished Hazel's dream about her date with Pete Dean who, filled with indignation about his blind date, "shot a death ray at well-meaning Jane."[40] Hazel's friend and Pete's cousin, Jane, arranged the blind date —after goading Hazel's half-hearted consent— in an attempt to alleviate Hazel's loneliness. One wonders why Hazel tries her luck. She is far from beautiful, her figure is plump, she has a slight squint, her feet are swollen, her fingernails psoriatic, her smile (hardly ever to be seen) is a sign of pain, her disposition is difficult and morose, and her imagination brings her strange fears and fantasies. Despite all this, her parents keep hoping that she will be invited to a ball, or taken to a dance. They even send her to a château in France, clearly to give her another opportunity to meet boys, although her father concedes that "Out of the lacquered night, a white-scarfed beau / Would never come for her; ..." How different is life for beauties like Belinda around whose coach "...crowd the white-glov'd Beaus." Unlike in Hazel's case, these beaux are not at all welcome, as they only serve to highlight how illusory such suitors are: "How vain are all these Glories..."[41]

---

[36] William Hazlitt, *The English Comic Writers* (London: O University Press, 1920), 189. See also Peter Quennell, *Hogarth's Progress* (London: Collins, 1955), 169.
[37] Hazlitt, *Comic Writers*, 177.
[38] Such attentions may lead, as in Belinda's case, to the loss of a lock, and in Lolita's case to the loss of her childhood.
[39] Zunshine, Pope's *Rape* and Nabokov's *Pale Fire*, 172.
[40] Pope, *Rape*, I 13; Nabokov, "Pale Fire," line 407.
[41] Nabokov, "Pale Fire," lines 333-34; Pope, *Rape*, V 13, 15.

Despite all her misfortunes, Hazel has moments of contentment as well: "...You remember those / Almost unruffled evenings when we played / Mah-jongg..."[42] One would like to learn more about this pastime: apart from studying, this is the only occasion that is mentioned which offers Hazel a kind of enjoyment. How different is Pope's poem, which presents 73 lines in canto III to describe Belinda playing ombre.

Another of Belinda's many pleasures is the company of her lapdog, Shock. Belinda is so fond of it that Shock is allowed to spend the nights in her room. Shock was a shaggy Iceland terrier, the same breed as Aunt Maud's Skye terrier.[43] Unfortunately, Sybil, Hazel's mother, "had the animal destroyed soon after its mistress's hospitalization, incurring the wrath of Hazel who was beside herself with distress."[44] The dog was partially paralyzed, which meant that it would have been a nuisance for Sybil but, at the same time, the dog's poor condition might have been an extra reason for Hazel to look after it. How curious that Hazel, with her many anxieties, was not permitted to keep the dog. The comfort provided by pets in one's life was noted by another Belinda, the heroine in one of Barbara Pym's novels: "Some tame gazelle, or some gentle dove, or even a poodle dog — something to love, that was the point."[45] In the variant on lines 417-421, Shade calls Pope's age "heartless" but Belinda, who has been advised that other things might be much more important than "beaux," has enjoyed her game of cards so passionately, and has been so fond of her poodle dog, seems in these respects to be better off than Hazel. As Michael Wood says, "she was surely more a victim of the manners of her time than anyone has to be or should be."[46]

Doubtless Hazel had loving and caring parents, but the future they desired for their daughter was rather illusory. We do not know the main reason that Hazel committed suicide (the incident with Pete Dean might only have actuated the event), but her parents' wish that she might find the same marital happiness as they enjoyed, probably did little to alleviate her predicament. As Wood has suggested, it was "[p]erhaps her other small hope

---

[42] Nabokov, "Pale Fire," lines 358-60.
[43] Quennell, *Hogarth*, 79. The second painting of Hogarth's *Marriage à la Mode* gives a fine illustration of an example of this breed.
[44] Nabokov, *Pale Fire*, 165.
[45] Barbara Pym, *Some Tame Gazelle* (London: Pan Books, 1993), 251. The title of Barbara Pym's novel is very unlikely the source for Kinbote's "tame gazelle" (Nabokov, *Pale Fire*, 133) as it was only published once during Nabokov's lifetime; no more likely is the poem by Thomas Haynes Bayly (1797-1839) "Something to Love" from which Pym borrowed her title.
[46] Wood, *The Magician's Doubts*, 195.

[…] that her parents would be able to think of something other than her sexual unattractiveness, put it out of their minds, and just love her."[47]

As Brian Boyd has uncovered, Hazel's life somehow continues after her death and she reappears as a butterfly, the Red Admirable that, at the brink of her father's death, showed "an almost frightening imitation of conscious play" in order to avert the impending murder.[48] Pope's poetry offers several instances of this sort of metempsychosis. In his *Elegy to the Memory of an Unfortunate Lady*, wherein the protagonist (like Hazel), committed suicide, Pope, after noticing her "beck'ning ghost" (like Shade heeding the swaying of the phantom of his little daughter's swing in line 57), envisions her as an airy being: "Fate snatch'd her early to the pitying sky / As into air the purer spirits flow."[49]

The sylphs in *The Rape of the Lock* are likewise reborn after such a transfiguration:

For when the Fair in all their Pride expire,
To their first Elements their Souls retire
[…]
Thence, by a soft Transition, we repair
From earthly Vehicles to those of Air [50]

The sylphs interfere with the lives of those on earth, as they "…thro' mystick Mazes guide their Way." Pope's sylphs resemble butterflies, as they have "Insect-Wings" which, when the sylphs waft through the air, show a magnificent variety of colors due to the perpetual mutation of reflected light: "Where Light disports on ever-mingling Dies, / While ev'ry Beam new transient Colours flings, / Colours that change whene'er they wave their Wings." The sylphs look like "*Zephyrs,*" and these are seen again in the description of butterflies in *The Dunciad*. "Of all th'enamel'd race, whose silv'ry wing / Waves to the tepid Zephyrs of the spring."[51]

In a note to line 421, Pope writes that he "seems to have an eye to Spenser, Muiopotmos" as it is from Spenser that Pope borrowed the image

---

[47] Ibid.
[48] Nabokov, "Pale Fire," lines 993-95. Brian Boyd, *Nabokov's* Pale Fire: *The Magic of Artistic Discovery* (Princeton: Princeton University Press, 1999).
[49] Alexander Pope, *Elegy to the Memory of an Unfortunate Lady, The Poems of Alexander Pope*, ed. John Butt (New Haven: Yale University Press, 1963), lines 24-25.
[50] Pope, *Rape*, I 57-8, 49-50.
[51] Ibid., I 92; II 59, 66-68, 58; *The Dunciad*, IV 421-2.

of silver wings.⁵² In "Muiopotmos: or The Fate of the Butterflie," Spenser suggests a mythological explanation for the colorful splendor of the wings of butterflies: Venus, out of jealousy, turned the nymph, Astery, into a butterfly and placed the many flowers the girl had gathered "in her wings."⁵³ Hazel's metamorphosis appears to have been preceded in Spenser's poetry. This cannot have escaped Nabokov's attention, as he had widely read the English poets (both major and minor) and, moreover, had a special interest in "lepidopterological images in English poetry."⁵⁴

PALE FIRE AND THE ESSAY ON MAN

In this section I will compare Shade's poem with Pope's *Essay* in terms of philosophical principles and ethical outlook. The *Essay on Man* has received a mixed response. Important critics like Samuel Johnson and Leslie Stephen did not appreciate *The Rape of the Lock*.⁵⁵ Nonetheless, the poem was translated into seventeen European languages and appeared in no fewer than ninety separate editions, and Kant found Pope's ideas superior to Leibnitz's.⁵⁶

---

⁵² See Pat Rogers, "Faery Lore and The Rape of the Lock," *The Review of English Studies*, New Series 25.97 (1974): 29, note 2.

⁵³ Edmund Spenser, "Muiopotmos: or the Fate of the Butterflie," line 142 (*The Poetical Works of Edmund Spenser* [London: O University Press, 1932]).

⁵⁴ Nabokov, *Speak, Memory* (New York: Vintage International, 1989), 129. Hazel's transition into a butterfly is so crucial that possible precursors are of interest as well. According to Pope (*The Poems of Alexander Pope*, ed. John Butt, page 217), sylphs have a Rosicrucian origin. This is not the case, as shown by Bonnie Latimer, "Alchemies of Satire: A History of the Sylphs in *The Rape of the Lock*," *The Review of English Studies* 57.232 (2006): 684-700. Belinda's guardian sylph is called Ariel, doubtless after Shakespeare's airy spirit from *The Tempest*. Pope's sylphs belong to a quartet of groups of spirits, each of them corresponding to "their first elements"; sylphs to air, salamanders to fire, nymphs to water and gnomes to earth (*Rape*, I 59-66). Pope could have found several instances of these elementary spirits in Milton, which Milton might have concocted from alchemical, Jewish and ancient Roman and Greek sources (see John Carey and Alastair Fowler, ed., *The Poems of John Milton* [London: Longmans, 1968], 175; and Merry Y. Hughes, ed., *Paradise Regained, The Minor Poems and Samson Agonistes* [New York: The Odyssey Press, 1937], 427).

⁵⁵ Johnson (*Lives*, 226) writes that Pope "was in haste to teach what he had not learned." Johnson, who could not deny the many poetic felicities of the *Essay on Man*, abhorred its lack of religious orthodoxy. According to Leslie Stephen, Pope's "reasonings in the *Essay* are confused, contradictory and often childish" (*Alexander Pope* [New York: Harper, 1880], 162).

⁵⁶ Maynard Mack, ed., Alexander Pope, *An Essay on Man* (London: Methuen and Co., 1950), xli and xlii.

Gerard de Vries

Although Pope says that his purpose was to "vindicate the ways of God to Man," the deistical tendencies seem to predominate, since he more often justifies "nature" than God.[57] Just as Shade's third canto can be seen as an explanation of the quest to which he devoted his "twisted life," Pope's *Epistle to Dr. Arbuthnot* can be regarded as an apology of his career as a poet.[58]

One of the final lines of Shade's third canto is most reminiscent of the first line of Pope's *Epistle*. "Darling, shut the door," Sybil says to her husband, John, as he strides in having returned from his visit to Mrs. Z., a journey that was crowned with his discovery of "the contrapuntal theme."[59] Pope's initial line, "Shut, shut the door, good *John!*..." is also associated with the poet's success, though in a more literal way. As a celebrity, Pope was often besieged by intruders seeking compliments, recommendations, suggestions or advice, who were to be kept out by John Searle, Pope's servant in his villa in Twickenham. By quoting Sybil's request, Shade might have privately celebrated his intellectual success as well.

Some of Nabokov's protagonists reappear in his later works. Pnin returns in *Pale Fire* and John Shade is represented in *Ada* as "a modern poet" while "the French thinker Delalande," copiously quoted in *The Gift* is, after twenty-two years, resuscitated in the Foreword to *Invitation to a Beheading*, which Nabokov wrote in 1959, one and a half years before he started to write *Pale Fire*.[60] Inspired by Delalande's thoughts, the author of *The Gift* states: "In our earthly house, windows are replaced by mirrors; the door, until a given time,

---

[57] Pope, *Essay on Man*, I 16. In the *Essay*, "God" is mentioned 56 times and "nature" is mentioned 65 times (*A Concordance to the Poems of Alexander Pope*, 2 vols., ed. Emmett G. Bedford and Robert J. Dilligan [Detroit: Gale Research Co, 1974], 6; 7; 523-24, 527). Cf. Nuttall's observation that "God is not a visible agent in Pope's story. The work on the spot is done by Nature" (*Pope's "Essay on Man,"* 201). Without equating nature and God as Nabokov did, they are most closely related: "All are but parts of one stupendous whole, / Whose body, Nature is, and God the soul" (Pope, *Essay on Man*, I 267-8). In his *Moral Essay, I, To Richard Temple, Viscount Cobham*, Pope writes: "Know, God and Nature only are the same" (154), though Thomas de Quincey argued that their sameness concerns their stability, as opposed to man's instability that is described in Pope's line 155 (Bateson and Joukovsky, *Anthology*, 223).

[58] Nabokov, "Pale Fire," line 180. Stephen, *Pope*, 182; Mack, *Pope*, 641.

[59] Nabokov, "Pale Fire," lines 831, 807.

[60] Nabokov, *Pale Fire*, 155; *Ada* (New York: Vintage International, 1990), 542; *The Gift* (New York: Vintage International, 1991), 309. Brian Boyd, *Vladimir Nabokov, The American Years* (Princeton: Princeton University Press, 1991), 417. In the Foreword to Nabokov's *Invitation to a Beheading*, Delalande is given a first name as well as the years of his birth (1768) and death (1849), which accurately register his literary age in 1959: the figures of each year (e.g. 1+7+6+8) add to 22.

is closed; but air comes in through the cracks."⁶¹ In *Look at the Harlequins!*, this image is employed once more and somewhat more resolutely: "maybe, the hereafter stands slightly ajar in the dark." A similar vision of a door opening to eternity is found in Lucretius's *On the Nature of the Universe*. Speaking of his great exemplar, the Greek philosopher Epicurus, Lucretius says that "he...longed to smash the constraining locks of nature's doors. The vital vigour of his mind prevailed. He ventured far out beyond the flaming ramparts of the world and voyaged in mind throughout infinity."⁶² Nabokov may have recollected this passage in his autobiography, *Speak, Memory*, when he mentioned his "bruised fists" caused by assailing the "walls of time" which kept him imprisoned. The same combative stance was displayed by Shade when he "...decided to explore and fight / The foul, the inadmissible abyss."⁶³ The same passage from Lucretius is echoed in Pope's *Essay on Man*, albeit with the emphasis on the upshot rather than on the pugilistic efforts: "He, who thro' vast immensity can pierce, / See worlds on worlds compose one universe."⁶⁴

In *Essay on Man*, Pope presents his concept of a harmonious and beneficent universe from the start, having been inspired by classical and contemporary authors who professed similar ideas. But Shade conceives his vision of the universe only after a long life of investigations, all fruitless, such as the instructions of the Institute of Preparation for the Hereafter (how to act as a ghost; how to deal with reincarnations; how to handle earthly relationships in Heaven), the lessons of cremationists and astronomers, the futile intimations from occultists and Freudians. And when he loses his daughter, his faith in a hereafter vanishes as well. But his hope is rekindled by a near-death experience, almost identical to that of Mrs. Z, and it is after visiting her that he finally envisages the way his life and afterlife are designed. What he sees is not a concatenation of "coincidence" and "nonsense," "but

---

[61] Nabokov, *The Gift*, 310. Pierre Delalande might be related to Joseph Jérôme le Français de Lalande (1732-1807), whom Nabokov mentions in his Commentary to *Eugene Onegin* (III 129). De Lalande was a French astronomer who believed in extraterrestrial life: "Imagination pierces beyond the telescope: it sees a new multitude of worlds infinitely larger" (http://www.astrobio.net/amee/spring_20003/retrospection_0.3htm).

[62] Vladimir Nabokov, *Look at the Harlequins!* (New York: Vintage International, 1990), 26. Titus Lucretius, *On the Nature of the Universe*, trans. R. E. Latham (Harmondsworth: Penguin Books, 1976), 29. Some translators have "gates" in stead of "doors" for Lucretius's *"portarum."* For a discussion of the influence of Lucretius's poem on Pope's *Essay on Man* see Miriam Lerenbaum, *Alexander Pope's "Opus Magnum" 1729-1744* (Oxford: Clarendon Press, 1977).

[63] Nabokov, *Speak, Memory*, 20; "Pale Fire," lines 178-79.

[64] Pope, *Essay on Man*, I 23-24. Mack, ed., Pope, *An Essay*, 15, note 23.

a web of sense." This is similar to Pope's comparison of the "scene of Man" with "A mighty maze! But not without a plan."[65]

Kinbote's comments on Shade's "web of sense" refer to a "maze" very similar to the one Pope uses to indicate the outward, inextricable appearance of man's life. Kinbote presents the reader with a passage from the *Letters of Franklin Lane* that "curiously echoes Shade's tone at the end of Canto Three." In this passage, Lane thinks about Aristotle and how he will take "the long ribbon of man's life to trace it through the mystifying maze of all the wonderful adventure...The crooked made straight." One can only admire the felicitousness of this passage, linking Shade's web with Pope's maze, a connection repeated by Lane's "ribbon," which perfectly fits Shade's textural images. Shade's "web of sense" results from the "pattern" in 'the game of worlds" played by extraterrestrial beings whose existence Shade has detected, although "...No sound, / No furtive light came from their involute / Abode,..." Shade seems to belong to those uniquely gifted people "...who thro' vast immensity can pierce,"[66] and thus can

> See worlds on worlds compose one universe,
> Observe how system into system runs,
> What other planets circle other suns,
> What vary'd being peoples ev'ry star.[67]

Pope's system is absorbed by another, which in its turn will be absorbed as well (like the planet earth which belongs to the solar system, which itself is part of a galaxy, etc.). This is reflected in Shade's vision of an intricate "system" of multiple sets of interlinked cells "[w]ithin one stem."[68]

Shade's discernment of a "correlated pattern in the game" might be connected to the purpose of the players of the game "...Coordinating these / Events and objects with remote events / And vanished objects. Making ornaments / Of accidents and possibilities"

might explain the "combinational delight" that Pope experiences in pervading "...the bearings, and the ties, / The strong connections, nice dependencies, / Gradations just,..." Of course the players of this "game of worlds" have to observe the rules that constitute this play, which explains how difficult it is to understand one of their moves or maneuvers in isolation:

---

[65] Nabokov, "Pale Fire," lines 809-10; Pope, *Essay on Man*, I 5, 6.
[66] Nabokov, *Pale Fire*, 261; "Pale Fire," lines 816-19; Pope, *Essay on Man*, I 23.
[67] Pope, *Essay on Man*, I 24-27.
[68] Nabokov, "Pale Fire," lines 704-706.

"Remember, Man, 'the Universal Cause / Acts not by partial, but by gen'ral laws." And it is by applying such rules or laws that "plexed artistry" emerges, "ornaments / Of accidents and possibilities" or that "...the whole worlds of Reason, Life, and Sense" turns out "In one close system of Benevolence." Although Shade presents his vision with firmness, he summarizes his newly won insight rather cautiously for Sybil: "I have returned convinced that I can grope / My way to some — to some — 'Yes dear?' Faint hope."[69] Hope is also Pope's resort, to which he turns in every missive of his *Essay*[70] as, for example, in the fourth epistle:

> For [Man] alone, Hope leads from goal to goal,
> And opens still, and opens on his soul,
> [...]
> Hope of known bliss, and Faith in bliss unknown.[71]

Despite the number of parallel passages, there are differences between the two poets. First of all, the door that stands ajar in Nabokov's imagery will not be used to look into the hinterland, but to profit from the air which "comes in through the cracks." In Lucretius's and Pope's poetry, the aspiration is to look into the universe.

Although the pyrrhonist, adverse to any claim of knowledge about the nature of things, will argue that this difference is chimerical, it is of great importance for those who are not intolerant of the possibility of supernatural phenomena. For Lucretius, the "door" opening to the universe is primarily a symbolic one because his great poem, covering an astonishing range of issues, is a testimony of his conviction that all visible and invisible things can be explained by nature and by nature alone. Pope justifies life on this planet by explaining the laws of nature (or nature's autonomy) and postulates that, because all we can understand is right, everything inexplicable must, analogously, be right as well. Shade, however, is primarily interested in the question of how to perceive and decipher the dim and dusky intimations which come from the beyond. To discern those tidings one has to rely on imagination rather than on ratiocination. The narrow openings are of importance to secure these messages. Of course, acknowledging the possibility of such messages entails the question about their senders. In Nabokov's novels, it is

---

[69] Nabokov, "Pale Fire," lines 813, 826-29, 973; Pope, *Essay on Man*, I 29-31; IV 35-36; Nabokov, "Pale Fire," lines 815, 828-29; Pope, *Essay on Man*, IV 357, 358; Nabokov, "Pale Fire," lines 833-34.
[70] Cf. Nuttall, *Pope's "Essay on Man,"* 123.
[71] Pope, *Essay on Man*, IV 341-46.

often close relatives or loved ones who try to admonish or assist those still alive. Although on three occasions Shade pairs the appearance or the image of a butterfly with his daughter or wife, he fails to make this association when a butterfly presents itself for the fourth time.[72] Likewise, those who play the game of worlds remain unidentified. In the *Essay on Man*, there are no such celestial beings who govern earthly life. There is no need for them to interfere, as providence has preordained the universe and its operation.[73]

Another difference of emphasis is related to ethical concerns. It can be said that the main argument of both poets, Shade and Pope, as far as their metaphysical pursuits are concerned, is expressed in these lines in the *Essay on Man*:

> All Nature is but Art, unknown to thee;
> All Chance, Direction, which thou canst not see;
> All Discord, Harmony, not understood.[74]

Pope is quite clear what this "Harmony" meant to him: "All partial Evil, universal Good."[75] Less clear is what "harmony" (resulting from the "web of sense," the "correlated pattern," or the "coordinating") means to Shade. Does harmony refer to "plexed artistry," the perfection of the "game of worlds," or the delights that "making ornaments" afford? Shade proceeds by enumerating several incidents yielded by this game.[76] Among the examples he presents is the "extinguishing [of] a short" life. One wonders how Shade, having lost his only child less than two years earlier, could have experienced "pleasure" in contemplating a game involving an identical loss. And one's confusion only increases after reading Shade's comment on a line from *Essay on Man*, — "Has unmistakably the vulgar ring / Of its preposterous age..." — knowing, as we do, that in a variant this age was even called "heartless." Here Shade gives Pope two inconsiderate digs: first that he was a callous poet and second that he merely copied contemporary thoughts.[77]

---

[72] Nabokov, "Pale Fire," lines 55-58, 269-271, 316-19, 993-97. See Boyd, *Nabokov's* Pale Fire.
[73] Although Lucretius's gods, like Shade's godlike beings, have lots of fun (as "...laughs with radiance lavishly diffuse [.]..." [96]), they are completely powerless (cf. Lucretius, *Universe*, 173-77).
[74] Pope, *Essay on Man*, I 289-91.
[75] Ibid., 292. This line is so crucial that it is repeated in epistle IV, line 114.
[76] As "promoting pawns" (Nabokov, "Pale Fire," line 819) belong to this game, Shade alludes to something similar to chess. From the examples given by Shade, it seems as if the only moves that are allowed are gambits.
[77] Ibid., 821-22, 815, 420-421; *Pale Fire*, Commentary 417-21. In his Commentary to *Eugene Onegin*, Nabokov mentions Pope's "thematic imitativeness" and his "Leibnitzian 'all is right'"

Why did Shade censure Pope's moral stance without offering some sort of clarification about the pleasure he found in discovering the deadly "game of worlds"?[78] Brian Boyd suggests that "Shade...feels the tender interest of the forces of imagination in his life, a sense of pattern even behind the anguish of his own loss" and that even an "allotment of pain, wantonly cruel in human terms, might be a necessary part of the pattern of tenderness."[79] This closely parallels Pope's argument: "'Tis but a part we see, and not a whole" and "...partial Ill is universal Good."[80]

Moreover, Pope explicitly discusses the incidents that Shade describes as parts of the "game of worlds." For example, "Kindling a long life" might be compared with Pope's lines: "Or why so long (in life it long can be) / Lent Heav'n a parent to the poor and me?"; and "extinguishing / A short one" with "Tell me, if Virtue made the Son expire, / Why, full of days and honour, lives the Sire?" Similarly, the "chunk of ice" that plummets from the sky and kills a farmer, is countered by Pope's "Shall gravitation cease, if you go by?" Both poets are convinced that whatever remains inexplicable in earthy life will be solved in the hereafter: "Life is a great surprise. I do not see why death should not be an even greater one," says Shade, while Pope recommends to "Wait the great teacher Death."[81]

Curiously, the two quotations Shade draws from Pope have no relation to the parallel passages discussed above. They come from a section in the second epistle:

Whate'er the Passion, knowledge, farmer or pelf,
Not one will change his neighbor with himself
The learn'd is happy nature to explore,
The fool is happy that he knows no more;

(III 30). However, Lerenbaum argues that Lucretius and Horace are Pope's major influences, and it is doubtful that Pope ever read a line of Leibniz (Stephen, *Pope*, 163; Nuttall, *Pope's "Essay on Man,"* 51). Moreover, Kant "was excited by the differences between Pope and Leibniz" (Nuttall, *Pope's "Essay on Man,"* 191).

[78] A comparable image is found in Shakespeare's *King Lear*: "As flies to wanton boys, are we to th' gods, / They kill us for their sport" (*The Complete Works of William Shakespeare* [Oxford: Oxford University Press, 1955], 4, 1, 36-37), but Gloucester certainly derived no consolation from this thought.

[79] Brian Boyd, *Nabokov's Ada: The Place of Consciousness* (Christchurch N.Z.: Cybereditions, 2001), 103-104. Cf. page 97: "perhaps [Shade] discerns the hidden justification of the game of life."

[80] Pope, *Essay on Man*, I 60; IV 114.

[81] Ibid., IV 109-110, 105-106, IV 125; Nabokov, *Pale Fire*, 225; Pope, *Essay on Man*, I 92.

> The rich is happy in the plenty giv'n,
> The poor contents him with the care of Heav'n.
> See the blind beggar dance, the cripple sing.
> The sot a hero, lunatic a king;
> The starving chemist in his golden views
> Supremely blest, the poet in his muse.
> See some strange comfort ev'ry state attend,
> And Pride bestow'd on all, a common friend;
> See some fit Passion ev'ry age supply,
> Hope travels thro', nor quits us when we die.[82]

Line 262 is of interest to a commentator editing a poem written by a neighbor who is killed by a bullet meant instead for the commentator. Line 267 is disapprovingly quoted by Shade. One may argue that Pope overstepped sensible boundaries by supposing gaiety among the disabled,[83] without offering any explication as he does with respect to the learned, the fool, the rich and the poor. But Shade might have remembered that Pope was a cripple himself,[84] and that Pope's appearance, like Hazel's, precluded intimate relationships that he longed for. Line 271 might raise the question of what "strange comfort" Hazel had to compensate for her "strange fears, strange fantasies, strange force." And the first hemistich of line 270 was borrowed by Shade for his book on Pope, a rather lofty title for a work "concerned mainly with Pope's technique."[85] In the *Essay*, it is the "starving chemist" who is supremely blest, a qualification extended to "the poet in his muse." Pope's "chemist" is the alchemist who seeks the transformation of base metals into precious ones, but whose ultimate aspiration is "the transformation of the soul."[86] The poet's muse is, of course, the source of inspiration; which must have been revered by Nabokov as it was a favorite image of Pushkin[87] and, in his Commentary to *Eugene Onegin*, Nabokov describes the journey of "Pushkin's Muse," following her through all its chapters. In Nabokov's view, the poet's muse is much more closely linked with Pushkin's creative genius than with Pope's "exceptional talent for placing the best words possible in the best possible order." The phrase "Supremely blest," with its winged meanings,

---

[82] Pope, *Essay on Man*, II 261-74.
[83] Cf. Nuttall, *Pope's "Essay on Man,"* 101.
[84] Mack, *Pope*, 553.
[85] Nabokov, "Pale Fire," line 344; *Pale Fire*, 195.
[86] E. J. Holmyard, *Alchemy* (Harmondsworth: Penguin Books, 1968), 158.
[87] In the index of Nabokov's edition of *Eugene Onegin* the entry "Muse(s)" is followed by fifty-five references.

seems to apply more to the author of Shade's book on Pope than to its subject, as it refers to Shade's search for the everlasting life of the human soul and his "unique" sense: his gift for imaginary visions.[88]

CONCLUDING REMARKS

Although Nabokov made numerous references to works of poets and prose writers in his oeuvre, the frequency of allusions to Pope in *Pale Fire*, as well as John Shade's scholarly and recreational affinity for Pope, makes the position of the Augustan poet unique. Subtexts associated with such literary allusions can serve various aims. Kiril Taranovsky, as quoted by Pekka Tammi, distinguishes three different functions for subtexts: they can help to create an image, to reveal a message, or to stage a polemic treatment.[89] These categories, however, seem too specific to apply to Nabokov's copious allusions to Pope. As Priscilla Meyer has shown, many of the references in *Pale Fire* contribute to its "cultural synthesis" of different literary and historical developments in the northern hemisphere.[90] Within this overarching concept, the Popean subtexts seem to have a particular role. Shade is meandering around Pope's examples, at times corresponding with them, at times markedly deviating from them.

Shade employs the same meter used by Pope, but not Pope's more characteristic heroic couplets. The focus on female beauty in Shade's canto II is as pronounced as that in *The Rape of the Lock*, but appreciation of it is highly dissimilar. Furthermore, some of Shade's philosophical views strongly resemble those expressed by Pope in the *Essay on Man*: the Lucretian interest in the universe; the presumption of coordination between unrelated events; and the selection of incidents which seem beyond vindication. These views are exquisitely epitomized in Pope's epigraph:

> All Nature is but Art, unknown to thee;
> All Chance, Direction, which thou canst not see.[91]

---

[88] Nabokov, Commentary to *Eugene Onegin*, III 303, 30; "Pale Fire," line 133.
[89] Pekka Tammi, *Russian Subtexts in Nabokov's Fiction, Four Essays* (Tampere: Tampere University Press, 1999), 9.
[90] Priscilla Meyer, *Find What the Sailor Has Hidden. Vladimir Nabokov's* Pale Fire (Middleton: Wesleyan University Press, 1988), 6.
[91] Pope, *Essay on Man*, I 289-90.

Michael Wood states that "Nabokov is plainly much attracted to this theory" as well.[92] However, the word "nature" means something different for Shade than for Pope. Pope's domain is primarily the visible world that operates by hidden forces which he would like to bare. Shade, on the other hand, is mainly interested in the invisible part of the universe, where the dead abide. Pope's aim is to illustrate by clever and ingenious arguments that nature makes sense, even when it looks like chaos. In Shade's view, earthly life can only make sense as a part of eternal life. And evidence for such a life can be derived from the dead, whose existence can be seen by those who are imaginative enough for this task. Shade mentions the possibility that the dead might return as animals by means of reincarnation, or as electric light, but expects that he may learn more of their windblown messages—the creaking of shutters, the rolling of marbles on the roof, the throwing of twigs at windowpanes—or their "'psychokinetic' manifestations" and roundlets of pale light which respond to recited alphabets.[93] However, as creation can be better understood by those who are creative themselves, Shade's artistic gifts appear to be a more successful medium through which he can probe the universe and find answers to its riddles.[94] Accordingly, it is not Pope's power of argumentation but rather his imagination that helps Shade to retrieve the "robust truth" promised by the "twin display" of the white fountain after it was destroyed by a misprint. And it is because of the patterns Shade discovers by means of artistic imagination that he can derive confidence about eternal life and find some pleasure in Hazel's preferring this life above her rather miserable earthly one.

Inspired by Newton's great example, many philosophers in the eighteenth century attempted to find similar comprehensive rules which might explain the way that nature controls earthly life.[95] Such deistic explanations rested heavily on the idea of a design, just as the orbiting of planets could be clarified by Newton's laws of gravitation. Next to astronomers and philosophers, artists may have similar aspirations, as they can create worlds based on plans only known to them. This idea is beautifully described by Pope in his *Essay on Criticism*:

---

[92] Wood, *The Magician's Doubts*, 170.
[93] Nabokov, "Pale Fire," lines 561-66, 653-54, 418, 479-480; *Pale Fire*, 165; 188.
[94] Nabokov, "Pale Fire," lines 766, 746. See de Vries, "'*Mountain, not fountain*,' *Pale Fire*'s Saving Grace," *The Nabokovian* (Fall 2009) in which the pivotal role of the reference to Pope's *Temple of Fame* is discussed.
[95] Cf. David Daiches, "Eighteenth-Century Philosophical, Historical, and Critical Prose, and Miscellaneous Writing," *A Critical History of English Literature* (London: Secker & Warburg, 1960), vol. 2, chapter 5.

> So when the faithful *Pencil* has design'd
> Some *bright Idea* of the Master's Mind
> Where a *new World* leaps out of his command,
> And ready Nature waits upon his Hand.[96]

This analogy, according to John Lyons, "leads Nabokov to his favourite narrative method."[97] Indeed, Nabokov often refers to the demiurgic qualities of an author. In *Bend Sinister*, for instance, he impersonates an "anthropomorphic deity" who responds to his own protagonist. In *Speak, Memory*, he attributes to "[t]he author" "the zest of a deity building a new world."[98] The parallel between writing and creating the world—the "heterocosmic analogue," as M. H. Abrams calls it—gained momentum in the eighteenth century, and would "sever supernatural poetry entirely from the principle of imitation."[99] This is the kind of poetry that Nabokov was interested in: "by poetry I mean the mysteries of the irrational as perceived through rational words."[100]

It looks as if Nabokov's *Pale Fire* gives his readers a metaphor of the world as he sees it: a plethora of magic and tragic incidents, bewildering at first sight, but with coincidences that may hold much more coherence than one is able to detect, even after much investigation. These complexities have been described by many authors, as Pope demonstrates, but it seems that the harmony detected by Shade is unprecedented.

---

[96] Pope, *Essay on Criticism*, 484-87.

[97] John O. Lyons, "*Pale Fire* and the Fine Art of Annotation," *Nabokov, The Man and His Work*, ed. L. S. Dembo (Madison: The University of Wisconsin Press, 1967), 157.

[98] Nabokov, *Bend Sinister* (New York: Vintage International, 1990), xviii; *Speak, Memory*, 291. In *Strong Opinions*, Nabokov ranks "the Almighty" among the "rivals" of a "creative writer" (32). See also *Lectures on Russian Literature* (London: Picador, 1983), 106. It is not only the world that is recreated by an artist, as Nabokov reaches out to the universe as well. The "real writer," he says in *Lectures on Literature*, "sends planets spinning" (New York: Harcourt Brace Jovanovich, 1980), 2; see also 379.

[99] M. H. Abrams, "The Poem as Heterocosm," *The Mirror and the Lamp* (Oxford: Oxford University Press, 1971), 272.

[100] Vladimir Nabokov, *Nicolai Gogol* (New York: New Directions, 1961), 55.

Conall Cash

PICTURING MEMORY, PUNCTURING VISION: VLADIMIR NABOKOV'S *PALE FIRE*

Astonishing things happen if one gives oneself over to the process of seeing again and again: aspect after aspect of the picture seems to surface, what is salient and what incidental alter bewilderingly from day to day, the larger order of the depiction breaks up, recrystallizes, fragments again, persists like an afterimage.[1]

In *Pale Fire*, Vladimir Nabokov stages a dialogue between two authors of his own invention, the poet John Francis Shade and his commentator Charles Kinbote. If a central tension of the novel is the seemingly chaotic disconnect between their two texts, then Nabokov's own authorial position appears to give order to this chaos, revealing a complex design behind

---

[1] T. J. Clark, *The Sight of Death: An Experiment in Art Writing* (New Haven / London: Yale University Press, 2006), 5.

the apparent mass of disordered parts. The bulk of criticism on *Pale Fire* has sought to elucidate just what this authorial design is, and how it functions. Those writers working broadly within a tradition of author-based criticism typically perform this elucidanation through a close analysis of the intricacies of the narrative, reaching a "solution" that confirms the unity and completeness of the text.[2] On the other hand, critics of a (broadly defined) poststructuralist bent have sought to dismantle the notion that any such solution might exist, or that there is a complete, unified, whole work beneath the chaotic surface.[3] Common in both of these approaches is a belief that it is alternately the presence (as the more traditionally formalist critics would have it) or absence (for the poststructuralists) of narrative coherence that constitutes the import of *Pale Fire*. Critics of all persuasions find that the novel elicits, indeed demands, a response to the problem of assessing this tension between chaos and order, between narrative coherence and its collapse into incoherence.

My contribution to this critical conversation turns to a relatively overlooked element of *Pale Fire*: the role of the visual arts of painting and photography.[4] Focusing on points in the text at which paintings and photos

[2] Notable examples of such criticism are Mary McCarthy, "A Bolt From The Blue," *The Writing on the Wall and Other Essays* (New York: Harcourt, Brace & World, Inc., 1970), 15-34; Brian Boyd, *Nabokov's* Pale Fire: *The Magic of Artistic Discovery* (Princeton, NJ: Princeton University Press), 1999; and the *Pale Fire* chapter of Vladimir E. Alexandrov, *Nabokov's Otherworld* (Princeton, NJ: Princeton University Press), 1991. In different ways, these texts are all concerned with uncovering the "tricks" and "riddles" of the novel, unmasking the "true" identities of characters and the "true" authorial roles of Shade and Kinbote. Their arguments are quite different: McCarthy makes a case for *Pale Fire* as a great, radical modernist novel; whereas Boyd and Alexandrov are chiefly concerned with Nabokov as a metaphysician, a traditionalist wearing the mask of a modernist, and hence they both tie their findings about the narrative of *Pale Fire* back to metaphysical questions of life and death.

[3] Major instances of such approaches to *Pale Fire* include Maurice Couturier, "The Near-Tyranny of the Author: Pale Fire," *Nabokov and his Fiction: New Perspectives*, ed. Julian W. Connolly (Cambridge: Cambridge University Press, 1999), 54-72; and Michael Wood, "The Demons of our Pity," *The Magician's Doubts: Nabokov and the Risks of Fiction* (Princeton, NJ: Princeton University Press, 1994), 173-205. To make their arguments about *Pale Fire* as a somewhat unstable, fraught text, Couturier and Wood each focus on aspects of the novel which do not seem to allow for a cohesive or definitive solution. For Couturier, this involves interrogating the different proposed solutions to the "authorial" question of *Pale Fire*, and taking up a reading which looks at the role of what he calls the "authorial figure," questioning the stake for this figure in creating a novel so maddeningly self-referential and insoluble. Wood makes similar, though not identical, claims focusing largely on the character of Hazel Shade and the problems her characterization offer to most critical understandings of both Shade and Kinbote as characters and as authors.

[4] There is some critical discussion of *Pale Fire*'s references to painting and photography, but it typically takes one of two directions, neither of which I will be following here. Gerard de

are evoked and described allows the opportunity for a fresh approach to this most labyrinthine of novels, and to the questions it poses about the reading process and narrative coherence. The pertinence of the relationship between writing and the visual arts in Nabokov's work can be observed if we consider a passage from one of his lectures to students at Cornell University.

> Curiously enough, one cannot *read* a book: one can only reread it. A good reader, a major reader, an active and creative reader is a rereader. And I shall tell you why. When we read a book for the first time the very process of laboriously moving our eyes from left to right, line after line, page after page, this complicated physical work upon the book, the very process of learning in terms of space and time what the book is about, this stands between us and artistic appreciation. When we look at a painting we do not have to move our eyes in a special way even if, as in a book, the picture contains elements of depth and development. The element of time does not really enter in a first contact with a painting. In reading a book, we must have time to acquaint ourselves with it. We have no physical organ (as we have the eye in regard to a painting) that takes in the whole picture and then can enjoy its details. But at a second, or third, or fourth reading we do, in a sense, behave towards a book as we do towards a painting.[5]

The experience of reading a book and that of regarding a painting are here presupposed as self-evident. Reading is a "laborious" process of "physical work" upon an object that dictates a certain temporal and corporal movement on the part of the reader, as he reads "from left to right," "learning in terms of space and time." The viewer of a painting, however, does not have this "element of time" standing "between [him] and artistic appreciation," for he is able to "take in the whole picture" at once. "Rereading" is seen as the solution to this problem, a way to overcome this "element of time," thereby making the reader's experience akin to the viewer's. A rereader is no longer concerned with "learning...what the book is about," and can now appreciate it as a single, still, unified object. When Nabokov states that "[a] good reader...is

---

Vries and D. Barton Johnson, in *Nabokov and the Art of Painting* (Amsterdam: Amsterdam University Press, 2006), painstakingly go through every reference to painting in *Pale Fire* and other Nabokov novels, only to reach the conclusion that the paintings "match the various themes in his novels, thus contributing to the profoundness of his art." Thus, paintings are seen to be fully and harmoniously integrated into the narrative world of the novel, rather than in any way problematizing this world. On the other hand, critical discussions of the photographs in *Pale Fire* tend to take them as evidence of a truth that is hidden by Kinbote's narrative voice (see, for example, Boyd, *Artistic Discovery*, 97; and McCarthy, "A Bolt from the Blue," 18). Neither of these perspectives offers any interrogation of what the formal characteristics of painting or photography may do to impact or disturb the written text.

[5] Vladimir Nabokov, *Lectures on Literature* (San Diego / New York / London: Harcourt, 1980), 3.

a rereader," he is perversely suggesting that to truly appreciate a literary text is to somehow move beyond textuality, beyond the very condition of its existence—language—into the lofty realm of painting.

In *Pale Fire*, the interaction Nabokov stages between literature and the visual arts seriously questions these presuppositions. The very idea of a timeless "first contact" with an image is elaborately deconstructed, as paintings and photographs shift meaning across the temporal plane of *Pale Fire*'s narrative. Similarly, the notion that reading is a "laborious" sequential process of accumulation leading towards the revelation of "sight" is both invited and mocked, as the text undermines all proposed solutions to its problems.[6]

The distinction established in the above quotation between the experience of the "whole" work of art and the enjoyment of its "details" is complicated and eroded in *Pale Fire*. As the Nabokov of the lecture sets out, literature and painting operate in precisely opposite ways in the temporal relation each establishes between "the whole" and "the details": the reader of a text must first sift through the details before finally "acquaint[ing]" himself with the whole, complete "picture" of the work; whereas the viewer of a painting *first* "takes in the whole picture," and "*then* can enjoy its details." In *Pale Fire*, however, Nabokov obscures this distinction by having one of his "authors," Kinbote, *write the visual* in the form of descriptions and interpretations of a series of visual art objects; the versions of paintings and photos in the novel are always written, always a part of the sequential process of narrative, enmeshed in temporality. In being written, or rendered ekphrastically, the images become enveloped within the "details" of narrative, and so lack the immediacy and wholeness that Nabokov in the Cornell passage above claims are essential properties of paintings. Instead, in *Pale Fire* he gives us written descriptions of, and reflections upon, the images as Kinbote engages with them, experiences them in time.

If Nabokov's ideal reader is a "rereader," then our task is to investigate how our experience of *Pale Fire*'s images shifts over time, as we (re)read. Does the process of reading and rereading allow us to get an unmediated vision of these images, and so lead us towards uncovering that ever elusive "truth" of *Pale Fire*, that point at which the text reveals itself as whole, like a painting? Or, will our readings and rereadings of these images lead us to rethink the model of reading set out by Nabokov in the Cornell lecture, wherein the process of

---

[6] Brian Boyd provides a useful summary of these proposed solutions in *Artistic Discovery*, 114-116.

rereading leads us to "behave towards a book as we do towards a painting?" What kind of readerly "behavior" is demanded by this text and its images?

Pale Fire presents us with two kinds of visual art objects—paintings and photographs—which function in quite different ways within the text. As will become apparent, the text is very much concerned with what we might call the "truth-value" of each of these forms of representation and, as such, leads the reader to make certain assumptions about how each form works, how it represents reality. As we move through the novel from the early appearance of several paintings to the photos that factor increasingly in the latter part of the narrative, we will need to pay attention to how the role of the image shifts, and how our initial assumptions about the value of each form are borne out or modified by our reading and rereading.

The first visual art objects that figure prominently in the novel are two paintings by Pablo Picasso, which appear in the very opening pages of Kinbote's commentary on John Shade's poem, "Pale Fire." The first painting is introduced at the starting point of what becomes the "Zembla story," the moment at which Kinbote's narrative begins to radically diverge from that of Shade's poem. On line twelve of his "Pale Fire," Shade describes the "crystal land" of snow and ice outside his window in upstate New York. Taking this as the cue to commence his own story, in the corresponding note Kinbote hypothesizes that these words are "Perhaps an allusion to Zembla, my dear country."[7] From here he introduces the starring character of his Zembla narrative, King Charles Xavier II, the last King of Zembla. One of the most unusual things about Charles Xavier, Kinbote tells us, is that he was not only a King, but also an academic at the local university, where he would "lecture under an assumed name and in a heavy make-up....All brown-bearded, apple-cheeked, blue-eyed Zemblans look alike, and I [Kinbote] who have not shaved now for a year resemble my disguised king (see also note to line 894)."[8] Not only was this King a university professor, like Kinbote; the two men also apparently "resemble" one another. The first of two Picasso paintings enters the scene at this point.

---

[7] Vladimir Nabokov, *Pale Fire* (New York: Vintage International, 1989), 33; 74.

[8] Ibid., 76. Kinbote's commentary is littered with instructions to skip backwards and forwards to other notes—this is one quite explicit way in which the "element of time," as Nabokov has it in his "Good Readers" lecture, is played with by the text. If we follow Kinbote's instruction here and skip to his note to line 894, we find ourselves at the point where the mystery of the "resemblance" between Kinbote and King Charles is unraveled, and the two men are finally revealed to be one and the same. When we come to an analysis of this note, in the conclusion of this essay, we will find that our reading of the significance of this revelation is deeply tied to the role allocated to images in the novel.

During these periods of teaching, Charles Xavier made it a rule to sleep at a *pied-à-terre* he had rented... One recalls with nostalgic pleasure its light gray carpeting and pearl-gray walls (one of them graced with a solitary copy of Picasso's *Chandelier, pot et casserole émaillée*), a shelfful of calfbound poets, and a virginal-looking daybed under its rug of imitation panda fur.⁹

Illustration 1: Pablo Picasso's *La Casserole Émaillée*, 1945

The parenthetical appearance of this 1945 Picasso still life brings color to the drab, gray scene Kinbote paints of Charles Xavier's office, and in so doing it lends a kind of color to Kinbote's story itself. The painting is the only detail given which connotes a specific time period, and it also implies a certain cultural sophistication on the part of both the King who hangs it on his wall and the critic, Kinbote, who is able to identify it. A claim is being made here for pre-revolutionary Zembla as a location of progressive Western modernity.¹⁰ Yet, in the midst of the grand, old-fashioned romance of Kinbote's Royalist narrative, this Picasso seems out of place, just as it looks out of place on Charles Xavier's wall; its color set off by the "light gray carpeting and pearl-gray walls," its cultural seriousness clashing with the tacky "rug of imitation panda fur." The placement of Picasso's still life seeks to add veracity to the scene through detail, but results in the opposite, as the painting becomes much

---

⁹ Ibid., 76. The actual title of this painting is *La Casserole Émaillée*. Henceforth I will refer to it by its usual English title, *Still Life with Candlestick*.

¹⁰ A revolution breaks out in Zembla in the 1950s, causing the King to flee the country.

Conall Cash

more than the signifier of place, period and status Kinbote intends it to be. It draws too much attention in the way it is set off against the rest of the room's décor and, for the first time, raises what will become a central question of the novel: how does Kinbote know all these minute details, down to the painting that hung on the wall of the King's secret office? This question becomes all the more pertinent due to the odd use of the pronoun "one" that immediately precedes the mention of the painting. If Kinbote does indeed "resemble" the King, as he has just told us, it seems that the line between the two begins to blur at this moment of recollection ("One recalls with nostalgic pleasure"), and the appeal to veracity that comes with the placement of the painting on Charles Xavier's wall only further impresses upon the reader the uncertainty of the distinction between recollection and invention. Just how much can we trust Kinbote's descriptions of this obscure world of Zembla, especially when his position as a character and an author seems to slide around so easily? What is being invented and what is being remembered? What is the true relationship between these two lookalikes?

Returning to the story of his arrival in the American college town of New Wye, Kinbote almost immediately introduces a second Picasso painting into his narrative as he describes his impressions upon first entering the house he rented from Judge Hugh Goldsworth, a neighbor of John Shade.

> Judge Goldsworth had a wife and four daughters. Family photographs met me in the hallway and pursued me from room to room, and although I am sure that Alphina (9), Betty (10), Candida (12), and Dee (14) will soon change from horribly cute little schoolgirls to smart young ladies and superior mothers, I must confess that their pert pictures irritated me to such an extent that finally I gathered them one by one and dumped them all in a closet under the gallows row of their cellophane-shrouded winter clothes. In the study I found a large picture of their parents, with sexes reversed, Mrs. G. resembling Malenkov, and Mr. G. a Medusa-locked hag, and this I replaced by the reproduction of an early Picasso: earth boy leading raincloud horse.[11]

We reach this second Picasso by way of an important set of photographs: family portraits of the Goldsworths, young and old. In replacing the photo of the judge and his wife with this second Picasso (also a picture representing two figures), Kinbote is making certain claims about the nature of the two representational forms, painted and photographic; in so doing he also reveals more about himself than he intends.

---

[11] Nabokov, *Pale Fire*, 83.

What does Kinbote find so objectionable about the photo of Judge and Mrs. Goldsworth and those of their four daughters, causing him to stash them away, out of sight? Evidently, he wishes to remove all traces of the Goldsworth family's presence in the house. This section of the novel is littered with similar examples — Kinbote deliberately ignores housekeeping instructions left by his landlord, even shipping out the family cat upon an unwilling cleaning lady — all of which suggest a kind of displacement anxiety on the part of this man recently arrived from a foreign country. To alleviate his feeling of exile, Kinbote pretends that he is the owner of the house, and so refuses to play the part of a tenant. To sustain this fantasy he removes the "evidence" of his landlord's presence (the photograph), replacing it with the reproduction of a painting that mocks the double Goldsworth portrait (the two austere, elderly, confusingly gendered figures replaced by the youthful, noble figures of the horse and the nude boy), and nostalgically recalls the Zemblan past, when a Picasso hung from the King's wall, long before Kinbote was plunged into exile.

But Kinbote's anxiety over the Goldsworth photos runs even deeper. They do not simply act as another reminder of the owner's presence in what our narrator pretends is his own home, as do the cat and the notes on housekeeping littered about the place, but also as evidence of Kinbote's utter alienation and exile in this new, unfamiliar environment. His isolation functions on two registers. First, there is a specifically sexual element to Kinbote's anxiety over these photos of the model heterosexual family. Let us look again at the names and ages of the four daughters: "Alphina (9), Betty (10), Candida (12), and Dee (14)." As one critic has observed, "the reversed order of daughters and letters implies a deliberate countdown, a comically confident case of family planning," as if it were anticipated from the time of Dee, the eldest daughter's birth, that there would be four female children, evenly spaced out, to complete the alphabetical "countdown."[12] Kinbote is "irritated" by the "pert pictures" of these wholesome American schoolgirls because they are emblematic of the entire ritualized process of procreation from which he, as a homosexual, is excluded. Even as the photographs hold the girls at a point of pre- or early-pubescence, Kinbote can readily imagine a near future when they will become "smart young ladies and superior mothers," and so continue the ceaseless process of generation, as Judge and Mrs. Goldsworth have done before them. For Kinbote, a gay man who perennially teeters between hedonistic abandon and suicidal despair over his sexuality, the adjacency of the picture

---

[12] Boyd, *Artistic Discovery*, 97.

of the Goldsworth parents to those of their growing children impresses too horribly upon him the heteronormativity from which he is excluded. When we speak of Kinbote as an "exile" in the moment he discovers and then hides these photographs, we are referencing two forms of exile: exile from home, from Zembla, and also exile from any kind of sexual agency or liberty in the decidedly conventional, heteronormative world of the New Wye intelligentsia.

The impending maturity of the Goldsworth girls also tells us something specific about how a photograph portrays its referent, the human being(s) captured within its frame. The photos make Kinbote anxious because of the very *impermanence* they signify, their status as placeholders of a moment that is gone as soon as it is captured. The faces of these girls are sickening to Kinbote, for in their smiles he sees anticipation of their heterosexual, procreative futures, peeking out of the photographic frame and refusing to remain still. Here referentiality works in a very different way than the referentiality of a painting. By giving us the recorded moment in its actuality, in its overwhelming presence as an apparently pure and unmediated representation, the photograph enacts a certain disconnect between the moment that is recorded and the moment of viewing. The very fact that the image is a clear representation of one unique instant serves only to emphasize that this captured moment is always past, that the individual caught in the frame is no longer the same individual at the time of viewing. This referential anxiety "irritates" Kinbote, as he is unable to contain the Goldsworth girls to their photographic images, to a permanent childhood.

When Kinbote stashes the photographs away and hangs in their place a print of Picasso's 1906 *Boy Leading a Horse*, he is working to overcome his feelings of geographical and politico-sexual exile by way of an unarticulated presupposition about the differing natures of photographic and painterly representation. He is horrified by the referential fragility of the photographs,[13] their presence forever hovering on the edge of absence, as Goldsworths young and old continue the fluid cycle of sexual reproduction. In the Picasso print with which he replaces the Goldsworth photo, Kinbote seeks out a permanence and stillness which recall the glory days of old Zembla, where

---

[13] By "referential fragility" I mean that the referent(s) of the image (in the case of these photos, the different members of the Goldsworth family) are fragilely held by the frame. The person referred to by the image is fully present within it, because (so it is believed) the camera captures the actual person without the mediation of artistic interpretation; *and* this referent is absent from the frame, because the uniqueness of this one past moment can never capture the individual in any timeless, essential image, for the individual is always pushing off into the future.

Illustration 2: Picasso's
Boy Leading a Horse, 1906

true art is fixed and absolute, and the youth of a child can be captured in its essence and intransience. The noble figure of the boy appeals to Kinbote not only because his sex and his state of undress suit our narrator's taste rather better than the Goldsworth girls, but also because of what he considers the eternality of this boy's youth, its stubborn refusal to be caught up in the temporality of procreation.

If the referential fragility of the photograph stems from the fact that the image is always assigned to a definitive past moment, the Picasso painting suffers no such fragility. Abstract and non-objective in its presentation, it has no individualized referent, so that the boy and the horse can rise to the level of essence, free from the temporal problem of photography. This boy is the essence of boyhood, this horse the essence of horseness. There is no implication that they exist in any other form; no fear that they will escape these essences, escape the fixity and permanence Kinbote assigns to them. This desire to essentialize can be noted in the (perhaps unconscious) alteration and extension Kinbote makes to the title of the painting: from *Boy Leading a Horse* to "earth boy leading raincloud horse." What this sometimes observant critic has evidently noticed here is that *Boy Leading a Horse* is a painting of two tones: the gray of sky and horse, the dusty orange of earth and boy. Each figure is perfectly at one with his environment, the horse with its head in the clouds and the boy firmly planted on the orange earth, in a permanence that must be the envy of the estranged Kinbote. His extended variation on Picasso's title serves to further essentialize these two figures, to mark them as immutable, forever youthful, and perfectly at home in their surroundings.

This painting works for Kinbote in much the same way as Nabokov used paintings in his Cornell lecture, with the suggestion that "the element of time does not really enter" into the experience of regarding a painting. Kinbote believes he has overcome the temporal problem of photographic referentiality with this painting of two abstracted, essentialized figures, a painting that links back to the Picasso hanging on Charles Xavier's wall in pre-revolutionary Zembla.[14] If photographs present Kinbote's text with a temporal problem, as they fail to contain their referents in time, then this painting offers a temporary alleviation of his anxiety over this problem. Having no specifically definable, temporally contingent referent, Kinbote's "earth boy leading raincloud horse" exists outside time, as an essentialized representation of youth and the permanence of art.[15]

The intransience and stability that the Picasso images signify for Kinbote are not enough to fully assuage his paranoia, however. While he attempts to set the nobility and purity of *Boy Leading a Horse* against the impermanence

---

[14] We may also observe that, even as the temporal movement of Kinbote's narrative has the Zembla scene occurring some years prior to our narrator's arrival at the Goldsworth house, the production dates of these two Picassos move in the opposite direction. *Still Life with Candlestick*, from 1945, would have been a very new painting when Charles Xavier had it on his wall; *Boy Leading a Horse*, from 1906, is over fifty years old when Kinbote uses it to replace the Goldsworth photograph. Time simultaneously moves forwards and backwards, and in the context of Kinbote's presentation of them, neither painting is ascribed a greater "modernity" than the other; instead, they are each seen as uniting past, present and future in the permanence of art, a permanence that can overcome Kinbote's anxiety over his personal exile and over the referential fragility of photography.

[15] Unlike a photograph, which must by its very nature have such a referent; being always contingent upon the specific object(s) it captures, objects which—whether living or inanimate—move and change in time.

and discomforting veracity of the Goldsworth photos, the painting is not entirely convincing in that role. It is, after all, a "reproduction," a copy among thousands of copies of this painting.[16] If a painting, even one of such essential power as this one, can be endlessly copied and reproduced (almost as if it were a photograph), then the refuge from reality that Kinbote desires to find in the immutability of painting is likely to prove fragile. To compensate for this problem, Kinbote must return to photography and make its problems—its fragility, its impermanence, its claim to a kind of artless, unmediated veracity—work *for* him, in support of his own narrative.

The first such attempt comes in this same scene of Kinbote's initial arrival at the Goldsworth house. While the family photographs cause him great anxiety, it seems that some other photos he finds as he snoops around his landlord's home have quite a different effect.

> The head of this alphabetic family had a library...but this consisted mainly of legal works...All the layman could glean for instruction and entertainment was a morocco-bound album in which the judge had lovingly pasted the life histories and pictures of people he had sent to prison or condemned to death: unforgettable faces of imbecile hoodlums, last smokes and last grins, a strangler's quite ordinary-looking hands, a self-made widow, the close-set merciless eyes of a homicidal maniac (somewhat resembling, I admit, the late Jacques d'Argus), a bright little parricide aged seven ("Now, sonny, we want you to tell us –"), and a sad pudgy old pederast who had blown up his blackmailer.[17]

Numerous hints are given throughout *Pale Fire* suggesting that Judge Goldsworth is an especially punitive dispenser of justice, casting "terrifying shadows...across the underworld,"[18] and this "morocco-bound album" suggests that he takes a certain sadistic pleasure in sentencing felons. When Kinbote finds the album and looks through it, he takes a similar pleasure in regarding the photographed faces of the criminals, many of whom, it seems, were executed not long after their photos were taken (as is indicated by those "last smokes and last grins"). In his disturbingly light-hearted descriptions of these photos, Kinbote amusedly contrasts the banality of the images with the horrific violence described in the accompanying texts, the "life histories" of the individuals behind the pictures, as when a pair of "quite ordinary-looking hands" is imbued with meaning when the accompanying text (perhaps from

---

[16] See quotation above (Nabokov, *Pale Fire*, 83): "this I replaced by the reproduction of an early Picasso."
[17] Ibid., 83-84.
[18] Ibid., 85.

a newspaper clipping or court document) informs Kinbote that they belong to "a strangler." Similarly, the bland images of a lone woman, a smiling young boy and an old man become, through the text, a mariticidal wife, a seven-year-old parricide, and a child rapist, respectively.

Flipping between the pictures and the text in this perverse scrapbook, Kinbote experiences a feeling of mastery and control in direct contrast to the anxiety he felt with the family photographs. If the photos of the Goldsworths made Kinbote anxious due to the impermanence they signified—tauntingly reminding him that the subjects are not contained in or by their images but will live on into "superior motherhood"—the finality of the images captured in the scrapbook gives him pleasure as he regards them, a pleasure derived from the feeling of mastery. For what awaits these people is not participation in the maddening cycle of heterosexual procreation, but death or imprisonment. This bleak future is signaled by the texts which, in telling the various characters' "life histories," also indicate their future prospects under Judge Goldsworth's sentence. The accompanying text fixes the meaning of the images: this person committed an appalling crime, was caught, and will be punished.

The more we learn about Kinbote, the more paranoid and fearful for his own safety we discover him to be. We have already noticed the anxiety he experiences from photographs that remind him of his civil and sexual disenfranchisement. When viewing the scrapbook photographs, however, the limiting power of the written texts enables him to experience mastery over the mortal fear that plagues him, as he sees himself in distinction from these captured (in both senses of the word) individuals. The pictures have their possibilities cut off by the text which Goldsworth has pasted into the book alongside them, just as the futures of these people have been cut off by Goldsworth's sentencing. The impermanence signified by the photos, their inability to truly *freeze* the subject in time, here works to overcome Kinbote's anxiety; the impermanence of the captured moment states that this person is now (at the moment Kinbote looks at the album) dead or incarcerated, the photo has not preserved them and they will not multiply.

To continue our discussion, a theoretical model will help to make sense of how photographs are functioning in *Pale Fire*. In his book *Camera Lucida*, Roland Barthes distinguishes what he calls two "elements" of the photograph. The first of these elements, the *studium*, is "a field of cultural interest," appealing to the intellectual curiosity of the viewer who gains some measurable cultural knowledge or experience from his encounter with the photograph, just as other forms of representation may communicate certain cultural knowledge. The second element, the *punctum*, is "that unexpected flash which sometimes crosses this field," "punctuates" the studium, disrupting the viewer in his pursuit of knowledge by presenting him with a certain stray detail that is inassimilable to the sensible, ordered meaning of the studium. The punctum "pricks" the viewer, draws him out of his position as the critical cultural observer, and addresses him directly, without mediation.[19] One of the most powerful examples Barthes gives of these two elements is based on his analysis of a photograph of a condemned prisoner, which he observes much as Kinbote observes the pictures of the condemned in Goldsworth's album.

> In 1865, young Lewis Payne tried to assassinate Secretary of State W.H. Seward. Alexander Gardner photographed him in his cell, where he was waiting to be hanged. The photograph is handsome, as is the boy: that is the *studium*. But the *punctum* is: *he is going to die*. I read at the same time: *This will be* and *this has been*; I observe with horror an anterior future of which death is the stake. By giving me the absolute past of the pose (aorist), the photograph tells me death in the future. What *pricks* me is the discovery of this equivalence.[20]

Illustration 3: Lewis Payne awaiting execution, photographed by Alexander Gardner, 1865

---

[19] Roland Barthes, *Camera Lucida: Reflections on Photography*, trans. Richard Howard (New York: Hill and Wang, 1981), 95.
[20] Ibid., 96.

As Kinbote looks at the photos of "last smokes and last grins," he too reads: *This will be* and *this has been*. Capturing an entirely discrete, isolated moment in time (what Barthes calls "the absolute past"), the photograph announces itself *as* past, as a moment which is gone—*this has been*. In so doing, the photographic image projects the viewer (Barthes or Kinbote) forward into a future from which it is absent because, at the moment of viewing, the photographed moment is always already gone, always dead—*this will be*. The Gardner portrait of Lewis Payne and Goldsworth's "last smokes and last grins" intensify this effect of the photographic image, for the figures they hold in their frames are quite literally absent from the present world. However, as Barthes reminds us, "Whether or not the subject is already dead, every photograph is this catastrophe."[21] With these photos, unlike those of the Goldsworth family, the punctum pricks Kinbote not with "horror," as the Payne photo pricks Barthes, but with pleasure derived from mastery, as he sees his own life, his own state of *being alive*, set aside in relief by the "anterior future of which death is the stake" for the photographed felons.

Kinbote uses the referential anxiety evoked by these photos for his own benefit, to mark himself as distinct from the condemned individuals captured in them. Kinbote does not have his "life history" written out in any scrapbook, nor is his future fixed to one of death or incarceration. Closing the book on Goldsworth's convicts, he remains secure in his mastery over death, a death to which they are sentenced and from which he is excluded. But lurking among these scrapbook photos is one that stands out distinctly from the others in the description Kinbote gives of it: "the close-set merciless eyes of a homicidal maniac (somewhat resembling, I admit, the late Jacques d'Argus)." The relation between text and image is not the same with this photograph as with the others in the series. Here Kinbote does not suggest a pictorial banality set off by a more sinister textual description; rather, the "close-set merciless eyes" of the photographed individual signify that there is something horrific about him even before it is revealed that he is a "homicidal maniac." Kinbote sets up this photo as distinct from the others by suggesting that its horror emanates from the picture itself, rather than from the "life history." Even more unsettling is the parenthetical remark that follows this description. What is special about this particular villain, and what does Kinbote mean when he "admits" (to whom is he admitting, anyway?) that the man "somewhat resembl[es]" somebody named Jacques d'Argus?

[21] Ibid.

The name "d'Argus" appeared a few pages previously in Kinbote's commentary: "Jakob Gradus called himself variously Jack Degree or Jacques de Grey, or James de Grey, and also appears in police records as Ravus, Ravenstone, and d'Argus."[22] "Jacques d'Argus," then, is an alias of Jakob Gradus, member of the Zemblan Extremist party, would-be assassin of King Charles Xavier II. Apparently Kinbote sees some resemblance between Gradus and the "homicidal maniac" he observes in one of Goldsworth's pictures. The significance of this resemblance can only be apparent to the rereader of *Pale Fire*, the reader who has returned to this point in the text after having reached the end: that reader who, in the words of the Nabokov of the Cornell lecture, "behave[s] towards a book as...towards a painting."[23]

We will here delay our rereading of this moment until we have reached the conclusion of the narrative in our own reading, and to do so we must delve deeper into the centerpiece of Kinbote's narrative, the Zembla story. By the time we return, we will have serious doubts about the idea that this act of rereading can ever achieve the true "vision" that Nabokov claimed for it in the Cornell lecture.

But to enter Zembla is not to leave behind the Goldsworth photographs. Rather, they are with us at the very point of entry into that world, for they are the locus of the *origin* of the Zembla narrative. Let us consider again the names of Goldsworth's four daughters, whose photographs so madden Kinbote, causing him to stash them away in a drawer: "Alphina (9), Betty (10), Candida (12), and Dee (14)." We have already remarked how the reverse order of names and ages indicates an elaborate design on the part of the Goldsworth parents, who have apparently anticipated the number, age and sex of their children from the time their first was born. But there is further design at work here. As several critics have noted, the names of these four girls seem uncannily similar to the names of the four members of the Zemblan royal family: King Alfin, Queen Blenda, their son Charles, and his wife Disa.[24] Just where has Kinbote's Zembla come from? If the names of its primary characters have been derived from the Goldsworth photographs, it would seem that the entire story, including the existence of Zembla itself, may have been imagined and created by Kinbote.

If "Alfin" and "Alphina," with a hint of "alpha" in their first syllables, suggest origins, then it is significant that the first extended Zemblan note in

---

[22] Nabokov, *Pale Fire*, 77.
[23] Nabokov, *Lectures*, 3.
[24] See Boyd, *Artistic Discovery*, 97.

Kinbote's commentary chiefly concerns King Alfin and, in so doing, acts as the originary moment of King Charles's life story. This note is figured around yet another set of photographs. Just as the lingering memory of the Goldsworth photos unconsciously influences Kinbote as he writes the Zembla story, so too will photographs play a major role in the very foundation of the Zembla he gives us—for, as we shall see, the mature life of King Charles, the hero of the Zembla saga, is born out of an encounter with photographs, an encounter similar to Kinbote's experience with the Goldsworth pictures.

As Kinbote develops the Zembla narrative alongside the story of his friendship with John Shade, his shaky hold on the reader's trust becomes increasingly difficult to maintain. If we are to be convinced that the story of King Charles Xavier II truly has influenced the writing of Shade's poem, as is Kinbote's wish, we will need greater evidence than we have so far been given. In a note to some lines from "Pale Fire" concerning the author's parents, Kinbote attempts to establish a point of sympathy between Shade and King Charles when he writes that, like Shade, the King "was unable to recall his [father's] face."[25] Both of their fathers died when they were children, and the memory of them faded as these boys grew into men. Shade describes the experience of this loss: "I was an infant when my parents died...I've tried / So often to evoke them that today / I have a thousand parents."[26]

There is a poignancy to Shade's realization that the mental effort of attempting to resurrect a faded memory has the effect of creating an infinity of phantom memories that lead him further and further away from any true image of his parents. At the same time, a certain compensation for this loss comes in the fact that his imagination can conjure "a thousand parents," and this joyous reveling in the inventive power of the human mind becomes, for Shade, more powerful than any traumatic memory of an originary loss.[27] The subtlety of Shade's understanding of memory, oscillating as it does between poignancy and playfulness, is emphasized in his use of the verb "to evoke" in describing his act of recollection. Kinbote unwittingly brings out the

---

[25] Nabokov, *Pale Fire*, 101.

[26] Nabokov, "Pale Fire," lines 71-74, 35.

[27] We might read something of Shade's (and Nabokov's) anti-Freudianism into this ("I loathe such things as...Freud," Shade writes in the final canto of "Pale Fire" [67]), as he rejects the idea of an inescapable, originary trauma (the death of the mother and father), and suggests that the powers of memory and imagination are capable not simply of repeating the traumatic episode, but of overcoming it and turning it into a kind of joy. Nonetheless, the poignancy of memory's inability to capture the true image of the parents is felt here, even if Shade seems to take a certain pleasure in the compensation that imagination offers him.

significance of this verb for Shade when he comments, "My friend could not evoke the image of his father. Similarly the King, who also was not quite three when his father, King Alfin, died, was unable to recall his face…"[28]

Kinbote emphasizes the "similarity" of these two experiences of the father's death in order to supply evidence for his insistent argument that the story of King Charles provided the hidden theme for Shade's poem. Yet this supposed connection only emphasizes a greater difference—that between evocation and recollection, between "evoking an image" and "recalling a face." Shade's lines acknowledge that memory is tied to invention and to fantasy, and that when a memory is too distant to retain, the inventive side has to overcompensate, evoking a series of images—out of imagination, out of other, unrelated memories and mental images—thereby creating a thousand phantom parents in place of the real, loved and loving ones whose memories he can never (re)capture. Kinbote, on the other hand, reduces this complexity to the banality of "the King… was unable to recall his [father's] face," as if memory were a simple, knowable instrument, which either succeeds or fails in its attempts to "recall" external stimuli, to revive and relive them in the mind.

As Kinbote continues his reflections on King Alfin's lost memory, he quickly makes an appeal to photography in its capacity to maintain and recollect the past. Unlike Shade, who understands memory to be an act of invention and imagination, Kinbote will not relinquish his belief that memory works in terms of true, complete recollection, which can be aided and enabled by photography.

> Similarly the King, who also was not quite three when his father, King Alfin, died, was unable to recall his face, although oddly he did remember perfectly well the little monoplane of chocolate that he, a chubby babe, happened to be holding in that very last photograph (Christmas 1918) of the melancholy, riding-breeched aviator in whose lap he reluctantly and uncomfortably sprawled.[29]

The photographic image described here holds three figures: King Alfin in riding breeches, at the very end of his life; the infant Charles Xavier, held uncomfortably in Alfin's lap; and a chocolate monoplane, held in Charles's hand, most likely just before he devours it. The adult Charles looks at this photograph and sees his father as a strange figure for whom he has no referent in his memory. Yet, he remembers the chocolate plane "perfectly well." The role Kinbote seems here to assign to photography reflects the manner in

---

[28] Nabokov, *Pale Fire*, 101.
[29] Ibid.

which he understands the workings of memory: the photograph acts as a kind of alibi for memory, confirming King Charles's recollection of one figure (the chocolate monoplane) and his non-recollection of another (his father). *These two, long since consumed figures really did exist,* the photograph says to Charles. One of them remains in his memory, the other does not. The photograph serves as evidence not just of the existence of these two figures, but as evidence of Kinbote's conception of memory as "recollection," wherein "real things" are either remembered or forgotten. The place of fantasy, invention and phantoms is somewhere wholly outside both memory and photography. Photography is seen here as a full, true representation of reality, a reality that memory alternately holds or loses, but with which it always has a fixed relationship. A true event or figure is either remembered or not: the role of photography is to prove this truth, the role of memory to decide which truths are most important.

We begin to realize the relevance of the seemingly trivial chocolate monoplane as we learn about the events surrounding King Alfin's death: "A very special monoplane, Blenda IV, was built for [Alfin]...and this was his bird of doom."[30] Alfin died while flying this "very special monoplane," named for his wife and Charles's mother, Blenda. The chocolate monoplane held by baby Charles in the photograph, then, was presumably a model of this special plane, intended to remind the son of his father's daring exploits. Through this object, young Charles experienced his father's death, so poignantly that its memory stays with him long after the memory of his father has faded.

As the description of this death scene continues, the interplay between memory and photography increases in significance.

> Something went wrong, and the little Blenda was seen to go into an uncontrolled dive. Behind and above him, in a Caudron biplane, Colonel Gusev...and the Queen snapped several pictures of what seemed at first a noble and graceful evolution but then turned into something else. At the last moment, King Alfin managed to straighten out his machine and was again master of gravity when, immediately afterwards, he flew smack into the scaffolding of a huge hotel which was being constructed in the middle of a coastal heath as if for the special purpose of standing in a king's way. This uncompleted and badly gutted building was ordered razed by Queen Blenda who had it replaced by a tasteless monument of granite surmounted by an improbable type of aircraft made of bronze. The glossy prints of the enlarged photographs depicting the entire catastrophe were discovered one day by eight-year-old Charles Xavier in the drawer of a secretary bookcase. In some of these

[30] Ibid., 103.

ghastly pictures one could make out the shoulders and leathern casque of the strangely unconcerned aviator, and in the penultimate one of the series, just before the white-blurred shattering crash, one distinctly saw him raise one arm in triumph and reassurance. The boy had hideous dreams after that but his mother never found out that he had seen those infernal records.[31]

Two different notions of memory and memorial, of how to remember the dead, are at play in this extraordinary scene. On the one hand, the "tasteless monument" constructed under the orders of Queen Blenda disgusts Kinbote because it does not accurately represent Alfin's life and death. Kinbote is particularly irked by the "improbable type of aircraft made of bronze" that caps Blenda's monument. He cannot tolerate this implausibility, cannot accept as a memorial for the dead something that is not a perfect representation of the lived past. This constructed aircraft is not a realistic flying vessel, but a mere artistic representation of the monoplane in which Alfin died, one that does not achieve absolute veracity. Kinbote objects to what he deems its aesthetic ugliness (its "tastelessness") and its aeronautical "improbability," its inability to function, to fly. Alfin's plane, like Alfin himself, went up in flames, and this constructed monument can refer to it, but cannot wholly represent it. On the other hand, there are the photographs taken by Blenda and Colonel Gusev of the incident itself. Unlike Blenda's "tasteless monument," these pictures hold a claim to true representation. In them, Alfin and his monoplane are preserved, truly memorialized, and the photographs act as real evidence of what happened in a way that the monument cannot. Yet these photos do not work simply as representations of reality, preserving it in a fixed, permanent state. They are not the still, unified, atemporal paintings evoked by Nabokov in his Cornell lecture; rather, they are unsettled and unsettling images, and the memory of them (the memory of memories) haunts young Charles in his dreams.

In the photographs described in this note, we find two "models" of Blenda IV, or "Little Blenda," the monoplane in which King Alfin died. The chocolate plane, captured in the photo of Alfin and baby Charles, is a playful little model, perhaps mass-produced as a reminder to the King's subjects of his daring and heroism, and a particular enjoinder to his small son of the dashing, manly prowess to which he, as the next King, is expected to aspire. The replica atop Queen Blenda's "tasteless monument," on the other hand, is constructed after the accident that destroys both the plane and the King. It is a memorial for the past, whereas the chocolate plane is a symbol of strength, dominion, *presence*: a presence that is in the process of being passed on into the future, as the

[31] Ibid., 103-4.

chocolate monoplane is passed from King Alfin into Charles' greedy hand, to be consumed and finally incorporated into Charles's body.

Yet when, long after his father's death, Charles sees the photo of his father and himself with the chocolate plane in his hand, it acts as a memorial in a way Blenda's deliberately designed replica never could. Photographed at this fleeting moment prior to its expected consumption, the chocolate plane does what the scrapbook photos did for Kinbote, and what the Lewis Payne photo did for Barthes: it simultaneously says *this will be* and *this has been*. The moment captured in the photograph is what Barthes calls the "absolute past," a moment at which King Alfin *was* alive, cradling his son; a moment at which the chocolate monoplane still existed. By giving the viewer of this image "the absolute past of the pose," the photograph "tells [him] death in the future." The absence of both King Alfin and the chocolate monoplane from the present world—the present from which Charles views the image—simultaneously emphasizes the *this will be* (death, consumption) and the *this has been* (the moment, captured forever on film). Blenda's "improbable" bronze memorial cannot achieve this, for the "absolute past" of the lived moment is not present in it. The memorial can only signify absence by *announcing itself* as doing so. The photograph announces only that it has captured the "absolute past" of this historical moment, without the rhetoric of "commemoration" and memorial that Kinbote classifies as "tasteless."[32] In Barthes's terms, the chocolate plane is the punctum of this photograph, pricking Charles as he views it, because this perishable item confirms both the truth of the image and the transience of the moment it has captured, its absence from the moment of viewing.

Our viewer experiences a similar tension with the photos of Alfin's death and the temporal problem they signify.[33] The descriptions do not emphasize the horror of impending doom, but rather Alfin's proud ignorance of that doom, the strength he shows at the moment of his greatest vulnerability. Kinbote describes Alfin as "strangely unconcerned" in the moments that lead to his death, observing that "one distinctly saw him raise one arm in triumph and reassurance." Here the "absolute past" and "future death" of the photographic image appear as emphatically as could be imagined, separated as they are by

---

[32] We should also note the pun at work in this adjective, "tasteless," and what it suggests about the contrast in Kinbote's description between the *chocolate* monoplane of the earlier photograph (which is assuredly *not* tasteless) and this bronze replica.

[33] Just who "our viewer" is in this scene is far from clear. We get Kinbote's descriptions and reactions, yet what he claims to be describing are King Charles's reactions, not his own. Occurring shortly before Kinbote explicitly reveals himself as the King, this note, like that concerning Picasso's *Casserole émaillée*, foreshadows that revelation.

a matter of moments; yet the image of Alfin offers "triumph and reassurance" in horrible contrast to the "future death" which is the reality of the subsequent events. Alfin's raised arm is the punctum of the photograph for our viewer, as the chocolate monoplane was of the earlier image, but in this case the punctum functions on two registers: that of the *detail*, and that of *time*.

Barthes identifies two versions of the punctum: that of time and that of intensity. The punctum of form is always manifested in a particular, often marginalized detail of the image; the punctum of intensity occurs through the problem of time, the simultaneity of the *this will be* of future death and the *this has been* of the captured moment in its "absolute past." The punctum of intensity, for Barthes, is not provoked by a specific visual detail but by the viewer's recognition of something temporally *outside* the image, not within the frame. With these two Alfin photographs, however, we find that Barthes's two puncta become one: the punctum of form is inseparable from the punctum of intensity. For in these photos it is quite explicitly a formal *detail* (the chocolate monoplane; the raised arm of King Alfin) that *pricks* the viewer, elicits this "intense" response, and announces the *temporal problem* of the image. It is the very specificity of the detail that announces the temporal fragility of what is captured in the photograph, and the presence of a temporality that is outside the image. These details tell us something that the intended rhetoric of the image does not. In the chocolate monoplane photo, the detail interrupts what the central figures in the image offer us, which is essentially a conventional, traditional conception of temporality, generation, and death. The "melancholy" face of the father with his son in his lap offers a somber portrayal of family lineage and continuation in the face of mortality, and this portrayal, this order, is disturbed by the little plane that zooms by in young Charles's hand. The plane becomes a foreboding sign of Alfin's future demise, of the utter randomness and unpredictability of death.

In what Kinbote calls the "penultimate" photo of Alfin's death scene, the triumphant, reassuring gesture of the King's arm similarly offers a counter narrative to what appears to be the intended rhetoric of the image: to capture the King as he faces his fear in the final moment before death. If the image's intended rhetoric offers us a grand narrative, with the hero facing death in his moment of truth, then the detail or punctum interrupts this message to once more announce the impossibility of making meaning or signification of death. The detail gives us the absolute past (for Alfin's arm will not be raised any longer, not even a moment after the photo is taken) and so tells us death in the future, death that cannot be codified or made to signify any grand notion of royalty, family, or history.

Kinbote offers the Alfin photographs and his detailed descriptions as evidence of his story's validity, as prove of the existence of the Zemblan characters and of his entire narrative.34 But here he gets caught up in the same trap that the *Casserole émaillée* painting caught him in. Purporting to describe the experience of King Charles, a character in his story, Kinbote is carried away by his own loquacity to the point where he reveals more than he could reasonably know or feel as a mere observer. His precise knowledge of what happened on the day of Alfin's death and his anger about the "tasteless monument" provide only further evidence for a suspicion the reader has long had in mind: Charles Kinbote and King Charles of Zembla are one and the same. In describing the experiences of this other character, Kinbote has really been describing his own memories. Furthermore, these memories are not the pure acts of recollection that Kinbote claims them to be. It does not take long for the reader to unmask the next layer of our narrator's identity, to discover what Mary McCarthy calls "the real, real story" of *Pale Fire*.35 Neither Charles Xavier nor Zembla truly exist; the story is too fantastical, Kinbote too unreliable. The only way the Zembla narrative can make sense is if we see it as Kinbote's *invented past*, a delusional story in which an exiled academic imagines himself to be the deposed King of a fictitious country. Kinbote attempts to use these photographs as supports for the veracity of his story, but his detailed descriptions insist too loudly on their legitimacy, providing evidence only of their own implausibility.

As we have seen time and again, the images in *Pale Fire* work upon memory and imagination in a complex variety of ways, blurring the distinction between fantasy and memory, narrative and reality. The passages devoted to the Alfin photos do indeed work towards discrediting Kinbote's story, unmasking him as delusional, but it would be unwise to presume too quickly that the "real, real story" which appears to be uncovered here is any less subject to the problematics of memory and invention than the "surface" story. In the final section of Kinbote's commentary, photography rears its head once more, further eroding the separation between the real and the imagined, between New Wye and Zembla. In his note to line 894 of Shade's poem, Kinbote describes a conversation amongst a group of academics in

---

34 Additionally, we might say that the placement of these photographs within the narrative offers them as evidence of the relevance of King Charles's life to John Shade's poem. If Charles's father really did die in this way, then the parallels to Shade's own parents are too great to be ignored. Note also that Shade's parents were ornithologists (line 72), Charles's father an aviator, and the parallel (implicitly intended on Kinbote's part) that this suggests.

35 McCarthy, "A Bolt from the Blue," 17.

the faculty club lounge of Wordsmith University.[36] Among them is a visiting German lecturer, who, upon seeing Kinbote, insists that he bears an uncanny resemblance to a certain foreign monarch.

> [The visitor] kept exclaiming, aloud and under his breath, that the resemblance was "absolutely unheard of...I had [he added] the honor of being seated within a few yards of the royal box at a Sport Festival in Onhava...We have a photograph of him at home." [...]
> Shade: "Take my own case...I have been said to resemble at least four people: Samuel Johnson; the lovingly reconstructed ancestor of man in the Exton Museum; and two local characters, one being the slapdash disheveled hag who ladles out the mash in the Levin Hall cafeteria."
> "I would rather say," remarked Mr. Pardon—American History—"that she looks like Judge Goldsworth" ("One of us," interposed Shade inclining his head)...
> "What a pity I cannot prove my point," muttered the tenacious German visitor. "If only there was a picture here. Couldn't there be somewhere—"
> "Sure," said young Emerald and left his seat....
> [Emerald] returned with the T-Z volume of an illustrated encyclopedia.
> "Well," said he, "here he is, that king."[37]

If we accept the so-called "real, real story," then we must interpret this scene as a fiction invented by Kinbote. There can be no visiting professor who has seen King Charles at a "Sport Festival," and certainly no photographs of the King, either at this visitor's home or in "the T-Z volume of an illustrated encyclopedia," for King Charles and Zembla are nothing more than the creations of our narrator's fantasy. Once more, Kinbote makes an appeal to photography as a support for his story, offering these photos as authentic "memories" of the King. Once the reader knows enough to read *against* Kinbote, s/he can see through this ploy and understand the photographs in this scene as a Kinbotean invention, a last desperate bid for plausibility.

Yet, these invented pictures of King Charles are not the only photographs evoked in the above passage. Obliquely lurking in the midst of this discussion of "resemblances" is a photo we have seen before, a photo that confirms another resemblance. John Shade begins to list the four people he is often said to resemble, but is interrupted before he can reach the last member of this list, the second of two "local characters." Who might this character be?

---

[36] See the discussion of Picasso's *La Casserole Émaillée*, in the opening section, for an early reference to this note.
[37] Nabokov, *Pale Fire*, 265-268.

Regarding the "disheveled hag" at the University cafeteria, another colleague suggests she looks "like Judge Goldsworth."³⁸ Shade's response ("One of us") provides the clue here: if the cafeteria woman may be said to resemble Goldsworth as easily as Shade—she may look like "one of us" as easily as the other—then it may be inferred that Shade and Goldsworth look very similar indeed. Goldsworth is the fourth person on Shade's list, the second of the two "local characters" he resembles.

Shade and Goldsworth's resemblance, revealed so off-handedly here, is vital to an understanding of the major event of the novel, Shade's death. In the death scene, described in the final note of the commentary, Shade and Kinbote are walking together from the poet's garden towards the Goldsworth mansion, the house next door in which Kinbote resides, when a gunman fires at them and shoots Shade dead. As Kinbote narrates it, the assassin is Jakob Gradus (*alias* Jacques d'Argus), sent by his Zemblan Extremist party to kill the disguised King of Zembla, Kinbote himself. Gradus misses his target and accidentally kills Shade. But by piecing together the supposed "real, real story" behind Kinbote's narration from the bits of information he gives us, we reach a very different conclusion. The "real, real" killer is one Jack Grey, an escapee from an insane asylum who has come to seek revenge on Goldsworth, the man who sent him there. Grey approaches Goldsworth's home, sees Shade and Kinbote outside of it, and fires at Shade, mistaking him for Goldsworth, the man he resembles.

With this vital knowledge in hand, the reader is now able to comprehend the significance of Kinbote's earlier horror at "the close-set merciless eyes of a homicidal maniac (somewhat resembling, I admit, the late Jacques d'Argus)" from Goldsworth's scrapbook. Knowing now that Jack Grey more than "resembles" Gradus or d'Argus, and that Goldsworth committed Grey to the asylum, we can decipher (retrospectively, as rereaders) that this photo is of Grey himself. Grey's eyes are seen as "merciless" because his gaze signifies the collapse of Kinbote's fantasy. This photograph *pierces* Kinbote's entire narrative, acts as an irruption of the real into his story: Grey is Shade's killer, Gradus/d'Argus but a delusional reimagining of Grey constructed to fit into Kinbote's paranoid fantasy.³⁹

---

³⁸ This "hag," who resembles Goldsworth, recalls Kinbote's description of Goldsworth's photo, in which he sees the judge as a "Medusa-locked hag."

³⁹ Of the many aliases used by Gradus throughout Kinbote's narrative, it is significant that the one chosen by Kinbote at this moment with the Jack Grey photograph should be "Jacques d'Argus," recalling as it does the classical figure of Argus Panoptes, the thousand-eyed giant. A recurrent reference in Nabokov's fiction, Argus is invariably used to signify

The Jack Grey photo and the illustrated encyclopedia pictures are each metonymic of the story they represent: the "real, real story" and the Zembla fantasy, respectively. One exists, the other does not—that is the official story, the "truth" which the perceptive reader discovers upon close rereading.[40] Both photographs are inserted into the narrative for the purpose of defining this reality/fantasy distinction. In the first instance, the Jack Grey photo dissolves Kinbote's claims to mastery and disproves his account of the events of Shade's death. In the faculty club scene, Kinbote attempts to elide this difference by incorporating photographic evidence into his fantasy, through the image of young Charles Xavier found in an illustrated encyclopedia. The good reader or rereader's response to this is to uncover the falsity of the scene itself, to expose this entire scene as a desperate attempt to make fantasy real.

Yet, there is a paradoxical element here that cannot be overcome. If the faculty club scene is invented, then so too is the evidence that Shade resembles Goldsworth. The conversation that reveals the resemblance has to have been made up by Kinbote, the very person who most wishes to keep that resemblance hidden. Alternatively, if this scene truly did occur within the New Wye narrative, then how can we account for the presence of the encyclopedia photograph, confirming as it does the existence of King Charles and of Zembla? At this moment the two narratives (the fantastic and the real) collide in these two photographs, and collapse into one another.

Photography acts as the location of this confrontation, not just between one narrative and another but also between narrative itself and what I will call the banal but inescapable *presence* of the image. We might even call this a collision between *studium* and *punctum*, between literary narrative as a form that attempts to give order to its world, and photography as a force that undercuts such attempts, that "breaks or punctuates the *studium*," as Barthes has it.[41] In *Pale Fire*, photographs stand out as *details* in themselves, disturbing the narrative as any written description of an image must disturb the temporal process of written text as it lingers on an unmoving

---

a kind of self-conscious fear. In this instance, Kinbote's horror at the destruction this photo performs upon his story provides him with an Argus-like fear of being watched, as the real world comes to sweep over his fantasy. For other Argus references in Nabokov, see *Laughter in the Dark* (Indianapolis: Bobbs-Merrill, 1938) and "An Evening of Russian Poetry," *The New Yorker* 21.3, March 3, 1945.

[40] The discovery of Jack Grey's identity as the "true" Gradus dates back to one of the novel's earliest readers, Mary McCarthy, who focuses on the same "scrapbook" passage discussed in this essay (McCarthy, "A Bolt from the Blue").

[41] Barthes, *Camera Lucida*, 26.

object. The image exists within time, swept up in the temporality of narrative as it moves from one point to the next, and also outside of time, remaining as a specific *detail*, a physical form that does not permit the human figures within it to be swept up by the flow of temporality, as they must do in order to participate in narrative.

In his Cornell lecture, Nabokov nominates the timelessness and permanence of painting as an aspiration for literature. This aspiration, he claims, may be attained through rereading, an act which is supposed to overcome the "element of time" present in the text. In *Pale Fire*, Nabokov has restaged this interaction between forms of representation, raising the stakes with the introduction of another visual form, the photographic. Photography presents a problem for the concept of permanence as an ideal to which literature may aspire, for, as photos are represented in the novel, they lead both text and image astray from the identities assigned to them in the Cornell lecture. Even as the text demands rereading in order to be understood, the overlaying narratives of *Pale Fire* mock any readerly attempt to move from the position of a reader to that of a viewer who "takes in the whole picture."

A second, related claim of the Cornell lecture is the proposition that the experience of reading and rereading can be understood as a temporal movement from "the details" to "the whole," from the gradual accumulation of narrative information to the eventual *realization* of the entire "picture." In this essay, I have attempted to pose a different formulation of this relationship through my analysis of the images in *Pale Fire*. These details, these written images, do not work towards the realization of a permanent, stable, whole image of the work. On the contrary, details *puncture* narrative coherence, rupturing all attempts to bring a fixed order to the mass of information that makes up the text: the Jack Grey photograph deflates Kinbote's version of events, revealing that John Shade's death has nothing at all to do with Zembla and its exiled king; but then, just as this new, "real, real" construction of events appears to establish *its* order over the text, the "illustrated encyclopedia" photo ruptures it, and order disperses once more. In this sense, these photographs, these *details*, act upon the text in a manner analogous to that in which the punctum of an individual photograph (the chocolate monoplane in the photo of young Charles Xavier and his father; the raised arm in the photo of Alfin's death scene) acts upon the studium of the image. Details function to disturb and discredit all constructions of "the whole" and, as we reread, these details definitively stand out as disturbers of order, mocking all attempts to impose a "real story" upon the text.

The photographic image by its very nature pulls away from permanence, and in so doing it pulls text away from coherence, from any notion of true representation. Acting as Barthesian puncta upon the studium of narrative sense, *Pale Fire*'s photographs dare to do that which no "solution" to the novel's problems can allow for: to be *present*, as *details*, without an ascribable meaning, yet with significant, destabilizing effects. In the Cornell lecture, Nabokov desires that the reader "behave towards a book as...towards a painting," but with these photographic puncta there is no place for any kind of readerly "behavior." The reader cannot "behave" in any way towards the punctum, for the punctum does not call upon him as an interpreter of meaning, but speaks directly to him, pricking and puncturing his understanding as a reader and interpreter of the text. In their failure to bring about the solution they so tantalizingly suggest, *Pale Fire*'s photographs ultimately demonstrate the falsity of permanence and objective "sight" as an ideal for a text, or any form of representation.

John A. Barnstead

TWO NOTES ON *PALE FIRE*[1]

1

In the Index to his edition of *Evgenii Onegin*, Nabokov discreetly applies the techniques of aesthetically-motivated misdirection and pleonastic ostension so elaborately developed in the Index to his novel *Pale Fire*. An example of the first of these techniques is provided in the first edition of Nabokov's *Onegin*, volume four, page thirty-eight, where the entry for "Guriev, K." sends any investigator trying to locate mention of this particular individual in Nabokov's elaborate commentaries to volume two, page three hundred forty-six, where, however, no mention of any Guriev is found.[2] Instead, when we follow up the page reference, we find footnote ten to Chapter Three, Stanza IX, which contains an extended discussion of the Prévost translations of Richardson's

---

[1] First appeared in *Nabokov Online Journal*, Vol. I (2007).
[2] Alexander Pushkin, *Evgenii Onegin: A Novel in Verse*, 4 vols., trans. with commentary Vladimir Nabokov (New York: Bollingen, 1964).

Clarissa Harlowe and *Sir Charles Grandison*, together with samples of the contemporary French reaction to them. The note has no conceivable connection to Guriev. It is preceded, however, by the last three lines of footnote nine, which read "seulement les souffrances de l'amour, mais les maladies de l'imagination dans notre siècle (*De l'Allemagne*, pt. II, chapter 28)." Perhaps only one suffering from les maladies de l'imagination dans notre siècle will go in search of Guriev K.?

Be that as it may, how is the investigator to proceed? The brute force method would be to read the two volumes of the commentaries straight through in search of the requisite Guriev. Nowadays, of course, one could simply scan the text into the computer and then do a search on "Guriev" but, whatever the degree of prescience one might wish to ascribe to John Shade in line nine hundred seventy-four of *Pale Fire*, it hardly seems cricket to resort anachronistically to a technology which was unavailable to Nabokov's *Onegin* readers at the time of publication.[3] Alternatively, we might suppose that a typographical error of some sort has occurred, and proceed on the basis of the numerical equivalent of *Pale Fire*'s word golf by examining the volume and page numbers that result from assuming that one of the digits in the provided volume and page number is off by one.[4] This yields the following possibilities to be tested:

Possibility 1.1. Volume *one*, page three hundred forty-six: alas, volume one has only three hundred forty-five pages.

Possibility 1.2. Volume *three*, page three hundred forty-six: this is an extended comment on the Decembrist rebellion, with attention paid particularly to Grand Duke Constantine.

Possibility 2.1. Volume two, page *two* hundred forty-six: a discussion of the *Dnieper Rusalka*, drawing attention to Ivan Zhdanov's erroneous back-transliteration of Karl Friedrich Hensler as "Gensler," perhaps the inspiration for the herald/Gerald connection that gives Emerald/Izumudrov his first name in *Pale Fire*.

Possibility 2.2. Volume two, page *four* hundred forty-six: at last we strike emeralds—er, gold! The pertinent part of the note reads: "He was Pushkin's schoolmate; 'les fameux écrivailleurs [those notorious scribblers], Pouschkine et Küchelbeker'—thus Grand Duke Konstantin couples their name in a private letter to Fyodor Opochinin, Feb. 16, 1826, from Warsaw, asking about a Guriev, if he is their classmate."

---

[3] *Onegin* had already been delayed for some seven years since its completion, due to various publishing difficulties.

[4] Vladimir Nabokov, *Pale Fire* (New York: Vintage International, 1989), 262.

Clearly Nabokov knows more than he is stating in this note, since the index entry, albeit misdirected, lists "Guriev, *K.*" rather than simply "Guriev." Who was this Guriev, K., and why was Nabokov so circumspect in the information he provided about him?

Konstantin Vasil'evich Gur'ev (1800-1833), as it happens, was a classmate of Pushkin's at the Lyceum, from which he was expelled in 1813 for "дурное поведение" ("improper conduct"), according to most available sources. The nature of this "дурное поведение" is clarified by Henri Troyat in his romanticized biography of Pushkin as "Greek tendencies," i.e., homosexual conduct.[5] In 1833, Guriev was serving as second secretary in the Russian embassy in Constantinople. According to Baron M. A. Korf, Gur'ev "умер задолго до 1854" ("passed away long before 1854").

Troyat, author of the only biography of Pushkin to allude to the Guriev affair available (in English or French) at the time that Nabokov published his edition of *Evgenii Onegin,* provides an example of Nabokov's second technique: pleonastic ostension. When one searches for "Henri Troyat" in the Index of *Eugene Onegin,* volume four, page ninety-eight, one finds the entry: "Troyat, Henri, *see* Tarasov." Turning to volume four, page ninety-five, we find: "Tarasov, L. ('Henri Troyat'), ²138, 139; *see also* P., PUSHKINIANA: *Pushkin.*"

The first of the volume two citations labels Troyat's biography "a compilatory *biographie romancée,* tritely written and teeming with errors (*Pouchkine, 2 vols., Paris, 1946*)." When one follows "P., PUSHKINIANA: *Pushkin*" one is sent to "²138 & n-9..." The circle is complete — although Nabokov fails to mention Troyat's birth name, Levon Aslan Torossian, and presumably could not know of his future conviction for plagiarism, which did not prevent him remaining a member of the Académie française until his death, as its oldest member.

2

Perhaps it is Alfred Appel, Jr.'s remark on page thirty-one in his book *Nabokov's Dark Cinema,* to the effect that the note (entitled "Trivia") to line ninety-one of *Pale Fire* "quotes rather than parodies two ads from 1937 and 1949 issues of *Life,* since their absurdity cannot be outdone," together with his juxtapositioning of the two on pages thirty-two and thirty-three, accompanied by the text of the complete note from the *Pale Fire* Commentary, that has prevented otherwise admirably assiduous critics from examining the matter further. What more, one might have thought, could be adduced?

---

[5] Henri Troyat, *Pushkin: A Biography* (New York: Pantheon, 1950), 55.

If one considers the text of the description, the *ekphrasis*, as it were, of the 1937 *Life* advertisement, one finds that the information it contains produces a mental picture closer to figure 1.1 than to figure 1.2.

Figure 1.1   Figure 1.2

The description of the 1949 *Life* advertisement[6] is more comprehensive: compare figures 2.1 and 2.2.

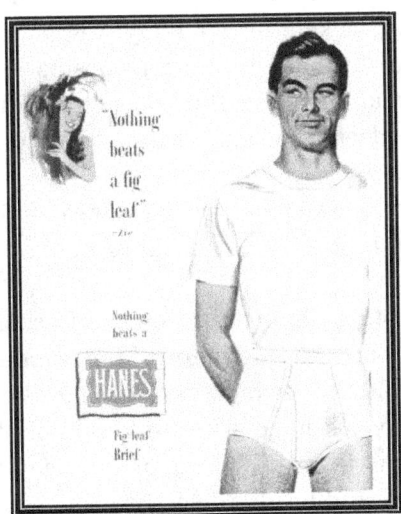

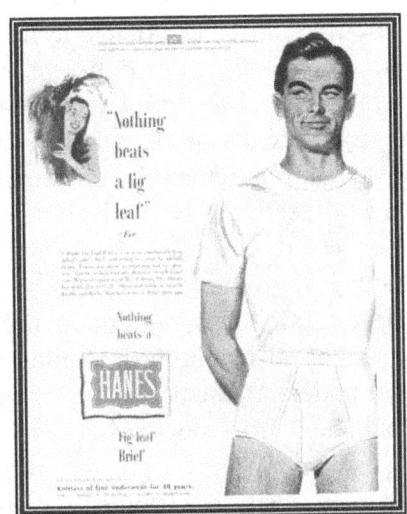

Figure 2.1   Figure 2.2

[6] *Life Magazine*, March 28, 1949, 127.

The pictorial, as opposed to the textual recreation of the 1937 advertisement is confined to a small portion of the left lower quarter; the advertisement itself is located on the right-hand page of the opened magazine. The visual apocope implied by the ekphrasis of the 1937 advertisement is particularly significant to the interpretation of line nine hundred seventy-four of *Pale Fire*; in light of which we can glean *two* versions of the word "right": in addition to the sense of "right" as "correct, proper," the line also has a directional/positional meaning, "right" as opposed to "left." A physical complementarity is established, then, between Kinbote, who concentrates almost exclusively on the *left* portion of the 1937 *Life* advertisement, and Shade, who states

> I feel I understand / Existence, or at least a minute part / Of my existence, only through my art, / In terms of combinational delight; / *and if my private universe scans right* [my italics] / So does the verse of galaxies divine / Which I suspect is an iambic line.[7]

It might also be noted that Aunt Maud, who presumably collected both advertisements, had suffered a stroke which clearly affected only one side of her body, since lines one hundred ninety-six through one hundred ninety-eight of *Pale Fire* state "We saw the angry flush / And torsion of paralysis assail / Her noble cheek" rather than her noble cheek*s*. Since she could still speak, it seems likely that the speech centre of her brain was *relatively* untouched by the stroke, implying that only the *right* side of her body was affected, presumably including her right eye, since the speech centre is located in the left hemisphere of the brain. Aunt Maud and Kinbote thus share a blindness to the right side of objects that reveals a deeper meaning when the 1949 *Life* underwear advertisement is considered.

In contrast to the 1937 advertisement, the 1949 ad for the Hanes Fig Leaf Brief is located on the *left* side of the magazine. The material printed on the *right* side is reproduced in figure 3.1.

Clearly, Kinbote's remark in the note to line ninety-one, referring to "clippings of an involuntarily ludicrous or grotesque nature," is a *model* of discreet understatement; although he amusingly juxtaposes the absurdities of the double-entendre slogans in the two advertisements, he outdoes himself by failing to mention the far greater grotesquerie in the pairing of an underwear advertisement with the gruesome pictures and lurid article about the suicide of Crown Prince Rudolph of Austro-Hungary.

---

[7] Nabokov, *Pale Fire*, 68-69.

Figure 3.1

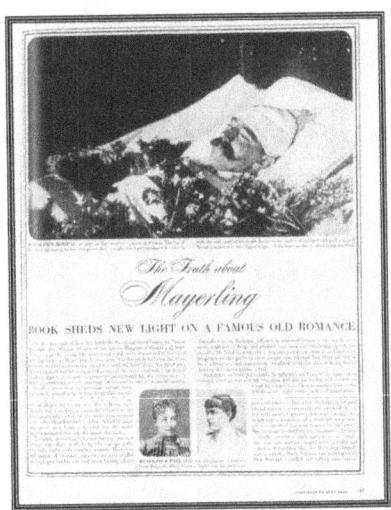

The article is, in fact, a review of Carl Lonyay's exposé, *Rudolph: The Tragedy of Mayerling*, which is described as presenting a different version of the death, "completely demolishing this romantic legend."[8] One may note the parallel between the caption to the picture of Rudolph's corpse lying in state at the emperor's palace in Vienna "flowers strewn over his trigger finger, which *froze in the crooked firing position*" and Kinbote's transposition to "his curved forefinger still directed towards the bell button he had just pressed" in his note to line one thousand (page two hundred ninety-three). One may relish the contrast between Kinbote/Charles the Beloved as a strict vegetarian, and Rudolph, "who liked to study the convulsions of dying animals."[9] Rudolph went Pushkin one better, and produced not merely a list of the women he had loved, but a *classified index*.

This new element connecting *Pale Fire* with the historical figure Crown Prince Rudolph of Austro-Hungary in the seemingly endless series of interlocking subtexts in the novel provides yet another illustration of Nabokov's unmatched ability to produce not just "a self-reflecting form, circular rather than linear, constituting its own autonomous and self-justifying world," but a work in which the question of whether art imitates life or life imitates art is rendered entirely unanswerable.

---

[8] Carl Lonyay, *Rudolph: The Tragedy of Mayerling* (New York: Scribners, 1949).
[9] *Life Magazine*, March 28, 1949, 127.

Juan Martinez

A FOLD OF THE MARQUISETTE: NABOKOV'S LEPIDOPTERY IN VISUAL MEDIA[1]

A book cover is a pragmatic affair, subject to a publisher's marketing concerns, and few authors exert any definitive degree of control over what is ultimately chosen. While some graphic artists, like Knopf's Chipp Kidd, work closely with writers, the cover has to fulfill needs that extend beyond the writerly domain to the financial responsibilities of the publishing company. Angus Philips identifies a few of the cover's functions including, among others, to target a reader and segment a market.[2] Whatever the cover's original intent, however, there

---

[1] First appeared in *Nabokov Online Journal*, Vol. III (2009).
[2] Angus Philips, "How Books Are Positioned in the Market: Reading the Cover," *Judging a Book by Its Cover: Fans, Publishers, Designers, and the Marketing of Fiction*, ed. Nicole Matthew and Nickianne Moody (Burlington: Ashgate Publishing, 2007), 22-23.

is no clean-cut separation of functions. The possible meaning inherent in one part of the book will frame our interpretation of other parts of the book. Covers, like other elements defined by Gerard Genette as paratexts, are capable of conveying vast amounts of information—such as highlighting certain facts about the author, or about the book's genre—while maintaining an illusory separation between form (a book cover illustration) and content (the book itself).[3] It bears repeating: this separation is illusory. A paratext may exist only outside a text, but it helps to determine the text's meaning, particularly when—as in Vladimir Nabokov's case—an image is closely aligned with the author. Butterflies follow Nabokov from cover to cover. That butterflies appear at all is not surprising, given Nabokov's lifelong, serious lepidopteral interest. But what are they doing? And why? And why are there so many of them?

In appropriating the signifiers of Nabokov's lepidopteral pursuits, graphic designers created a series of texts whose most salient messages borrow from traditional, folkloric associations of science to signify an integrated high aesthetic, an aesthetic composed of equal parts apoliticism, highbrow seriousness, and an objective, decontextualized mandarin artistry. This appropriation is seen in the movement from Nabokov's assertions about his dual pursuits—lepidoptery and literature—in published interviews to the visual depiction of these statements in a 1969 *Time* magazine cover, a 1998 *New Yorker* illustration, and a series of representative paperback and hardback covers. The designers appropriated the aura of science—its privileged position—to further reify Nabokov's extraordinary control over his critical reception and public image.

These associations, in turn, reassert received concepts of science, with the scientist as a neutral figure removed from the concerns and distractions of the real world, an understanding reinforced by the scientific community itself, as Charles Taylor and Thomas Lessl point out, to demarcate the community's uniqueness and superiority. The meaning in question is an informal, diffuse, and elusive popular understanding of science. This perception is informal because it presents itself indirectly, as do so many other mythologies. It is diffuse and elusive because its strongest quality is that it is assumed, never stated. As Barthes points out, myth relies on reassuring us of core values without ever resorting to explicit articulation; it is the thing that "*goes without saying.*"[4] This folkloric understanding of science, as Thomas Lessl

---

[3] Gerard Genette, *Paratexts: Thresholds of Interpretation*, trans. Jane E. Lewin (Cambridge: Cambridge University Press, 1997).

[4] Barthes, "Myth Today," *Visual Culture: the Reader*, ed. Jessica Evans and Stuart Hall (London: Sage Publications, 1999), 58.

writes, is tied to "various ideals of intellectual morality," which reinforce, through informal, often unattributed diffusion, a popular conception of the scientist's "rationalism, skepticism, and disinterestedness."[5] Science is understood to be set apart, not merely demarcated but also neutral, above any social concern. Indeed, it cannot be seen as superior without first being seen as essentially separated; as Taylor points out, "attributed superiority assumes a prior act of differentiation."[6] Embedded in the identity-forging narratives explored by Lessl and Thomas are many of the traits associated, rightly or wrongly, with the scientific field, and with the ways in which it is privileged: "Symbol systems devised by institutional cultures must be capable of saying to outsiders in some compelling fashion: '*This* is who we are, and *that* is who you are — behave accordingly.'"[7] Science, then, is commonly thought of as superior, rational, disinterested, neutral, difficult, and capable of inducing wonder and fear; it is not for regular folk; it is reserved for extraordinary individuals.

In stressing the link between art and science, and in blurring the line between his two pursuits, Nabokov claimed the privileged status of a scientist. In the first interview of *Strong Opinions*, Nabokov writes that his "pleasures are the most intense known to man: writing and butterfly hunting."[8] Nevertheless, when asked to respond to this statement, and to compare one pleasure to the other, Nabokov denies their connection: "They belong essentially to quite different types of enjoyment."[9] This distinction, however, is not consistent throughout the range of interviews; earlier Nabokov answered a variant of the same question with the statement: "in a work of art there is a kind of merging between the two things, between the precision of poetry and the excitement of pure science."[10] The statement is significant not simply because it blurs the traditional boundaries between the understood attributes of the fields (science is supposed be precise, poetry exciting), but also because, immediately before conflating art and science, Nabokov insists on separating one field from the other. "My interest in butterflies," he writes, "is exclusively scientific."[11] Nabokov achieves an extraordinary, highly

---

[5] Thomas Lessl, "The Galileo Legend as Scientific Folklore," *Quarterly Journal of Speech* 85 (1999): 148-149.

[6] Charles Taylor, "The Rhetorical Ecology of Science," *Defining Science: A Rhetoric of Demarcation* (Madison: University of Wisconsin Press, 1996), 19.

[7] Lessl, "Folklore," 147.

[8] Vladimir Nabokov, *Strong Opinions* (New York: Vintage Books, 1990), 3.

[9] Ibid., 39-40.

[10] Ibid., 10.

[11] Ibid.

persuasive act of self-definition: he claims access to two seemingly disparate fields, art and science; borrows the terminology and connotative aura of one to color the other (thus further reinforcing the uniqueness and rarity of science and its participants); and then stresses the demarcation between the fields. The artist and the scientist are both inaccessible. Nabokov may sound as though he is subverting the myth of the scientist, but he is not; he is merely laying claim to science's privileged status by associating his art with his science.

After the success of *Lolita*, Nabokov was able to exert a great deal of control over his interactions with mass media. In the foreword to *Strong Opinions*, Nabokov explained his criteria: "The interviewer's questions have to be sent to me in writing, answered by me in writing, and reproduced verbatim. Such are the three absolute conditions."[12] Given this statement, and given the passion and considerable space that *Strong Opinions* allots to butterflies — over forty general references to the insect and its hunt, with an additional score made to various individual species[13] — it is no surprise to find that Nabokov's authorial image has been linked to lepidoptery; the latter has become shorthand for the former. It is clear, moreover, that Nabokov was aware of this association and was actively involved in forging it.

Nabokov's deliberate insertion of a leitmotif does not escape his foremost biographer, Brian Boyd, whose "Nabokov, Literature, Lepidoptera" contrasts Socrates' connection to hemlock with Nabokov's connection to lepidoptery: "But while Socrates did not *choose* to be forever linked with hemlock, Vladimir Nabokov made butterflies his lifelong personal mark."[14] Boyd remarks on Nabokov's tremendous success in connecting the arc of his life to butterflies, one foreshadowed by a 1907 photograph of the writer posing in front of his butterfly-collecting books at age eight. Boyd also qualifies: "Yet designers who would not dream of picking hemlock for the cover of a new book on Socrates again and again pin butterflies to the lapel of Nabokovian jackets."[15] Indeed, the book that contains Boyd's comment, *Nabokov's Butterflies*, has a butterfly pinned to its jacket, though of course it is a volume devoted to the subject, but

---

[12] Ibid., xv.
[13] These butterfly references can easily be found in John DeMoss, "An Index to *Strong Opinions*," *Zembla*, Jeff Edmunds, ed., November 10, 2006, http://www.libraries.psu.edu/nabokov/demossp1.htm, starting with a simple search under "B," for butterflies, and moving on (as instructed by DeMoss) to individual species.
[14] Brian Boyd, "Nabokov, Literature, Lepidoptera," *Nabokov's Butterflies*, ed. Brian Boyd and Robert Michael Pyle (Boston: Beacon Press, 2000), 2.
[15] Ibid.

so do other scholarly works, such as *The Cambridge Companion to Nabokov* and *Imperia N.: Nabokov and Heirs*.[16]

More surprising are the cartoons, magazine covers, and book jackets where Nabokov and butterflies are conflated without an explicitly stated purpose—where no butterfly would be thought to be called for. Over fifty such texts are available, of which the following are striking and representative: a 1969 *Time* magazine cover, a 1970 Fawcett Crest *Ada* cover, the Vintage paperback reissues of the early 1990s, the hardcover and paperback variants of Nabokov's collected stories (Knopf 1995 and Vintage 1996, respectively), and a 1998 *New Yorker* cartoon of the writer.[17]

These visual artifacts share some striking patterns of meaning, which will be discussed below, although they were not chosen because of these patterns. Rather, they are worth a closer look because they provide a representative—if arbitrary—sample across a wide range of time, from the late 1970s to the late 1990s. They can also be safely assumed to possess what Roland Barthes defined as *intent*, an essential element of the advertising image (and one shared by most commercial graphic designers), since "the signification of the image is undoubtedly intentional; the signifieds of the advertising message are formed *a priori* by certain attributes of the product and these signifieds have to be transmitted as clearly as possible."[18]

Since these images were all vetted by relatively large committees, where clear commercial as well as communicative interests were at stake, they reveal an insistence on certain signifying undertones. These nuances are particularly striking in that none of the designers seem to feel a strong need to explain the butterfly images. They are treated as a kind of commonly understood shorthand, a sign from which a larger meaning (Nabokov's

---

[16] Julian Connolly, ed., *The Cambridge Companion to Nabokov* (Cambridge: Cambridge University Press, 2005); Yuri Leving and Evgeniy Soshkin, ed., *Imperia N: Nabokov and Heirs* (Moscow: New Literary Observer, 2006).

[17] Several websites feature Nabokov covers. One of the most exhaustive, Bert Smeets, "A Vladimir Nabokov Coverage," http://axxc.nl/vn/vn.htm (accessed January 8, 2009) offers a rich catalog of editions, many of which include butterfly imagery. While some of these are featured in the Appendix, the site contains far more illustrations; some, such as a series of Turkish paperbacks, use the butterfly as a recurring, readily identifiable motif: http://axxc.nl/vn/vn-tr.htm. (Vintage International, discussed below, does so as well.) Dieter E. Zimmer, "Covering Lolita," *The Dieter E. Zimmer Homepage*, November 6, 2008, http://www.d-e-zimmer.de/Covering%20Lolita/LoCov.html (accessed January 8, 2009) also provides a remarkable collection of *Lolita* book covers which—here and there, competing with nymphets in various stages of undress—also features some butterflies.

[18] Barthes, "Rhetoric of the Image," *Visual Culture: the Reader*, ed. Jessica Evans and Stuart Hall (London: Sage Publications, 1999), 33-34.

actual scientific contribution to lepidopteral taxonomy, for example) has been obscured. A traditional Barthesian examination of these images would denote the butterfly as the Signifier of Nabokov's entomological interests, which in turn would be the Signified; together, they would form a Sign. This is image-making, which Barthes would call "a mode of signification," a myth "constructed from a semiological chain which existed before it."[19] The undertones are often connected to other aspects of lepidoptery, so that it is not simply the iconography of the butterfly that is present but also the tools to collect and classify the specimen (the net and the pins). The movement from Nabokov's scientific life can be understood as the first-order semiological system — with a clear Signifier and a corresponding Signified — to its place as a kind of myth. Myth occurs, according to Barthes, when "what is invested in the concept [of the image] is less reality than a certain knowledge of reality; in passing from the meaning to the form, the image loses some knowledge." Barthes stressed that meaning is not fully erased, merely "impoverished."[20]

A trajectory similar to Nabokov's scientific background is translated into visual rhetoric. However, this conversion does not necessarily result in the impoverishment of meaning, erased and replaced by a kind of empty myth-making self-assertion, of Nabokov's science turned to window dressing, since in juxtaposing one to the other, the designers seem to be enriching the potential meanings of each connotative field. I am suggesting that in including signifiers of Nabokov's science in graphic design, the artists are following the same train of thought as that behind the writer's statement conflating science with poetry, so that the boundaries between art and science are intentionally blurred and, moreover, the roles traditionally assigned to one are passed to the other. Art enriches the connotative field of science and vice versa.

It is important to note that butterflies, in all of the visual texts under consideration, are never solely aesthetic objects. That is, they are never far from the scientific connotations associated with Nabokov's life. The first image, the 1969 cover of *Time* (Figure 1),[21] provides some insight into this connection.

The cover was occasioned by the imminent release of Nabokov's longest, most challenging novel, *Ada*, after the spectacular popular success of *Lolita* and the critical success of *Pale Fire*. On the cover, Nabokov's portrait is orbited by a smaller series of signifiers. From left to right, and considerably smaller than the towering, three-quarter depiction of an unsmiling Nabokov, we see

---

[19] Barthes, "Myth Today," 51, 53.
[20] Ibid., 53.
[21] *Time*, 23 May 1969.

Figure 1

Saint Basil's Cathedral; a small reproduction of a pencil portrait of Nabokov's mother; a large brown butterfly; three tiles of Russian *Scrabble*; and a small blue butterfly. The banner in the top-right corner of the cover reads, "The novel is alive and well and living in Antiterra," referring to the setting, *Ada*'s parallel universe. The small blue butterfly acts as an anchor to the illustration, the last place one's eyes will rest as they travel from top to bottom and from left to right. The butterflies are also significant in that they play a role in the novel (Ada, the novel's namesake, collects butterflies), while also contributing to the shifting identity of the author (since he is also an avid butterfly collector). The illustration blends aspects of Nabokov's personal life (the portrait of his mother) to those shared by both the fictive and the actual (the butterflies, the *Scrabble* tiles). It portrays Nabokov's disengagement from the orbiting visual elements, and is particularly interesting because it is so *serious*.

This seriousness signifies "important." The *Time* magazine banner suggests that the novel is not dead; it is "alive and well" in an age where so many writers and critics were preoccupied with the death of the form, a common complaint at this time, one not limited to the novel. Jean Luc Godard, a year earlier, declared the death of cinema in the end titles of *Week End*.[22] The

---

[22] Jean Luc Godard, *Week End* (France: Script Director, Jean-Luc Godard; Music, Antoine Duhamel, 1967).

Figure 2

Anti-Novel, as exemplified by Alain Robbe-Grillet, was still in vogue, as was the formalist and fabulist fiction of John Barth, Thomas Pynchon, and Donald Barthelme (among others) — all authors who questioned the idea behind a traditional, mimetic approach to fiction. Barth titled his 1967 essay on his work and that of his peers "The Literature of Exhaustion," which suggested (somewhat misleadingly) dead-ends and depletion.[23] Nabokov's portrait in *Time* suggested a renewal and an alternate entryway into novel-writing. A serious, unsmiling Nabokov carried with him a seriousness of purpose — saving the novel.

The unsmiling Nabokov also suggested what Amy Reading, in analyzing the 1962 *Newsweek* Nabokov cover (Figure 2), described as the "indisputably highbrow" connotations of any literary endeavor. With "Nabokov frowning into the middle distance of writerly inspiration beneath the smiling visage of Sue Lyon," we have the author of *Lolita* turning away from the actress who played Lolita in the Stanley Kubrick film adaptation.[24]

Nabokov's disengagement from Sue Lyon in Figure 2 is similar to that shown in the *Time* cover in Figure 1. These images can be viewed as

---

[23] John Barth, "The Literature of Exhaustion," *The Atlantic Monthly*, August 1967, 29-34.
[24] *Newsweek*, 25 June 1962. Amy Reading, "Vulgarity's Ironist: New Criticism, Midcult, and Nabokov's *Pale Fire*," *Arizona Quarterly* 62.2 (2006): 77.

indicative of the 1962 *Newsweek* and 1969 *Time* designers' understanding of what Reading terms "highbrow" art, an art deeply concerned with class connotations and just as deeply concerned with avoiding midcult status. To succeed as highbrow art, the image must portray the artist as a dispassionate creator, one who is above any crass commercial concerns.[25] This dispassionate quality—what may be considered a kind of objectivity in a highly subjective field—helps to explain the separation of the author's portrait from its surrounding set of signifiers. In *Time*, Nabokov's eyes are directed at the viewer while ignoring the whirling visuals of novel and life orbiting his face. In *Newsweek*, Nabokov is celebrated as the creator of *Lolita*, but his eyes are neither focused on the viewer nor on Sue Lyon.

This lack of engagement is commonly associated with a popular understanding of the scientist as a fully objective, fully neutral figure in a white lab coat, whose interaction with the outside world is never motivated by subjective forces. This figure exists both inside and outside of what Taylor deemed "the rhetorical ecology of science," a realm separate from political or social constraints, carved off from other pursuits and performed in a kind of inviolate black box.[26] By conflating the seemingly irreconcilable claims of art and science—the precision of one, the excitement of the other—Nabokov seems to be claiming the privileges of the latter for the former; he is insisting on the separate legitimacy of each field ("My interest in butterflies is purely scientific") while also disrupting these traditional demarcations. As such, when the *Time* and *Newsweek* designers underscored the image of the "highbrow" Nabokov as a disinterested figure, they were also borrowing, indirectly, from the traditional image of the objective scientist and of science "as a practice whose uniqueness from other pursuits, most notably politics, demanded special, even deferential treatment."[27]

Nabokov was, as *Strong Opinions* makes clear, self-avowedly apolitical. "I do not," he maintains, "have any neatly limited political views," though he also states that "what is bad for the Reds is good for me."[28] This stance is important in that it was widely considered one of the obstacles blocking Nabokov from a Nobel Prize in literature; according to a 1998 *New Yorker* article, the prize committee was assumed to be sympathetic to leftists and antipathetic to political conservatives. Of particular interest in the *New Yorker*

---

[25] Midcult would regard art as a commodity, as something to be consumed, while highbrow art would claim to be above commercial interests.
[26] Taylor, "Rhetorical Ecology," 19.
[27] Ibid., 3.
[28] Nabokov, *Strong Opinions*, 113.

Figure 3

Vladimir Nabokov is one of the most lamented non-laureates.

article is the accompanying cartoon (Figure 3), whose approach mirrors that of the *Newsweek* and *Time* covers.[29]

As in those images, most striking about this cartoon depiction of Nabokov is the seriousness and the disengagement of the pose. Nabokov has his arms crossed, and refuses to engage the viewer; instead, his attention is directed to a butterfly on the upper-right corner. The caption reads, "Vladimir Nabokov is one of the most lamented non-laureates." Here, Nabokov has a decidedly disinterested bent, and he seems more preoccupied with the butterfly than with the business of prizes. He may be a "lamented non-laureate," but none of the woe is coming from him. His attention is elsewhere. The cartoon's composition and Nabokov's depicted disdain echo Reading's definition of highbrow culture: it is fundamentally serious and avowedly disinterested. Nabokov's stance is to be understood as somehow above the concerns of ordinary citizens. This stance, again, finds some parallels in the commonly understood definition of the scientist, so that the signifier of Nabokov's scientific background—his interest in butterflies—is used to portray his neutrality, his apolitical nature, and his self-imposed removal from a race for a prize.

If the butterfly, when paired with a likeness of Nabokov, seems to reinforce some of the author's statements about his work, his politics,

[29] Michael Specter, "The Nobel Syndrome," *The New Yorker*, October 8, 1998, 50, 53.

and his interests, what happens to this sign when it is shown without the writer? The butterfly often appears on Nabokov book covers, and one can conclude that the designers make certain assumptions about the connection between Nabokov and the image of the butterfly. The first (safest and most basic one) is that designers assume that their audience will make a natural link between the writer and the butterfly. They may make this assumption because of the rich biographical material connecting one to the other. They may also simply work from an informal network of received knowledge. Again, Roland Barthes' concept of myth is particularly useful here, since the substitution of Nabokov for a butterfly works largely out of a shared connotative field; the man and the butterfly are so similar that one sign can substitute the other. Or, perhaps the butterfly signifies enough to contain the other. The butterfly, the designers may think, is all that is needed to evoke Nabokov. It is also possible that designers feel satisfied with the butterfly's impact—the butterfly fulfills its potential for signification both as an adequate emblem of the book's contents and a useful advertisement to market and sell it.

Most appealing to designers, perhaps, is that the butterfly is an inherently beautiful icon, with an easily recognizable outline and a colorful, symmetrical pattern. Also, the butterfly has been assigned, as Boyd points out, some of the same recurring thematic concerns that appear in Nabokov's fiction: the transcending of death, the possibility for change, the elusive and highly ornate nature of art, the complexity and specificity and harmony of nature.[30] But neither these correspondences nor the inherent appeal of butterflies can fully explain their inclusion in Nabokov-related graphic design. After all, as Boyd also indicates, "it would be perfectly possible to read a thousand pages of his best fiction...and another five hundred pages of his short stories and not even realize that he was a lepidopterist."[31] If anything, the substitution of the butterfly for Nabokov (or for Nabokovian themes) is rendered strange because it seems so natural, and because it happens so often and goes so unquestioned, particularly in a graphic context where the image often stands as the primary signifier with little, if any, contextual help. The designer, in other words, is assuming that the audience will be familiar enough with the connotative qualities of the butterfly to find the design rich in meaning, concordant with all rhetorical purposes, striking, and appealing.

[30] Boyd, "Nabokov, Literature, Lepidoptera," 19-21.
[31] Ibid., 17.

Figure 4

It helps of course that no book-cover image stands alone, so that the image of the butterfly is not the sole content-rich code in the visual artifact. Text is also included, often at the top, and it directs — or denotes — the possible meanings of the image, a function described by Barthes as pointing the viewer "towards a meaning chosen in advance."[32] Barthes explains that, in a primarily graphic environment, text acts as an anchor, since an image on its own is potentially "polysemous." Images "imply, underlying their signifiers, a 'floating chain' of signifieds, the reader [is] able to choose some and ignore others."[33]

Along with text, the two most important anchoring elements of Nabokov covers are the title and the byline. The butterfly image is anchored by both. In the case of the 1970 Ted CoConis illustration for the Fawcett Crest *Ada* cover (Figure 4), the text serves to further anchor the image: "The New Bestselling 'Erotic Masterpiece' by the Author of LOLITA."

[32] Barthes, "Rhetoric of the Image," 38.
[33] Ibid., 37.

Although the phrase "Erotic Masterpiece" is pulled from a *New York Times Book Review* (the full quote is reproduced on *Ada*'s back cover),[34] its major purpose seems to underscore the titillation of the image itself—a kaleidoscopic, vaguely psychedelic butterfly-shape composed of symmetrically arranged nude women. This image is only superficially different from the cover illustrations and the cartoon discussed above. While at first blush it may seem that this is a drastically different approach to the butterfly motif, it does share a preoccupation: the image's strict symmetry and its insistence on blurring the boundaries between one representation (the butterfly outline) and the other (the nude women) are both indicators of an apolitical, decontextualized mandarin aestheticism—one in which direct representation, and hence a direct appeal, is eschewed. The illustration is so highly stylized that it shares the previously discussed visual artifacts' remove from the actual.

The blurring of the signifiers—combining a series of nudes to create a butterfly—serves also as another indicator of highbrow seriousness. The image may be playful, but a careless viewer (the illustration warns) will miss the larger import. This caution is twofold. A casual glance at the cover may only reveal a butterfly. Too close an examination of the image may uncover the nudes, but the viewer may then miss the larger outline formed by the individual figures. Equally significant is the hybrid nature of the image. It echoes the fusion of Nabokov's public image as scientist and novelist, and the butterfly motif as a purely aesthetic, code-free visual but also shorthand for the double nature of the author, whose last name is cropped by the image.

This juxtaposition of Nabokov's name and the butterfly's wing creates a visual bridge. The reader will scan the page from top to bottom, moving from the initial, anchoring, denotatively-limiting blurb, to the large letters spelling out the title (*Ada*), to the byline and, in the byline, to the fusion of name to graphic—effectively moving from Nabokov to wing. There is a strong link between one and the other: Nabokov is closely linked to the butterfly, or (an equally likely connotation) the butterfly embodies many of the thematic concerns in Nabokov's life and works.

A similar interpretation may be applied to the uniform Vintage-edition paperback covers of the early 1990s, whose use of the butterfly image is more subtle; the butterfly is neither the dominating element nor expected to bear

---

[34] Vladimir Nabokov, *Ada* (New York: Fawcett Crest, 1970). Alfred Appel, "*Ada*: An Erotic Masterpiece That Explores the Nature of Time," *The New York Times*, May 4, 1969.

Figure 5

Figure 6

Figure 7

the bulk of the signifying force. Instead, it is a small component, acting almost as a punctuation mark or an arrow: it either serves as the final resting place for the eyes or it links disparate components of the design together. The Vintage covers for *The Defense* (Figure 5), *Bend Sinister* (Figure 6), and *The Gift* (Figure 7) are representative of the uniform series as a whole, though a few of the paperbacks — no more than three — do omit the butterfly.

The covers are usually dominated by a blurred and otherwise altered photograph that bears some relation to a theme or major plot point in the novel, along with a blurb. Nabokov's byline appears as a framing device on the upper-left in heavy, high-contrast font, so that the butterfly, particularly on the covers of *The Defense* and *Bend Sinister* (where it is placed on the bottom-right), acts as the byline's corresponding bookend: the name and the iconic butterfly together provide a kind of unifying logo for the series — the small butterfly as much a brand, a personal corporate trademark, as the Vintage logo on the bottom-left.[35]

On the cover of the Vintage paperback edition of Nabokov's collected *Stories* (Figure 8), a nearly complete butterfly outline is created by negative space stenciled out of the larger design of a butterfly wing.

This design — particularly the blank outline — shares some of the elements discussed above with respect to the other covers, but it is particularly

---

[35] Vladimir Nabokov, *The Defense* (New York: Vintage International, 1990). Vladimir Nabokov, *Bend Sinister* (New York: Vintage International, 1990). Vladimir Nabokov, *The Gift* (New York: Vintage International, 1991).

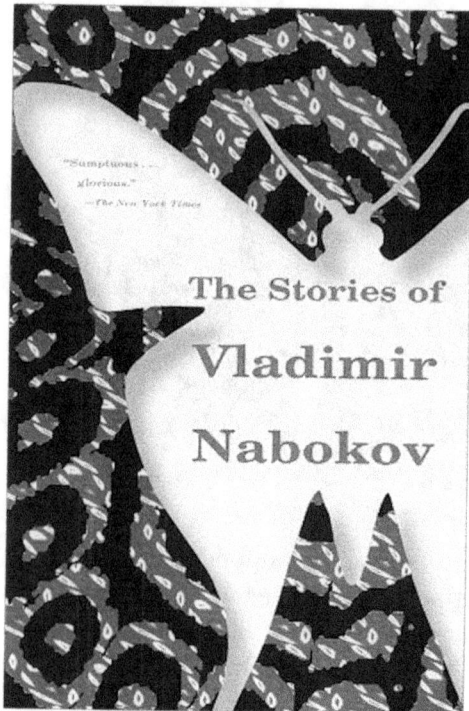

Figure 8

interesting in that the image is constructed out of two successive layers of butterfly imagery: a wing close-up and a butterfly outline. Moreover, the image is twice abstracted A recognizable butterfly pattern is made strange by removing all contextual clues; the reader can only see the pattern, not the wing on which the pattern would be imprinted. It is further abstracted by the creation of a white, butterfly-shaped field at the center of the design in which the author and title are presented: Nabokov, the author, framed by an outline of Nabokov, the lepidopterist. This abstraction and use of repetition is not far removed from the 1970 Fawcett Crest *Ada*.[36] Both stress the primacy of the image over any apparent or inherent intent; the image seems to exist primarily as a celebration of itself as an ornate, intricate representation. Both, however, also signify Nabokov. As on the *Ada* cover's cropping of byline to wing, the Vintage *Stories* cover joins the writer to the outline.

This fusion is perhaps more apparent if one assumes that the outline created by negative space has been cut out of the cover. That is, the silver and

---

[36] Vladimir Nabokov, *The Stories of Vladimir Nabokov* (New York: Vintage International, 1997).

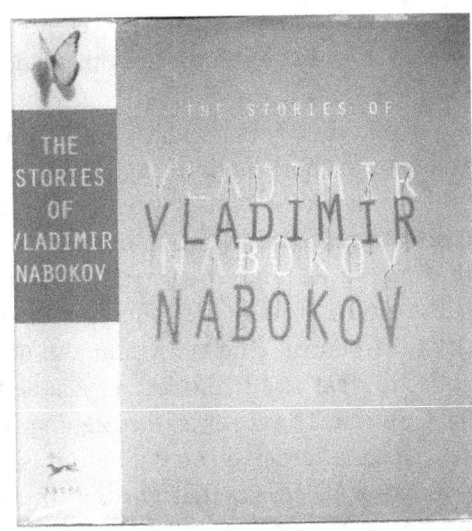

Figure 9

black pattern is the first layer, closer to the viewer, whereas the white of the butterfly shape is deeper; the *trompe l'oeil* effect is that of someone having cut into the book, revealing its contents. The book becomes a specimen box, the specimens being the individual stories. However, the connection between a butterfly collection and a story collection is made much more succinctly, and much more clearly, in the earlier, hardcover release of the same book by Knopf (Figure 9).

Nabokov's name is pinned to a blue background, each letter a specimen. Again, the designer deliberately blurs the line between artist and scientist. There is no longer the need, it seems, for the pictorial representation of the butterfly—its iconography, and the signifying force behind it (Nabokov's lepidopteral interests and accomplishments), are embedded in the collection tools. The designer's intent is clear, since a specimen collection is not terribly different from an omnibus gathering of a writer's short work. Moreover, in marrying at least two disparate meanings, the designer is again working with a backlog of visual knowledge commonly assumed of any Nabokov-minded reader: that the author was interested in the study and classification of butterflies. The letters, pinned to the background, become butterflies.[37] This easy—if dizzying—reversal of traditional iconography may not be exactly what Nabokov had in mind when he talked of "the precision of poetry and the excitement of pure science," but it highlights the shifting role of science

[37] Vladimir Nabokov, *The Stories of Vladimir Nabokov* (New York: Knopf, 1995).

in Nabokov's connotative aura. Here, as elsewhere, the butterfly points to the same values explored on the magazine covers, the *New Yorker* cartoon, and the paperback artwork.

The pinned letters are particularly interesting in that they present Nabokov's short fiction as subject to collection, categorization, analysis, and dispassionate observation. The absence of any human figures—even a disengaged human figure, a Nabokov portrait, for example, looking off into the middle distance—suggests a kind of absolute abstraction. So does the substitution of letters for pictures or photographs of butterflies. Not only is the field neutral (the color and the unseen source light are both mild), but so is the text itself: the letters are slim and contrast only slightly with the background. The cover is once again presented as part and parcel of highbrow seriousness. It may be playful, but it is playful without claiming any particular interest or place. Furthermore, in presenting a book of fiction as a scientific specimen, the design makes some of the same claims explored earlier; it is, as in the *Time* and *Newsweek* covers, declaring an authenticity traditionally associated with science.

This legitimacy has much to do with understood notions of the scientist as a disinterested observer. Nabokov, as a lepidopterist *and* a writer, is presented in these designs as a kind of mystic figure, since the designers conflate artistic creation and scientific inquiry, thus turning both creation and inquiry into mysteries to which access is denied to all but a select few. The writer paired to his butterfly studies becomes a larger-than-life character, estranged from the ordinary. These visual artifacts create a double myth, each design turning into a signifier of several concurrent messages—highbrow seriousness, apoliticism, the neutral or disengaged aesthete, the precision of poetry, the excitement of science—that, simultaneously, reflect a Barthesian myth about our culture. By pairing scientist to artist, setting them apart in their own little field of meaning, each figure is exoticized by the presence of the other. The butterfly iconography turns Nabokov into a strange figure. The aura of the scientist, and the graphical manifestation of a natural, scientific specimen to be collected and studied, becomes a means to make the writer both instantly recognizable (butterfly=Nabokov) and immediately inaccessible (science=difficult).

Nabokov delighted in playing with that image. Whether he knew he would succeed or not is open for debate, though *Strong Opinions* shows him to be anything but uncertain. His opinions are strong—and witty, and clear, and beautifully articulated. They do not leave much room for debate. (They could not; they were all produced in writing, then corrected and reshaped to the author's satisfaction before being released to the world.) Nonetheless, echoes of Nabokov's lepidopteral aura reverberate in the strangest places. For instance, when he was hired to adapt *Lolita* to a movie for Stanley Kubrick, Nabokov wrote himself into a scene:

> The Butterfly Hunter. His name is Vladimir Nabokov. A fritillary settles with outspread wings on a tall flower. Nabokov snaps it up with a sweep of his net. Humbert walks toward him. With a nip of finger and thumb through a fold of the marquisette Nabokov dispatches his capture and works the dead insect out of the netbag and onto the palm of his hand.
> HUMBERT   Is that a rare specimen?
> NABOKOV   A specimen cannot be common or rare, it can only be poor or perfect.
> HUMBERT   Could you direct me —
> NABOKOV   You meant "rare species." This is a good specimen of a rather scarce subspecies.[38]

Humbert goes elsewhere for directions. Unfortunately, neither this scene nor much else that Nabokov wrote ever made it to the screen: Kubrick cut nearly every word written by the author and changed the rest beyond recognition. The butterflies, however, have made their way into just about every other part of Nabokov's world; his contributions to taxonomy have been recognized in two books and numerous specialized journals. And the butterflies also continue to appear — in one strange form or another — in all sorts of Nabokov-related graphic design, further blurring the line between art and science, artist and scientist. Each butterfly illustration is a good specimen of a rather scarce subspecies: a person capable of specializing and succeeding in two seemingly disparate, disconnected fields; offering further proof that neither arena is as inviolate or isolated as one might think.

However, the hazy line does not extend beyond the writer's accomplishments, since the graphic design celebrating them has further exoticized science. In using the signifiers of Nabokov's science as shorthand for the writer's art, the designers may have unwittingly discouraged the viewer from participation in one of Nabokov's fields of interest. Nabokov played a part in this separation, but the designers seem primarily responsible for turning a meaningful activity into window dressing. He complained, in letters, of errors in cover design, saying that "the only symbol a broken butterfly is of is

---

[38] Vladimir Nabokov, *Lolita: A Screenplay. Novels 1955-1962* (New York: Library of America, 1996), 769.

a broken butterfly."[39] Broken or not, the butterflies were not without meaning, since their incorporation into the writer's iconography further mythologized and rarefied the scientist. Nabokov, of course, was not one to shy away from demarcation—from laying claim to exceptionality and exclusivity. In the foreword to *Strong Opinions*, he writes: "I take every precaution to ensure a dignified beat of the mandarin's fan."[40] The differentiation takes advantage of the aesthetic appeal of lepidoptery while simultaneously removing the viewer from it. This separation is problematic not simply because it further alienates the public from science, but also because the appropriation of scientific imagery strips the signifier (the butterflies) from its most elemental signifieds (for example, taxonomy, population sightings, migration patterns, and species extinctions). The butterflies, like science, become something to admire from afar—curious, pretty and strange, but off limits and untouchable.

---

[39] Vladimir Nabokov, *Selected Letters*, ed. Dmitri Nabokov and Mathew J. Bruccoli (San Diego: Harcourt Brace Jovanovich/Bruccoli Clark, 1990), 384.
[40] Nabokov, *Strong Opinions*, xv.

GOAL BOX

INTERVIEW

An Interview with
Dmitri Nabokov
by Suellen Stringer-Hye

"*LAURA* IS NOT EVEN THE ORIGINAL'S NAME"[1]

PREFACE

When Yuri Leving, editor of *Nabokov Online Journal* (NOJ), asked me in 2008 to interview Dmitri Nabokov for an issue of NOJ I was delighted. I had already interviewed Stephen Schiff, screenwriter for Adrian Lyne's ill-fated film adaptation of *Lolita*; Stacey Schiff, who had not yet won the Pulitzer for her biography of Véra Nabokov; and Azar Nafisi, author of the bestseller, *Reading Lolita in Tehran*. As an interviewer, it was only natural to inquire about the fate of the manuscript of *The Original of Laura*, Nabokov's unfinished novel, which any student, scholar or fan of Nabokov knew was locked away in a vault somewhere awaiting Dmitri's decision as to whether it would be allowed to live for all eternity or die according to Nabokov's deathbed

---

[1] First appeared in *Nabokov Online Journal*, Vol. II (2008).

GOAL BOX

instructions. So when I asked Dmitri, somewhat innocently, what his plans were for *Laura*, I never expected that it would ignite a worldwide conflagration, starting when Dmitri forwarded a transcript of the still unpublished interview "*Laura* is not even the original's name" to *Slate Magazine* columnist Ron Rosenbaum. Rosenbaum's public plea to Dmitri first to save and later to destroy the manuscript was echoed during 2009 by writers, artists and journalists around the globe. We now know the outcome of Dmitri's deliberations. The book has been published and whether to burn or not to burn has been settled. The already iconic Chip Kidd book cover design conveys the continuing shadowy presence that publication of *The Original of Laura* did not erase.[2] Like Pluto, I suspect scholars will be trying to determine how to classify this last of Nabokov's utterances for many years to come. The hand lettered card, with the artistically resonant and graphically interesting list of synonyms for efface, destroy, and rub out, itself provides sufficient justification for publication. Like a glow worm, like the Cheshire Cat's grin, *The Original of Laura* is both there and not there for all time. Of the many hundreds of reviews, both critical and favorable, of Dmitri's decision and of the text itself, "A Glorious Mess" which appeared in *New York Magazine* stands out: "It could be Nabokov's very last brilliant joke: a black hole of textuality that he conjured and then slipped into, pulling his pencil behind him."[3] I'm glad I asked.

20 March 2010

Suellen Stringer-Hye: While you are often very forthcoming on Nabokv-L with corrections to mistranslations or misstatements of fact, certain puzzles in Nabokov's writings, such as the identity of Kinbote and Shade and the subsequent authorship of *Pale Fire*, remain unsettled. In the case of *Pale Fire*, do you think there are inherent textual ambiguities without resolution, or do you have "inside knowledge" that might help to illuminate these questions? Do you ever feel like you need to "hold back" what you know for fear of interjecting a bias into the scholarly discourse?

Dmitri Nabokov: I have been accustomed since childhood to reading my father's books with a flow of receptivity. I might check an occasional stumbling block to comprehension, but not interrupt with scholastic snags

---

[2] Kidd is a graphic artist with Knopf, the publisher of *Laura*.
[3] Sam Anderson, "A Glorious Mess," *New York Magazine*, November 15, 2009, http://nymag.com/arts/books/reviews/62036/

the spinal thrill, the continuity of reading pleasure. As Vladimir Nabokov once said, reading is rereading: it is in subsequent passes that one can plunge into conjecture regarding the author's intentions, the multiplicity of levels, and real or apparent textual ambiguities. That much said, one of the more delicate questions regarding *Pale Fire* has been that of its actual or virtual authorship; i.e., who, within the context of the novel, invented Kinbote? Who invented Shade? When, early on, this dilemma began to be debated, I popped the question to my father. As closely as I can remember, his reply was "It does not matter much; let's just say that each invented the other." I shared this "inside knowledge" with Brian Boyd. It seemed, at the time, to set in motion a certain series of thoughts that Boyd appreciated and found useful. Simple enough. More profound conjectures, of course, are up to the reader.

Online resources can yield precious finds. One can, however, wiki-woogle ad infinitum and find a plethora of coincidences and irrelevancies, all the while missing the gist of Nabokov's writing. Misquotations, sometimes the result of translational blunders, occasionally do require attention. An egregious case of both resulted when the leftist writer Alberto Manguel, parroted by his Venezuelan analogue Fernando Báez in a 2005 statement to the IPS [Inter Press Service], parlayed a grotesque (and perhaps politically propitious) mistranslation into the charge that my father had "burned *Don Quixote* in front of his students," a crime that qualified him as one of "the worst enemies of books," more culpable than the military forces presumably acting as a result of "the US-led invasion of Iraq." Nabokov had lectured on Cervantes as visiting professor at Harvard in 1951. What he subsequently said, in a 1967 interview in the *Paris Review*, was

> ...What I intend to do is publish a number of twenty-page essays on several works...all based on my Cornell and Harvard lectures. I remember with delight tearing apart [figuratively, of course] *Don Quixote*, a cruel and crude old book, before six hundred students in Memorial Hall...[4]

The accusation, in the context of the "biggest cultural disaster since 1258," as Marxist Humberto Marquez had qualified the events in Iraq, was quickly picked up by the less informed, or sometimes more disingenuous, members of the media.

I would, however, like to clarify the matter. My father's scholarly evaluation of what is an iconic novel to many in no way reflects his or my

---

[4] Interview by Herbert Gold, The Art of Fiction, *Paris Review* 40.41 (Summer—Fall 1967): 1-19, http://www.theparisreview.org/viewinterview.php/prmMID/4310

feelings toward Spanish writers in general, or toward his faithful readers in the Spanish-speaking world, or toward our marvelous Spanish publisher Anagrama. He also said of the novel, which he most certainly did not burn,

> We are confronted by an interesting phenomenon: a literary hero gradually losing contact with the book that bore him; leaving his fatherland, leaving his creator's desk, and roaming space after roaming Spain. In result, Don Quixote is greater today than he was in Cervantes' womb. He has ridden for three hundred and fifty years through the jungles and tundras of human thought—and he has gained in vitality and stature.[5]

For my part, some of my most satisfying singing engagements have been in the Spanish-speaking world—Colombia, Venezuela, Puerto Rico, and the Gran Teatro del Liceo in Barcelona. And it was upon ascending the 18,700-foot summit of Mexico's Mount Orizaba that I recalled the famous Petrarchan sonnet of Keats, "On First Looking into Chapman's Homer," in which he mistakenly has "stout Cortez," instead of Balboa, gazing down, from a lower elevation, on Vera Cruz.

I am not deterred by a fear of skewing scholarly discourse if I believe in the truth of a fact or the validity of an opinion that I express. Besides, an occasional skew can be fun. But when a peculiarly obsessed individual seriously threatens me—as, in fact, has happened—for not confirming his guess with regard to a lucrative "solution" he imagined is concealed in *Pale Fire*, things have gone too far. As they have when a nasty little online adventurer presumes that, being musical, the son of a famous author, and unmarried, I am perforce of his sexual stripe.

Suellen Stringer-Hye: You have devoted a considerable part of your life to administering Vladimir Nabokov's legacy. How comfortable are you with dealing with the non-artistic and non-literary side of your father's affairs (e.g., solving financial issues, facing copyright infringements, post-Soviet bureaucrats, etc.)? Do you ever feel like your own pursuits were eclipsed by the necessity to handle the business side of the Nabokov estate?

Dmitri Nabokov: Fortunately, I have good agents. They have taken over many of the ever-increasing administrative burdens that my mother and I had previously sustained, but certainly not all of them. Still, I hope to eke out the time to complete certain projects of my own. What *does* make me uncomfortable are dinner companions who ask "Hasn't your father written

---

[5] Vladimir Nabokov, *Lectures on Don Quixote*, ed. Fredson Bowers (San Diego; New York; London: Harcourt Brace Jovanovich, 1983), 111-112.

INTERVIEW

anything better than that [*Lolita*]?" Or delightedly declare, "I saw a show of his — *Evita*."

During the Soviet period, samizdat versions of my father's works were reproduced by whatever means were at hand, such as the (then illegal) mimeograph. Of course, more sophisticated means like the fax and the computer were still beyond the official horizon in Russia, and therefore some of the copying even had to be done by hand. Sources for the texts were often copies brought to the Moscow Book Fair by the late, much lamented Carl Proffer and his wife Ellendea, with an eye closed to pilfering.

Ironically, as legal and semi-legal pirate versions of Nabokov's works proliferated during Perestroika, they were often such travesties of the originals, and so poorly annotated, that the old samizdat versions based on the Proffers' Ardis editions, and on previous exile editions, remained the most faithful. Finally, there was a substantial improvement with the advent of the new copyright bill recently signed into law by President Putin.

Theoretically, this change placed Russian publishing on a par with that of many western countries. Unfortunately, though, a vast stock of pirate editions was left to be sold, and certain new ones continued to appear. It would take unreasonable amounts of time and effort to check every Nabokov work produced in Russia and to comment thereon, and such an effort might indeed eclipse much of my other work. Hence some fish of varying size continue to slip through the net.

Suellen Stringer-Hye: Nabokov was always "supremely indifferent" to the critics. Are you, as his son and the executor of his estate, equally so?

Dmitri Nabokov: If one paid attention to every single silly error or misstatement, that too would be a full-time job. Sometimes I am tempted to intervene, especially if the result will be humorous. I most definitely do so if my father's honor or mine, or a gross misstatement of fact, is at stake. Otherwise, the critics have a right to their own opinions.

Of course, one of the most offensive critical cracks was that of certain dour post-Soviet pundits affirming that *Lolita* and other of Nabokov's writings suggest a malignant contempt for America and all things American. Nothing could be further from the truth.

Father once said, "I am as American as April in Arizona." And I am a witness to his longing to return one day to the American Southwest. Besides, one must remember that a bit of good-natured satire need not be considered hostile.

Suellen Stringer-Hye: What do you think about your own public image? Nabokov said, "To myself I appear as an idol, a wizard, bird-headed, emerald-gloved, dressed in tights made of bright-blue scales."[6] How do you see yourself?

Dmitri Nabokov: Nabokov also expressed, in the following celebrated passage, the hope that:

> One day a reappraiser will come and declare that, far from having been a frivolous firebird, I was a rigid moralist, kicking sin, cuffing stupidity, ridiculing the vulgar and cruel — and assigning sovereign power to tenderness, talent, and pride.[7]

The image of the idol, the bird-headed, emerald-gloved wizard in tights made of bright blue scales, and that of the frivolous firebird, somehow echo Nabokov's nom-de-plume, the fabled, many-colored phoenix-owl Sirin, with an admixture of the conjuror-cum-acrobat in his scintillating costume.

My love of things mechanical might have suggested an incarnation as some motorized Sirin. But no, what matters to me is not the public image but (as in Father's case) the private. I would like to be able to consult my own conscience, now or later, and find that what good I have done prevails over the mediocre, while the harm must remain my burden like a bad credit score. The credit-score racket, incidentally, should be avoided. It commonly ascribes debts one never dreamt of incurring, and recourse is a slow and iffy proposition.

Suellen Stringer-Hye: What is the current status of your own novel?

Dmitri Nabokov: I shall be quite frank. I completed a kind of novel some years ago. Some people I respect spoke well of it, but something was wrong. Having toyed with it this way and that, I remain incompletely satisfied. Since I think there was some good stuff in it, I may yet rework it.

Suellen Stringer-Hye: What is your current thinking on how to handle the unfinished manuscript of *The Original of Laura*?

Dmitri Nabokov: *Laura* is a spellbinding thing, and at the same time a terrible thorn. It is difficult to imagine that such a delicately nuanced work may be properly perceived, especially in its somewhat fragmentary state. I am aware, Ron, that time is rumbling on and I may soon head for the Clarens Cemetery and the Nabokov grave, only a bone's throw from my home on the hillside above. One must, however, consider the following: in the fall of 1990 one Brandon S. Centerwall, under the title "Hidden in Plain Sight: Nabokov and Pedophilia," propounded, by some convoluted logic, the thesis that my father's never having used the word "molest" in *Lolita* was sufficient proof that *Lolita* was a thinly disguised re-creation of the molestation that

---

[6] Vladimir Nabokov, *Poems and Problems* (New York: McGraw-Hill Book Co., 1970), 105, 113.
[7] Vladimir Nabokov, *Strong Opinions* (New York: McGraw-Hill Book Co., 1973), 193.

he supposedly underwent at the hands of his Uncle Ruka (Rukavishnikov). This idiocy, bordering on the criminal, underwent a plagiarism bordering on the insane some years later, thanks to a certain Joanne Morgan, whose own presentation bore astounding similarities to that of Centerwell (or "wall"—it does not matter, for either way he is off the wall).

Meanwhile, another meddler, named Penny Something or other, was busy with a mad hypothesis of her own, namely that the incestuous situation in Ada was an echo of my father's strolls in the Caucasian hills while awaiting the family's departure from Yalta, strolls during which he instructed his beloved younger sister Hélène in the rudiments of entomology and the niceties of prosody. Having seen the perfidy wrought upon *Lolita*, *Ada* and other of Nabokov's works by such monstrous nincompoops as the above, I have toyed with the idea—lest the vulnerable *Laura* suffer the same kind of fate—of being an obedient son and destroying the manuscript. On the other hand, wouldn't it be fun, before my time does run out, to have a last spin in a remaining Ferrari or in my fast boat? But woe is me! The transmission of the boat's right engine needs urgent service, so perhaps "destitute Dmitri" (in the words of an unastute ass named Augustine) should jettison his principles and publish? Or, instead, should he sell the lectern and the chess set together with his soul?

All kidding aside, I never seriously considered burning, nobody has made me change my mind, and I shall publish. I had hoped, in honor of my father's birthday, to make this announcement with more flourish and more detail—for there will be entertaining details—but publishing exigencies must prevail. Fioritura will be incorporated as an online addendum when the time is ripe.

Here I might mention certain suppositions in a much more innocent vein than those of the Pennys and Joannes, regarding the *Original*, or the original of the *Original*, expressed by the articulate Ron Rosenbaum in the New York *Observer*. Mr. Rosenbaum's candidates and conjectures may sound plausible from certain points of view, but I can reassure him that I have no need to "prove him wrong," for *The Original of Laura* is in no way inspired by Petrarch or by Otto Preminger's film or by echoes of *Pale Fire*.

Incidentally, I would say that the opening quatrain of Petrarch's poem No. 141 in the *Canzoniere* (in the 2004 translation by David Young)[8] disproves rather than proves any nexus to *Pale Fire*, for the simple reason that its image involves a butterfly not a bird, flying not into a window, but, in

---

[8] David Young, trans., The Poetry of Petrarch (New York: Farrar, Straus and Giroux, 2004).

search of light, into someone's eyes. Nabokov's sense of zoological and other detail was so precise that it would have been extremely unlikely for him to associate creatures from two vastly different biological domains.

I am flattered by having been compared to Hamlet; perhaps, indeed, a bare bodkin ought to be considered when facing certain agonizing decisions. But the Kinbotes and their conjectures merit little comment. I can assure Mr. Rosenbaum that this is the wrong path, as are the many other proposals that have appeared at Nabokv-L and elsewhere.

Besides, the notion of conceptual, aesthetic origin is so vague and so arbitrary that I would not assign much importance to it in this context. I have, of course, read and reread what exists of *The Original of Laura*, while smoothing the handwritten cards into a more legible typescript, and can assure Mr. Rosenbaum that I know whereof I speak. This does not diminish the respect I have for his intelligently voiced ratiocination. Finally, or semi-finally, "Laura" is not even the original's name.

Suellen Stringer-Hye: Throughout *Strong Opinions*, Nabokov identifies himself as an American writer and many American artists, writers, filmmakers and even a sitting Supreme Court Judge have been influenced by him. While scholars often debate the "Americanness" of Nabokov's work, what do you think it meant to Nabokov to be considered an American writer?

Dmitri Nabokov: I have already mentioned his thoughts about his personal sense of Americanness. With regard to the nationality of his writing, I recall a comment by the eminent Russian writer Andrei Bitov, on a television program we did together: "Nabokov was a Russian writer who ventured forth and conquered the cosmos." At the same time, it is curious to imagine how things might have gone had Russia not been raped by the Reds. Nabokov might never have left to move elsewhere, might never have married Véra Slonim, or settled in the United States, or written *Lolita*. He might have composed only in his native tongue, and pursued lepidoptera in his native country, with perhaps an occasional foray to some exotic land. There would, of course, have been no *Pale Fire* either, no *Ada*, and no *Pnin*. I would not be writing this reply, because I would not exist.

Suellen Stringer-Hye: Do you think that Nabokov's legacy has been trivialized by pop-culture or is Nabokov simply a writer capable of straddling high and low culture, and are misunderstandings, misrepresentations and misappropriations the price of that feat? Or, of course, something else altogether?

Dmitri Nabokov: As far back as I can remember my father relished certain facets of pop culture: he would call the feminine type that Brigitte made famous by the affectionate Russianized diminutive "bardoshka." He perused with enormous mirth the terminally *poshlyi* "Rex Morgan, MD" and his nurse June. He relished Charlie Chaplin's Hitleresque character bouncing the inflatable globe (even if he liked the real-life Charlie a lot less). He enjoyed Laurel and Hardy and the Three Stooges with me and was amused when I imitated Charlie Chan saying "our methods are simple but effective." He would take me to the kids' Saturday matinee at the Harvard Square Cinema and the short-subject theatre at Boston's South Station and share my mirth. At the same time, he was sufficiently prescient to realize that a man of his stature could not avoid a certain amount of kidding and trivialization, and had enough confidence in his art to know that it would not be thereby diminished. He continued unperturbed to cast a condescending eye at the bikini ads, the pop-song lyrics, the army of starlets and demimondaines parading under the Lolita banner.

It took a misdeed of mine to irritate him briefly: while I was in Milan for operatic reasons, a questionable publicity agent persuaded me to host a mock Miss Lolita contest. My father, who had rigorously kept his distance from the casting of the Kubrick film, saw a photograph of me with half a dozen superannuated aspiring nymphets draped across my satin bed. Next came a furious cable: "Stop Lolita publicity immediately!" It was almost like old times, some thirty years later, to encounter the charming La Scala ballerina we had designated to win that competition, her beauty undiminished, in the atrium of the Piccolo Teatro, where I had gone to see Luca Ronconi's outstanding theatrical adaptation of my father's *Lolita* script (incidentally, to set the record straight, I had been invited to play the butterfly-hunting VN in a brief cameo appearance, but was unable to take part not because I was unqualified—as one scandal sheet gloatingly suggested—but because I had arrived from an engagement abroad too late for even one rehearsal on the difficult track-covered stage, and was the first to decline).

Suellen Stringer-Hye: You have said that Stacy Schiff's biography *Véra* did for your mother what Brian Boyd's two volume biography *The American Years* and *The Russian Years* did for your father. Boyd however, in his 1999 review of that book said, "this is not the biography Véra deserves."[9] Do you think Boyd was correct in that assessment? What aspects of Véra Nabokov's life and works would you want remembered?

Dmitri Nabokov: A difficult question, first of all because Stacy Schiff is a friend of mine, and an indiscreet bon mot of mine has already caused an

---

[9] Brian Boyd, "Handmaid to Genius," review of Stacey Schiff's *Véra*, The Globe and Mail, Toronto, May 15, 1999, http://www.theglobeandmail.com/

unfortunate temporary falling out between us. On one hand, I should have moderated my praise; on the other, I should have mellowed my criticism. The main difficulty was the pressure to which the publisher was subjecting poor Stacy, making it impossible to check certain details.

My mother's beautiful eyes were wide open to everything around her. She had an incredible rainbow of talents and interests. She might start an evening by reciting to me, from memory, Pushkin's "Bronze Horseman," and then listen with undiminished attention and comprehension as I explained the intricacies of the special limited-slip differential with which my race car had been equipped.

There are people of multiple good or middling talents who never follow through to the hilt with any of them, as if they were afraid to find themselves amid big fish in a big pond. My mother radiated affectionate interest on all the good things around her, and her abilities might have made her a substantial fish in any one of multiple ponds. Yet, from the moment she first heard Vladimir Nabokov give a public reading, she knew that he would emerge as an immensely gifted writer. Thereupon, she relegated to the background her own prodigious and varied talents to become his lifelong helpmeet in every sense. In her own profoundly personal way, she assigned sovereign status to tenderness, talent and pride, and was well rewarded by my father's total devotion.

Véra Nabokov's literary taste and talent were exceptional, and manifested themselves in certain touches she lent to her husband's work, to my translations, and to a few unsung writings of her own. Nabokov considered her his best critic, and her remarks, though rare, always to the point.

In the fall of 1980, I was the victim of a serious accident that confined me for three months to the overheated penumbra of the Lausanne Hospital's burn unit. No visitors were allowed inside. The Swiss weather was getting colder. The only way Mother could converse with me was by speaking into an intercom, sitting outside in her wheelchair in the feeble warmth of an overhead infrared heater. I would make things even dimmer by dousing the soft light so that she could not clearly see my grafted and bandaged state. On one occasion, as the television played softly off to my left, she asked, "Don't you see what's going on behind you?" She had always loved animals with a particular gentleness, and was calling my attention to one of those wonderful nature documentaries that appear on certain channels.

My father had died in her presence and mine, in a different part of the same hospital complex, some three years earlier. As we drove home after his death to Montreux, Mother, who was not a weepy widow, and had declined the consolatory embrace of a well-meaning duty nurse (who did not understand that my mother was a very private person, immensely affectionate with those close to her, but inhibited when sharing such intimate grief with a stranger), suddenly said in a soft voice, "Let's hire an airplane and crash." She, who almost always splendidly controlled herself, quickly thought better of that idea (I already knew how to fly, and she too had once taken lessons, but neither of us held a license—so there would have been a pilot's fate to ponder, as well as other logistical considerations).

Somehow the image evolved in certain quarters of a heartless harpy with her handgun, shooing and shooting intruders away from her husband. In it was partly the result of sophomoric humor ("actually, he is blind, and she is his seeing-eye dog" went one quip), partly of her utter loyalty, which at times entailed strength, as when she delivered her ill husband's lecture on a moment's notice, or dealt with certain jackals of the publishing or cinema world. But such an image has nothing to do with the Véra Nabokov that should be most vividly remembered. No, Stacy—it is the loving, tender, marvelously human and humane Véra I have previously described. And the fact that you and I may not have fully agreed in the past in no way diminishes my fondness for you. I'll say something more: in fact, in certain very nice ways, you remind me a little of my mother.

Suellen Stringer-Hye: In the summer of 2009 the Vladimir Nabokov Collection in the Library of Congress will become open for scholars. How do you think this will change the state of archival research in Nabokov scholarship?

Dmitri Nabokov: As things have stood so far, I have tried not to deny access to the truly deserving. I don't think I or the decision-makers who succeed me shall change this policy, and I hope that archival research will continue to flourish under the expert supervision of Alice Birney and her staff. The same should be said of Isaac Gewirtz and Stephen Crook of the New York Public Library, which holds much of the Nabokov Archive.

Suellen Stringer-Hye: What do you consider the current state of Nabokov scholarship—both in the West and in Russia?

Dmitri Nabokov: Notwithstanding a remaining imprint of the Soviet boot, a sinister shadow of the Soviet soul, the specter of Freud and friends, and the bizarre comments of such pundits as Norman Podhoretz redux (who abruptly reversed his loyalty to *Lolita*), there are occasional brilliant scholars in both camps. A fair and detailed reply to this question would require considerable time and space.

Suellen Stringer-Hye: "Because there is no such thing as reading… only rereading. Fondling details is essential to being in this group." Thus reads the description of the Facebook group called Nabokov Junkies, which claims over 500 members. Clearly Nabokov stays relevant to young readers in ways that many of his contemporaries do not. In what ways do you think Nabokov studies will evolve? In what directions would you guide inquiry?

Dmitri Nabokov: Toward the thrill of experiencing beauty, to the originality with which it manifests itself, to the charming details of its summits rather than the cavils of the boulder field at its base. I think it is less important to search for the ways in which Nabokov is "relevant" to younger readers than to applaud the relevance itself, however variegated it may be. New areas of study do, of course, remain among a number of unpublished items: for example, the dreams — his own and those of his wife, in 1964 — that Nabokov recorded to investigate the validity of certain oneiric hypotheses. The commentary must be sensitive and moral, and its criterion not one of social correctness.

Suellen Stringer-Hye: How do you estimate the future market of Nabokov rarities (manuscripts, first editions, dedication inscriptions, memorabilia, etc.)? For example, how successful were the recent auctions of VN's books (Tajan in Europe, Horowitz in the USA)?

Dmitri Nabokov: There are differences between Nabokov's memorabilia and those of O.J. I suppose the main one is morality, since murder has never been one of our options for recovering purloined property. The Tajan auction was remarkably unprofessional and poorly prepared. Glenn Horowitz has placed some items well and holds a refreshed reserve of valuable Nabokoviana.

I think we all realize that O.J.'s leftovers, like home-run baseballs and illustrious billiard cues, will not represent much to the public mind or the public purse a century or two from now. On the other hand, a trinket like VN's pince-nez, which I presented to the Nabokov Museum in St. Petersburg, the period lectern at which he composed, or the Staunton championship chess set on which his father had taught him to play, will likely be cherished for centuries.

The point, however, is not the edition, the inscription, or the chance object. The essence of a great writer is intangible and inestimable: it is what he has written, not the font or the format in which one enjoys it. Nor do the exact words scribbled on a football helmet or a baseball glove carry much weight for posterity. As for the value of autographed first editions, I can by chance give an example from a recent email. I and others on Nabokv-L recently received a request for help in finding an autographed copy of *Pale Fire* that was desired for gift-giving purposes. I was able to furnish some information because I happened to know that at least one such presentation copy exists on the rare book market, and can be bought for $17,500 or thereabouts. Certain exceptional rarities have been sold for sums well into six figures. Don Johnson has contributed the authoritative comment that Vladimir Nabokov autographs are extremely rare and extremely expensive. Rarity, of course, generates value.

In any case, the item that was most precious to me—an original first edition of *Lolita*, lovingly inscribed to me by my father—was stolen from the flimsy New York cellar of an ill relative where I had improvidently left it for safekeeping when departing for Europe in December of 1959. While taking part in the 1983 Cornell Nabokov Festival, I learned from a fellow participant, who was to become a close friend of mine, that it had been purchased for two dollars, and had become a prize possession of a Cornell graduate student whom my colleague had visited. My acquaintance apparently lacked the fortitude to demand immediate restitution of the stolen goods, and advised me somewhat lackadaisically after the fact. I would have acted much more forcefully. When, some time later, my friend attempted to trace the culprit, he said the man had vanished. I was deeply hurt by the whole incident, and would probably greet a civil return with a gentlemanly reward. Otherwise, as the guilty party or a subsequent recipient stews with his conscience, I hope for their sake that neither will come face to face with me or my heirs. I am, however, getting closer, and a Bryn Mawr fund raiser of some summers past seems to play a part.

Suellen Stringer-Hye: In 1969, Philip Oakes of *The Sunday Times*, London, asked Nabokov, "Which is the worst thing men do?" to which he responded "Stink, cheat, torture."[10] These words echo against the oft-heard debate about the necessity for torture in the "war on terror." While not overtly political, Nabokov often defended the motives and actions of the United States Government. Do you think it would have saddened him that his beloved adopted country might use torture to defend its freedoms?

Dmitri Nabokov: Stinking recently hit the TV headlines on two occasions in a row: that of a janitor who was fired for his bad breath, and the (human) love birds who failed to mate because of reciprocally unacceptable pheromones. Cheating, whether on grade school exams or on official documents, will regrettably remain a part of daily life. For example, one has only to glance through the Internet to find an ad with all the appurtenances

---

[10] Philip Oakes, [An Interview with V. Nabokov], *The Sunday Times*, London, June 22, 1969 (quoted from Nabokov, *Strong Opinions*, 135).

of legitimacy for "Fake Doctors [sic] Notes: use it for anything you want to be excused from; no one on the Web can beat our price!!!, [etc.]; fake excuses, doctors notes, work excuses; indistinguishable from the real thing!" And one has but to consult the current news to see how kiddies are indoctrinated into our cheating society by their own parents, to wit: a six-year-old girl entered her essay in a contest in the hope of winning tickets to a pop-music concert. She won the prize, whereupon it was discovered that the sob story she had recounted about the death of her father was a total fake. It turned out, moreover, that she had been coached from beginning to end by her mother.

If I were overseer of the world (as I sometimes fantasize) there are many changes I would consider. For instance, I would eliminate shopping malls, which seem to spawn mass shootings. I would cancel popular holidays that promote the most vicious human instincts. While I was at it, I might also consider the option of a third term for a current president if it is obvious that nobody can do the job better, thereby postponing by at least a year the energy, time, and expense of a futile election. When an election did become necessary, I would abolish the mention of religion in political contexts. I would drastically limit the expenditures that all the hoopla entails, and redirect all leftover funds, through strictly controlled channels, to the poor and the ill, upon whom we bestow such abundant lip service.

As for torture, which has become a current event on a par with the Fox Channel's "Daily Britney," and is energetically and indiscriminately practiced in various Middle Eastern and other countries, I would, seriously speaking, willingly torture anyone who despises life sufficiently to kill others, gratuitously and nonchalantly, while sacrificing his own to some obscene credo. Such a view might have saddened my father. While I cannot speak for him for the moment, I suspect nevertheless that, in the end, he would agree with me that there appears to be no way to discourage suicide bombers other than making their punishment, if they survive or are arrested before the fact, more protracted and more painful than the death they seek.

Had my father been allowed to live on, he might have something to add to his list of vile deeds: the shameless official denial, in a supposedly decent country, of the collective horrors committed, without the shadow of a doubt, by a large part of mankind.

I refer to a report that appeared on international television in December of 2007 that the teaching of the Holocaust had been forbidden in a major British city (apparently as the result of strong pressure from Moslem quarters). I might mention here that I was born into a family utterly devoid of racial or religious prejudice. This was the continuation, on my father's side, of the liberal aristocratic tradition of his own father, who consistently condemned injustice toward the weak and the poor. He, like his son, had not an ounce of Jewish blood, but was a ferocious opponent of anti-Semitism in general, and pogroms in particular. My father would have been embittered by the echoes of the infamous Black Hundred, such as those evoked in an excellent piece by Gavriel Shapiro on vile vignettes in the form of a cartoon depicting, amid the typical clichés of Fascist caricature, a rotund Rothschild scuttling with bags of cash toward the leaders of the Provisional Government, among them an insultingly nuanced elder Nabokov, with the caption, "Russia sells out to the Jews."[11]

Suellen Stringer-Hye: Do you have a favorite Nabokov book?

Dmitri Nabokov: Probably *Pale Fire*.

Suellen Stringer-Hye: "The years are passing and soon no one will know what we know." Is there one detail about the Nabokovs that is generally not known, or hasn't been included in the biographies, that you would like to pass on?

Dmitri Nabokov: They were utterly unique, and their union surpassed arithmetical addition: by a one-in-a-billion aberration, they found each other, and one plus one became much more than two. There are many things I recall: the way my father called my mother "dushen'ka" (darling), the way she referred to him by the Russian diminutive "papochka."

On a warm day in the fall of 1980, my mother received a phone call from the Lausanne hospital's burn unit. I was calling to say I had had a "minor" accident on the autoroute on my way to a dental appointment, and would not be able to meet her for lunch at the Montreux Palace as planned. Nor, it turned out, would she see me at close quarters for the three months I have already mentioned, for I was to remain under intensive care with extensive burns and a fractured neck. She was profoundly shocked, and immensely supportive during those months and the seven-month rehabilitation that followed. It was her love that nurtured me through some pretty tough times to a miraculous, nearly total recovery.

On an idyllic morning in the spring of 2001, long after Mother's death, I was descending a gentle seaside trail not far from a vacation place I had on Sardinia's Costa Smeralda. Suddenly, for no apparent reason, I lost my balance and fell forward. Already during the previous winter, while skiing with a Palm Beach friend at Villars in the Swiss Alps, I had been disturbed by

---

[11] Gavriel Shapiro, *Delicate Markers: Subtexts in Vladimir Nabokov's "Invitation to a Beheading"* (New York: Peter Lang Publishing, 1998).

GOAL BOX

an unfamiliar lack of assurance while turning at speed, in perfect conditions, on what had long been familiar terrain. I soon dismissed what had happened, attributing it simply to a bad day. But my fall in Sardinia, as I soon found out, was the first true harbinger of polyneuropathy, a debilitating illness that was to deprive me not only of skiing but of my entire physically active way of life, and confine me to a wheelchair whose Ferrari-red color would be the only relic of my energetic past.

    I have never ceased missing my parents, and their abstract presence has always remained my inspiration. Yet I am relieved that they were spared, in the material world at least, having to suffer for me anew. They might have shared my thought that Fate speaks to us in strange, sometimes emphatic ways. At the very onset of what would be my father's fatal illness, I was to depart for a distant shore to perform a task, for a noble cause, that was not only risky but that might have altered the whole course of my life. My father's illness made it impossible for me to go. As for the fiery crash of my Ferrari on the Lausanne autoroute in 1980, it put a stop to my increasing involvement in a sport—offshore powerboat racing—that was consuming me, and preventing me from giving my best where it belonged.

    With regard to my beloved parents, there are other things, too—things that I know, but cannot try to express, for I would then find myself in a multidimensional, kaleidoscopic labyrinth with no issue.

1 January—22 April, 2008

>

ONE TOUCH PASS

NABOKOV ACROSS THE LINES

Samuel Schuman

"WHICH IS SEBASTIAN?" WHAT'S IN A (SHAKESPEAREAN AND NABOKOVIAN) NAME?

My brother he is in Elysium.[1]

I remember you did supplant your brother...[2]

In his very clever note "See Under Sebastian," Gennady Barabtarlo speaks for many readers of Nabokov's *The Real Life of Sebastian Knight* when he says "Something in the name of Sebastian Knight has often made me pause and wonder." He observes that the name is quite uncommon in the Russian social circle into which Sebastian was born and, partly for that reason, there "seems to be something deliberate about Sebastian." Barabtarlo

---

[1] Shakespeare, *Twelfth Night*, The Complete Signet Classic Shakespeare (New York: Harcourt Brace Jovanovich, 1972), I. ii., line 4.

[2] Shakespeare, *The Tempest*, The Complete Signet Classic Shakespeare (New York: Harcourt Brace Jovanovich, 1972), II. i., lines 273-274.

suggests that "Sebastian Knight" is a near-perfect anagram of "Knight is absent," with only a single "a" left out.[3]

The plot of the novel involves the search of the living narrator, "V," to find, both physically and biographically, Sebastian, his half brother. "V" recounts his desperate rush to reach the bedside of the dying Sebastian, only to fall victim to a grotesque case of mistaken identity which results in his watching over the final moments of the wrong man, and to discover that Sebastian has already died and disappeared. Sebastian is, as Barabtarlo points out, "absent." The story then focuses on "V's" attempt to reconstruct the biography of Sebastian, an effort which ultimately seems as frustrated as the rush to his death bed. At the end of the work, in a phrase dramatically reminiscent of the Humbert Humbert / Claire Quilty tussle in *Lolita*, "V" proclaims "I am Sebastian, or Sebastian is I, or perhaps we both are someone whom neither of us knows."[4] I do not dispute Barabtarlo's anagrammatic explanation for the name "Sebastian." But I do propose an alternative, or supplemental, interpretation: that there are two characters named Sebastian in Shakespeare's works and, in both cases, they function primarily in their role as brothers of other characters, as does Nabokov's Sebastian. In his controversial *Nabokov: His Life in Art*, Andrew Field noticed "the Shakespearean echoes in the characters' given names."[5]

In Shakespeare's *The Tempest*, Sebastian is the caustic and malevolent brother of Alonso, King of Naples. Early in the play, Antonio, who has usurped his brother Prospero's position as Duke of Milan, tempts Sebastian to emulate him, slay Alonso, and take over the throne of Naples.

> Antonio: Say this were death
> That now hath seized them, why, they were no worse
> Than they are now. There be that can rule Naples
> As well as he that sleeps....O, that you bore

---

[3] Gennady Barabtarlo, "See Under Sebastian," *The Nabokovian* 24 (Spring 1990): 24-25.

[4] Vladimir Nabokov, *Lolita* (New York: Vintage, 1997), 299: "I rolled over him, he rolled over me, we rolled over us..."; and *The Real Life of Sebastian Knight*, New Directions edition (Norfolk, CN.: James Laughlin, 1951), 205.

[5] Andrew Field, *Nabokov His Life in Art* (Boston: Little, Brown, 1967), 28. Later (210) discussing the characters in "The Waltz Invention" Field notes that "As in *The Real Life of Sebastian Knight*, Viola Trance's name refers to Shakespeare's *Twelfth Night*. She is described as "a smart woman of 30 in black masculine dress Shakespearean-masquerade style" by Samuel Schuman, "Nabokov and Shakespeare: The Russian Works," *The Garland Companion to Vladimir Nabokov*, ed. Vladimir E. Alexandrov (New York: Garland, 1995), 516.

> The mind that I do! What a sleep were this
> For your advancement! Do you understand me?
> Sebastian: Methinks I do....I remember
> You did supplant your brother Prospero.
> Antonio: And look how well my garments sit upon me...
> Sebastian: Thy case, dear friend,
> Shall be my precedent. As thou got'st Milan
> I'll come by Naples. Draw thy sword.[6]

Sebastian embraces the plot, but it is foiled when Ariel wakes the sleeping shipwrecked nobles.

In the play's final scene, in which Prospero reveals himself to Alonso and his party, including Antonio and Sebastian, many readers of *The Tempest* have noted that Antonio says not a word to Prospero, who has forgiven him: no apology, no recognition of his malfeasance. Sebastian offers a couple of comments during this scene, but his words do not clearly convey either regret or continued culpability. He remarks on the drunkenness of Stephano, then teases him, then accuses Caliban, Stephano and Trinculo of robbing the "luggage"—stolen apparel—in which they appear. Without violating Shakespeare's words, a theatrical director of *The Tempest* could easily present Sebastian at play's end as either an unrepentant fratricidal plotter, or as relieved and pleased by Prospero's restoration and the generally just and happy conclusion of the action (Alonso's son Ferdinand will wed Prospero's daughter Miranda, and they will become the rulers of Naples).

Clearly, Sebastian is in *The Tempest* in order to be a *brother*, set in parallel with Antonio, the evil brother of Prospero: Sebastian and Alonso echo and reinforce the fraternal relationship between Prospero and Antonio. Interestingly, it is also almost exclusively in the part of *brother* that we see Shakespeare's other Sebastian, in *Twelfth Night*. (Of course "Knight" and "night" are homophones.) Twins Viola and Sebastian are separated in a shipwreck, and Viola, the play's protagonist, believes Sebastian perished. Disguising herself as a boy, Viola enters the service of the Duke of Illyria, wooing, on his behalf, Lady Olivia. She, believing the gender altering disguise, falls in love with Viola who calls herself "Cesario." After much comic mischief in the subplot, Sebastian appears, and Olivia promptly asks him to marry her, not knowing that she is speaking to Viola's twin brother rather than "Cesario"; Viola disguised as a male. The confusion is cleared up when Viola and Sebastian finally appear together, to the amazement of all.

---

[6] Shakespeare, *The Tempest*, II. i., lines 264-296.

> Duke: One face, one voice, one habit, and two persons—
> A natural perspective that is and is not....
> Antonio: How have you made division of yourself?
> An apple cleft in two is not more twin
> Than these two creatures. Which is Sebastian?[7]

The play concludes with Olivia paired with Sebastian, the Duke with Viola.

A. M. Lyuksemburg, who annotated the translation of *The Real Life of Sebastian Knight* into Russian, suggests that the reference to "a packet of sugared violets" in Nabokov's work "introduces the Shakespearean motifs."[8] "Viola," of course, is the scientific name of the family of plants commonly called "violet." Thus, *Twelfth Night*'s Viola becomes *The Real Life of Sebastian Knight*'s many violets. There are several references to violets in Nabokov's novel, including these three:

1. When Sebastian's mother comes to pay him a visit (the only time she does so), "she thrust into Sebastian's hand a small parcel of sugar-coated violets."[9]

2. When later, as a boy, "V" discovers the key to a drawer Sebastian keeps locked, opens the drawer, and finds "a small muslin bag of violet sweets."[10] This could well be the same violet sweets his mother gave Sebastian earlier. Are violets a kind of "key" to the *Twelfth Night* motif in *The Real Life of Sebastian Knight*?

3. Still later, when "V" goes through Sebastian's belongings after his death, he finds in his brother's bathroom: "The glass shelf, bare save for an empty talc-powder tin with violets figured between its shoulders, standing there alone, reflected in the mirror like a coloured advertisement."[11] It does

---

[7] Shakespeare, *Twelfth Night*, V. i., lines 215-223. Note that Antonio is a sea captain, and friend of Sebastian.

[8] A. M. Lyuksemburg in V. V. Nabokov, *Sobranie sochinenii amerikanskogo perioda v 5 tomakh*, vol. 1 (St. Petersburg: Symposium, 1997), 555. I am grateful for the assistance of Professors Priscilla Meyer and D. Barton Johnson for, in the first case, pointing out this commentary in the Russian edition and, in the second, for translating and summarizing it. There are a multitude of Violas in Nabokov's other works as well, some of which are clearly Shakespearean. As early as 1923, a year before his poem "Shakespeare," Nabokov's collection of early poems entitled "Grozd'" included a Russian poem with an English title, "Viola Tricolor." In "The University Poem," the narrator and Violet attend a performance of *Hamlet*. Yuri Leving, V. Nabokov. *Sobranie sochinenii russkogo perioda v 5 tt.*, vol. 2 (St. Petersburg: Symposium, 1999), 567.

[9] Nabokov, *Knight*, 10. These are discussed insightfully in Priscilla Meyer, "Black and Violet Words: *Despair* and *The Real Life of Sebastian Knight* as Doubles," *Nabokov Studies* 4 (1997): 37-60.

[10] Nabokov, *Knight*, 17.

[11] Ibid., 37.

not seem overreaching to suggest that what is being "advertised" here are the paired violets — the tin and its reflection; identical twins Viola and Sebastian "reflected in the mirror."

Yet another interesting link between Shakespeare's comedy and Nabokov's novel comes when Viola, in the play's final scene, proves her identity to her twin Sebastian by noting that her father died when she was thirteen.[12] Of course, her twin Sebastian was exactly her age. The very first sentence of Nabokov's work tells us that "Sebastian Knight was born on the thirty-first of December, 1899..." Later, we learn that his father died early in 1913, when he would have been thirteen, as was Shakespeare's Sebastian when he lost his father.[13]

Russian author Viktor Shklovsky, whose works recently began appearing in English, wrote extensively on Shakespeare. He comments on a triangular connection:

> Therefore, to the question of Tolstoi: "Why does Lear not recognize Kent and Kent — Edgar[?]" [O]ne may answer: because this is necessary for the creation of the drama[,] and the unreality disturbed Shakespeare no more than the question "Why cannot a Knight move straight?" disturbs a chess player.[14]

There are further references to Shakespeare in *The Real Life of Sebastian Knight*, most prominently, to *Hamlet*. Sebastian declares that one of the things he most likes about England and English is "a purple passage in Hamlet."[15] When "V" catalogs a list of books he finds on Sebastian's book shelf, the list begins with *Hamlet* and ends with *King Lear*. And, amusingly, "V" describes Sebastian pulling the leg of his secretary, Mr. Goodman:

> Sebastian speaking of his very first novel (unpublished and destroyed) explained that it was about a fat young student who travels home to find his mother married to his uncle; this uncle, an ear-specialist, had murdered the student's father. Mr. Goodman misses the joke.[16]

---

[12] Shakespeare, *Twelfth Night*, V. i., line 244.
[13] Nabokov, *Knight*, 5-7.
[14] Viktor Shklovsky, "The connection between devices of syuzhet construction and general stylistic devices" (Normal and London: Dalkey Archive Press, 2005 [Orig. pub. 1919]). See also *The Knight's Move*, trans. Richard Sheldon (Urbana-Champaign: The Dalkey Archive Press, 1995 [Orig. pub. 1923]). I am grateful to Dr. Yuri Leving for pointing out this connection to me. See also Dale Peterson, "Knight's Move: Nabokov, Shklovsky and the Afterlife of Sirin," *Nabokov Studies* 11 (2007-08): 25-37.
[15] Nabokov, *Knight*, 68. Priscilla Meyer, "Violet Words," 42, believes the "purple passage" is Queen Gertrude's citation of purple, "violet" flowers when speaking of Ophelia's death.
[16] Nabokov, *Knight*, 64.

There are both obvious and subtle thematic links between Nabokov's novel and the two Shakespeare plays. Clearly, *Twelfth Night*, with the confusion between Viola and Sebastian (as well as the gender confusion between Viola and Cesario, her male disguise) parallels the Sebastian / "V" theme of *The Real Life of Sebastian Knight*. In both works, characters mistake the identity of other characters and, more originally, key characters seem to mistake their own identities. A similar theme, in a more minor key, operates in *The Tempest*. Here, too, characters do not really know each other: Ferdinand does not know until the last scene that Miranda is the daughter of a former Duke of Milan; Caliban does not realize that Stephano and Trinculo are comic incompetents; Alonso and Sebastian do not recognize that their actions are being overseen by Prospero. At the end of the First Folio edition of *The Tempest*, the setting is described, tellingly and mysteriously, as "The Scene, an un-inhabited island." What does this mean? That "no one" lives there? What about Prospero and Miranda? What about Caliban and Ariel and the spirits?

These queries lead us from the issue of "identity" to what has been called the "metadrama" or "metafictional" level of both plays. Prospero's moving soliloquy in Act IV recognizes that *The Tempest* is a play, set in a theater:

> Our revels now are ended. These our actors,
> As I foretold you, were all spirits and
> Are melted into air, into thin air;
> And, like the baseless fabric of this vision,
> The cloud-capped towers, the gorgeous palaces,
> The solemn temples, the great globe itself,
> Yea, all which it inherit, shall dissolve,
> And, like this insubstantial pageant faded,
> Leave not a rack behind. We are such stuff
> As dreams are made on, and our little life
> Is rounded with a sleep.[17]

The Tempest was long seen, understandably but probably incorrectly, as representing Shakespeare's farewell to the stage in Prospero's farewell to his magic art. Most modern students of the play would not subscribe to the autobiographical reading, but would still find it almost unavoidable to see the parallels between Prospero's art and that of his creator.

Similarly, *Twelfth Night* is shot through with self-referential images of the theater. Thus, when Olivia asks Viola in the disguise of Cesario if s/he is

---

[17] Shakespeare, *The Tempest*, IV. i., lines 148-158.

a "comedian" (actor), Viola's response is "I am not that I play."[18] When Feste, the Clown, taunts Malvolio, he compares himself to the traditional character in the Morality plays: I'll be with you again / In a trice / Like to the old Vice.[19] And, of course, the play ends with the same character proclaiming: But that's all one, our play is done, / And we'll strive to please you every day.[20]

Self reflexivity—writing fiction about writing fiction—is generally characteristic of Nabokov's work, and *The Real Life of Sebastian Knight* is certainly no exception. As Stephen Jan Parker has pointed out, the novel is a work of art which is an exploration of "the nature of art."[21] Discussing the narrator "V's" explanation of Sebastian's aesthetics, Vladimir E. Alexandrov notes how close Sebastian's literary philosophy and practice are to Nabokov's "metaliterary themes and praxis."[22] He cites "V's" description of an artist who creates "not the painting of a landscape, but the painting of different ways of painting a certain landscape." (In *Pnin*, Victor, the title character's son, paints a picture of the sky...as reflected in the complex curve of an automobile fender.) In describing Knight's book *The Prismatic Bezel*, "V" observes that the work "can be thoroughly enjoyed once it is understood that the heroes of the book are what can be loosely called 'methods of composition.'"[23] Priscilla Meyer observes that not only is *The Real Life of Sebastian Knight* a book about doubles, it has, itself, a "double": the novel *Despair*.[24] Nabokov, then, like Shakespeare, creates a work of art about the workings of art.

Finally, in Shakespeare's *Twelfth Night* and *The Tempest*, and Nabokov's *The Real Life of Sebastian Knight*, the shared name "Sebastian" leads us to what may be the deepest theme of both authors—that magical place where the motifs of identity and self-reflexive art come together. "I am Sebastian, or Sebastian is I, or perhaps we both are someone whom neither of us knows," says "V."[25] If "V" is "Viola," seeking her lost brother, "V" is also "Vladimir," whose literary works are very much like those of Sebastian Knight. "V" and Sebastian are both someone neither of them knows: they are their creator and

---

[18] Shakespeare, *Twelfth Night*, I. v., lines 180-181. See Anne Richter, *Shakespeare and the Idea of the Play* (London: Chatto and Windus, 1962), 130-136.
[19] Shakespeare, *Twelfth Night*, IV. ii., 122-124
[20] Ibid., V. i., lines 408-409.
[21] Stephen Jan Parker, *Understanding Nabokov* (Columbia: The University of South Carolina Press, 1987), 128.
[22] Vladimir E. Alexandrov, *Nabokov's Otherworld* (Princeton, NJ: Princeton University Press, 1991), 143.
[23] Nabokov, *Knight*, 95.
[24] Meyer, "Violet Words," 37-60.
[25] Nabokov, *Knight*, 205.

they are the creations of their creator. Is Shakespeare's Viola actually Viola, or is she Cesario, her male counterpart; or is she the male actor playing both Viola and Cesario; or is she, ultimately, the words Shakespeare found to create Viola, Sebastian, Cesario and *Twelfth Night*? "A great while ago the world begun, / Hey, ho, the wind and the rain; / But that's all one, our play is done, / And we'll strive to please you every day."[26] If *Twelfth Night* is really a play of mistaken identity, the biggest identity mistake of all is to forget that Viola and Sebastian are figments of Shakespeare's imagination. At the end of *The Tempest*, Shakespeare reminds the audience that they *are* an audience, that they have been watching "actors," who "were all spirits and are melted into air, into thin air." In the play's epilogue, the actor playing Prospero continues to play Prospero, and also plays the actor playing Prospero:

> Now my charms are all o'erthrown,
> And what strength I have's mine own,
> Which is most faint. Now 'tis true
> I must here be confined by you,
> Or sent to Naples. Let me not,
> Since I have my dukedom got
> And pardoned the deceiver, dwell
> In this bare island by your spell
> But release me from my bands,
> With the help of your good hands...[27]

The real *The Real Life of Sebastian Knight* is a novel, a fiction, in which the title character owes his name, at least in part, and his reality—the reality of art—to two other fictional persons invented by Shakespeare.

---

[26] Shakespeare, *Twelfth Night*, V. i., lines 406-409.
[27] Shakespeare, *The Tempest*, Epilogue, lines 1-10.

Marta Pellerdi

AESTHETICS AND SIN: THE NYMPH AND THE FAUN IN HAWTHORNE'S *THE MARBLE FAUN* AND NABOKOV'S *LOLITA*

There have been some noteworthy attempts in the past to compare similar features and motifs in Nabokov's works to those in Hawthorne's tales and romances. Although it has been a general tendency to accept that the literary structures and patterns in Nabokov's work have European sources, critics such as Leona Toker, Robert Kiely and Elizabeth Freeman have discovered several links between Nabokov and Hawthorne in their efforts to trace the American literary influence in Nabokov's writings.[1] The

---

[1] Leona Toker sets up analogies between other novels and stories by Nabokov and Hawthorne in *Nabokov: The Mystery of Literary Structures* (Ithaca: Cornell University Press, 1989). See also Toker's "Nabokov and the Hawthorne Tradition," *Scripta Hierosolymitana* 32 (1987), 323-49. According to Toker, "there are elements in Nabokov's art which he had always shared with

basis of the seemingly far-fetched literary connection is Nabokov's description of Hawthorne in *Strong Opinions* as a "splendid writer."[2] Kiely, in particular, finds parallels between *The Marble Faun* and *Lolita* in the faun theme and in the way the two authors relate to readers, neither of them having "much faith" in their audience.[3] He quotes from Hawthorne's *The French and Italian Notebooks* in which the nineteenth century American author recognizes the thematic possibilities of placing the faun's character in the center of a literary investigation. After seeing a copy of Praxiteles' Faun in the Villa Borghese and in the Capitol sculpture gallery of Rome Hawthorne wrote: "Their character has never, that I know of, been wrought out in literature; and something very good, funny, and philosophical, as well as poetic, might very likely be educed from them."[4] By placing the character of Humbert, who seems to be the modern reincarnation of the faun-satyr, into the focus of a literary investigation in *Lolita*, Nabokov is attempting to do something similar, although there is no substantial proof of whether Nabokov had ever read Hawthorne's *The Marble Faun*.[5] Yet, a "very good, funny and philosophical, as well as poetic" work of art in is created, a text in which the fate of the nymph, Lolita, is full of "pathos" and tragedy, like the faun's in Hawthorne's work.[6]

---

what may be called the Hawthorne tradition; upon his arrival in America these elements developed with particular vigor" (324). Chapter Seven of Robert Kiely's *Reverse Tradition: Postmodern Fictions and the Nineteenth Century Novel* (Cambridge: Harvard University Press, 1993), 152-175, entitled "The Reader without a Country: Nathaniel Hawthorne's *The Marble Faun* after Nabokov," mainly discusses Hawthorne's romance, but some similarities between the two authors and their works are noted. See also Elizabeth Freeman, "Honeymoon with a Stranger: Pedophiliac Picaresques from Poe to Nabokov" *American Literature* 70.1 (1998): 109-154.

[2] Vladimir Nabokov, *Strong Opinions* (New York: McGraw-Hill, 1973), 64.

[3] Kiely, *Reverse Tradition*, 152.

[4] Nathaniel Hawthorne, *The French and Italian Notebooks*, The Centenary Edition, vol. 14, ed. Thomas Woodson (Columbus: Ohio State University Press, 1980), 173, 178, quoted in Kiely, *Reverse Tradition*, 154. In *The Marble Faun*, the four friends, Miriam, Donatello, Kenyon and Hilda admire "a copy of a bronze statue" of the Faun "then believed to be by Praxiteles (c.370-c.330 BCE), [which] stands in the Hall of the Dying Gladiator in the Capitol." Susan Manning, "Explanatory Notes," *The Marble Faun*, Nathaniel Hawthorne, ed. Susan Manning (Oxford: Oxford University Press, 2002), 364, number 8.

[5] If he did, then the book may have been recommended to him by Edmund Wilson in the 1940s when they were still close friends. In a letter to Newton Arvin (May 24, 1946) Wilson writes that Hawthorne's *The Marble Faun* is a "remarkable book" which he "admire[s] the most" among Hawthorne's works. "Edmund Wilson on Writers and Writing," *The New York Review of Books*, March 17, 1977, http://www.nybooks.com/articles/8577?email (accessed November 12, 2009). I am indebted to D. Barton Johnson for this observation and the reference.

[6] Hawthorne, *The French and Italian Notebooks*, 178, quoted in Kiely, *Reverse Tradition*, 154.

The Marble Faun and *Lolita* are American classics.[7] A period of almost one hundred years separates them: Hawthorne's romance was published in 1860; Nabokov's novel first appeared in Paris in 1955. While Hawthorne's work served as a travel guide to American tourists visiting Rome in the second half of the nineteenth century, Nabokov's *Lolita* offers readers a description of familiar American scenes. Nabokov's faun is transported across the Atlantic and placed into the "broad and simple daylight" of shadowless North America with "suburban lawn[s], mountain meadow[s]" and motels as a backdrop for his story.[8] As an American writer, Hawthorne felt that he owed an explanation to his readers, in the preface to his last major work, as to why he had placed the setting of his romance in Popish Rome:

> No author, without a trial, can conceive of the difficulty of writing a Romance about a country where there is no shadow, no antiquity, no mystery, no picturesque and gloomy wrong, nor anything but a common-place prosperity, in broad and simple daylight, as is happily the case with my dear native land... Romance and poetry, like ivy, lichens, and wall-flowers, need Ruin to make them grow.[9]

Nabokov, however, uses the "ivy" and "Ruin" of classical literature, the faun of the Arcadian dream world created and adapted by other artists throughout the centuries, placing him in New World surroundings to show that he is "trying to be an American writer and claim only the same rights that other American writers enjoy."[10] Hawthorne's romance is the first in a long line of international novels (taken up later by Henry James), in which American innocence is contrasted with European experience, usually in a European environment. While Hawthorne was an American writer in Europe writing about American and European artists in the Old World and about Arcadian innocence, Nabokov was a Russian-American author writing about a European pedophile with artistic inclinations in America and his ardent desire for and

---

[7] *The Marble Faun*, however, came under serious critical attack in the twentieth century. See R. W. B. Lewis, "The Return into Time: *The Marble Faun*," *Nathaniel Hawthorne*, Modern Critical Views, ed. Harold Bloom (New York: Chelsea House Publishers, 1986), 25-31. According to Lewis, "The novel's plot verges more than once on incoherence," and it is "not the best and probably not the second-best of Hawthorne's novels" (25). See also Nina Baym, "*The Marble Faun*: Hawthorne's Elegy for Art," *Nathaniel Hawthorne*, ed. Harold Bloom (New York, 1986), 99-114. To Nina Baym, the book "appears confused and self-contradictory" (99).

[8] Vladimir Nabokov, "On a Book Entitled *Lolita*," in *Lolita* (New York: Vintage Books, Random House, 1997), 315.

[9] Nathaniel Hawthorne, *The Marble Faun*, ed. Susan Manning (Oxford: Oxford University Press, 2002), 4.

[10] Nabokov, "On a Book Entitled *Lolita*," 315.

violation of a twelve-year-old girl. The undercurrent of incest runs through the main theme of both works. In *The Marble Faun*, it is an ambiguous and elusive subtheme that remains unexplained. In *Lolita*, it is presented as "the parody of incest" by the faunish stepfather, Humbert, who reasons, this, "in the long run, was the best I could offer the waif."[11] This article attempts to elucidate how the revival of the Arcadian creatures, the metaphorical faun and the nymph, seem particularly suitable for both writers in expressing the distinctions between life and art. With different emphases, both works show the consequences of a choice between the ephemeral, but moral quality of life and the timeless, but morally indifferent or dubious aestheticism of art.

In *The Marble Faun*, Donatello, the Count of Monte Beni, a descendent of half-human, half-beast mythical creatures, undergoes a transformation into a human being through suffering and repentance after he commits murder. In *Lolita*, Humbert does not undergo any such change; instead, he seems to be misplaced in time as a revived faun-satyr in a human guise, transplanted by the author from an Arcadian world into the land of modern America. This is why he cannot control his bestial passion and cannot make a distinction between flesh and blood little girls and Arcadian-demoniac nymphets. While the growth of the artistic powers and tastes of the American artists Kenyon and Hilda in *The Marble Faun* are affected by the moral development of their friend Donatello, they must eventually choose between rejecting or accepting the inevitable relationship between art and sin.[12] Humbert, however, simply and mercilessly confuses life with art. Thus, he rejects the moral standards of American life; and instead chooses to substitute life for the "refuge of art," which does not have moral dimensions, and in which all manifestations of the imagination, including pedophilia, are possible.[13]

Hawthorne identified his four longer works as romances rather than novels. He attempted to define "the romance" in several prefaces to his works.[14] Richard Chase, Joel Porte and many others adopted Hawthorne's

---

[11] Nabokov, *Lolita* (New York: Vintage Books, Random House, 1997), 287.

[12] Thus, Hawthorne raises dilemmas concerning Calvinist-Puritan convictions (represented by Hilda), which do not accept sin and experience, and their relationship to art or "education" as leading to a "loftier Paradise" than Adam's (Hawthorne, *Faun*, 357). Kenyon has to surrender the lesson learned through Donatello's story in favor of Hilda. See Agnes McNeill Donohue's work on Hawthorne's religious confusion, "his disturbed and distressed response to Calvinism versus Roman Catholicism," *Hawthorne: Calvin's Ironic Step-child* (Kent, Ohio: The Kent State University Press, 1985), 268.

[13] Nabokov, *Lolita*, 309.

[14] In the preface to *The House of the Seven Gables*, for instance, Hawthorne makes the distinction: the novel is "presumed to aim at a very minute fidelity, not merely to the possible, but to the

definition of the essential characteristics of the genre. Chase emphasized the special American features and tradition of the romance as opposed to its European version.[15] According to Porte, Hawthorne's

> attempts to describe this special fictional entity center not only in discussions about a particular kind of treatment but also in a persistent association of the romance with certain themes. Chief among these... is the notion of the continuing force of past experience, especially guilty or sinful experience, in the life of the present.[16]

According to this description, what makes a given work a romance is the theme itself, not just the way the theme is handled. In the case of *Lolita*, "past experience, especially guilty or sinful experience, in the life of the present" is displayed. If romances, as Michael Davitt Bell proposed, are a "convenient label for *any* qualities... typical of American fiction or even of American life generally," then Humbert's confession, written in consequence of his guilt, can be regarded as a parody of a modern romance.[17] Nabokov's *Lolita* clearly fits into the American literary tradition not only by parodying certain superficial and philistine aspects of American culture, but also by focusing on the themes of innocence and corruption and their relationship to art.

In *The Marble Faun*, Donatello, the Count of Monte Beni, is the faun come to life, and resembles the ancient statue of the Faun of Praxiteles to a striking degree:

> The whole statue—unlike anything else that ever was wrought in that severe material of marble—conveys the idea of an amiable and sensual creature, easy, mirthful, apt for jollity, yet not incapable of being touched by pathos..... Perhaps it is the very lack of moral severity of any high and heroic ingredient in the character of the Faun, that makes it so delightful an object to the human eye and to the frailty of the human heart.[18]

---

probable and ordinary course of man's experience." The romance—"while, as a work of art, it must rigidly subject itself to laws, and while it sins unpardonably so far as it may swerve aside from the truth of the human heart—has fairly a right to present that truth under circumstances, to a great extent, of the writer's own choosing or creation." Nathaniel Hawthorne, *The House of the Seven Gables* (Boston, New York: Houghton, Mifflin, 1894), v.

[15] Richard Chase, *The American Novel and its Tradition* (Baltimore: The John Hopkins University Press, 1993).

[16] Joel Porte, *The Romance in America* (Middletown, Conn.: Wesleyan University Press, 1969), 96.

[17] Michael Davitt Bell, *Culture, Genre, and Literary Vocation: Selected Essays on American Literature* (Chicago: University of Chicago Press, 2000), 36.

[18] Hawthorne, *Faun*, 10.

The likeness intrigues Donatello's friends, Miriam, Kenyon and Hilda, who are artists living in Rome. The main difference between the mythic, half-animal, half-human creature and humans, except physical features, is the former's lack of moral conscience. Miriam, a European artist with a shady background, expresses a wish to change places with the faun and summarizes the difference between humans and the Arcadian creatures:

> Imagine, now, a real being, similar to this mythic Faun; how happy, how genial, how satisfactory would be his life, enjoying the warm, sensuous, earthy side of Nature; revelling in the merriment of woods and streams; living as our four-footed kindred do — as mankind did in its innocent childhood, before sin, sorrow, or morality itself, had ever been thought of!... For I suppose the Faun had no conscience, no remorse, no burthen [sic] on the heart, no troublesome recollections of any sort; no dark future neither![19]

Donatello's life is full of Arcadian joy and innocence, until he commits the murder that turns him into a fallen man who will have to bear the burden of his guilty conscience. He is in love with Miriam, who is referred to as a nymph in Chapter IX (entitled "The Faun and Nymph"). Although Miriam is "the more inclined to melancholy,"[20] she romps about in the Borghese grove with Donatello in a scene which provides a

> glimpse far backward into Arcadian life, or, farther still, into the Golden Age, before mankind was burthened [sic] with sin and sorrow, and before pleasure had been darkened with those shadows that bring it into high relief, and make it Happiness.[21]

The dark-haired, dark-eyed, young and beautiful artist of English-Jewish background is persistently followed all over Rome by a mysterious older man whose past is guiltily intertwined with Miriam's. Near the end of the book, when Miriam reveals some details about her shadowy past to Kenyon, the American sculptor, she also speculates about the possible reason for her pursuer's unnatural behavior:

> Looking back upon what had happened, Miriam observed, she now considered him a madman. Insanity must have been mixed up with his original composition, and developed by those very acts of depravity which it suggested, and still more intensified by the remorse that ultimately followed them.[22]

---

[19] Ibid., 13.
[20] Ibid., 65.
[21] Ibid., 66.
[22] Ibid., 335.

"Depravity" refers to "insanity which often develops itself in old, close-kept breeds of men, when long unmixed with newer blood," which is a euphemistic way of referring to incest.[23] Miriam, however, is not a completely innocent nymph. While there is only a shadow of suspicion cast upon her for having been involved in a gruesome crime in the past, she becomes an accomplice, an inciter, as it were, to Donatello, who throws her mysterious pursuer off a precipice when he sees the desire unintentionally expressed in her eyes. Both the nymph and the faun of Hawthorne's romance have to repent, but much of the book is about Donatello's suffering and transformation into a human being. Thus, the story of the innocent faun and the morally ambiguous nymph becomes a "developmental narrative of the Fall of Man".[24] Graham Clarke, in summing up the main characteristics of *The Marble Faun*, concludes: "To put it at its most obvious the book is almost wholly concerned with the nature of art and the art-making process..."[25] Janice M. Fuller goes one step further, stating that many critics overlooked the fact that Hawthorne's romance is concerned with "the relationship between art and life or the ideal and real."[26] The marble statue of the faun comes to life in Hawthorne's romance only to find that "[l]ife has grown so sadly serious, that such men must change their nature, or else perish."[27] Nabokov's Humbert, however, is incapable of changing his cruel nature in *Lolita*. In both works of fiction "Life and Art are elaborately parallel worlds...but neither provides a key to 'solve' the mysteries of the other."[28]

Although Humbert expresses remorse after he loses his nymphet, he would, if he could, in the same way as Miriam's madman, "follow [her] forth with fresh impulses to crime."[29] While Humbert seems to feel sorrow at past deeds, he laments losing Lolita more than he regrets the crime that he committed against her. At one point he feels that it would be "[b]etter [to] destroy everything than surrender her."[30] In the execution scene, years after

---

[23] Ibid., 334.
[24] Manning, "Introduction," xi.
[25] Graham Clarke, "To Transform and Transfigure: The Aesthetic Play of Hawthorne's *The Marble Faun*," *Nathaniel Hawthorne: New Critical Essays*, ed. Robert Lee (Totowa, N.J: Barnes and Noble, 1982), 132.
[26] Janice M. Fuller, "Hawthorne as Protomodernist: The Relationship of Flesh and Marble in *The Marble Faun*" *Postscript* 5 (1988): 25, http://www.unca.edu/postscript/postscript5/ps5.3.pdf (accessed August 6, 2009).
[27] Hawthorne, *Faun*, 356.
[28] Manning, "Introduction," xxiii.
[29] Hawthorne, *Faun*, 335.
[30] Nabokov, *Lolita*, 235.

Dolly's escape, he recites a poem to Clare Quilty in which he is still "dreaming of marriage in a mountain state / aye of a litter of Lolitas."[31] After he murders Quilty, Humbert realizes that there is no way he can give back to Dolly the childhood which he robbed from her. His autobiography becomes a public confession, written to atone for the sins he committed against her. Unlike Donatello, however, "Humbert is a vain and cruel wretch," as Nabokov warned readers, "who manages to appear 'touching.'"[32]

When Humbert describes the source of his passion for nymphets, he recalls his first love, Annabel Leigh, echoing Poe's "Annabel Lee."[33] Humbert stresses that when the germs of his ruthless obsession were born, he and Annabel were coevals: "When I was a child and she was a child, my little Annabel was no nymphet to me; I was her equal, a faunlet in my own right, on that same enchanted island of time…"[34] Unfortunately, he does not remain a simple "faunlet" and, after growing up, he becomes more like a lecherous faun, or satyr, and develops an obsession for nymphets. When speaking about his desire for nymphets, Humbert consistently sees himself as having the attributes of the pagan faun: the animalistic "ape ear[s]," "hairy hand[s]" and "timid claws."[35] But Humbert's case is not simple; his malady is a longing for a "more poignant bliss" which only the females that he labels as "nymphets" can provide and to which twelve-year-old Dolly unfortunately belongs.

> Between the age limits of nine and fourteen there occur maidens who, to certain bewitched travelers, twice or many times older than they, reveal their true nature which is not human, but nymphic (that is, demoniac); and these chosen creatures I propose to designate as "nymphets."[36]

In other words, not all little girls are nymphets to Humbert. But some of them are, and one of them happens to be Dolly. At the beginning of Humbert's confession, he admits that he "was perfectly capable of intercourse with Eve, but it was Lilith he longed for." When Humbert's imagination transforms Dolly into Lolita, the little girl begins to assume the attributes of a female demon.[37]

---

[31] Ibid., 300.
[32] Nabokov, *Strong Opinions*, 94.
[33] Andrew Field, *Nabokov: His Life in Art* (Boston: Little Brown and Co., 1967), 338.
[34] Nabokov, *Lolita* 17-18.
[35] Ibid., 48; 60; 56.
[36] Ibid., 16.
[37] Ibid., 20. See Olga Voronina, "The Tale of Enchanted Hunters: *Lolita* in a Victorian Context," *Nabokov Studies* 10 (2006): 147-174, on *Lolita* and Victorian authors' fascination with "the figure of [the] 'demon-child'" (150).

The critic Michael Wood sees the reader as having a major role in finding the child to whom Humbert seems to be blind: "[t]he 'actual' Lolita is the person we see Humbert can't see, or can see only spasmodically."[38] Lolita suffered, sobbing "in the night—every night, every night—the moment [Humbert] feigned sleep." Humbert is deeply aware that Lolita will never be able to forget that she has been "deprived of her childhood by a maniac," and since he seems to condemn himself for what he has done to her, the only way he can try to save his soul is to apply "the melancholy and very local palliative of articulate art."[39]

Humbert thus combines cruelty, lechery and moral decadence with elitist views on art; elitism that he shares with his creator, Nabokov. Although Humbert may consider the real Dolly conventional, when he sees himself as a faun, she becomes the nymph, namely the ideal, the beautiful, the inaccessible Lolita, all that an artist would strive to attain. Brutal and animalistic, Humbert's nature is dark and gloomy; in other words, he is a lustful faun who seems to be out of place in the modern American world. His character evokes another figure in Nabokov's much earlier work. In 1928 Nabokov wrote a poem in Russian entitled "Лилит" ("Lilith"), and in a footnote in *Poems and Problems* advised readers to refrain from making analogies between this poem and his later writings.[40] But there is also a common, initial source for both the poem and *Lolita*. In "Lilith," the unnamed speaker of the poem believes that he has died and is in heaven. The atmosphere is congenial, and he is surrounded by fauns when he glimpses a little nymph-like girl, Lilith, "graceful as a woman," who reminds him of "the miller's youngest daughter," the girl he longs for.[41] When he is invited to enjoy his pleasure, he is interrupted at the crucial moment by the girl drawing away from him. Disappointed, "writhing with agony," he finds himself "outside in the dust," surrounded by "goat-hoofed" creatures, and knows "abruptly that [he is] in Hell."[42] The "obscenely bleating" fauns seem more like devils and the little

---

[38] Michael Wood, *The Magician's Doubts. Nabokov and the Risks of Fiction* (Princeton: Princeton University Press, 1995), 117.

[39] Nabokov, *Lolita*, 176, 283.

[40] Vladimir Nabokov, *Poems and Problems* (New York, Toronto: McGraw-Hill, 1970), 51-55. Nabokov remarks in a footnote: "Intelligent readers will abstain from examining this impersonal fantasy for any links with my later fiction" (55). According to Christine Clegg, however, "[w]hat is most intriguing about this instruction to look no further is that the 'links' between 'Lilith,' *Lolita* and *The Enchanter* are plainly there to see." Christine Clegg, *Vladimir Nabokov: Lolita. A Reader's Guide to Essential Criticism* (Duxford, Cambridge: Icon Books, 2000), 14.

[41] Nabokov, *Poems and Problems*, 51.

[42] Ibid., 55.

girl's identity as Lilith, the female demon, is thus substantiated.[43] The theme of disruption and frustration at the end of the poem evokes the plight of the faun in Stéphane Mallarmé's *Afternoon of a Faun*. Although Humbert does not directly refer to Mallarmé, the French symbolist poet's texts always hover in the background.[44] Humbert is similar to the unnamed speaker in "Lilith": the description of his diabolic desire for the nymphet also matches the faun's desire for the nymphs in Mallarmé's poem, and their intentions are the same: "Ces nymphes, je les veux perpétuer" ("I would perpetuate these nymphs") the faun declares.[45] This reverberates in Humbert's words: "A greater endeavor lures me on: to fix once for all the perilous magic of nymphets."[46]

The primary inspiration from Mallarmé resulted in the poem about fauns, Hell and the desire for the demonic "Lilith." Later, when Nabokov was in America and writing in English, he might have had Mallarmé's faun and this Lilith in mind when he created Humbert and his Lolita. Humbert, the faun in *Lolita*, shares certain qualities with Mallarmé's faun: he is brutal and devoid of human tenderness and understanding, only caring for his own pleasures, regarding his nymph as "prey" who is "forever ungrateful," and becoming frustrated when Lolita, "spurning the spasm with which [he] still was drunk," finally manages to escape.[47]

Mallarmé also inspired Claude Debussy's musical version of *Afternoon of a Faun*, which was deemed a scandalous performance of The Russian Ballet in 1912, where the role of the faun was enacted by the famous dancer-choreographer, Vaslav Nijinsky.[48] Besides being considered overtly sexual

---

[43] Ibid., 53.

[44] Vladimir Nabokov, *Bend Sinister* (Harmondsworth: Penguin, 1986), 10. Nabokov draws attention to the theme of interruption in the Introduction to *Bend Sinister*, which is suggested by the "fractured parts" of lines taken from Stéphane Mallarmé's *L'Après-Midi d'un Faune. Oeuvres complètes. Poésies*, ed. C. P. Barbier and C. G. Millan (Paris: Flammarion, 1983), 264-267.

[45] Mallarmé, *Oeuvres*, 266; *Stéphane Mallarmé: Selected Poems*, trans. C. F. MacIntyre (Berkeley, Los Angeles: University of California Press, 1957), 47.

[46] Nabokov, *Lolita*, 134.

[47] In the Introduction to *Bend Sinister*, Nabokov offers his own translation of the line "Sans pitié du sanglot dont j'étais encore ivre" as "spurning the spasm with which I still was drunk" (10). Together with the previous line "Cette proie, à jamais ingrate se délivre" (Mallarmé, *Oeuvres*, 267), in MacIntyre's English translation (*Mallarmé: Selected Poems*, 52) it sounds like: "this prey, forever ungrateful, frees itself, / not pitying the sob that still bedrunkened me."

[48] In "'Ballet Attitudes': Nabokov's *Lolita* and Petipa's *The Sleeping Beauty*," *Nabokov at the Limits: Redrawing Critical Boundaries*, ed. Lisa Zunshine (New York: Garland, 1999), 125, note 1, Susan Elizabeth Sweeney mentions the literary link between *Lolita* and Nijinsky's performance in *Afternoon of a Faun* by The Russian Ballet. "He [Nabokov] may have had in

at the time, Nijinsky's Faun, according to contemporary ballet historian, Cyril W. Beaumont, "appeared to be of a race apart, or another essence than ourselves, an impression heightened by his [Nijinsky's] partiality for unusual roles, which were either animal-like, mythological, or unreal."[49] The production, according to Farfan, presented the "sexual queerness of the Faun."[50] Nabokov probably heard of the famous and controversial production because of the scandal it caused, and there are some hints in *Lolita* that can be interpreted to underline this possibility. For example, the famous performance is indirectly alluded to in a photo in Gaston Godin's room showing Nijinsky in the costume of the faun "all thighs and fig leaves." Nijinsky is again evoked by Humbert when he is trying to shoot Quilty in the final, parodistic, slow-motion execution scene and he sees Quilty "[rising] from his chair higher and higher, like old, gray, mad Nijinsky, like Old Faithful, like some old nightmare of mine, to a phenomenal altitude" only to land on his feet again and turn into a "normal robed man."[51] Nijinsky's interpretation of the "mythical half human/half animal Faun" in the famous ballet, even if somewhat different from the original Mallarmé text, was crucial to "the emergence of modernism" and played an important role "in the circulation of modern ideas about gender and sexuality."[52] Nijinsky's formalist and perfectionist approach in producing his artistic interpretation mirrors Nabokov's own efforts in his works.[53] The ballet's "ambiguous moral tone" and its controversial reception also coincide with the shock that *Lolita* caused its first readers.[54] Nijinsky's production demonstrated a "strange commingling of the archaic and the decadent."[55] Similar to Hawthorne's

---

mind Nijinsky's performance as the Faun in *L'Après-midi d'un Faune*, since in Gaston Godin's photograph of him the dancer appears as 'all thighs and fig leaves.'"

[49] Cyril Beaumont, *Vaslav Nijinsky* (London: C. W. Beaumont, 1932), 25, quoted in Penny Farfan, "Man as Beast: Nijinsky's Faun," *South Central Review* 25.1 (Spring 2008): 76, http://muse.uq.edu.au/journals/south_central_review/v025/25.1farfan02.pdf (accessed August 6, 2009).

[50] Farfan, "Man as Beast," 82.

[51] Nabokov, *Lolita*, 181-182, 302-3.

[52] Farfan, "Man as Beast," 76; 88.

[53] "Nijinsky was the first to demand that his whole choreographic material should be executed not only exactly as he saw it but also according to his artistic interpretation. Never was a ballet performed with such musical and choreographic exactness as *L'Après-midi d'un Faune*." Bronislava Nijinska, *Bronislava Nijinska: Early Memoirs*, ed. and trans. Irina Nijinska and Jean Rawlinson (New York: Holt, Rinehart and Winston, 1981), 427, quoted in Farfan, "Man as Beast," 78.

[54] Farfan, "Man as Beast," 83.

[55] Edward C. Moore, "Ballet Russe Makes Matinee Call at Grand" (New York: New York Public Library Manuscripts and Archives Division), quoted in Farfan, "Man as Beast," 83.

Donatello, Nijinsky's faun was modeled on the "condition of man prior to any awareness of sin."[56] The problems of art and sin versus reality and virtue are central to the texts of both *Lolita* and *The Marble Faun*, as we shall see.

Of the many works of art described by the narrator of *The Marble Faun* in his story about artists in Rome, another one, besides the Faun of Praxiteles, is particularly detailed and seems central to the main theme of innocence and corruption in the romance. The painting of Beatrice Cenci, erroneously attributed to Guido Reni at the time, made a deep impression on contemporary writers and artists and becomes "an intense presence" in *The Marble Faun*.[57] Shelley was inspired by the actual story behind the painting and wrote the historical tragedy *The Cenci* (1820) on the taboo topic of how innocence combats incest and evil. Melville's Lucy in *Pierre; or the Ambiguities*, a book that was written a few years earlier than Hawthorne's romance, and which treats the theme of incest more directly, also admires the painting. In *The Marble Faun*, after witnessing the murder, both Miriam and Hilda assume the expression of Beatrice Cenci in Hilda's copy of Guido Reni's picture, which portrays her just before she was executed for having plotted the murder of her abusive father. When Hilda sits next to the copy she produced of Guido Reni's painting, and looks in the mirror, she sees that "Beatrice's expression, seen aside and vanishing in a moment, had been depicted in her own face" and "[i]t was the knowledge of Miriam's guilt that lent the same expression to Hilda's face."[58]

With the knowledge of her friend's guilt and the assumption that, by witnessing the murder, she may also have become an accomplice, Hilda, who had unreservedly admired the works of the Old Masters until then, becomes fatigued by museums and galleries and the works of the great masters. She was a talented copyist, but after the murder she loses her talent and "it is questionable whether she was ever so perfect a copyist, thenceforth." According to Clarke, "she is not only initiated into a knowledge of sin, she is forced to acknowledge its existence as a primary element in the aesthetic and artistic process."[59] Hawthorne also makes clear that, as a consequence of such knowledge, Hilda acquires a refined critical taste in art, becoming capable of distinguishing the fake from the real:

---

[56] Eric Hellman, "The Scandal of Nijinsky's Faune," *Ballet Review* 22.2 (1994): 18, quoted in Farfan, "Man as Beast," 82-83.
[57] Manning, "Introduction," xxi.
[58] Hawthorne, *Faun*, 160.
[59] Ibid., 291. Clarke, "Transform and Transfigure," 134.

[she] saw into the picture as profoundly as ever, and perhaps more so, but not with the devout sympathy that had formerly given her entire possession of the Old Master's idea. She had known such a reality, that it taught her to distinguish inevitably the large portion that is unreal, in every work of art.[60]

But by recognizing the role of sin in artistic creation, Hilda also turns away from it. From this point onwards she is incapable of losing herself in art. She cannot "understand...how two mortal foes—as Right and Wrong surely are—can work together in the same deed." Nor can she accept that "a mixture of good there may be in things evil."[61] Hilda also rejects Miriam's views on the role of experience and sin. She refuses to see sin as a "blessing in strange disguise," "a means of education" in the history of mankind, which Kenyon half believes. The sculptor at the end of the romance attempts to summarize the "moral of [Donatello's] story."

> Sin has educated Donatello, and elevated him. Is Sin, then—which we deem such a dreadful blackness in the Universe—is it, like Sorrow, merely an element of human education, through which we struggle to a higher and purer state than we could otherwise have attained. Did Adam fall, that we might ultimately rise to a far loftier Paradise than his?[62]

Hilda is "shocked...beyond words" and reminds Kenyon of the "mockery [his] creed makes, not only of religious sentiment, but of moral law." Kenyon chooses to agree with Hilda rather than lose her. However, this does not dispel the ambiguity of the ending. In his contemplation of the key role played by sin in the artistic process and in the education of mankind, the author himself appears perplexed. By describing Donatello's act of murder and illustrating his extreme suffering and remorse, Hawthorne is also aestheticizing it, adopting an attitude to art that the inflexible Puritan, Hilda, would never accept.[63]

Thus, the Protestant-American artists, Hilda and Kenyon, turn away from Miriam and Donatello. Unlike the faun in Nabokov's novel, Hilda and Kenyon choose life and each other—moral reality instead of art—on the basis of religious convictions that exclude the possibility of aestheticizing sin. Miriam as nymph and Donatello as faun (the European characters of the story) also choose life through penitence, and the four friends leave the picture galleries

---

[60] Hawthorne, *Faun*, 291.
[61] Ibid., 298.
[62] Ibid., 337, 356-57.
[63] Ibid., 357. Here Hawthorne seems to be battling with the demonic attractions of Catholicism but conscientiously choosing Protestantism instead.

of Rome. Miriam and Donatello are dressed as a peasant and Contadina the last time they appear together before readers, demonstrating that there is no longer any difference between them and the ordinary citizens of Rome. Through contrition and penitence, Donatello has now undergone a complete transformation from an innocent creature into a moral being. Miriam, having acknowledged the role of sin in the artistic process, will have to dedicate herself to repentance and praying for Donatello.

Lolita, just like *The Marble Faun*, is also full of artistic references, mainly to literary works. It seems that Nabokov's faun, Humbert, has a propensity for both pedophilia and highbrow aesthetics. In other words, Humbert's moral decadence is fused with a taste for literary decadence. This aspect of his controversial nature has persistently baffled critics. Humbert's erudition manifests itself in the numerous literary allusions he scatters throughout his autobiography. The intertextual quality of Nabokov's writings was noticed by his earliest critics, and much has been said about the similarities between the literary references and the patterns they form. The theme of art and sin links *Lolita* to the Hawthorne tradition, as we have seen but, if one looks closely, the English subtext of *Lolita* is constructed upon texts mainly from French and English literature, especially from the Symbolist period.[64] The allusions to past writers and their works bolster Humbert's intention of convincing his readers that his case is not abnormal, since it has precedence in the lives of renowned poets.

> After all, Dante fell madly in love with his Beatrice when she was nine, a sparkling girleen, painted and lovely, and bejeweled, in a crimson frock, and this was in 1274, in Florence, at a private feast in the merry month of May. And when Petrarch fell madly in love with his Laureen, she was a fair-haired nymphet of twelve running in the wind, in the pollen and dust, a flower in flight, in the beautiful plain as descried from the hills of Vauclus.[65]

Humbert forgets to add, however, that Dante was only one year older than Beatrice at the time, and Petrarch's Laura was at least eighteen.[66] By omitting and falsifying details, he is trying to persuade his readers that he truly regrets having ruined Lolita's childhood, but at the same time he also wants them to condone his immorality. Through Humbert's direct or indirect literary

---

[64] According to Priscilla Meyer, *Find What the Sailor Has Hidden: Vladimir Nabokov's Pale Fire* (Middleton, Conn.: Wesleyan University Press, 1988), 6, the Russian tradition is at the root of the subtext of *Lolita*.
[65] Nabokov, *Lolita*, 19.
[66] Morris Bishop, *Petrarch and his World* (Bloomington: Indiana University Press, 1963), 64.

references, Nabokov also points to the exclusively literary dimension of Humbert's character. Humbert's text feeds on other texts; it is a rewritten and compiled, distorted version of other literary texts.[67]

Humbert is an elegant stylist and, after losing Lolita, he regrets that he is left with "only words to play with." As a foreigner whose mother tongue is not English, Humbert experiments with the language of his new homeland. He is of English and "mixed French and Austrian descent, with a dash of the Danube in his veins." While Humbert is trying out English words and sounding alternately informal, archaic and erudite, Nabokov is doing the same—he declares in the postscript that on his part *Lolita* was "a love affair" with the "English language."[68] Humbert provides readers with various pieces of information from his European past, which explain his erudition and the numerous allusions in his text. In Paris as a student, he "switched to English literature, where so many poets end as pipe-smoking teachers in tweeds." Later, after finishing his studies, he worked as a teacher of English in France and then "started to compile that manual of French literature for English-speaking students (with comparisons drawn from English writers) which was to occupy [him] throughout the forties." The influence of this work is faintly detected in Humbert's memoir. Perhaps it is not an exaggeration to remark that the texture of *Lolita* is very much like a "manual of French literature" for English readers "with comparisons drawn from English writers," as Humbert claims.[69]

Mallarmé's *L'Après-Midi d'un Faune*, like Nijinsky's ballet, shares characteristics with especially decadent poetry of the time, but nymphs and fauns cultivating the pagan spirit appealed to other artists as well. This tendency in France parallels the aesthetic movement in the English literature whose first representatives were D. G. Rossetti, Walter Pater and Oscar Wilde (in England). Pater's *Marius the Epicurean* demonstrated a return to a Hellenistic, impressionistic view of life, which Pater's followers later developed into sensuality; a form of hedonism in lifestyle, the (self)-criticism of which is found in Wilde's *The Picture of Dorian Gray*. Aestheticism meant elitism in art, or "art for art's sake," and the decadents felt they were fulfilling a purpose by fighting against mediocrity and conventionality. In other words, they extended aestheticism to the sphere of non-textual existence. And Humbert feels entitled to do the same. That is, he confuses Arcadia

---

[67] See C. R. Proffer, *Keys to Lolita* (Bloomington: Indiana University Press, 1968); and Vladimir Nabokov, *The Annotated 'Lolita*,' ed., intro. and annotated Alfred Appel, Jr. (New York: Vintage Books, 1991).

[68] Nabokov, *Lolita*, 32, 9; and "On a Book Entitled *Lolita*," 316.

[69] Nabokov, *Lolita*, 15, 16.

with Terra (to borrow from *Ada*), myth with "reality," art with life. While anything is possible in art, this is not the case with life. Faunish in his tastes and passionately longing for nymphets, Humbert is a belated disciple of the decadents, transplanting the decadent spirit of late nineteenth century Europe to twentieth century modern America. We see this in the clues that Quilty leaves behind, such as his home address: "Aubrey Beardsley, Quelquepart Island." Similarly, Beardsley, the town where he settles with Lolita for a short time, again echoes the name of the fin-de-siècle artist Aubrey Beardsley, who not only captured the pagan artistic spirit of the times in his pen and ink drawings of Wilde's *Salomé*, but whose illustrations also inspired George Barbier's drawings of Nijinsky as faun in 1912 and 1913.[70] The rather covert references to Wilde, Swinburne, and Aubrey Beardsley also point to the Victorian period, when the lives of many decadent artists were viewed with horror. George Steiner observed that "it is difficult to dissociate *Lolita* from the English versions of art nouveau, from the coloration of Beardsley, Wilde, and Firbank."[71] Humbert's problem is that America proves too Victorian in matters of nympholepsy, and too conventional for his aesthetic tastes, but still capable of exerting a powerful influence over him — at least in the person of Lolita.

While art and sin are problematically linked to Catholicism for the American artists in Hawthorne's romance, in *Lolita*, aestheticism and Catholicism are logically conjoined. Like many decadent artists (Wilde, Swinburne, Verlaine and Huysmans or Beardsley), Humbert also seeks forgiveness for his sins in Catholicism, but is unsuccessful in his efforts:

> A couple of years before, under the guidance of an intelligent French-speaking confessor, to whom, in a moment of metaphysical curiosity, I had turned over a Protestant's drab atheism for an old-fashioned popish cure, I had hoped to deduce from my sense of sin the existence of a Supreme Being.... Alas, I was unable to transcend the simple human fact that whatever spiritual solace I might find, whatever lithophanic eternities might be provided for me, nothing could make my Lolita forget the foul lust I had inflicted upon her.[72]

---

[70] Nabokov, *Lolita*, 251. Léon Bakst, the costume and set designer for the Russian Ballet, also portrayed Nijinsky as faun in one of his famous paintings. Nabokov was probably acquainted with this work as well. According to Sweeney, "Ballet Attitudes," 124, the Nabokov family had a collection of Bakst's works in St. Petersburg; among them "the rose-and-haze pastel portrait" of Nabokov's mother. This is confirmed in Vladimir Nabokov, *Speak, Memory: An Autobiography Revisited* (Harmondsworth, Middlesex: Penguin Books, 1987), 148.

[71] George Steiner, *Extraterritorial: Papers on Literature and the Language Revolution* (London: Faber and Faber, 1972), 10.

[72] Nabokov, *Lolita*, 282-3.

While the Catholic form of Confession worked for the Puritan Hilda in Hawthorne's *The Marble Faun*, Humbert cannot find peace in his hopeless imitation of the nineteenth century decadents. He will have to put his confession into writing to find some form of spiritual solace for his sins, but he knows that no redemption is possible for having "deprived" Lolita "of her childhood."[73] Like many decadent artists of the past, Humbert cannot distinguish moral decadence from artistic decadence. Aestheticism as a way of life was only an exterior manifestation of the quest for Beauty, and this is perhaps one reason why Humbert, in his faun-like state, persistently, but unobtrusively, attempts to defend his immorality with literary allusions.

Both *The Marble Faun* and *Lolita* explore the differences between the separate spheres of reality and art. The artist protagonists in *The Marble Faun* are taught to view art as necessarily linked with sin and corruption, but they are able to dissociate it from life which, they conclude, must be moral, and so they abandon art for life rather than confuse the two spheres. Humbert, however, will never learn to distinguish between them because he will always give precedence to "ecstasy" as a faun in a literary world "where art...is the norm," omitting "curiosity, tenderness, [and] kindness," the attributes by which Nabokov defined the term "aesthetic bliss."[74] While readers can witness the process of Donatello's suffering and transformation into a human being in Hawthorne's romance, Humbert, Nabokov's lecherous faun, cannot undergo this change because he is constantly confusing "reality," the moral world around him, with the morality (or immorality) of the world of art from which he issued. His victim, the little American "nymph," Lolita, is just an ordinary child and not the "Lilith" of his dreams. All he can do is immortalize the corruption of his nymphet in his memoir, but he will forever remain captive in the literary prison of his hellish passion, caught between two worlds: the moral reality of America (which Nabokov created for him) and the world of nineteenth century decadent art and artists and literary texts in which he feels at home.

---

[73] Ibid., 283.
[74] Nabokov, "On a Book Entitled *Lolita*," 315.

Mikhail Efimov

NABOKOV AND PRINCE D. S. MIRSKY

1. DOUBLE AGENT, CONFUSED ÉMIGRÉ

D. S. Mirsky (Prince Dmitri Petrovich Svyatopolk-Mirsky, 1890-1939) was a brilliant historian of Russian literature and a literary critic, one of the most enigmatic and intriguing personalities in the history of Russian culture in the twentieth century. The descendant of Rurik (and of Catherine the Great, *via* his mother, Countess Bobrinsky), he was the son of the Tsarist Minister of Internal Affairs. Mirsky's *A History of Russian Literature* was written in English in the 1920s and remains a cogent and insightful handbook for all students of Russian literature.[1] Mirsky's

---

[1] D. S. Mirsky, *A History of Russian Literature. From Its beginnings to 1900*, ed. Francis J. Whitfield (New York: Vintage, 1958). Sir Isaiah Berlin's famous assessment of Mirsky's *History* is usually placed on back covers of the standard edition: "[Mirsky's] histories of literature... possess learning, elegance, wit, intellectual gaiety, and an incomparable style and sweep and power of communicating impressions and ideas."

education uniquely combined European and Russian cultures; from his "English governess, Miss Trend, came the initiation into the English language that flowered into mastery unmatched by that of any other Russian writer save Nabokov."[2]

The trajectory of Mirsky's life was no less controversial than his literary views. After his military service in General Denikin's army, Mirsky was a White émigré who held an academic position in London, and became one of the most provocative literary critics in the Russian emigration milieu. Mirsky was known for his inclinations towards Eurasianism. The proponents of this émigré political movement in the 1920s believed that Russian civilization did not belong in the "European" category and, to a certain extent, even justified the Bolshevik Revolution as a necessary reaction to the rapid modernization of Russian society. Mirsky's views resulted in a kind of political journalism and activities that linked him to the leftist and anti-émigré pathos. Mirsky later joined the British Communist Party, and in 1932 repatriated to the USSR with Maxim Gorky's support.[3] With a little time out for trips to the provinces, Mirsky lived in Moscow until his arrest in 1937. He remained a prisoner until his death in the Far East in January 1939.[4]

According to G. Smith,

> Mirsky's overlooking or ignoring Nabokov's writing is perhaps the most surprising negative feature of his works on current Russian literature to the retrospective observer, until we reflect on how rarely it is that anybody genuinely cares for the work of the generation that is succeeding their own.[5]

Nabokov's opinion on Mirsky is well-known. He admitted in the late 1940s,

> Yes — I am a great admirer of Mirsky's work. In fact, I consider it the best history of Russian literature in any language including Russian. Unfortunately I must

---

[2] G. S. Smith, Preface and Introduction, "D.S. Mirsky. Literary Critic and Historian," *Uncollected Writings on Russian Literature*, Modern Russian Literature and Culture: Studies and Texts, vol.13, ed. G. S. Smith (Berkeley: Berkeley Slavic Specialties, 1989), 20.

[3] Hilton Kramer, "The Strange Case of D. S. Mirsky," *The New Criterion* (January 2002), http://www.thefreelibrary.com/The+strange+case+of+D.+S.+Mirsky.-a082260382) notes, "[u]nlike so many other victims of the Terror, Mirsky may be said to have written his own death warrant by choosing to return to the Soviet Union from a decade-long exile in Britain at the very moment that Stalin was declaring war on intellectuals like himself as class enemies."

[4] Smith, *Uncollected Writings*, 20.

[5] G. S. Smith, *D. S. Mirsky: A Russian-English Life, 1890-1939* (Oxford, New York: Oxford University Press, 2000), 90. I am deeply and gratefully indebted to Smith's fascinating, and to date the only, biography of Mirsky.

deprive myself of the pleasure of writing a blurb for it, since the poor fellow is now in Russia and compliments from such an anti-Soviet writer as I am known to be might cause him considerable unpleasantness.[6]

This came as a response when Knopf editor Robert M. Glauber approached Nabokov about endorsing the one-volume edition of Mirsky's *History*. Nabokov "refused, with the best of motives."[7] Apparently, Nabokov was unaware of the fact that Mirsky perished in the Soviet concentration camp a decade earlier. Nonetheless, his concern for Mirsky's reputation, let alone his safety, is quite remarkable. However, almost twenty years prior to that exchange, Nabokov named Mirsky *"merzkii Mirsky"* ("vile Mirsky," a paronomasia in Russian) in a private letter to his friend and literary critic, Gleb Struve.[8]

How should one interpret this double standard? Does it testify to Nabokov's duplicity or is it mere inconsistency? The aim of the present note is to reconstruct the relationship between Nabokov and Mirsky and to offer some explanations to this complex question.

2. FROM EPIGRAM TO ADMIRATION

Nabokov must have heard of Mirsky and his work long before Mirsky's name appeared in Nabokov's letters. The mid-1920s was Mirsky's zenith as a literary historian, when he published his major works: *Modern Russian Literature* (London, 1925), *Pushkin* (London and New York, 1926), and *A History of Russian Literature from the Earliest Times to the Death of Dostoevsky (1881)* (London and New York, 1927).

However, Mirsky's name may have been significant to Nabokov in a slightly different, and more polemical, context. Mirsky's notorious lecture, "The Ambience of Death in Pre-revolutionary Russian Literature," delivered in Paris on April 5, 1926, was widely discussed in the Russian émigré Diaspora.[9] One of the main targets criticized in that lecture was the poet

---

[6] Vladimir Nabokov, *Selected Letters 1940-1977*, ed. Dimitri Nabokov and Mathew J. Bruccoli (San Diego: Harcourt Brace Jovanovich/Bruccoli Clark, 1990), 91.
[7] Smith, *Russian-English Life*, 295.
[8] Vladimir Nabokov, "Pis'ma V. V. Nabokova k G. P. Struve. Chast' vtoraia (1931-1935), publikatsiia E. B. Belodubrovskogo i A. A. Dolinina. Kommentarii A. A. Dolinina [April 25, 1932], *Zvezda* 4 (2004): 146.
[9] D. S. Mirsky, "Veyanie smerti v predrevoliutsionnoi russkoi literature," *Vyorsty* 2 (1927): 247-254.

Vladislav Khodasevich, Nabokov's poetic inspiration and mentor. In the first volume of *Vyorsty* (1926), Mirsky disapprovingly wrote: "Khodasevich is a small Baratynsky from the underground, the favorite poet of those who do not love poetry."[10] Khodasevich, who published a major volume of *Collected Poems* (*Sobranie stikhov*) in 1927, considered this statement tantamount to a declaration of war. One of the consequences was the anti-Mirsky campaign led by Khodasevich.[11] Notably, Nabokov welcomed Khodasevich's book with an enthusiastic review.[12]

The Prince's name appeared in Nabokov's correspondence with Gleb Struve after Nabokov learned about Mirsky's return to the Soviet Union from England. Struve aimed for the career vacancy that resulted from Mirsky's departure, and was subsequently appointed as Mirsky's successor to the School of Slavic studies at London University. The early 1930s, the time before Struve's appointment, may be considered an apogee of Struve's and Nabokov's literary friendship. Nabokov shared his professional opinions freely and it was then that Mirsky's name surfaced a few times in his letters: "I will be very happy for you if you could replace the Prince (by the way, have you read his penitential article in *The* [Soviet] *Literary Gazette*?)."[13] Soon thereafter he again expressed a hope that "success will crown [Struve's] English affairs."[14] Finally, at the beginning of June 1932, Nabokov sincerely congratulated his friend who assumed the teaching position of Russian literature at London University. Nabokov even added a rhymed epigram mocking the Prince:

> Dear Gleb Petrovich,
> I have just received your letter and rush (though I'm in bed) to answer and to congratulate you very, very much! It is splendid, lovely news. I have no doubt of your success in England. It's wonderful. [...]

---

[10] On the context of this statement see M. Efimov, "Baratynski kak predmet i siuzhet literarurnoi polemiki (Nabokov, Khodasevich, Adamovich) [Baratynsky as subject and topic of literary polemics (Nabokov, Khodasevich, Adamovich)], *Nabokov Online Journal* IV (2010).

[11] Smith, *Russian-English Life*, 150-154 comments, "[t]he spectacle of the two most gifted critical minds of the emigration tearing at each other in the way Mirsky and Khodasevich did is one of the most dismal in the unhappy story of Russia Abroad."

[12] Vladimir Nabokov, Review of Vladislav Khodasevich, *Collected Poems* [*Sobranie stikhov*] (Paris: Vozrozhdenie, 1927), *Rul'* [*Rudder*], December 14, 1927. Reprinted in V. V. Nabokov, *Sobranie sochinenii russkogo perioda v 5 tomakh*, vol. 2 (St. Petersburg: Symposium, 1999), 649-652.

[13] Nabokov, "Pis'ma k Struve. Chast' vtoraia" [April 25, 1932], 146.

[14] Ibid. [May 20, 1932], 147.

> *There'll be more sense from Gleb*
> *than from wicked Svyatopolk!*
>
> [*Iz Gleba vyidet bol'she tolka,*
> *chem iz durnogo Sviatopolka!*]
> Yours V. Nabokov.[15]

This is not the only abusive epithet Nabokov used to describe Mirsky. In his letter of December 2, 1932, Nabokov responded to the news that Struve had read a lecture on Nabokov's art:

> It is very, very pleasant to me that you—and not someone else—have lectured about me. I heard that your first talk on Bunin went excellent. I wish you, my dear, a tremendous success. I am more than positive that you will achieve much in England. As for vile Mirsky, apparently he is coming to Paris (where, as people say, he, Babel and others will be editing some journal).[16]

The picture is quite unambiguous: "bad Svyatopolk," "vile Mirsky," an author of the "penitential article in *The Literary Gazette*," the prospects of publishing a magazine in collaboration with the Soviet writer, Babel—everything testifies to Nabokov's irritation with the Prince. His attitude toward Mirsky is understandable given that, in 1932, Nabokov was at the peak of his creative energy and he considered Gleb Struve both a reliable literary ally and a potential helper; Struve's path as an English Professor also seemed promising to Nabokov. On the contrary, Mirsky's personal fate and the evolution of his literary tastes hardly represented any interest for Nabokov in 1932. The fact of Mirsky's converting to the Soviet belief was, for Nabokov, a sufficient reason to dismiss Mirsky and to deem him "merzky." Presumably, Nabokov did not forget Mirsky's attacks on Khodasevich and this played a role in shaping his opinion of the former aristocrat turncoat. It would be a while until Nabokov would take another, more sober look at Mirsky's contribution to scholarship and reassess his class adversary's critical "strong opinions."

---

[15] Ibid., 147, 148.
[16] Ibid., 150.

3. REEVALUATION

Mirsky's name appeared again, almost ten years later, in Nabokov's correspondence with Edmund Wilson in the United States. On September 18, 1941 Nabokov wrote from Wellesley: "I happen to be working on the question of the exact relationship between [John] Wilson's *City of the Plague* and Pushkin's version [*The Feast during the Plague*]. Apparently Mirsky did not see the original. I shall send you my notes later on."[17] It turns out that Edmund Wilson was an especially significant figure in the relationship between Nabokov and Mirsky. As Simon Karlinsky put it,

> [during Wilson's visit to the USSR in 1935] an encounter with the literary historian D. S. Mirsky stimulated Wilson's interest in Pushkin, an interest which lasted for the rest of his life and which was so important in bringing him together with Nabokov. It was in order to read Pushkin in the original that Wilson undertook to learn Russian at the end of his trip.[18]

Another remarkable exchange of letters concerning Mirsky occurred in 1942 when Wilson criticized his fellow critic in a letter to Nabokov:

> Mirsky speaks of the versification of one of Pushkin's dramas — I forget which — as showing the flexibility of Shakespeare's later plays. When I read the play, I found that this was ridiculous. Besides the verse of Shakespeare's later plays, Pushkin seems pedantically regular [...] It may be that neither you nor Mirsky, trained on classic Russian verse, quite realizes what English verse is like.[19]

---

[17] Vladimir Nabokov, *The Nabokov-Wilson Letters. Correspondence between Vladimir Nabokov and Edmund Wilson 1940-1971*, ed. and annotated Simon Karlinsky (New York: Harper & Row, 1979), 47. As B. Averin and M. Malikova note, "the juxtaposition of John Wilson's drama in verse [...] and *Feast during the Plague* has been researched in some studies. One of the first is the paper 'About the sources of "The Feast during the Plague"' (1925) by N. V. Iakovlev. D. P. Svyatopolk-Mirsky (1880-1939) has also written about it in his *A History of Russian Literature from the Earliest Times to the Death of Dostoevsky* (1926)." Vladimir Nabokov, "Iz perepiski s Edmundom Uilsonom," Per. s angl. S. Taska. Prim. B. Averina i M. Malikovoi, *Zvezda* 11 (1996): 128.

[18] Simon Karlinsky, *Nabokov-Wilson Letters*, 5. Twenty years after his meeting with Mirsky in Moscow, Wilson published a paper on Mirsky: "Comrade Prince," *Encounter* 5.1 (1955): 10-20. On Wilson and Mirsky see Smith, *Russian-English Life*, 279-291, 295. Wilson met with Mirsky in Moscow in 1935. In 1934 Mirsky published his notorious article "The Problem of Pushkin" (D. Mirskii, "Problema Pushkina" [*A. S. Pushkin: Issledovaniya i materialy*] / Plan toma, organizaciya materiala, literaturnaya redakciya, podbor materiala i oformlenie I.S. Zil'bershteina i I.V. Sergievskogo. M.: Zhurnal'no-gazetnoe ob'edinenie, 1934: 91-112 (*Literaturnoe nasledstvo*, vol. 16-18).

[19] Edmund Wilson, *Nabokov-Wilson Letters* [April 29, 1942], 59, 60.

A few months later Wilson added: "I was disappointed in *Каменный Гость* [*The Stone Guest*], and don't quite see why Mirsky thinks it a masterpiece [...] What are the theories about *Домик в Коломне* [*The Little House in Kolomna*] of which Mirsky speaks? There *is* something a little queer about it?"[20] In the letter dated August 24, 1942, Nabokov clarified both points to Wilson. Nabokov remembered Wilson's passing comment on Shakespeare and brought it up again here in connection with Mirsky, after a dozen letters had been exchanged between them since April.

> I do not recall what Mirsky says about Pushkin's Shakespearean flexibility; but I do know that there is absolutely nothing regular or pedantic about Pushkin's iamb. Except perhaps in *Boris Godunov* (which is a failure).[21] Pushkin does nothing but vary and almost dislocate the iamb [...] Incidentally we are not trained, Mirsky and I, on classic Russian verse; we are trained on the verse of Blok, Annensky, Bely and others who revolutionized the old ideas about Russian versification and introduced into Russian verse breaks and substitutions and mongrel meters that are far more syncopic than anything even Tyutchev had dreamed of.[22]

Later, in 1943, Wilson suggested to Nabokov the candidacy of Helen Muchnic as a translator, attesting her to be Mirsky's student in London.[23]

No doubt, Wilson was strongly influenced by Mirsky's writings. In fact, in 1948 he was accused of an intellectual plagiarism of sorts by Stanley Edgar Hyman. In his book, *The Armed Vision*, Hyman objects that Wilson was "using other people's insights and research without giving them credit: 'On Russian literature Wilson used D. S. Mirsky's two histories and his study of Pushkin, de Vogüé's *Le Roman russe* and many of the specific insights of Vladimir Nabokov.'"[24] It would be safe to presume that for Nabokov, who lived in America in the 1940s, Mirsky became a distant (both chronologically and topographically) ally in establishing his position, in the new cultural milieu, as heir to the Russian cultural tradition from Pushkin to the Silver Age.

---

[20] Ibid. [August 8, 1942], 68.
[21] Cf. Mirsky, *History*, 58: "*Boris Godunov* must rather be regarded as one of the immature and preparatory works of Pushkin, less mature and less perfect than much that had preceded it—than *The Gypsies*, for instance, or the early chapters of *Onegin*."
[22] Nabokov, *Nabokov-Wilson Letters* [August 24, 1942], 71-72.
[23] Wilson, *Nabokov-Wilson Letters*, 92.
[24] Karlinsky, quoted in *Nabokov-Wilson Letters*, 206.

4. NABOKOV AS A CLOSE READER OF MIRSKY

Analyzing Nabokov's lecture on Dostoevsky, Hugh MacLean remarked that

> [t]he only critics Nabokov does mention are two who wrote in English, D. S. Mirsky (as support for the view that the authenticity of Dostoevsky's Christianity is in question) and, of all people, Petr Kropotkin, the "anarchist prince," whose Lowell lectures on Russian literature had seemed quaintly old-fashioned in their prejudices even when delivered in 1901.[25]

The "shadow" of Mirsky appears in *Nikolai Gogol,* Nabokov's first biographical study written in English.[26] Nabokov's well known definition of *poshlost'* (platitude, banality) in *Nikolai Gogol* seems to have its origins in Mirsky's *A History of Russian Literature.*[27] In the chapter on Gogol, Mirsky wrote: "The aspect under which he sees reality is expressed by the untranslatable Russian word *póshlost,* which is perhaps best rendered as 'self-satisfied inferiority,' moral and spiritual."[28] And further "Chichikov is the greatest of Gógol's subjective caricatures — he is the incarnation of *póshlost.*"[29]

It is difficult to determine whether Nabokov's acquaintance with and attentive reading of Mirsky's *History* was a direct result of his starting his academic career in the United States. In the preparatory notes to Nabokov's

---

[25] H. McLean, "Lectures on Russian Literature," *The Garland Companion to Vladimir Nabokov,* ed. Vladimir E. Alexandrov (New York: Garland, 1995), 267. On Kropotkin's Lectures see Smith, *Russian-English Life,* 83. As Smith points out, "Kropotkin was originally a professional geographer; the writings by him and his peers in the great age of Russian geography during the last 35 years before 1914 were among Mirsky's favorite reading, and provided him with a rich source of metaphor" (333). It is curious to compare this preference of Mirsky with the geographic writings utilized in Chapter 3 of Nabokov's *The Gift.*

[26] Vladimir Nabokov, *Nikolai Gogol* (Norfolk: New Directions, 1944). Stekhov states that Svyatopolk-Mirsky's *A History of Russian literature* (1927), published seventeen years prior to Nabokov's book, was the only English-language work mentioned in *Nikolai Gogol*: "Everything that D. Svyatopolk-Mirsky has discovered and has noticed in the realm and the nature of Gogol's art Nabokov has used in his book." See A. V. Stekhov, "Strategiya literaturnogo obrazovaniya i taktika chteniya V. Nabokova v knige 'Nikolai Gogol'" [The strategy of literary education and the tactics of reading of V. Nabokov in "Nikolai Gogol"], *Pedagogika iskusstva* 3 (2009), http://art-education.ru/AE-magazine/archive/nomer-3-2009/stechov_06_09_2009.htm.

[27] This was overlooked in a paper on this subject by S. Davydov, "Poshlost," *The Garland Companion to Vladimir Nabokov,* ed. Vladimir E. Alexandrov (New York: Garland, 1995), 628-633.

[28] Mirsky, *History,* 158.

[29] Ibid., 160.

lectures, Stephen Jan Parker found the following jottings: "Text books. Guerney A Treas. of Russian Lit. I recommend Mirsky and my book on Gogol."[30]

There is some traceable evidence of Nabokov's close reading of Mirsky's *History* in his *Lectures on Russian Literature*.[31] In a section devoted to Turgenev, Nabokov noted: "Bazarov, the representative of this younger generation [of nihilists], is aggressively materialistic; for him exists neither religion nor any esthetic or moral values. He believes in nothing but 'frogs'..."[32] In *A History of Russian Literature* Mirsky had written of Turgenev: "This nihilist, with his militant materialism, with his negation of all religious and aesthetic values and his faith in nothing but frogs..."[33] Nabokov simply paraphrases Mirsky's original text. Another faithful though unattributed borrowing from Mirsky, who wrote "In *Smoke* (1867) he gave full vent to his bitterness against all classes of Russian society,"[34] is echoed in Nabokov's "[I]n *Smoke* he expressed his bitterness against all classes of Russian society."[35]

Later there was yet another resemblance of Mirsky's *History* in Nabokov's *Lectures*:

> Turgenev felt much more at home among his French confreres than among his Russian equals (with most of whom, including Tolstoy, Dostoevsky, and Nekrasov, he sooner or later quarreled), and there is a striking difference between the

---

[30] Stephen Jan Parker, "Nabokov's Montreux Books: Part II," Nabokov: Autobiography, Biography and Fiction, *Cycnos* 10.1 (1993), http://revel.unice.fr/cycnos/index.html?id=1307. Here Nabokov refers to Bernard Guilbert Guerney, *A Treasury of Russian Literature* (Philadelphia: Blakiston, 1945).

[31] In the Russian edition of B. Boyd's second volume of Nabokov's biography, *Vladimir Nabokov: Amerikanskie gody: Biografiia / Per. s angl.* M.: Izdatel'stvo Nezavisimaia Gazeta (St. Petersburg: Symposium, 2004) — the insert between pp. 544-545 — there is a reproduction of a photo on two pages of Nabokov's notebook (the entry from September 16-19, 1954): "325. [...] Reserve: Slovo, Avvacum, Mirsky." It is possible that Nabokov intended to use in his course "The Russian literature in translations" ("Literature No. 325-326"), the book edited by Mirsky: *The Life of the Archpriest Avvakum by Himself*. Translated from the Seventeenth Century Russian by Jane Harrison and Hope Mirrlees, with a Preface by Prince D. S. Mirsky (London: Hogarth Press, 1924). Smith, *Russian-English Life*, 98 stated that Mirsky's foreword was "one of his best pieces of historical writing."

[32] Vladimir Nabokov, *Lectures on Russian Literature*, ed. Fredson Bowers (New York: Harcourt Brace Jovanovich/Bruccoli Clark, 1981), 67. As H. McLean, "Lectures," 262 notes, "[w]ith the chapter on Turgenev we begin what were evidently Nabokov's unrevised lecture notes."

[33] Mirsky, *History*, 196.

[34] Ibid., 197.

[35] Nabokov, *Lectures on Russian*, 67.

impressions he produced on foreigners and on Russians. Foreigners were always impressed by the grace, charm, and sincerity of his manner. With Russians he was arrogant and vain.[36]

He impressed foreigners with his charm and graceful manners, but in his encounters with Russian writers and critics he at once felt self-conscious and arrogant. He had had quarrels with Tolstoy, Dostoevski, Nekrasov.[37]

A fragment from Nabokov's lecture on Dostoyevsky, in which he mentions Mirsky, is of special interest:

> The very best thing he ever wrote seems to me to be *The Double*. It is the story — told very elaborately, in great, almost Joycean detail (as the critic Mirsky notes), and in a style intensely saturated with phonetic and rhythmical expressiveness — of a government clerk who goes mad, obsessed by the idea that a fellow clerk has usurped his identity. It is a perfect work of art...[38]

The text from "of a government clerk" until the end of the sentence is a literal citation of Mirsky; the first part of the phrase follows Mirsky accurately except in the characterization of details such as "almost Joycean." This phrase is markedly absent in Mirsky's text.[39] Shoshana Knapp was the first to detect Nabokov's close reading of Mirsky, as well as the strange absence of proper acknowledgment. Knapp considers the possibility that Fredson Bowers, who edited the lectures for publication,

> is responsible for the buried citation. The reference to Mirsky seems to show that Nabokov wanted to indicate a quotation. As the text stands, however, the lecture gives credit only for the original material (the parallel with Joyce) and withholds credit for the borrowed material (the rest)."[40]

Finally, Mirsky is implicitly present in Nabokov's lecture on Maxim Gorky: "I have heard intelligent people maintain that the utterly false and sentimental story 'Twenty-six men and a Girl' is a masterpiece."[41] As Hugh McLean points

---

[36] Mirsky, *History*, 197.
[37] Nabokov, *Lectures on Russian*, 68.
[38] Ibid., 104.
[39] Mirsky, *History*, 184. "It is the story, told in great detail and in a style intensely saturated with phonetic and rhythmical expressiveness, of a government clerk who goes mad, obsessed by idea that a fellow clerk has usurped his identity. It is painful, almost intolerable reading."
[40] See the pioneering note by Shoshana Knapp, "Nabokov and Mirsky," *The Nabokovian* 13 (1984): 35-36.
[41] Nabokov, *Lectures on Russian*, 305-306.

out, "[o]ne of those 'intelligent people,' incidentally, was D.S. Mirsky, who said it in print, but Nabokov does not name him here."[42]

To sum up, Nabokov utilizes Mirsky's text in various ways—from using it as a reliable source (as in the lecture on Turgenev) to postulating, with its help, some important theoretical ideas (or enriching them as in case of "almost Joycean details" in the lecture on Dostoyevsky). Knapp is right in that identifying the cases of borrowing is definitely not to impugn Nabokov's integrity but to point out the hybrid qualities of the lecture genre,

> even when practiced by a genius, and to offer, if it is needed, a sort of reassurance to Nabokov's admirers: if a sentence in one of Nabokov's edited lectures seems too awkward or conventional to have been written by Nabokov, it probably wasn't.[43]

5. LITERARY REFLECTIONS

Returning to the European period of Nabokov's biography, one should notice an additional possible intersection leading covertly to Mirsky. In the letter of August 13, 1935, Nabokov asked Struve about a possibility of delivering lectures on Russian or French literature in England, or of getting any type of a literary grant. He mentioned two Western scholars who might be helpful in arranging this: M. Baring and B. Pares.[44] This plea yielded nothing, but the two names mentioned by Nabokov are quite interesting. Sir Bernard Pares (1867-1949) was Mirsky's long-term chief, the founder and head of the School of Slavonic and East European Studies at London University. The departure of Mirsky to the USSR was accompanied by a scandalous break in their relationship with Pares. Maurice Baring (1867-1949) was not only a long-term friend and supporter of Mirsky in England, but also his family's friend in the pre-Revolution era, and visited the Mirskys in Russia. Baring's collaboration with Mirsky in the 1920s is one of the illustrious pages of the Russian-English cultural dialogue.

---

[42] McLean, "Lectures," 272. Cf. D. S. Mirsky, *Modern Russian Literature* (London: Oxford University Press, 1925), 93: "Gorky in these years had a decided leaning towards poetry. He wrote verse, but his highest poetic achievement as well as the best written of his early stories is 'Twenty-six Men and a Girl,' a little masterpiece of powerful poetry made out of vile reality. There is, however, more promise of the real Gorky in *Foma Gordeyev*, the life story of a young merchant of Saratov. It is chaotic and formless, but displays a great power of detailed and sagacious observation."

[43] Knapp, "Nabokov and Mirsky," 36.

[44] Nabokov, "Pis'ma k Struve. Chast' vtoraia," 161.

According to Gennady Barabtarlo's recent discovery, the manuscript copy of the third chapter of Nabokov's first English novel, *The Real Life of Sebastian Knight*, contains "a deleted paragraph which among Knight's 'not very numerous friends-literati' mentions a well-known English philologist Maurice Baring."[45] Nabokov composed *The Real Life of Sebastian Knight* in Paris from December 1938 to January 1939. Mirsky died in the concentration camp in June 1939, a fact that remained unknown to Nabokov even ten years later.[46] Nabokov could have been well aware (even *via* his friend Struve) of the Mirsky-Baring connection; although it is difficult to explain why, after initially including Baring in a circle of Knight's friends, Nabokov later changed his mind.[47]

I am far from trying to describe all possible cases of Nabokov and Mirsky crossings, from the concurrences in their opinions to purposeful polemics.[48] My hope, though, is that the present note will demonstrate that juxtaposition and historical contextualization of texts by the two authors is not an entirely senseless occupation.

---

[45] Vladimir Nabokov, *Istinnaia zhizn' Sevast'yana Naita*. Per. s angl. G. Barabtarlo (St. Petersburg: Azbooka-klassika, 2009), 284.

[46] Some émigrés did know about it; Georgii Ivanov wrote: "[G. Adamovich] is not a renegade like Roshchin or a high-society snob tempted by Bolshevism, like the deceased Svyatopolk-Mirsky, who perished on Kolyma." See G. Ivanov, "Konets Adamovicha" ["The End of Adamovich"], *Vozrozhdenye* 11, 1950, *Sobranie sochinenii v 3 t.* vol. 3 (Moscow: Soglasie, 1993), 607.

[47] Mirsky dedicated his *Contemporary Russian Literature* to M. Baring. Also the title of Baring's book of memoirs, *The Puppet Show of Memory* (London: W. Heinemann, 1922) had to at least intrigue Nabokov.

[48] Such subjects as "Mirsky's Chekhov and Nabokov's Chekhov," Nabokov's studies of Pushkin and Mirsky's book "Pushkin" (1926), and even Hugh McDiarmid's views of Nabokov and Mirsky, are beyond the scope of my present note.

CORNER FLAG

INTERVIEW

An Interview with
Alvin Toffler
by Yuri Leving

"LOST IN TRANSIT"[1]

PREFACE

Of the twenty-two interviews that Vladimir Nabokov compiled in his *Strong Opinions*, the one he gave to interviewer Alvin Toffler for *Playboy* magazine in 1963 is the second longest. In addition to the interview with Nabokov, the Tenth Anniversary Issue of *Playboy* magazine (January 1964) featured such items as Philip Roth's "An Actor's Life for Me," Pablo Picasso's "The Wisdom of Pablo Picasso," and Ernest Hemingway's "Advice to a Young Man." The issue culminated in a retrospective tribute to Hollywood legend, Marilyn Monroe.

In this interview, in response to Toffler's question as to whether he believed in God, Nabokov formulated his famous maxim: "I know more than I can express in words, and the little

---

[1] First appeared in *Nabokov Online Journal*, Vol. III (2009).

INTERVIEW

I can express would not have been expressed, had I not known more."[2] As Galya Diment comments,

> It is somewhat ironic that Nabokov's rare (for interviews) reflections on higher consciousness appeared, of all places, in Hefner's *Playboy*. Nabokov, who obviously was fond of paradoxes of all kinds, may have done it intentionally — but even if that were the case, the sentiments he expresses in response to Toffler's question appear to be quite genuine.[3]

Alvin Toffler, who conducted the *Playboy* interview with Nabokov, was born in 1928. He is an American writer and futurist; his works discuss the digital revolution, communications, and technological singularity. A former associate editor of *Fortune* magazine, he has been described in the *Financial Times* as the "world's most famous futurologist."[4] His early work focuses on technology and its impact on humanity, while later writings explore the increasing power of twenty-first-century military hardware, weapons and technology proliferation, and capitalism. His books include: *Future Shock* (1970), *The Third Wave* (1980), *Powershift: Knowledge, Wealth and Violence at the Edge of the 21st Century* (1990), *War and Anti-War* (1993), and *Revolutionary Wealth* (2006). He is married to Heidi Toffler, also a writer, futurist, and his co-author who joined his interview with Nabokov in 1963, and also this conversation in 2009.

Yuri Leving: Nabokov's interview for *Playboy* magazine is one of the most quotable, along with those he granted to his former student Alfred Appel, Jr. What was the secret behind the success of this substantial conversation?

Alvin Toffler: I have vivid memories of my meeting with Nabokov. My wife, Heidi, and I stayed in Montreux for a week, in the hotel. We gave Nabokov written questions because he refused to be interviewed face to face.

Heidi Toffler: I suspect that one of the reasons was because he had some stammer when he spoke in public. Nabokov made a BBC television interview about his butterfly collecting, and one afternoon he put it on and we watched it. It was a very lovely program. I think Nabokov was simply kind to us because, although he refused to answer our questions verbally and insisted on writing the answers, we would meet with him every afternoon and have

---

[2] Vladimir Nabokov, *Strong Opinions* (New York: McGraw-Hill, 1973), 45.
[3] Galya Diment, "Strong Opinions," *The Garland Companion to V. Nabokov*, ed. V. Alexandrov (New York: Garland, 1995), 691.
[4] Nathan Gardels, "Lunch with the FT: He has seen the future," *Financial Times*, August 18, 2006.

tea, and chat for half an hour or so. So we were waiting there until he finished answering all the questions.

Yuri Leving: Did you submit the questions prior to your arrival at Montreux?

Alvin Toffler: We had a rough draft of questions we wanted to ask Nabokov beforehand, and changed them slightly as a result of some of his answers or oral comments. But we had no idea ahead of time that he would refuse to give a face-to-face interview.

Yuri Leving: The week in Switzerland in mid-March 1963 was totally unplanned?

Alvin Toffler: We simply had no choice but to stay! We would write questions and give them to Nabokov. Then he had a chance to think about what he wanted to say, and he wrote his answers down instead of giving an immediate response.

Yuri Leving: Where did you stay while in Montreux?

Alvin Toffler: It was a luxurious place. We stayed at the same hotel where the Nabokovs lived.

Yuri Leving: You must have stayed at *Le Montreux Palace*, built in 1906. What were your impressions?

Alvin Toffler: What struck me was the environment. It was an elegant place which was virtually empty during the off-season. There was an eerie feeling about this super top-level hotel. Very few people were present at the time. We would sit at a table in a large restaurant, and waiters would serve us with great flair. But we probably were the only clients there.

Yuri Leving: Who funded the trip, especially an unforeseen extra week that you had to spend in the expensive tourist premises?

Alvin Toffler: I don't think *Playboy* funded it in advance, but they paid for the work-related travel after we got back and submitted them a bill. There was no problem.

Yuri Leving: You mentioned the BBC television interview shown to you by Nabokov. I am curious: how was this done technically in the pre-VCR era?

Alvin Toffler: I don't know. He just set up the equipment and showed it to us. It was on a reel and shown on a projector of some kind.

Yuri Leving: Speaking of other gadgets, were you recording the conversations?

Heidi Toffler: We brought our tape recorder, but Véra wouldn't allow us to make any recordings.

Alvin Toffler: Our child, Karen, was with us — she was ten years old at that time. She loved staying at the hotel. We would go around town, and I remember how Nabokov's son, Dmitri, played a game of table football with her. He also spent some time with us during the week.

Yuri Leving: You were almost the same age as Dmitri at that time. In your letter to Nabokov you mention attaching an article that you published, which Dmitri was interested to see.[5]

Heidi Toffler: One afternoon when we were sitting and having tea with Nabokov, I used the word "ploy" in our conversation. Nabokov immediately got up, went to the dictionary and read all the meanings of the word "ploy," and then said: "This is very unusual! This is the fourth or fifth meaning of 'ploy' and now it's moving up in the usage scale." We were both amazed that he was so concerned about the language usage and nuances of the word's meaning. So he questioned me about the sense and context in which the word was used. Vladimir and Véra monitored language intensely.

Yuri Leving: Where did the conversations take place—was it in the Nabokovs' suite or at the bar downstairs?

Alvin Toffler: It was in their suite. They had a nice balcony with a view. I don't actually recall where Véra Nabokov was at that time. Véra was the one who would let us in and, essentially, she was the one who determined when we would come and meet her husband. She was clearly his business manager and partner, and I wouldn't be surprised if she also was a partial co-author.

Heidi Toffler: No, I don't think so.

Alvin Toffler: Not necessarily in a literal sense, but my guess is that she knew the language as well as Nabokov. They were very close, and I think she was a part of whatever he was.

Yuri Leving: Did you feel it was enough time for you to see Nabokov every day for half an hour? When the time was up, would Nabokov simply stand up, thank you, and say, "See you tomorrow"?

Alvin Toffler: Basically yes.

Yuri Leving: How do you remember him as a man?

Heidi Toffler: Very charming, very erudite, and very pleasant.

Yuri Leving: How did you prepare for the questions? Had you read his other novels which you quote—*Invitation to a Beheading* and *Bend Sinister*? It also seems from your questions that you had read a great deal of critical reviews of Nabokov's works.

---

[5] 20 June 1963. The correspondence between Nabokov and Toffler is now part of the Berg Collection, New York Public Library. —*Ed. note*.

Alvin Toffler: The press in the early 1960s was still filled with *Lolita*. It was in the news occasionally, and still controversial. We always did quite a bit of research for our interviews, and Nabokov was no exception.

Yuri Leving: How were the potential candidates for interviews picked? Were your questions screened or selected by *Playboy* prior to an interview?

Heidi Toffler: We suggested the person. The editor usually either accepts your idea or rejects it based on whether he thinks that this is the right moment for publication, whether the interview is well done, and if the person warrants the readers' interest, so there has to be this "magic moment."

Alvin Toffler: Let's put it this way: the interview section of *Playboy* was the serious part of the journal. The columns, I think, were very well done. Murray Fisher, an associate editor, was very intelligent and knowledgeable. Besides that, he was a good editor who made interesting choices. By and large most of the topics were suggested by us, although I talked with Murray, and he might say, "By the way, don't forget to ask about 'X.'" In March 1963 we were in Europe, and the suggestion to interview Nabokov came from us. We read *Lolita*, of course, and probably *The Real Life of Sebastian Knight* before that.

Yuri Leving: Nabokov was an ideal candidate and his relationship with *Playboy* had been forged since 1958. Who else did you interview for the magazine, and what was your favorite conversation?

Alvin Toffler: We conducted some political interviews; for instance, with the historian, Arthur Schlesinger. We did Jimmy Hoffa, the corrupt union leader. Our Ayn Rand interview is still being published by her advocates (Rand didn't like giving interviews). I recently visited a Book Fair at the UCLA campus. There was a whole "Ayn Rand" tent. And, the interview was there. It was still selling! Nabokov and Ayn Rand certainly belong to the most memorable ones.

Yuri Leving: Let me get back to your interview with Nabokov and the way it was reprinted later in *Strong Opinions*. In his brief introduction to the *Playboy* interview in *Strong Opinions*, Nabokov states that the "present text takes into account the order of my interviewer's questions as well as the fact that a couple of consecutive pages of my typescript *were apparently lost in transit.*"[6] Could you illuminate the mystery of this loss, if it happened indeed and was not invented by Nabokov?

Alvin Toffler: I have no idea. That must have been after we completed the interview. Probably, he refers to something that he added and sent to

---

[6] Nabokov, *Strong Opinions*, 20.

Playboy later. The original typescript might be in our archive; we donated our early papers to Columbia University.

Yuri Leving: It would be interesting to compare the two versions; however, there is no mention of any lost or added materials in the writer's 1963-1964 correspondence with the editors of the journal. In a very Nabokovian manner this can be just a trick, an invented mystery, as is the case with an enigmatic pseudo-Latin phrase from the same introductory paragraph which ends with the exclamation, *Egreto perambis doribus!* Could you explain this last phrase: maybe Nabokov referred to some inside joke?

Alvin Toffler: No, and what does it mean?

Yuri Leving: This is a good question. Most probably this is dog Latin, used as a humorous device similar to a famous phrase also evoking the means of transportation: "Brutus sic in omnibus / Caesar sic intram" ("Brutus sick in omnibus / Caesar sick in tram"). My knowledgeable colleague, Omry Ronen, whom I asked about that, thinks that it can be a playful translation of some standard slogan in American public spaces like restaurants, movie theaters, etc.: "Exit by both doors," since *doribus* is an ablative of English *door*. In addition, in the 1960s the Playboy clubs used to be decorated with brass plaques that read, "Si Non Oscillas, Noli Tintinnare," which roughly translates from Latin as "If You Don't Swing, Don't Ring." The same inscription is above the front door of Hugh Hefner's Chicago mansion today. In short, the metaphoric meaning is: "Read as you wish, either in the interviewer's or in my manner," but some additional erotic hints may be inherent, too.

Speaking of inscriptions, did you ask Nabokov to sign any books for you?

Alvin Toffler: Unfortunately, no.

Yuri Leving: What do you regret *not* asking Nabokov? Or what would you have asked him now if there were another such opportunity?

Alvin Toffler: If we could speak with him today about that event, I would ask what consequences this interview had—or whether it had any significant impact one way or another. Obviously, Nabokov went on to write more and more, and he turned into one of the most important writers of his time. As to Dmitri, I don't know much that has happened to him since then. All I remember about him is that he was interested in opera when we met.

Yuri Leving: A sketch of the Playboy bunny logo by Nabokov went for $17,925 at Christie's International in 2003. Could you imagine at the time of your meeting with Nabokov that he would become a cultural icon four decades later?

Alvin Toffler: No, of course, I couldn't imagine that. Nor that this interview would still be remembered.

Yuri Leving: And even quoted—the latest proof is the French scholar Maurice Couturier's memoir in volume III of the *Nabokov Online Journal* ("A Forty-year Journey in Nabokovland").

© A. Toffler, 2009. Used by permission.

Alvin Toffler: It was a very interesting encounter for us—and a serious one. On the one hand, once we got to Montreux and Nabokov refused a regular interview we had no recourse but to agree to his terms. On the other hand, if I recall correctly, there was no way for the reader to know that the interview was conducted in such an odd way. *Playboy* did not indicate that these were written answers, did it?

Yuri Leving: Obviously, Nabokov invested much time and effort in this conversation, meeting with you over the week to work on details. Why do you think he chose such a venue as a men's magazine with a dubious reputation for an important interview in the first place?

Alvin Toffler: I think that at the time Nabokov was being bombarded with negative coverage that accused *Lolita* of obscenity and so on. *Playboy* made a comfortable environment for him in which to be interviewed.

Heidi Toffler: Especially since he could control the answers because he wrote them himself.

Yuri Leving: For how long had you been contributing to *Playboy* prior to this Nabokov interview? Could you describe the creative atmosphere of the editorial board, inside *Playboy* magazine, in the late 1950s and early 1960s?

INTERVIEW

Alvin Toffler: We did some other freelance interviews. But neither of us ever "worked" at Playboy. I went to their headquarters a couple of times, but there were only two or three key people with whom I actually met: Murray Fisher and the originator of the *Playboy* enterprise, Hugh Hefner. I don't remember his attitude to Nabokov but there is an episode that might be relevant to the whole issue. Once I was working on a nonfiction story, and there was a line in it that I thought might be dangerous legally and that could bring on a possible lawsuit. And I said to Hefner: "Of course, you are the boss: if you want to delete that — you can." Without hesitation he answered: "No, run with it." So that was interesting: Hefner didn't shy away for fear of a controversy or lawsuit.

Yuri Leving: Have you also met with Auguste Spectorsky, the literary editor who created the more serious half of *Playboy*'s split personality? There is an opinion that while the *Playboy* publisher's tastes run to fried chicken, cool jazz, and Los Angeles weekends, Spectorsky preferred Continental cuisine, Mozart, and Caribbean sailing. When "Spec" joined Hefner in 1956, it was a slick erotic magazine in search of some intellectual balance to nude girls.

Alvin Toffler: We met maybe twice, but mostly our contacts were by telephone. Spectorsky was a real driving force of the magazine behind the scenes.

Yuri Leving: What have you personally learned from Nabokov in your own prolific career as a professional writer?

Alvin Toffler (laughs): As a journalist I was surprised that Nabokov would insist on writing his answers rather than speaking them. This was an odd experience. By that time we'd spent a few years living in Washington and, as a correspondent, I was interviewing congressmen, senators, and big shots on a daily basis, so interviewing was not a novel experience for me. Nonetheless, it surprised me that Nabokov wanted such total control. Again, it probably makes sense because he was under attack and in the center of controversy, because of *Lolita*.

Yuri Leving: What do you mean by saying that "he was under attack" — did he project any defensive mood?

Alvin Toffler: Not once when we sat down with him to do that interview. Heidi and I would formulate questions and then send them upstairs. Hey, Heidi (*addresses his wife who participates in our conversation via telephone*), I am looking through the ceiling window as I am speaking right now, and there is a squirrel running right over my head, as we talk!

Yuri Leving: The appearance of a butterfly would impress me even greater! But a squirrel is also a "Nabokovian creature," holding quite a symbolic presence in the novel *Pnin*. This actually reminds me of how at the Nabokov conference in Nice in the early 1990s, during the closing remarks by one of its organizers, a huge butterfly suddenly flew into the hall through an open window, which was, of course, interpreted as the Master's divine intervention.

This leads to my concluding question: considering Nabokov's sci-fi short story "Lance" (1951), as well as the author's interest in the American flight to the moon, was he a sort of a "futurist," the term that is most often applied to your own career?

Alvin Toffler: He was an allegorist rather than futurist.

MIDFIELD LINE

FORUM

Priscilla Meyer
(*Wesleyan University*)
Christine Raguet
(*Université Sorbonne Nouvelle-Paris 3*)
David Rampton
(*University of Ottawa*)
Corinne Scheiner
(*Colorado College*)

TEACHING NABOKOV[1]

Yuri Leving: *Every discipline has its own language and its own pedagogical needs. How would you try to set them out for Nabokov Studies?*

David Rampton: One of the best teachers I had at university taught a Shakespeare course I audited as a graduate student. As an undergraduate, I had taken the same course with someone else. Unfortunately, it was the late 1960s, and the very impressive Shakespeare scholar running the class thought giving lectures simply confirmed the dynamics of the authoritarian power structures we should be intent on destroying. A very dreary, 35-person, equal opportunity "seminar" was the result, in which students earnestly exchanged their stock responses, and Shakespeare was more or less forgotten, while the professor dreamily surveyed the wreckage, her credibility gone but her egalitarian

[1] First appeared in *Nabokov Online Journal*, Vol. II (2008).

credentials intact. The professor I was hoping would help me fill in the resultant gap was Geoffrey Durrant, a Wordsworth specialist, and he read Shakespeare's plays as great dramatic poems, working his way through them in painstaking and brilliant fashion. When we did *Hamlet*, I think we spent at least half an hour on the title and first two lines: "Who's there?" "Nay, answer me: stand and unfold thyself." That course made an indelible impression on me, and for years I have tried to do something similar with the Nabokov novels I routinely teach, usually in courses on twentieth-century fiction.

Christine Raguet: In France, Nabokov is taught in various departments: English and American Studies, Slavic Studies and Comparative Literature Studies, which means that he is either taught in the original language or in translation, which implies different approaches, either centered on thematic readings or stylistic readings. When I teach, I always try to help students delve into the complexities of language. This is all the more true when I ask them to compare translations and originals, and not to deliver a judgment as such, but to simply have an objective poetic approach to textuality.

Yuri Leving: *Knowing a subject well does not guarantee teaching a subject well. What would you like students to get from Nabokov's writings?*

Priscilla Meyer: To learn to be literary detectives, which means learning to attend to detail—hence to patternings at every level, from etymology to referentiality.

Christine Raguet: I'd like my students to discover the pleasure of the text: "The mind, the brain, the top of the tingling spine, is, or should be, the only instrument used upon a book."[2] The tingle in the spine really tells you what the author felt and wished one to feel. This is what students should come to.

Corinne Scheiner: As John Updike famously remarked, "Nabokov writes prose the only way it should be written, that is, ecstatically." It is precisely this ecstasy, this joy in and of language, that I want students to get from Nabokov's writings; what Nabokov termed "aesthetic bliss."[3]

David Rampton: What strikes me as so interesting about these responses by Priscilla, Christine, and Corinne, is how clearly they show the extent to which Nabokov has influenced the way we read him, and how crucial it is to get students to approach his work, at least at first, on his own terms. All

---

[2] Vladimir Nabokov, *Lectures on Literature* (New York: A Harvest Book, 2002), 4.
[3] Vladimir Nabokov, "On a Book Entitled *Lolita*," in *Lolita* (London: Weidenfeld & Nicolson, 1997), 314.

this emphasis on sleuthing out patterns and aesthetic bliss is also a somewhat unfashionable position in the academy at the moment, which makes it that much more important that we make as convincing and enthusiastic a case for it as we can. These answers also make me think about how helpful it is to show how the pleasures of a Nabokov text are more multifaceted than some of his strictures imply. I'm thinking of those moments in the lectures, in the chapter on Dickens's *Bleak House* for example, where he says that he is giving "a lesson in style, not in participative emotion."[4] We can savor the shiver in the spine and the emotions elicited by what is being depicted. In fact, sometimes they're inextricably bound together.

Yuri Leving: *Teaching raises the most profound issues about how people learn, about freedom and control, about open-mindedness and didacticism. Now that Nabokov is a part of the academic curriculum, what specific considerations are there to teaching his art in the age of political correctness?*

Priscilla Meyer: Whatever I teach involves attempting to enter the new universe of the book under discussion. The book is the teacher; we are its adepts. Nabokov parodies simplistic approaches to literature—sociological, moral, psychological; political correctness could be considered in the context of these parodies and juxtaposed to Nabokov's mockery of forms of real prejudice; for example of anti-Semitism in *Lolita*, the stereotyped roles of blacks, the sexual exploitation of girls.

Corinne Scheiner: In my experience, it is *Lolita* more than any other of Nabokov's works that raises issues regarding open-mindedness, primarily because students conflate the author with his characters or forget that they are reading an imaginative work in which the characters are fictional constructs. They are often unwilling or unable to examine the novel apart from its subject matter and, hence, are likely to focus solely on moral questions derived from the plot. Two brief examples should serve to support my claim (and I am sure others have similar stories to tell): 1) once, when I guest lectured on *Lolita* in an English department senior seminar, a student asked me, in all seriousness, if Nabokov was a pedophile; and 2) when I approached a colleague about team teaching a course on Nabokov, she was at first hesitant, remarking "I didn't like that novel because I really didn't like Humbert Humbert and what he did." It is imperative that we remind students (and colleagues) that Nabokov's skill as a writer enabled him to create fictional worlds and characters that feel so real and that, appropriately, our

---

[4] Nabokov, *Lectures on Literature*, 94.

focus should be on what he identified as the "structure, style, [and] imagery" of his texts.[5]

Christine Raguet: Even in the supposedly very open-minded French system, we observe resistance to some issues as those at stake in *Lolita*. Some of my female students came up to me and declared that they could not stand the plot; therefore, they would not attend class. So, it is important to teach that fictional situations are, as Hamlet said, nothing but "words, words, words."

David Rampton: Again, I'm struck by the unanimity here, which might well seem strange to those who are skeptical about Nabokov's humaneness, even thoughtful readers who profess to liking him a lot—I'm thinking of the curious exchange between James Wood and Richard Lamb in *Slate* a few years back.[6] It's important when discussing *Lolita* to talk about how adept Nabokov is at making energetic evil attractive *and* how large his capacity for pity was. Students enjoy engaging in this kind of debate. They often surprise their colleagues, particularly the ones who can heartily enjoy the most outrageous kind of politically incorrect humor on television but insist on something else from great literature.

Yuri Leving: *Many researchers think about Nabokov's texts as literary problems. How can we solve them in an academic environment; what tools should we use? How do you teach new material that challenges literary conventions?*

Christine Raguet: This is one of the things French students enjoy: facing new challenges. Obviously, they are attracted to unconventional texts and happy to get keys to their decoding. They often find the English text difficult, as they read the original, and when the text is tough to decode, they try to find some help in the translations at hand; but once they start mastering the subtleties of the text, they really want to get into the deep structures and nuances of the original. In the French tradition, one of the favorite exercises is "close reading," which means that short excerpts are studied in every detail, such as narrative devices at work, narrative voice, metaphors, the rhetoric of the passage, different types of speech, etc., and the students are supposed to become familiar with the stylistic specificities of the author.

Priscilla Meyer: I don't think that Nabokov's texts challenge literary conventions more than, for example, Joyce's or Woolf's do. The problem of teaching each author's new language to undergraduates is to break them of the respect for the unearned generalization they acquire in high schools, to

---

[5] Nabokov, "On a Book Entitled *Lolita*," 314.
[6] http://www.slate.com/id/2000072/entry/1002648/.

learn to work from the detail outward to larger categories of meaning; not the reverse. (I teach only undergraduates at Wesleyan). A monograph course, as mine is, allows students to experience the accumulation of resonance of Nabokov's themes and devices throughout the semester, and eventually to realize that Nabokov appears to have patterned his entire oeuvre as a spiral. (One student once told me that she'd come to Wesleyan because there was a course offered on Nabokov).

Corinne Scheiner: Certainly, some of Nabokov's texts, such as "The Vane Sisters," contain codes for the reader to decipher, and one can lead students through the process of decoding the text. However, overall I find it much more productive to think of Nabokov's texts not as problems but as innovations. To fully appreciate them as innovations, students must have a basic understanding of traditional literary conventions. Only then can they begin to examine Nabokov's texts as challenges to, parodies of, and departures from these conventions. *Pale Fire* provides perhaps the most obvious example. When I teach the text, I do not tell students anything about its fictional structure. I have them read it in its entirety, and begin our discussion by asking students how they read the text: did they skip the introduction or did they read it? Did they read the notes in conjunction with the poem or did they read the poem as a whole and then read the notes? Did they flip back and forth between the two parts of the text or did they follow Kinbote's advice and rip the text in two? Did they read the index or did they skip it? In short, did they approach the entire text as a fictional construct, that is, *as a novel*, as the subtitle of the work directs them to do? We then discuss traditional conventions of the novel and of scholarly editions of poems and how *Pale Fire* plays with such conventions. Finally, I have them reread the novel to see what additional clues they can find (and which perhaps they overlooked on their first reading) within the text as to its parodic nature. Similarly, I have students closely examine the fictional preface of John Ray Jr. in *Lolita* and the footnotes in *Ada* to see how Nabokov plays with traditional uses of paratext. Thus, as Christine Raguet and Priscilla have described, our focus is always on close reading, on the specific, on details.

Yuri Leving: *What is the most suitable format (lecture, seminar, electronic discussion, presentations, multimedia, etc.) that you found useful for instruction when teaching Nabokov? How does that shape the way you teach?*

Corinne Scheiner: All of the courses I teach are seminars and therefore are primarily discussion based. It is essential that students learn how to close-read texts, particularly texts as rich as Nabokov's.

David Rampton: Nabokov concludes his *Lectures on Literature* by saying: "The work with this group has been a particularly pleasant association between the fountain of my voice and a garden of ears—some open, others closed, many very receptive, a few merely ornamental, but all of them human and divine."[7] Lecturing was never described more lovingly, and I'm pretty sure that, with an author this complex and erudite, many Nabokov specialists still feel that they have a useful role to play in modified fountain mode. But we are here to discuss other methods as well. I'm very interested in hearing from my colleagues about teaching (say) *Lolita* in the twenty-first century, a much discussed topic of late; Nabokov and comparative literature; and multimedia approaches to his work (including observations about what use can be made of all those awful films). If someone has suggestions about how better to convey what a humorous writer he is, I would be grateful to hear about that as well.

Priscilla Meyer: Perhaps overexposure to the Soviet period makes me wary of lecturing, just as I discourage undergraduates studying a literary work from reading criticism before they have developed their own reading. I abjure quoting a printed "authority" as if it were proof of anything, and refuse to provide such by lecturing something that could be taken as authoritative; that is likely to be misunderstood; and can be propagated in any form independent of the student's own critical thought. I find that the best way to develop that critical capacity is in seminars (no more than twenty-five students) in which they respond in class discussion to topics announced on the syllabus, sometimes beginning from short written class responses.

Christine Raguet: Seminars offer the most appropriate format to invite active participation from the students and help them become familiar with the texts they study.

Yuri Leving: *How can we make lectures on Nabokov more engaging and more demanding of student thought and feedback? How do you determine what to focus on, and what method do you employ to pace the material?*

David Rampton: I tend to linger over titles, opening sentences, and first pages: the epitaph as epigraph that begins *Laughter in the Dark*, for example (and the striking differences between it and the opening of *Camera Obscura*); the dazzling first lines of Hermann's mad monologue in *Despair*; the epigraph to *The Gift* and Fyodor's impressions of the sights and sounds of a Berlin Street, and so on, all the way through the equally distinctive openings of *Sebastian Knight*, *Bend Sinister*, *Lolita*, *Pale Fire* and *Ada*—here

---

[7] Nabokov, *Lectures on Literature*, 382.

is Nabokov's plenty. Quite recently, someone told me that this is how Wayne Booth taught Nabokov to undergraduates—by letting them read over his shoulder, as it were, and that too encouraged me to go on doing it. Close reading is of course a fundamental part of any worthwhile critical approach, but this sort of analysis, the kind that focuses on carefully crafted detail and its thematic resonances; minute particulars and felt moments; the play between surface effects and deep structures; and the voices created by distinctive styles and characterized by their iterations—this has always seemed to be the most rewarding way to proceed when trying to teach students what makes Nabokov such a pleasure to read and why they should know more about him. Approaching his work in this way also means showing how much he has in common with a range of writers whose novels lend themselves to similar treatment: not only Sterne and Dickens and Joyce and Proust, the sort of list he would approve of, but also James and Faulkner and Woolf and Bellow, the kind of writers he was not so interested in.

Corinne Scheiner: One can engage in the type of lingering, attentive, close reading David describes in a seminar format as well. After discussing and demonstrating how to close read, I ask students to come to class each day with a passage that they have close read and to be prepared to share it with the class. We usually begin our discussion of the text at hand with several of these passages. A student leads off with his or her reading of a passage and other students join in, offering complementary, supplementary, or contradictory readings. Doing so helps avoid the professor-as-fountain mode of lecturing described above and enables the "magical moments of astonished discovery" that Priscilla discusses below.

Christine Raguet: When Nabokov is on the syllabus, only one novel is selected, which means that I have to decide what I want to teach; their fluency in English being the reference. They necessarily need dictionaries to understand every detail, but they know long in advance what they have to read. It is also important to give them very precise directions as to the theories they need to know and use to understand how narrative structure, characters, voices, sounds, time, tenses, and figures of speech function. My main objective has always been to lead them into the intricacies of the text. They generally respond positively and are happy to be able to tackle a difficult text.

Yuri Leving: *To what extent should we introduce Nabokov students to the discipline of comparative literature and culture, theories of literary criticism?*

Corinne Scheiner: Rather than discussing to what extent we should introduce comparative literature to the student of Nabokov, I would argue for the necessity of introducing Nabokov to the student of comparative literature. To me, Nabokov is the ideal author for students of comparative literature due to his bi-discursivity (that is, his continual creation in both Russian and English), his use of multiple languages within a given text, his practice of self-translation, his familiarity with multiple languages and literary traditions, and his frequent and seemingly effortless moves among them. Indeed, Nabokov seems far more at home in a comparative literature setting than he does in a traditional national literature setting, be it either Russian or English.

It is also productive to examine Nabokov's texts in conjunction with literary criticism and theory. For example, several of Nabokov's texts, in particular *Pale Fire*, poke fun at critical practices and thus lend themselves beautifully to a discussion of literary criticism and theory. Moreover, many excellent studies of Nabokov's texts work from very specific theoretical perspectives with which students may not be familiar. Therefore it is quite helpful to provide them with background on or key readings from those different theoretical schools.

David Rampton: Both of Corinne's points about Nabokov's usefulness seem to me extremely well taken. Of course, one can just as easily find a central place for his work when teaching nineteenth century Russian literature, twentieth century Russian literature, American literature, modernism, postmodernism, the contemporary novel, autobiography, comic verse, the lyric, translation, editing—the list is a very long one indeed.

Yuri Leving: Describe your pedagogical practices in teaching Nabokov.

Corinne Scheiner: As a Nabokovian and a Nabokophile who teaches comparative literature, I try to include at least one of Nabokov's texts in every course I teach. I regularly teach *Pale Fire* in the introductory course to the major (Introduction to Comparative Literature), in a lower-level course on self-conscious fiction, and in an upper-level course on the novel (Practice in Comparison: The Novel as a Genre). However, I teach only one course devoted solely to Nabokov (Nabokov's Butterflies), which I team teach with a colleague at the department of biology. Bearing in mind Nabokov's claim that "in a work of art there is a kind of merging between...the precision of poetry and the excitement of science,"[8] we begin our study of the work of art that is Nabokov's *oeuvre* by reading *Speak, Memory* to discover how his interests in literature and butterflies merge in his life. We move on to a study

---

[8] Vladimir Nabokov, *Strong Opinions* (New York: McGraw-Hill, 1973), 10.

of the field of Lepidoptera and the central questions contained therein, focusing particularly on systematics, mimicry, and behavioral and ecological evolution.

Throughout the course, we read several of Nabokov's literary works — novels, short stories, and poems — in conjunction with his scientific writings, and explore how Nabokov's knowledge of these lepidopteral concepts, and others drawn from the study of the natural world, play out in his work as a writer. For example, we pair systematics and taxonomy with *The Eye* to explore notions of identity and identification; we examine the scientific phenomenon of metamorphosis and Nabokov's literary rendering of it in "Christmas"; we study Nabokov's thoughts regarding mimicry and patterning and how he employs these concepts in "The Poem," and "The Vane Sisters"; and we examine the question of resemblances, true and false, both in families of butterflies and in Nabokov's stories, "The Admirable Anglewing" and "Conversation Piece, 1945." Students continually experience "the precision of poetry" by engaging in close reading of Nabokov's texts. As one student wrote in her journal, "Details, Details, Details. It's all Details."

During the course, they also experience "the excitement of science" as they engage in hands-on lepidopterological activities: they learn to catch butterflies, moths and other insects in a nearby park; they learn how to kill them (using both Nabokov's preferred method of pinching the thorax and the less intimate method of placing the catch in a kill jar); they learn how to spread the butterflies and moths they catch; and they learn how to identify their specimens. The course culminates in a week-long field trip in which we re-enact one of Nabokov's butterfly-hunting expeditions in the Southwest and catch butterflies ourselves. Nabokov wrote much of *Lolita* during such trips; hence, while on the road we read and discuss *Lolita*.

Christine Raguet: In American Studies in France, Nabokov is a prominent figure, but does not represent the canon. As such, he is always introduced as a master of prose writing. When asked about Nabokov, French students are mostly familiar with the figure of Lolita, without having read the book. This is why I like them to discover it first. They are supposed to have read the complete book (annotated version) before the first seminar. They also receive a bibliography to guide their reading. I give them a plan of my course, which is organized along an alternation of "thematic" presentations and approaches to the novel and of a selection of excerpts to be studied in detail. They are invited in turn to individually prepare their own presentation to the whole group, which will be discussed afterwards and readjusted to the text and to Nabokov criticism.

Yuri Leving: Nabokov remarked in *Strong Opinions:* "*Every lecture I delivered had been carefully, lovingly handwritten and typed out, and I leisurely read it out in class.*"[9] *Share your methodologies, strategies and activities during a course devoted to Nabokov.*

David Rampton: I'm intrigued by this remark, because it reminds us of just how much of his time and energy Nabokov devoted to teaching, how carefully he proceeded, how instructive it is to think about how he went about it, and how studiously we should avoid imitating some of the things he did best. He is obviously a pretty impressive close reader in his own right, as the Gogol book, the published lectures, and the annotations to *Onegin* make clear. His insistence on the importance of rereading is as appropriate for our distracted age as it was for his students half a century ago. He unfailingly conveyed an enormous enthusiasm for the writers he admired, something that studies of pedagogical methods consistently identify as the *sine qua non* of the exercise. And he repeatedly reminds us to what extent teaching is a function of personality, with all that that implies about what can be learned and what cannot; how important making the sound of a human voice come through still is; and how important it is that that voice be one's own.

Nabokov's critical precepts have influenced my teaching a lot. His modified version of Arnoldian touchstones, positive and negative, intrigues me still; his conviction that salutary chills or goose bumps represent the height of aesthetic achievement still seems profound and important; and *Strong Opinions*, with its ringing endorsements and sweeping dismissals, still strikes me as an extraordinarily insightful book. But "the manner dies with the master," and that means finding one's own way forward in the end. Reading Nabokov's books as described above is to approach them in ways similar to the ones he uses when he talks about literature; reading them in light of their historical context, symbolism, and general ideas (admittedly a somewhat ambiguous formulation)—things he tended to ignore when teaching—one is simply taking advantage of the academic freedom he so fiercely defended. I think it is instructive to compare his article on Pushkin ("Le vrai et le vraisemblable") to those that appeared alongside it in the *Nouvelle Revue Française*; or notions of the totalitarian state in *Bend Sinister* and *1984*; or self-reflexive gestures in late Nabokov and Vonnegut, and students tend to learn a lot from such juxtapositions.

Priscilla Meyer: It's one thing for Nabokov to do what he says in *Strong Opinions*. Even his reading whole pages from the texts being studied

---

[9] Nabokov, *Strong Opinions*, 104.

was doubtless a formative experience for his students. Lacking that genius, I prefer to try to facilitate the occasionally quite magical moment of astonished discovery that emerges in class discussion. On the first day of class, before uttering a single word, I play a recording of Nabokov reading "An Evening of Russian Poetry." I then hand out a photocopy of the poem and we discuss it for the remainder of the 120-minute class. Students tend to refer to the poem throughout the semester as they find its themes and images in Nabokov's novels. I like writing "НАБОКОВ" mirror-imaged on the blackboard.

Readings begin with *Eugene Onegin.* They read enough chapters in James Falen's English translation to get a sense of the stanza and Pushkin's playfulness, and then in Nabokov's literal translation for its greater semantic precision. I provide a guideline for dipping into Nabokov's Commentary, emphasizing his ideas about "Proshla liubov', iavilias' muza" and the cool distance that is the essential fourth step of artistic creation. Nabokov's diatribe against Nikolai Brodsky's commentary to *Onegin* prepares them to understand the impetus behind Fyodor's biography of Chernyshevsky. Nabokov's scorn for the concept of the "superfluous man" is a useful antidote to the "social analysis" beloved of beginning readers.

Reading *Onegin* provides students with their own portable Petersburg and a sense of the importance of Pushkin for Russian literature and for Nabokov. They can notice the *Onegin* stanzas framing *The Gift*, the parodic love triangle in that novel, the Pushkinian intonations (even if taken from his prose) of Fyodor's attempt at a biography of his father. It also allows them a means of identifying the hidden Russian dimension of *Lolita*—and hence gaining leverage on the distinction between Humbert and Nabokov—when asked to consider Nabokov's novel as a parody of a literal translation of *Onegin* in the USA of the 1950s. They are prepared to think this way by writing their own "translation" of *Onegin* into the USA of their own decade (Onegin is often a New York swell, Tatyana from Maine, Vermont or the midwest; some have produced wonderful rap versions—"Yo, 'Negin,").[10]

Following *Onegin*, we read *Speak, Memory* as a kind of biographical and methodological baseline for reading the novels. Knowing the biography from the horse's mouth allows students to understand, for example, Sebastian Knight as like Nabokov but precisely *not* Nabokov. Tracing the circle of items in the index (jewels, pavilion, stained glass, colored hearing) shows them the nature, method and importance of motifs for Nabokov's work and convinces them of their intentionality.

---

[10] See http://pmeyer.web.wesleyan.edu/nabokov/index.html.

The second paper is a four-page motif study, to be presented in class, with an appendix comprising each complete sentence containing the motif, to be distributed to everyone in the room, so that the collective can develop the presenter's interpretation using their data. The cumulative effect of twenty-five motif studies stuns students as they discover Nabokov's ability to control so many fine strands in multiple works over so many years. In the final class (as a postlude to *Pale Fire*) we read "Signs and Symbols" which treats the distinction between referential mania and meaningful interpretation of the universe, and "The Vane Sisters" which explicitly confirms the theme of Otherworld.

Intensive exposure to Nabokov has a deep effect on many (Dan Handler a.k.a. Lemony Snicket complained during the semester, "I can't stop reading Nabokov!"). Half-way through the term students start emailing that they have started noticing squirrels after reading *Pnin*, or have just seen "A jet's pink trail above the sunset fire." They make the books their own, and this is the immortality which teachers can share with Nabokov.

RED CARD

ARCHIVE

Yuri Leving

"THE BOOK IS DAZZLINGLY BRILLIANT...BUT"[1] TWO EARLY INTERNAL REVIEWS OF NABOKOV'S *THE GIFT*

The first English-language review of *The Gift* appeared long before the novel became available to non-Russian readers. The text of this internal review remains unpublished and buried in the Nabokov manuscript collection at the Library of Congress. It was written in 1938 by Alexander I. Nazaroff, a Russian-American who lived in New York from the 1920s. Nazaroff authored several insightful books on Russian history and literature,[2] and also served as a frequent reviewer

---

[1] A. Nazaroff, internal review of *The Gift* for Bobbs-Merrill, typescript (Washington, D.C.: Vladimir Nabokov Collection, Manuscript Division, Library of Congress).

[2] Among them, *Tolstoy the Inconstant Genius* (New York: Fredrick A. Strokes, 1929); and *The Land of the Russian People* (Philadelphia: J. B. Lippincott, 1944).

and commentator on Russian cultural issues for *The New York Times*. In 1934, Nazaroff published an article in Russian in *Novaya Zarya* [*The New Dawn*], entitled "Sirin—the New Star in Literature," in which he gave Nabokov an extremely high place among the leading new talents emerging in both émigré and Soviet literature.[3]

In a letter accompanying his two-page review of *The Gift*, commissioned by the Bobbs-Merrill publishing house, Nazaroff tried to give a painstaking explanation of the pros and cons of its possible publication in the United States. Although unbiased, this appraisal, unfortunately, recommended against introducing the novel to American readers. As a keen observer, Nazaroff realized that contemporary audiences were not yet mature enough for such a complex work as *The Gift*. Essentially he was correct: it would take several decades, and the explosion of the *Lolita* "time-bomb" (in Nabokov's own words), before even the most perceptive critics would be ready to turn their attention to Nabokov's finest achievement in Russian.

Nazaroff began his letter, "I always have regarded V. Nabokoff [sic] as by far the most talented, brilliant and original of the young Russian writers (no matter whether Soviet or émigré) and perhaps of the young European writers in general," adding that a publishing firm which takes up the job of "establishing" Nabokov in the USA "sooner or later will be well rewarded for it, if even, in the beginning, the task appears to be ungrateful." Moreover, Nazaroff thought that Bobbs-Merrill made a good choice by introducing the writer to American readers with his *Laughter in the Dark*, though he refrained from advising them to add *The Gift* to that line-up: "But I am not at all sure that [this novel] would be the right selection for following up your effort." Nazaroff's doubts were based on the following considerations:

> 1. In its general type, *The Gift* sharply differs from that which hitherto was the common run of Nabokoff's novels. No matter how Nabokoff has always been fond of original (and often inimitably brilliant) tricks and artifices of composition and style, *Laughter in the Dark, Luzhin's Defense, The Exploit*,[4] and *Despair* are "normal" novels; they either have a well-constructed and developed dramatic plot (*Laughter in the Dark, Despair*), or are built "biographically" around one central character which holds the reader's interest (*Luzhin's Defense, The Exploit*); withal, they all firmly stand on the ground of reality (although Nabokoff often "alleviates" that reality and fascinatingly plays with it).

---

[3] Alexander I. Nazaroff, "Sirin—the New Star in Literature," *Novaya Zarya* [*The New Dawn*], August 11, 1934.

[4] *Podvig* (1931-32), later translated as *Glory* (1971).

Now, in contradiction to this, *The Gift* is not a realistic novel. I even am not sure that it can be called a novel at all. It is an ultra-sophisticated and modernist piece of introspective, almost "non-subjective" writing which, in composition, may be likened to James Joyce's *Ulysses*.

2. The narrative is—very loosely—centralized around Godunov-Cherdyntsev,[5] a young Russian émigré poet living in Berlin. At moments the author completely identifies himself with his hero; at others, without warning, he dissociates himself from him and speaks of him "from outside." The book follows no factual narrative thread of any kind; from beginning to end, it is a detailed disclosure of Godunov-Cherdyntsev's inner world, in which pictures of Berlin's streets or of the young poet's present life in a poor émigré's room, reminiscences of Cherdyntsev—the father's (who was an explorer) trips to Pamirs, the young man's reflections on life, poetry and literature and, above all, the constant watching of the intricacies of his own creative artistic process mingle in a succession which is determined not by any "outside logic" but by the free play of associations in his mind alone. The book thus is a crazy quilt of bits of reality drowning in the author's (or his hero's) "inner comment" on them. *The Gift*, no doubt, is a correct title for the work, for the unconquerable urge of Cherdyntsev's mind to digest artistically and transfigure by his imagination all things (including the most trivial ones) with which he comes in contact is the leitmotif of his narrative.

In the second half of the book, the author, to the reader's astonishment, inserts a comparatively very long biography of N.G. Chernyshevski, a famous Russian critic of the XIX century, which, supposedly, has been written by his hero Cherdyntsev; the biography is followed by long quotations from the comment made on it by various Russian reviewers and by the author's reaction to that comment. It is only towards the end of the book that this strange deviation finishes and that the reader finds himself again in the crazy quilt of Cherdyntsev's introspection.

In the third section of his evaluation, Nazaroff displayed his profound understanding of Nabokov's text. In fact, he presented one of the most favorable accounts ever produced by someone who was not among the writer's friends or sympathetic readers (as were Vladislav Khodasevich and Gleb Struve), a skill later found probably only in the lucid review of *Pale Fire* by Mary McCarthy, who described it as "a jack in the box, a Fabergé gem, a clockwork toy, a chess problem, an infernal machine."[6]

---

[5] The reviewer writes "Cherdyntzev" and refers to the novel title without the definite article—changed here and elsewhere in quotes to conform to Nabokov's transliteration and the accepted norm.

[6] Mary McCarthy, "A Bolt from the Blue," *New Republic* (June 1962): 21-27. Rpt. in McCarthy, *The Writing on the Wall and Other Literary Essays* (London: Weidenfeld and Nicolson, 1970) and in Introduction to V. Nabokov, *Pale Fire* (Harmondsworth: Penguin, 1991), v.

> Now, one who accepts and likes that [introspective] type of literature can pronounce but one verdict on *The Gift*; with the exception of the deviation on Chernyshevski (which is decidedly weak), the book is dazzlingly brilliant—one is tempted to describe it as a work of genius. The author's unique gift to convey to the reader the most complicated characterization of human beings or implications of thought, emotion and humor by a gliding, imperceptible stroke of the pen; the nervous burning and palpitation in the light and precipitous flight of his phrases which often, with a truly miraculous grace and plasticity, embrace the whole universe in a few casual words; the abnormal keenness of his eye which notices every human gesture and immediately discloses a whole "inner panorama" behind it; and a colossal spiritual culture, erudition and amount of knowledge touched off by imagination and fantasy in whose divine flight there is something of madness—all this renders the very texture of his pages so fascinating that one cannot tear oneself away from them. But how many American readers will appreciate that fascination?[7]

Among the amusing incidents surrounding the difficult publication history of *The Gift* were critics' attempts to provide Nabokov with some practical advice for improvement. The novel could be turned into a more readable piece, according to such well-wishers, either by revising the subject matter, or writing it in a more accessible manner. Alexander Nazaroff, for example, went as far as suggesting to Bobbs-Merrill a more suitable author for the possible English-language biography of Nikolay Chernyshevsky: "[Nabokov's Fourth Chapter] left me with an unpleasant feeling, but also gave me an idea that a book on Chernyshevski would be a good one to publish if you could get someone like E. H. Carr, the author of a recent brilliantly interesting life of Bakunin, to write it."[8] Others were less radical, and did not go beyond offering "friendly" advice:

> With only *The Gift* to judge by, a friendly reviewer might be tempted to urge Mr. Nabokov toward a style of broader strokes and coarser texture, as being more suited to the amplitudes of the novel. Such advice, however, would merely go to demonstrate that writers seldom can derive much benefit from their critics and ought never to attend to them.[9]

Despite the crescendo of positive remarks, Nazaroff nonetheless concluded with a decision unfavorable to Nabokov:

---

[7] A. Nazaroff, internal review (Vladimir Nabokov Collection).
[8] Ibid.
[9] Donald Malcolm, "A Retrospect," *New Yorker* XL, April 25, 1964, 198-204.

Obviously, this type of a work can appeal only to a very limited group of not only exceptionally cultured, but also ultra-sophisticated readers. Worse still, since the chief source of interest lies not in _what_ Nabokoff tells, but in _how_ he tells it, that is to say, in his unsurpassed verbal mastery, the book is bound considerably to fade out in translation [Emphasis in the original].

I can see in advance how an American will shrug his shoulders in disappointed astonishment over some of the passages which hold a Russian reading the original literally spellbound. In a normal-type realistic novel that, of course, would not be an insurmountable obstacle—the dramatic or human interest would make up for it; but in a piece of introspective writing this is a serious thing indeed. Finally, the appearance of this book in this country, where Nabokoff is not known, may easily scare away from him numbers of readers who would thoroughly enjoy his earlier, "normal" novels.

All this leads me to believe that *The Gift* is not a thing to be published in America—or, at least, not a thing to be published at the present time, when Nabokoff's reputation has not yet been established. Besides *The Gift*, he has so many truly excellent and perfectly "understandable" and "normal" works, from *Luzhin's Defense* to *Despair*; I am of the opinion that, at the present moment, it would be much better both for the publisher and for the author to pick out one of them.

Altagracia de Jannelli, Nabokov's literary agent at the time, forwarded a copy of Nazaroff's detailed analysis to Europe where the writer read it with ardent interest. As a result, Nabokov entered into an argument with the publisher's internal reviewer via an intermediary—quite an unusual step for someone who publicly dismissed all kinds of critical opinions. Nabokov's staunch desire to publish the novel uncensored, at all costs, meant even the compromise of publishing it first in English translation. In the atmosphere of a disintegrating Russian émigré community, and while Russian critics were virtually silent, Nabokov made his choice. On July 14, 1938, Nabokov wrote to his agent from Hotel de la Poste, a small mountain resort in Moulinet, France:

On the whole I rather liked N.'s description of *The Gift*, although it is very superficial—there is a lot more in my book both for the connoisseur and the lay reader. Here are some objections:

The Gift is thoroughly realistic, as it tells the story of a definite person, showing his physical existence and the development of his inner self. As he is an author, I naturally show his literary progress. Moreover, the whole story is threaded on my hero's love-romance, with the underground work of fate revealed—an essential point which N. has entirely missed. My style and methods have nothing in common with Joyce (though I greatly appreciate *Ulysses*). The novel is not 'a crazy quilt of bits'; it is a logical sequence of psychological events: the movements of stars may seem crazy to the simpleton, but wise men know that the comets come back.

> I don't understand why the reader should be "astonished" at the "insertion" of my hero's work (Chernyshevski's biography). The preceding chapters lead up to it and, as samples are given of all my hero's literary production, it would have been an impossible omission to leave his chief book out. Moreover, at this point, my hero's interpretation of Chernyshevski's life (which, incidentally, took me four years to write) lifts my novel to a wider plane, lending it an epic note and, so to say, spreading my hero's individual butter over the bread of a whole epoch. In this work (Chernyshevski's life), the defeat of Marxism and materialism is not only made evident, but it is rounded out by my hero's artistic triumph.
>
> As to the interest which *The Gift* might represent to the foreign (American) reader, I want to repeat that I know how to translate the book in such a way as even to avoid the necessity of footnotes. "Human interest" means Uncle Tom's cabin to me (or Galsworthy's drivel) and makes me sick, seasick.
>
> Your faith in my work is of the greatest value to me and I thank you warmly for your kind words.[10]

Since Nabokov refers to the reviewer only as "N.," it is likely that de Jannelli used only the first letter of Nazaroff's name when she was sending a typed copy of the original—her regular practice as evident from her correspondence with other publishers.

Most probably Alexander Nazaroff's identity remained unknown to Nabokov for a long time. In her letters to Nabokov, Altagracia de Jannelli referred to the anonymous critic consistently as "N." Dmitri Nabokov, who translated and published this communication in *Selected Letters*, listed "N" in a footnote as an "unidentified person."[11] Upon reconstructing the entire polemic, it is now possible to restore the real name and to correct the bibliographic note in the folder of the Nabokov archive in the Library of Congress. The latter dates Nazaroff's review as "1942" with a question mark; the accurate date is 1938.

Nazaroff's comments should be viewed as a rare instance of critical acumen. Although Nabokov claimed in response that his style and methods had nothing in common with Joyce, this is true only in part. Perceptive as Nazaroff was, he pointed out not just "style and methods," but also the psychological depth of the protagonists' minds and the general similarity in the artistic universes of *The Gift* and of *Ulysses*. Considering that the Chernyshevsky chapter had not yet been published and that Nabokov's status as an intellectual celebrity was still far into the future, Nabokov likely came to especially appreciate, in retrospect, the comparison of his novel with Joyce's

---

[10] Nabokov, *Selected Letters*, 27-28.
[11] Ibid., 28.

Ulysses, and the characterization of *The Gift* as an "ultra-sophisticated," "modernist piece of introspective writing."

In a last-ditch effort to override Nazaroff's internal opinion, which so oddly blended ecstatic praise with cool, rational market considerations, de Jannelli forwarded a copy of Nabokov's letter to D. L. Chambers, the president of the Bobbs-Merrill company. In her note dated August 2, 1938, she explained: "This was sent me in reply to my sending him the copy of Nazaroff's silly review. I know it will make no difference, but I am simply sending you this because I would like you to hear what the author himself has to say of his work." The agent was right in her assumption, as it did not bring about the desired change in the decision. Two days later, Chambers politely thanked de Jannelli for her "courtesy in letting [him] see a copy of Mr. Nabokoff's very interesting comment on Mr. Nazaroff's review of *The Gift*" and wished all success with adapting *Laughter in the Dark* to the stage or screen (another project that Nabokov was trying to pursue at that time with the help of his American agent).

Nazaroff's review was by no means "silly," as Altagracia de Jannelli hastily called it in her letter to the Bobbs-Merrill president. On the contrary, it remains one of the most vivid examples of shrewd critical feedback on Nabokov's *The Gift*.

"LIKE RISING BREAD FORGOTTEN BY THE BAKER..."[12]

Another early internal review of *The Gift* that survives in the Library of Congress archive was also written by a contemporary and former compatriot of the author. This second reader appears to have been less sophisticated than Alexander Nazaroff, although this in no way makes the document less distinctive, first and foremost as an illustration of "naïve reading." Charles Scribner's Sons Publishers commissioned this short review by a Russian émigré whose name was never mentioned in their correspondence with Nabokov's literary agent. Founded in 1846, Charles Scribner's was well known for publishing Ernest Hemingway, F. Scott Fitzgerald, and Thomas Wolfe, among others; several Scribner titles and authors garnered Pulitzer Prizes and National Book Awards. After the Bobbs-Merrill fiasco, Altagracia de Jannelli offered a possible translation of *The Gift* to this respected firm.

---

[12] L. T. Iglehart, Jr., "Served By Vladimir Nabokov: A Rich, Slavic Pudding," *St. Louis Globe-Democrat*, June 1–2, 1963, 4F.

RED CARD

On 16 September, 1938, John Hall Wheelock of Charles Scribner's Sons returned the manuscript of *The Gift* to Mme. de Jannelli. In accordance with the agent's request, Wheelock also enclosed his reader's report along with the cover letter to Mr. Perkins[13] (which was not copied to Nabokov). "When you have examined these, will you kindly return them to me? We don't usually do this, but perhaps it may help you in guiding Mr. Nabokoff," wrote the editor.

The unknown external reader opened his remarks with an apology for taking considerable time to read the book — "it seems to take much longer to write about it. I am terribly sorry about the delay. It is not entirely my fault." Despite the cautious preamble, it is clear that the reader made a genuine effort to work his way through the dense forest of modernist fiction, a category that he admits he was not particularly used to.

> What the author sets out to do in this book is to give his reader the inside dope on the inner life of a person endowed or cursed with the gift of creative imagination. It is through the eyes of such person, in this instance a poet, Godunov-Cherdyntzev [sic], or rather through his reactions, that we see the events and the characters of the book. The result is that we do not see them clearly, but as if we were looking through a double screen which makes their outlines not only vague, but also crooked. It is a stunt, and as such it is successful and amusing. Whether it is original or not, I cannot tell, because I do not read enough modernist literature.

The critic found it especially irritating that Nabokov uses various "stunts" that confuse the conservative reader and blur the line between reality and imagination.

> Another favorite stunt of the author is to make his hero live in his imagination for ten or twelve pages and then suddenly, without warning, jerk both him and the reader back to reality, so that the reader never quite knows where either of them is. For instance, the hero would be looking at an old tree with the swing which he and his sister used to enjoy so much in their childhood; then he would walk away from that tree and take the reader with him over the paths and avenues of his old country estate, talking to his father, and smelling buckwheat fields and what not; and then it will all suddenly vanish and the bewildered reader will find himself in front of just any old tree in the crowded public park in Berlin.

The reviewer was especially upset with what he believed to be unmotivated and confusing transitions within the narrative:

---

[13] Maxwell Perkins (1884-1947) was an influential literary editor who worked with writers such as Ernest Hemingway, F. Scott Fitzgerald, and Thomas Wolfe. Hemingway's *The Old Man and the Sea* (1952) was dedicated in memory of Perkins.

Or our hero will be holding a discussion with another poet, whom he meets in a park, about the respective merits of this or that Russian literary style, and after twenty pages of this discussion the other poet will suddenly break the flow of our poet's ideas by some trivial remark in German, because he really wasn't that other poet, but just a German unemployed resting on a bench, who happened to recall the image of this other poet to our poet's restlessly creative brain.

At a certain point the bleary-eyed critic felt that he had to defend his methodology, but instead just resorted to an expressive simile, almost foreshadowing the title of one of the American reviews which appeared twenty-five years later:

> I am talking so much about these tricky stunts because they are the best thing about the book. The story itself, the characters and the events, do not have the amusing quality of these tricks. The book itself has no form; it sprawls around like rising bread forgotten by the baker. It seems that in making his hero a fellow writer[,] the author thought he had provided himself sufficient excuse for stringing together all sorts of heterogeneous subjects, practically everything he had ever heard of or thought about, and trying to squeeze them into this book. Some of the subjects he had thought about might be interesting to people well acquainted with Russian poetry, Russian literature, and Russian literary criticism of the latter half of the last century. They would not be interesting to others, and even to me they fail to redeem a dull book. There is no real plot and no suspense whatever. The characters of the hero and his friends and acquaintances, Russian émigrés in Berlin, are drawn with indifferent disapproval rather than sympathy, with dull mockery rather than humor.[14]

It was not only the novel's plot and subject matter that the reviewer found weak; the author's language also came under fire from the carping critic. Nabokov's colloquial Russian, he suggested, "seems to have suffered from his many years of absence from his native land." The dialogue, the evaluator continued, did not sound authentic to him, though he admitted parenthetically that he too had been away from Russia for a long time.

In what is generally a confused response, the anonymous reader stated that *The Gift* "was a real disappointment," and that it was not worth translating and publishing because of its length, its contemplative nature, and the fact that it deals with subjects that would be accessible and interesting only to readers who are well acquainted with the nuances and ongoing polemics of Russian literature and criticism. The critic's suggestions to the publisher appear to be in tune with what Nazaroff had earlier expressed to Bobbs-

---

[14] Iglehart, "Slavic Pudding," 4F.

Merrill. In his opinion, novels like *The Defense* (which he briefly recounted, though omitting the title) were much more accessible and more suitable for the purpose of introducing the Russian writer to the American public.

> Several years ago I read another book by the same author built very much on the same idea — only there the hero was a chess-player. The reader was made to live in the same way in his head. The book was short and lively and interesting. I remember that I liked it and recommended it to Simon and Schuster, for whom I was doing the reading. And I think [that this novel] would be a much better book to translate. I met the author in Paris and liked him too...

One suspects that this final personal mention was meant to imply opposite of what it stated explicitly.

A long pause followed these two internal reviews, and it was twenty-five years later before *The Gift* was once again exposed to the scrutiny of the English-speaking audience.

DANGEROUS PLAY

CONFERENCE

Marie Bouchet

"REVISING NABOKOV REVISING" NABOKOV CONFERENCE IN KYOTO

April 24-27, 2010
Organized by the Nabokov Society of Japan

"Revising" is a word rich with implications. Advancing Nabokov studies would be impossible without discussing how Nabokov revised his works as he translated them, as well as our own view of Nabokov's standing and of which of his works should be subject to revision, especially since the publication of *The Original of Laura*, and the subsequent backlash and refracting waves of canon revisionism. Moreover, the 2010 Nabokov conference in Kyoto was not confined to this theme since "revising" makes it possible to focus on a wide range of issues, from close examinations of specific textual revisions to broad cultural issues dealing with the way that Nabokov's work is currently read and received around the world.

After a delightful opening reception on March 24, 2010, the conference started with three papers dedicated to the *Lolita* screenplay. Andrei Babikov (The Culture Center of Ukraine in Moscow) presented the first paper, entitled "Nabokov's Revisions of *Lolita* in the Screenplay." Mr. Babikov, who has translated the published screenplay into Russian, tackled the notion of revising through a singular example of Nabokov's revision of his own work. Babikov focused on motifs and networks of allusions that Nabokov added or strengthened in his screenplay, which should not be considered a simplified version of the novel, but as a work in its own right: an "implied film," as Michael Wood put it. In the discussion that followed, Susan Elizabeth Sweeney wondered whether the screenplay had been designed for a film meant to be viewed more than once, or for people who had read *Lolita*. The presenter's opinion is that the *Lolita* screenplay is a text for readers.

Jacqueline Hamrit (University of Lille III, France) in her "Generic Glidings and Endless Writing from *The Enchanter* to *Lolita: A Screenplay* through *Lolita*," underscored the cross-generic writing at stake in the nymphet story. She demonstrated that these texts illustrate not only the difference between showing and telling in literary terms, but also between literary narrative and cinematic showing. Dr. Hamrit analyzed the shift from third- to first-person narration and the absence of such a filter in the screenplay, as opposed to the conservation of the mother-child-husband scheme. Nabokov's awareness of the camera's presence and function in his screenplay was also underlined.

In the paper entitled "Nabokov Revising Nabokov: The *Lolita* Screenplays," Julian Connolly (University of Virginia) focused not only on the changes in the medium of the work (from verbal narrative to screenplay), but also on literary allusions and characterization. Connolly rehearsed some of the major differences between the two versions of the screenplay (such as the opening), and insisted on toning down all erotic contents, even though Nabokov kept some indications of Humbert's pedophilia, later deleted by Kubrick. Julian then interrogated the intertextual aspect of the screenplay, noting that only the references to Poe were kept, and almost all other references dropped. Finally, he analyzed the absence of some of the novel's characters (Monique, Gaston Godin) and the expansion of both the role and personality of others (Quilty and Lolita).

The next set of papers focused on Nabokov's linguistic peculiarities and writing strategies. In "Nabokov's 'Natural Idiom': From 'First-rate' Russian to 'Second-rate' English," Shun'Ishiro Akikusa (University of Tokyo) carried out a stylistic comparison of Nabokov's Russian and his self-translation into English. Dr. Akikusa demonstrated that the most unique feature of Nabokov's

Russian style is the fact that he deliberately utilizes the grammar, usage and idiom which native speakers unconsciously internalize. Nabokov's writing style is to bring out all the possibilities of Russian, and it is different from his English, which often evidently violates the rules of idiomatic usage. Moreover, Akikusa noted that in Nabokov's self-translations into Russian, some features of his English were transferred into the Russian equivalents.

Marie Bouchet (University of Toulouse, France) developed an analysis focusing on the notion of displacement in Nabokov's fiction in terms of structure, characterization, and style. She analyzed the syntactical and phonological displacements at play in the characterization of Pnin, and the recurrence of a rather infrequent device in *Lolita*, the hypallage, one of Humbert's favorite. Hypallages perform the syntactic displacement of an adjective or adverb, which qualifies an item other than the one it logically should. This transgression of syntactical borders renders the limits between words porous, and invites the reader to replace the adjective or adverb, and thus play the displacement game offered by the text.

The first plenary speaker of the conference was Maurice Couturier (University of Nice), who presented his findings on the process of annotating the translation of *Lolita* for the second volume of the Pléiade edition of Nabokov's works (due to appear in 2010 in France; Couturier is its chief editor). Professor Couturier focused on two types of annotations. First, he analyzed the contents of Nabokov's cards held at the Library of Congress, going over the ample material that Nabokov gathered from newspapers, magazines, and books on such topics as the development of a girl's body at puberty, sex, teenage slang, legal jargon, and literary references. Couturier then concentrated on intertexts such as Vigneau's *Lolita* and *Nocturnal Revels* which could have served Nabokov as sources for the name of Charlotte Haze, as well as potential echoes of the French literary works which the author passed on to his French-speaking narrator, Humbert Humbert. According to Couturier, these two sets of annotations tend to show that desire and sex are much more important in *Lolita* than Alfred Appel, Jr. suggested in his annotated edition.

Tadashi Wakashima (Kyoto University) presented a paper entitled "Another Road to *Lolita*: A Transatlantic View," in which he considered the possible reasons why Graham Greene notoriously praised *Lolita*. Professor Wakashima explored the so-called "mushroom jungle"—a horde of lurid paperbacks which gained large popularity in postwar Britain. His goal was to trace how *Lolita* could be mistakenly considered as a typical product of that popular genre.

In her paper "Revising Nabokov Revising the Detective Novel: Vladimir, Agatha, and the Terms of Engagement," Catharine T. Nepomnyashchy (Columbia University) examined the way in which Nabokov revised the detective novel by incorporating it into his own novels, via possible references to Agatha Christie. Dr. Nepomnyashchy analyzed *Lolita*, *Despair* and *The Real Life of Sebastian Knight*, showing how Nabokov appropriates popular fiction's power to seduce the reader. According to Nepomnyashchy, Nabokov posed the problem of the function of literature in an age when it was challenged by politics and competing forms of culture.

Maya Medlock (Yamaguchi University) studied "the theme of tears" in *Lolita*, pointing out that though much attention is given to Lolita's tears in the novel, we do not really relate to Humbert's tears. Humbert repeatedly mentions his own tears and sobs, which almost overwhelm those of Lolita.

In "Some Spiritual Subtexts Hidden in *Transparent Things*," Akiko Nakata (Nanzan Junior College) noted the subtexts alluding to spirituality, which she called, following Boyd, "stories behind the story behind the story." The difficulty to notice these indirect quotations indicates that these subtexts are incorporated in the text to be found but also to remain concealed, as Nabokov often does with the theme of death.

In "*Bend Sinister*'s Mad Dash or How to Impersonate an Anthropomorphic Deity," Leland de la Durantaye (Harvard University) analyzed the ending of *Bend Sinister* and discussed the image of creator and creation at the end of this work, linking it to larger aesthetic and ethical questions in Nabokov's writing. Professor de la Durantaye demonstrated that the question of suffering goes beyond any political intent, and related it to some basic features of Nabokovian art.

Kazunao Sugimoto (Aichi Shukutoku University) summed up the common features of what he called "Nabokov's Orpheus Stories," namely the narratives in which male protagonists lose their beloved and struggle in vain to find a way to get her back. Studying "The Return of Chorb," *Mary*, "Ulthima Thule," and *Lolita*, Kazunao stated that the last attempt to get back the lost beloved often appears to be the act of becoming the "author" of a story.

In his paper entitled "Saving Jewish-Russian Emigrés," Maxim D. Shrayer (Boston College) considered Nabokov's Jewish concerns and explorations, analyzing works from Nabokov's Russian short fiction. Dr. Shrayer underscored the pattern of characters rescuing or attempting to rescue Jewish children, and interpreted Nabokov's Berlin fiction as an implicit warning addressed to the émigré community.

Entrance to the Kyoto hotel hosting the conference

Yuri Leving, Kyoto conference photographs, 2010 ©

1 Samuel Schuman

2 Bronwen and Brian Boyd, Ellen Pifer, Tadashi Wakashima, Akiko Nakata

3 Brian Boyd

4-5 Walking tour of Ginkakuji and Shisendo

6 Maxim D. Shrayer, Maria Malikova, Mitsunori Sagae

4

5

6

7 Susan E. Sweeney, Leland de la Durantaye

8 Michael Wood

9 Mitsyoshiu Numano

7

8

9

The next three papers dealt with Nabokov's autobiography. Maria Alhambra (University of East Anglia) focused on the paratext of *Speak, Memory* (map, index, and photographs) and the unpublished chapter sixteen. Subsequently, Siggy Frank (University of Nottingham) focused specifically on the photographs reproduced in Nabokov's memoirs, and analyzed the relation between the text and the images—the photograph and the caption chosen by Nabokov. The photographs provide an echo to Nabokov's intense, mainly visual, experience of remembering, as if his mental pictures were juxtaposed with the actual photographs.

In her paper, entitled "Folding His Magic Carpet: Nabokov's *Speak, Memory* and *Lolita*," Ellen Pifer (University of Delaware) attempted to trace the creative evolution of the nymphet theme by focusing on Polenka, the young daughter of the Nabokovs' head coachman, with whom young Vladimir exchanged glances of desire. She demonstrated how, in the memoir as in the novel, the triumph of memory over time's arrow is often tinged with remorse.

The second plenary speaker of the Kyoto conference was Brian Boyd (University of Auckland), who had also provided the conference's title theme. In his talk "Nabokov as Psychologist: Routes for Exploration," Professor Boyd suggested it was time to revise or refresh our sense of Nabokov by considering him as a serious psychologist, though not without a playful touch. He outlined Nabokov's scientific curiosity, his gift for precise observation, and artistic inventiveness applied to psychology. Indeed, much of his famous antipathy to Freud derived from his own passion for psychology. Following Nabokov's claim that "all novelists of any worth are psychological novelists," Boyd demonstrated how Nabokov, not only a brilliant observer of the world of nature and human kind, had subtly understood the workings of man's mind. He did this by analyzing in detail a short excerpt from *Ada*, which illustrates Nabokov's use of various mental processes now well known to specialists of the cognitive systems in the human brain.

Nobuaki Kakinuma (Kobe Shoin Women's University) gave a talk in Russian, entitled "From the Notes to *Eugene Onegin* to *Pale Fire*: Comparing the Annotations of Nabokov and Lotman." Kakinuma proposed that Lotman's notes can be read as a criticism of Nabokov's far from strictly scientific commentary to *Eugene Onegin*. The ambiguities of Pushkin's original compositional directions provide extreme stimulation to the unbridled imagination of Nabokov as a writer.

In his paper, Mitsuyoshi Numano (University of Tokyo) focused on the "stylistic exuberance" of *The Gift*, which became all the more obvious as he was translating the novel into Japanese (to make Nabokov's masterpiece in Russian available to Japanese readers). Mitsuyoshi explained how the syntactical constraints of the Japanese language rendered the task of translating Nabokov's long and convoluted sentences, frequently resorting to relative pronouns and participles, excruciatingly difficult. Translating the abundant alliterations and assonances of Nabokov's text also proved complicated, especially because such stylistic ornaments do not sound as poetic and elegant in Japanese as they do in Russian.

A French psychiatrist and Nabokov amateur, Jean-Pierre Luauté, gave a talk entitled "Was Nabokov a Psychologist?: About *Despair* and Nabokov's Inflexible Criticism of Freud's Doctrine." As a specialist on the various clinical conditions in which the phenomenon of the double appears (currently designated as Delusional Misidentification Syndrome), Mr. Luauté evaluated the "syndrome of the subjective double" and suggested that the first to discover this particular condition was none other but Nabokov who, in *Despair*, gave its exact description. Jean-Pierre Lauté and his colleague would have liked to call this disorder the "Nabokov syndrome," but unfortunately the writer's name had already been ascribed to another condition, namely the mental-spatial impairment Vadim displays in *Look at the Harlequins!*, which P. L. Assoun mistakenly assumed that Nabokov had suffered from as well.

In a paper, "'Almost Completed But Only Partly Corrected': Enacting Revision in Nabokov's Novels," Susan Elizabeth Sweeney (College of the Holy Cross) examined the practice of revising as part of Nabokov's creative process. Dr. Sweeney considered various versions, revisions, additions, and self-translations with modifications that not only mark Nabokov's works in their making, but are also thematically reflected in his fictional worlds, as most of his novels, in fact, present themselves as manuscripts still being composed by a first-person narrator.

Maria Malikova (Pushkinskii Dom) focused on Nabokov's "Shishkov cycle" ("A Phantom Russian Poet: Vladimir Nabokov's Poetics and Position in the Late 1930s—Early 1950s"), a series of poems written under the pseudonym Vasilii Shishkov. It is commonly accepted that Nabokov triumphantly played a practical joke on the most famous and influential Russian émigré literary critic, Georgii Adamovich, who out of sheer partiality had consistently dismissed Nabokov's Sirin poems but enthusiastically welcomed them disguised under the Shishkov mask. However, Dr. Malikova showed that Adamovich's reading of those poems should not be viewed only through the narrow lens of the comic misidentification story: the scholar revealed a much more complex context of the rivalry, and underscored Adamovich's acute insights into the essence of Nabokov's later Russian poetics.

Masataka Konishi (Tokyo Gakugei University) presented "Nabokov's Paradox," a paper in Russian, in which he analyzed the recurrence of mathematical motifs in Nabokov's novels from the end of the 1930s to the mid-1940s. According to Dr. Konishi, the presence of such mathematical paradoxes and conundrums is paralleled not only to self-reference, as part of the metafictional aspect of Nabokov's novels, but also to his interest in the otherworld.

Stephen Blackwell (University of Tennessee) offered a revision of Nabokov's relationship with the work of Dostoevsky, showing how Nabokov developed important Dostoevskian devices in his work; one such device, the "loophole," was pushed to new limits. Following Bakhtin's analysis of Dostoevsky, Professor Blackwell demonstrated that Dostoevsky was the first to introduce a heightened sensitivity to the finalizing power of language through characters that continually seek transcending their own and others' narratives about them; but it was Nabokov who developed that approach by crafting narratives which extrude and dramatize their own entrapping potential.

In his paper "Nabokov and Hemingway: The Fish That Got Away," Yuri Leving (Dalhousie University) claimed that Nabokov's attitude toward American achievements in literature was neither black nor white. In 1954, the émigré Chekhov Publishing House proposed that Nabokov undertake a possible translation of *The Old Man and the Sea*. Contrary to the associate editor's fears, Nabokov did not reject the idea with "indignation" and he seriously considered translating Hemingway's masterpiece into Russian. Despite the fact that Nabokov's Russian translation of *The Old Man and the Sea* never materialized, the unpublished correspondence at the Berg Collection (NYPL), presented by Professor Leving, sheds new light on this unrealized project.

Sam Schuman's (University of Minnesota) talk, "'The Sun's a Thief': Nabokov and Shakespeare—A Quantitative Approach," summarized his substantial work-in-progress of annotating every reference to Shakespeare in the Nabokov English-language cannon. Schuman explained his method (defining types of references) and presented some of the results obtained so far. The more Nabokov continued composing in English, the more numerous were the references to the Bard in his prose.

After visiting two wonders of Kyoto—Ginkakuji and Shisendo—and a delightful walk under the cherry blossoms, the last plenary speaker of the

Kyoto Nabokov Conference, Michael Wood (Princeton University), lectured on "The Afterlife of Sebastian Knight." Amidst the enchanting setting of Hakusasonso, Professor Wood analyzed the structure of inquiry that Nabokov establishes in *The Real Life of Sebastian Knight,* as well as its recurrence through later novels and stories. He also wondered whether the notion of the "original" of Laura was designed precisely to recall the "real life" Sebastian Knight may or may not have. The point was not to suggest that *The Real Life of Sebastian Knight* was a source or model for Nabokov's later work, but that it provides a distinctive theoretical framework through which much of that work may usefully be seen.

PENALTY AREA

BOOK REVIEWS

Graham Vickers, *Chasing Lolita: How Popular Culture Corrupted Nabokov's Little Girl All Over Again*, Chicago Review Press, Chicago, 2008; ISBN 9781 55652 6824, 247 pp. Bibliography. Index. Illustrations. No price available.

Graham Vickers opens his work *Chasing Lolita* with a declaration of his mission as "separating the miss from the myth."[1] This somewhat vague and uncannily catchy quote sets the tone reasonably accurately for the vague and catchy book that follows it. Just what this is supposed to mean is further complicated when the author cites his inspiration as a throwaway comment by Dmitri Nabokov, on the set of the 1997 film adaptation of his father's great work, that "there was surely a book to be written about the bizarre and kitschy nature of the Lolita legacy."[2] If not irremediably contradictory, these two concepts certainly seem to deal with two distinct issues, and Vickers creates further problems for himself by asserting that

---
[1] Vickers, *Chasing Lolita*, 1.
[2] Ibid.

his real interest actually lies in how Lolita has been understood among different classes of readers. Thus, the introduction offers us three spheres of contemplation, yet we emerge from the book with none of them satisfied.

The substance of *Chasing Lolita* consists of an impressive archive of cultural references to Nabokov's controversial heroine in literature, film, music, theatre, fashion and journalism. These range from the obvious major cinematic adaptations to a Swedish operatic rendition. Among the more interesting examples are *Reading Lolita in Tehran: A Memoir in Books*, a compilation of discussions raised in a covert book group for Iranian female students; and *Lo's Diary*, an Italian author's apparently unsuccessful attempt to restore Lolita's voice—Vickers finding no more praiseworthy adjective for it than "curious."[3] In each case, a history and context is presented, along with a dissection of the work in terms of its success in recreating the novel, particularly the portrayal of the eponymous protagonist. When simply considered as a body of research, this detailed chronicling is very valuable, not to mention accessible, but it lacks the meaningful and directed analysis required to turn it into a book of critical worth.

In terms of content, a lot of examples are not satisfactorily justified, most ostensibly a wealth of tenuously linked Hollywood anecdotes explained as "a label being applied retrospectively."[4] On the appealing but questionable grounds that *Lolita* should be considered "a literary lighthouse...casting its light backward as well as forward,"[5] Vickers traces the history of the sexualization of young girls on the American screen, from the silent era to present day. He notes twenty-six-year-old Lilian Gish's 1919 portrayal of an abused twelve-year-old, and thirteen-year-old Brooke Shield's infamous performance as child prostitute *Pretty Baby* in 1978. While there is clearly some interest and relevance to be gained from these examples, Vickers seems too distracted by his need to include every possible instance to actually draw it out.

The segment on Marilyn Monroe is a case in point. Vickers ascribes Monroe's popularity to "childish feminine innocence wrapped up in an adult body."[6] What relevance this bears to Lolita, who held such a great attraction to her eventual stepfather because of her childlike body (which Vickers repeatedly points out), is highly dubious. In relation to the 1950s icon, the question is asked "Did Lolita, at 'about thirteen,' start laying plans to become

---

[3] Ibid., 208. Azar Nafisi, *Reading Lolita in Tehran: A Memoir in Books* (New York: Random House, 2003); Pia Pera, *Lo's Diary* (Northwood, Middlesex: Foxrock Books, 1999).
[4] Vickers, *Chasing Lolita*, 57.
[5] Ibid., 1.
[6] Ibid., 71.

a sex symbol?"[7] This solitary reference to the supposed core of the book's endeavors is not only a total non sequitur, but remains entirely unanswered. Instead, the author spends a full chapter reliving Monroe's career and comparing her success to that of her contemporaries. Such unnecessary attention to irrelevant detail, combined with an apparent inability to focus any discourse on a given topic, undermines whatever intellectual contributions *Chasing Lolita* may have offered.

This lack of direction is extended by the inclusion of numerous scandals involving movie industry figures who have at one time been accused of pedophilia. Predictably, Roman Polanski, Woody Allen and Charlie Chaplin are named, as well as earlier, now less remembered cases such as Errol Flynn and D. W. Griffith. Again, these examples could be used as the basis for different arguments and hypotheses, yet leave many questions not so much unanswered as unasked. Why is there such a high incidence of pedophilia amongst Hollywood celebrities? Why have these cases almost invariably been tolerated? Admittedly, such issues contribute little to the myth of Lolita, Lolita's kitsch legacy, or varied understandings of Lolita along class divisions, but neither does the inclusion of these examples, and there seems very little reason to bring them up without effectively linking them to some ulterior argument.

The chosen material does not contribute to a separation of "miss from myth." On the contrary, it encourages a very literocentric, or perhaps, more accurately, Nabokov-centric, tendency to see Lolita in everything. One exception to this is in the chapter "Tabloids and Factoids" which argues that the term Lolita has come to refer to seductive young girls, and "carries with it a certain assumption of guilt" that in some way excuses whatever role the older man may have in the affair.[8] This seems to be the heart of what Vickers is trying to investigate — what exactly Lolita has come to mean as a commonly understood description and how accurately it relates to Nabokov's character. Had Vickers ignored his three proffered objectives in the introduction and concentrated on this one aspect, which overlaps each of them, *Chasing Lolita* would arguably provide a much more valuable platform for both literary and social discourse. As Vickers summarizes in the conclusion, "[Lolita] has been corrupted in a variety of ways, but each corruption tells us something not about her but about us."[9] He fails, however, to elaborate on how and why these "corruptions" are so revealing.

[7] Ibid., 72.
[8] Ibid., 173.
[9] Ibid., 231.

Zoe Aiano

Just as the introduction establishes the flaws to follow, with the phrase "separating the miss from the myth" sacrificing meaning for style (and tabloid style at that), the conclusion encapsulates many of *Chasing Lolita*'s shortcomings. The conclusion is hung on two questions—"One: was the book a dramatization of Vladimir Nabokov's own sexual proclivities? Two: doesn't discussing *Lolita*—doesn't the very existence of the book—make pedophilia more socially acceptable?"[10] Neither of these seems to relate to any of the content preceding them or to each other, and would appear to be asked solely for the sake of inclusion. Furthermore, they are not answered properly; as Vickers writes "The second question is so stupid that it does not really deserve an answer... The first question is almost as stupid."[11] This can account for why the questions are only considered in the summary rather than the body of the text. It still does not explain, however, why Vickers chose to doubt his readers' intelligence by asking them at all, nor why he feels obliged to provide long-winded responses to questions he has already condemned.

The book closes with the assertion that "Happily, the 'real' Lolita can always be perfectly restored for anyone who cares to read or reread Nabokov's novel."[12] This negates any meaning to be found in cultural responses to Lolita, as it implies that their distortion of the character is more important than their interpretation. It also overlooks the question of subjectivity, which is a vital element of Nabokov's writing. The entire first segment of *Chasing Lolita* is dedicated to assessing the extent to which we should trust Humbert Humbert's description of Lolita, since his is the only perspective we are given. Surely one of the reasons *Lolita* has inspired such a myriad of legacies is that the book's inherent moral and narrative ambiguity lends itself to infinite interpretation. Regardless of this, it is a perplexing note to end on, if not quite as confounding as the last words, which simply describe Vickers's favorite scene.

It seems more reasonable to consider *Chasing Lolita* a collection of interesting and accessible vignettes of twentieth century child pornography—which merely uses *Lolita* as a frame or point of reference—than a work intent on "separating the miss from the myth."[13] Despite its overarching failure to follow a single argument through to a conclusion, it is a pleasant and easy read with a broad enough scope to offer some new information to every reader.

Zoe Aiano
Glasgow

[10] Ibid., 229.
[11] Ibid.
[12] Ibid., 231.
[13] Ibid., 1.

Approaches to Teaching Nabokov's Lolita, edited by Zoran Kuzmanovich and Galya Diment. The Modern Language Association of America, New York, 2008; ISBN 978-0-87352-943-3, xiv+190 pp. Prefaces to series and volume. Notes on contributors. Bibliography. No price available.

It is difficult to imagine a more useful handbook for teaching *Lolita* than this one. It goes a long way towards its aim of helping teachers to make "Nabokov's chocolate mousse prose" accessible to students.[1] The first section of the book contains a usefully comprehensive chronology of Nabokov's life, continuing with a detailed and insightful analysis of many different materials relating to the study of *Lolita,* including a full account of the complex publication history of the text. But the real meat of this book is in Part 2. The variety of stimulating strategies for teaching *Lolita* described, in some detail,

---

[1] Kuzmanovich and Diment, ed., *Teaching Nabokov's* Lolita, Preface to the volume, page unnumbered.

should comfortably achieve the book's stated aspiration of preventing "students falling into platitudes."[2]

The first critical essay, "Only Words to Play With: Teaching 'Lolita' in Reading and Writing Courses" certainly tackles a critical platitude. In "Is *Lolita* a dirty book?"[3] Samuel Schuman explores the issue of what kind of book *Lolita* actually is. In an approach typical of many of the other essays in the collection, he describes how he explored Nabokov's text with first-term students, employing a varied complex of practical teaching techniques.

In describing her approach to the text in "Teaching *Lolita* in a Course on Ethics and Literature," Marilyn Edelstein explores Nabokov's conflicting statements on the novelist as moralist. "Since *Lolita* foregrounds and complicates ethical questions,"[4] Edelstein goes on to describe how she exposed her students to various classic texts of literary criticism from Plato to Kant, exploring the relationship between ethics and literature. After introducing a seemingly unpromising connection between Tolstoy and Nabokov, she describes how she explored Tolstoy's famously non-aesthetic view of the purpose of art in his treatise *What is Art?* with her students. Edelstein includes a discussion of Tolstoy's view of the two types of religious art, the "lower" of which conveys "negative feelings of indignation and horror at the violation of love."[5] Tolstoy's essay would now seem to possess an obvious, if previously unsuspected, interest for students of *Lolita* and, in her own study of the text, Edelstein includes a discussion of Humbert Humbert as a "negative" ethical example, in Tolstoy's sense.

It is clear that among the most interesting essays in this continually challenging and engaging book are those which relate *Lolita* to Russian literature and culture, firmly locating Nabokov in a Russian milieu. In the first such essay in the volume—"Teaching *Lolita* with Dostoevsky and Poe in Mind"—Dale E. Peterson, quoting Mikhail Bakhtin, relates the position of Humbert Humbert with his "supremely self-conscious narration" to "Dostoevsky's unattractive and slippery narrators."[6] The justice of this

---

[2] Ibid., 27.
[3] Samuel Schuman, "Only Words to Play With: Teaching 'Lolita' in Reading and Writing Courses," *Teaching Nabokov's Lolita*, 31.
[4] Marilyn Edelstein, "Teaching *Lolita* in a Course on Ethics and Literature," *Teaching Nabokov's Lolita*, 44.
[5] L. N. Tolstoy, *What is Art?*, trans. Aylmer Maude (Indianapolis: Bobbs-Merrill, 1978), 152.
[6] Dale E. Peterson, "Teaching *Lolita* with Dostoevsky and Poe in Mind," *Teaching Nabokov's Lolita*, 73. M. Bakhtin, *Problems of Dostoevsky's Poetics*, trans. and ed. C. Emerson (Minneapolis: University of Minneapolis Press, 1984), 233.

observation is at once obvious and certainly ironic, given Nabokov's well-documented hostility toward Dostoevsky.

In his essay "Russian Cultural Contexts for *Lolita*," Julian W. Connolly links the "demonic nymphet,"[7] Dolores Haze, to the similarly bewitching folklore-figure of the *rusalka* in works by Pushkin and Gogol. Connolly suggests a particular link to the "drowned maiden" of Gogol's short story "A May Night, or The Drowned Maiden." He posits a further fruitful connection between Nabokov and Dostoevsky in linking Stavrogin's (suppressed) confession in "At Tikhon's" to the "Dostoevskian grin" Humbert Humbert admits to enjoying as he contemplates how marriage to Charlotte Haze would grant him ready access to Lolita—a young girl of much the same age as Stavrogin's victim in *The Devils*.[8]

In her essay "Teaching *Lolita* Through Pushkin's Eyes," Priscilla Meyer reminds us that Nabokov was working on his translation of *Eugene Onegin* (1950-57) while writing *Lolita* (1947-54), and she discovers (perhaps well-hidden) similarities between the two, including: the action of both texts spans five years; the heroine of each grows from "provincial miss to inaccessible grown woman"; the "hero" in both books returns from lengthy travels, only to be rejected by his love; Onegin kills Lensky, Humbert kills Quilty. Finally, both Pushkin and Nabokov offer the reader the possibility of creative confusion of the personae of author, hero and narrator.[9] We might add that in Canto IV (stanza VIII) of *Eugene Onegin*, Pushkin reveals that Tatiana was thirteen years of age when she first met Onegin.[10]

It is well known that Nabokov was a keen cinema patron when he was young.[11] Galya Diment explores the possible creative influences of early Russian film on Nabokov in her piece "From Bauer's Li to Nabokov's Lo: *Lolita* and Early Russian Film." She describes the influence of Poe on Nabokov, and on Evgenii Bauer—an important director in early Russian cinema, whose films dealt with themes that "brim with dark psychological twists and turns of the kind that Nabokov appreciated."[12]

---

[7] Julian W. Connolly, "Russian Cultural Contexts for *Lolita*," *Teaching Nabokov's* Lolita, 89.
[8] Ibid., 93.
[9] Priscilla Meyer, "Teaching *Lolita* Through Pushkin's Eyes," *Teaching Nabokov's* Lolita, 95, 98.
[10] Alexander Pushkin, *Eugene Onegin*, trans. Stanley Mitchell (London: Penguin Classics, 2008), 79.
[11] Vladimir Nabokov, *Speak, Memory: An Autobiography Revisited* (London: Penguin Books, 2000), 182.
[12] Galya Diment, "From Bauer's Li to Nabokov's Lo: *Lolita* and Early Russian Film," *Teaching Nabokov's* Lolita, 103.

Nabokov would certainly have appreciated the ironies apparent in Marianne Cartugno's "Teaching *Lolita* at a Religious College." This essay discusses the importance of the context in which a given text is read. In particular, Cartugno fruitfully juxtaposes reading and exploring *Lolita* at a Christian college in the United States with the experiences of the brave women in Azar Nafisi's memoir *Reading "Lolita" in Tehran*, who explored the text in secret in what she calls "a place of transgression" somewhere in the capital of the Islamic Republic of Iran.[13]

Nabokov would surely have seen the irony of his super-subtle text *Lolita* being dissected in the strongholds of two rival theologies, both so alien to his belief in the primacy of aesthetic values over all others, and of good writing over the merely second-rate. This book will certainly assist students of Nabokov in very practical ways, both to appreciate the good writing in *Lolita*, and perhaps to become better writers themselves. As Samuel Schuman says in his "Only Words to Play With: Teaching *Lolita* in Introductory Reading and Writing Courses," "it is impossible to read *Lolita* carefully and not recognize when one writes poorly."[14]

Joseph Lynch,
University of Glasgow

---

[13] Azar Nafisi, *Interview with Azar Nafisi, Samarkand Quarterly* 3-4 (2003-2004): http://libstaff.library.vanderbilt.edu/LIBTECH/Stringer/samarkand.html.

[14] Schuman, "Only Words to Play With," *Teaching Nabokov's Lolita*, 34.

***Verses and Versions: Three Centuries of Russian
Poetry*, selected and translated by Vladimir Nabokov,
edited by Brian Boyd and Stanislav Shvabrin. Harcourt,
Orlando — Austin — New York — San Diego — London, 2008;
ISBN 978-0-15-101264-0, xxxv+442 pp. Notes. Indices.
No price available.**

In this handsome and beautifully referenced book, Brian Boyd and Stanislav Shvabrin have brought together Nabokov's translations of short Russian poems into English, completing a project which Nabokov had planned. The book includes translations previously published in the 1940s in the anthologies *Three Russian Poets* and *Pushkin, Lermontov, Tyutchev*. It also incorporates translations made during Nabokov's laborious work on *Eugene Onegin*, and unpublished texts from the Nabokov archives in New York and Montreux. As Boyd explains in the preface, the rather fragmentary nature of the book is due, in part, to the fact that it is a posthumous compilation: the selection of poems is "more accidental than it would have been" had

Nabokov overseen it.[1] *Verses and Versions* is as much a sourcebook on Nabokov as it is on Russian poetry, and no less interesting for that.

The poets whose work is most generously represented here are the three nineteenth century poets in Nabokov's anthology: Pushkin, Lermontov and Tyutchev. Also included are some of their more prominent forbearers, contemporaries and successors, such as Lomonosov, Karamzin and Zhukovsky, Fet and Nekrasov, as well as the work of some less well known poets, such as Aleksey Koltsov. The choice of twentieth century poets is highly selective: Blok, Khodasevich, Mandelshtam and, surprisingly, Okudzhava. (As is often the case with Nabokov, what he leaves out is as interesting as what he includes). Each translation is printed next to the original version of the poem, and the editors have provided a website giving transliterated versions for those who do not read Russian.

In addition to the translations, the book includes short biographical and critical articles on each poet, penned by Nabokov, as well as a number of his comments on the activity of literary translation. In these notes, Nabokov is revealed in a number of different guises. He is, by turns, a fascinating, poetic and opinionated literary critic—writing of Lermontov's talent for creating "a fluid and iridescent medium wherein reality discloses the dreams of which it consists";[2] a ferocious baiter of those who substitute travesty for translation—such as Lowell, who receives a battering for his misleading adaption of a Mandelshtam poem; and a learned and generous guide to the work of those he regarded as truly great, such as Pushkin and Khodasevich. He even appears in the unfamiliar role of devoted father, in a set of notes for an album of songs recorded by his son Dmitri in the 1970s. Here, Nabokov's usual uncompromising tone is noticeably softened.

The book opens with some notes on translating poetry, in which the author's strong opinions are at their most evident. (Not for nothing did one writer brand him "Nazistic Nabokov," "the verbal sadist").[3] Nabokov was fond of drawing up lists of unreasonable rules regarding the "perfect translator" (including one that the translator "should be of the same sex as his author"),[4] and of delivering highly subjective statements as if they were undisputed facts (for instance: "the Russian sense of blueness belongs to a different series than the Russian 'remember' does").[5] His comments are couched in

---

[1] Boyd and Shvabrin, ed., *Verses and Versions*, xxiv.
[2] Ibid., 274.
[3] Ibid., xxvi.
[4] Ibid., 15.
[5] Ibid., 10.

an oppressive rhetoric reminiscent of that of the fire-and-brimstone preacher or the hanging judge, bristling with words like "ignorance," "sin," "evil," "frailty," "hell," "turpitude," and "crime."

Nabokov's translations, however, speak far more eloquently and humbly than his diatribes. They bear witness not only to his phenomenal talent but also to the difficulty of the tasks he set himself in trying to render the most melodious of Russian lyrics into English. In the earlier translations, there are concessions to what Nabokov called the "into" language[6] that must have cost him dearly—such as the word "frail" included in his translation of Lermontov's "The Sail" for the sake of the rhyme. In some cases, there are various versions of a single poem which chart Nabokov's growing disillusionment with free, rhyming translation. Eventually, around 1950, literal translation takes over entirely. Nabokov described his "stratagem" in his famous poem on translating *Onegin*, also included in *Verses and Versions*:

> I traveled down your secret stem;
> and reached the root, and fed upon it;
> Then, in a language newly learned
> I grew another stalk and turned
> Your stanza patterned on a sonnet
> Into my honest roadside prose
> All thorn, but cousin to your rose.[7]

The more prosaic thorns in the collection, like Pushkin's "Demon," produced in this later period, function as elegant cribs to be read side by side with the Russian (or the transliteration). But more interesting by far is the material relating to the period when Nabokov was still producing literary roses. In his translations of such poets as Karamzin and Zhukovskii, Nabokov reveals a rare ability to capture an archaic poetic diction. The translations of Tyutchev, dating from the 1940s, are particularly beautiful. Nabokov's version of "Nightfall" retains the melodic qualities and rhyme of the original without sacrificing imagery and sense. A delightful example of the way Nabokov recasts Russian into English is the line "A liquid shiver, swift and sweet" for "*I sladkii trepet, kak struia.*" In "Reconciliation," there are more conspicuous departures from the original, which are justified by the result.

---

[6] Ibid., 14.
[7] Ibid., 16.

> *A uzh davno zvuchnee I polnei*
> *Pernatykh pesn' po roshche razdalasia,*
> *I raduga kontsom dugi svoei*
> *V zelenye vershiny uperlasia!*

Nabokov's version:

> —while thrush and oriole make haste to mend
> their broken melodies throughout the grove
> upon the crests of which was propped the end
> of a virescent rainbow edged with mauve.[8]

The translation is lovely and largely faithful to the essence of the Russian original, but it reveals touches of Nabokov's style: the unusual, slightly prosaic "propped" and the rainbow embroidered (for the sake of scanning) with the rare and melodious "virescent." Although Nabokov declared that the translator must "possess the gift of mimicry and...impersonate (his author) with the utmost degree of verisimilitude,"[9] his own voice can, on occasion, be heard ringing through in his English versions (in Lermontov's "Angel" "*skuchnye pesni*" is rendered "dull little ditties"—a characteristically Nabokovian turn of phrase).

The best translations in the collection are of blank verse, which provide just the right scope for Nabokov to show his virtuosity. On reading Khodasevich's wonderful "The Monkey," side by side with Nabokov's English version, the translator's extravagant claims for its author do not seem far-fetched. Best of all, though, are the translations of Pushkin's *Little Tragedies*. Just about any line of these can be selected at random to illustrate how Nabokov finds inventive ways of retaining the rhythm and the melodic qualities of the Russian. In "The Covetous Knight," for instance, "*bleshchushchie grudy*"—"glittering heaps" (the coffers filled with gold) is rendered as "brimming glory"; and "*tiazhelykh dum*" ("heavy thoughts") as "inner gloom." "Mozart and Salieri" is the crowning glory of the book, as near perfect as a translation can be, and poignant, as Nabokov echoes in Salieri's words:

> I cut up music like a corpse; I tested
> The laws of harmony by mathematics.
> Then only, rich in learning, dared I yield
> To blandishments of sweet creative fancy;

---

[8] Ibid., 241.
[9] Ibid., 9.

and in Mozart's exclamation: "If all could feel like you the force of harmony!"[10]

This wonderful book will bring us closer to feeling, as Nabokov did, the force of harmony in some of the best poetry ever written in Russian.

Rose France,
University of Edinburgh

[10] Ibid., 173.

Vladimir Nabokov, *Tragediia gospodina Morna: P'esy, lektsii o drame*, introduced and edited by Andrei Babikov, Azbuka-klassika, St. Petersburg, 2008; ISBN 978-5-91181-768-8, 638 pp. Introduction. Commentaries. Illustrations. Hardcover. No price available.

Over time, most of the characters populating Nabokov's novels have managed to enter Russia one way or another; at first quietly tucked away in the brittle pages of *samizdat* editions, and later, in the post-perestroika era, announcing their arrival with colourful editions or — in the case of some of the more Kinbotean characters — unashamedly slipping through the net of international copyright in cheaply produced pirated copies. Ironically, the one character of Nabokov's fiction whose sole *raison d'être* is returning to Russia had to wait longer than any of the others. After more than eighty years he has finally arrived. Enter Kuznetsov, the man from the USSR, the secret double agent of Nabokov's second play (written between *Mary* and *King, Queen, Knave*). With this new edition of Nabokov's dramatic work, which for the first time includes the complete original Russian version of *The Man from the USSR*, "the process of returning Nabokov's heritage to its homeland is now finally completed," as the publishers proudly announce.

Nabokov's brilliance as a novelist has long overshadowed his work as a dramatist, and the fragmented publishing history of his plays in Russian and in translation has hardly helped to promote his playwriting. Nabokov wrote a number of small one-act closet dramas and four major plays during his Russian period. His first play, *The Tragedy of Mr Morn* (*Tragediia Gospodina Morna*, written 1923-4), remained unpublished during his lifetime while, of his next drama, *The Man from the USSR* (*Chelovek iz SSSR*, written in 1926), only the first act was printed in the Russian émigré newspaper *Rul'*.[1] Two dramas written in the second half of the 1930s, *The Event* (*Sobytie*) and *The Waltz Invention* (*Izobretenie Val'sa*), were published in émigré journals, but the *Waltz Invention* was the only play published in English translation during the author's lifetime.[2] Posthumously, *The Man from the USSR* was published in English translation together with *Event* and *The Waltz Invention*, some one-act closet dramas, and the lectures on theatre which Nabokov gave at Stanford in 1941.[3] *The Tragedy of Mr Morn* is still awaiting its English translation. A first Russian edition of the plays included only the material available in Russian publications, hence neither *The Tragedy of Mr Morn* nor the complete text of *The Man from the USSR* were included.[4] A more recent German edition of Nabokov's dramas included all four of his plays and the minor dramas, but was directed towards a more general readership than previous iterations.[5]

This new edition of Nabokov's plays, introduced and edited by Andrei Babikov, combines not only the four major plays (including separate earlier outlines and preparatory sketches for *The Tragedy of Mr Morn*), but also all of Nabokov's early one-act plays: "The Wanderers" ("Skital'tsy"); "Death" ("Smert'"); "The Grand-Dad" ("Dedushka"); "The Pole" ("Polius"); "Ahasuerus" ("Agasfer"); a libretto Nabokov wrote together with Ivan Lukash; and "The Mermaid" ("Rusalka"), Nabokov's conclusion to Pushkin's unfinished verse drama. In addition, this volume provides Russian translations of Nabokov's

---

[1] Vladimir Nabokov, "Chelovek iz SSSR," *Rul'*, January 1, 1927, 2-3.
[2] Vladimir Nabokov, *The Waltz Invention*, trans. Dmitri Nabokov (New York: Phaedra, 1966).
[3] Vladimir Nabokov, *The Man from the USSR and Other Plays*, intro. and ed. Dmitri Nabokov (San Diego: Harcourt Brace Jovanovich, 1984).
[4] Vladimir Nabokov, *P'esy*, ed. Ivan Tolstoi (Moscow: Iskusstvo, 1990). *The Tragedy of Mr Morn* was subsequently published separately in the Russian journal *Zvezda* 4 (1994): 9-98.
[5] Vladimir Nabokov, *Gesammelte Werke: Dramen*, vol. XV/1, ed. Dieter Zimmer (Hamburg: Rowohlt, 2000).

lectures on theatre, and reprints Dmitri Nabokov's excellent introduction to his father's plays in Russian translation. Additional archival materials are hidden away at the back among the notes to the plays, including excerpts from Nabokov's lectures on Soviet drama, and his speech for his role as the murderer of Tolstoy's *Kreutzer Sonata* at a "literary trial" in 1920s Berlin.

The lucid and informative introduction should be read together with a sort of supplementary preface to the commentaries at the end of the book. Here Babikov draws together published sources and new archival material, outlining a wider and more complex background to Nabokov's playwriting than has been available to date. Babikov's exhaustive search of Nabokov's personal correspondence adds much color to his account. For example, Nabokov's predictable condemnation of fellow émigré Roman Gul"s play *Azef*, as a most talentless, extremely trite drama ["bezdarneishaia, poshleishaia p'esa"]; or Nabokov's amusing anecdote of how he came to play the role of Pozdnyshev in the "literary trial."[6] The wider discussions on the dramatic art which took place among Russian émigrés, and constitute essential contexts for Nabokov's ideas of theatre, are also particularly interesting. Babikov makes a convincing case for Vladimir Veidle and Iulii Aikhenval'd as clear influences on Nabokov's thinking in this regard.

The dramas in this volume have been edited with great care. Major discrepancies between the *Zvezda* edition of *The Tragedy of Mr Morn* and the original manuscripts and typescripts have been removed. For instance, where the *Zvezda* version had mediocrity and meanness ["posredstvennost' i *podlost'*"], the Azbuka edition has reinstated the correct reading based on the actual manuscript; an early example of Nabokov's penchant for the peculiar Russian concept of vulgarity and pretentiousness ["posredstvennost' i *poshlost'*"].[7] A few further examples illustrate Nabokov's dictum that sometimes "the difference between the comic side of things, and their cosmic side, depends upon one sibilant."[8]

'lucha i *tainy*'[9]
[rays and secrets]
'lucha i *teni*'[10]
[rays and shadows]

---

[6] Andrei Babikov, ed., *Tragediia gospodina Morna*, 10; 544.
[7] Ibid., 16; 152, emphasis added.
[8] Vladimir Nabokov, *Lectures on Russian Literature* (Orlando, Fl.: Harcourt Books, 1981), 57.
[9] Nabokov, "Tragediia," *Zvezda*, 18, emphasis added.
[10] Babikov, ed., *Tragediia*, 155, emphasis added.

'[…] stikh i s iazyka sletit / ognem i *lepestkom*'[11]
[and the verse flies from your tongue as fire and petal]
'[…] stikh i s iazyka sletit / ognem i *lepetom*'[12]
[and the verse flies from your tongue as fire and prattle]

'*Tristramovo staran'e* koldovskoe'[13]
[the magical endeavor of Tristram]
'*Tristanovo stradan'e* koldovskoe'[14]
[the magical suffering of Tristan]

The other dramas in this collection have been edited with the same level of precision. The first act of *The Man from the USSR* is reprinted and then followed by an accurate reproduction of the typescripts in the original Russian. The edition finds a productive compromise for *The Waltz Invention* that abides by the original publication, but includes detailed notes on further revisions which Nabokov made in 1939 and in the later English translation. All other dramas are faithfully reprinted according to the published versions authorized by Nabokov.

The commentaries to the plays are informative and useful in that they suggest lines of enquiry which invite the reader to dig deeper rather than impose specific readings of the dramas. Some interesting literary allusions and references are also uncovered, such as Nabokov's dialogue with Blok's 1912 poem "Miry letiat. Goda letiat. Pustaia…" in *The Tragedy of Mr Morn*, or the allusions to Merezhkovskii's play *Sil'vio* in *The Waltz Invention*. Some comparatist pitfalls, however, are obvious here. For example, stage directions in the first scene of *The Waltz Invention* that describe the view of a mountain through a window, are strangely associated with the beginning of Bernard Shaw's *Heartbreak House* where the "hilly [not mountainous] country in the middle of the north edge of Sussex […] is seen through the windows of a room." Does this mean that there is also a connection to, say, Shaw's *Arms and Men*, which also has the view of a mountain through a window? To paraphrase Nabokov, sometimes a leaf is just hopelessly green. That said, on the whole, the commentaries are helpful and in some cases essential.

This volume is so strikingly elegant that its aesthetic aspects should not go unmentioned. The cover shows a detail from Somov's painting "Harlequin

---

[11] Nabokov, "Tragediia," *Zvezda*, 18, emphasis added.
[12] Babikov, ed., *Tragediia*, 155, emphasis added.
[13] Nabokov, "Tragediia," *Zvezda*, 69, emphasis added.
[14] Babikov, ed., *Tragediia*, 244, emphasis added.

Siggy Frank

and Death," alluding to Nabokov's indebtedness to the theatricality of Russia's Silver Age, while the fly paper is a color reproduction of the Russian artist Iurii Annenkov's sketches for Nabokov's play *The Waltz Invention* (the production never materialized). Further reproductions of images interspersed throughout the text provide interesting illustrations of the staging of Nabokov's plays—beyond the well known photograph of Nabokov amid the cast of the Gruppa troupe in Berlin—such as a photograph of the staging of *The Event* in the popular Russian émigré magazine *Illiustrirovannaia Rossiia*. A flyer and the program for the production of *The Event* by a Russian theatre troupe in New York serve as a reminder that Nabokov's plays were actually staged rather than merely read. The illustrations are another indication that Babikov has literally left no (archival) leaf unturned to reveal new sides of Nabokov, the dramatist.

In the best Russian tradition of carefully compiled critical editions, Babikov has restored a part of Nabokov's work which could have easily gone astray somewhere along the way to his homeland. Through what can only be termed a "labor of love," Babikov has performed a crucial service to Russian-speaking Nabokov scholars and readers, and not least to Nabokov's legacy, by opening the way for a thorough analysis and examination of the writer's dramatic oeuvre. This beautifully produced and intelligently edited volume can rightfully claim to have returned to Russia the last piece of Nabokov's baggage long lost in transit and translation.

Siggy Frank,
University of Nottingham

Pekka Tammi, *Russian Subtexts in Nabokov's Fiction: Four Essays*, Tampere University Press, Tampere, 1999; ISBN 951-44-4584-8, xiii+187 pp. Notes. References. No price available.

Nabokov's often playful use of subtexts, and critics' accounts of spotting them, is certainly not a new topic. In his four short essays, Tammi aims to bring these subtexts into clearer focus, and to lay the groundwork for their categorization. In doing so, we might be able to glean what function subtexts play in certain Nabokov works, and determine thematic patterns between his works and the broader sphere of Russian literature, stretching back to Pushkin.

Tammi's approach is patiently methodical and begins at the beginning, as it were, with a short analysis of the first known works to identify and examine literary subtexts, namely Kiril Taranovsky's critical essays on the poetry of Osip Mandel'shtam. Taranovsky's definition of subtext, quoted by Tammi, is "an already existing text (or texts) reflected in a new one."[1] While Taranovsky acknowledged a "surface" plot in Mandel'shtam's poetry that was intelligible to all readers, he noted that there was also a subtext that imbued every semantic element of the piece with additional or enhanced meaning—whether this subtext was present in Mandel'shtam's canon, or in the broader sphere of literature. Looking outside the closed system of a work, therefore, allows greater overall comprehension of its meaning. Of course, many readers do this intuitively, establishing connections and motifs almost unconsciously. Systemizing this process, combining these strands into effective interpretation, is Tammi's challenge.

Tammi admits that there is a leap from examining subtexts in poetry to those in prose—that is, we cannot expect every word of a prose piece to be imbued with subtextual meaning—but does not see this as a problem with a writer as allusively rich as Nabokov. A greater problem, Tammi acknowledges from the start, is the open-endedness of determining subtexts, which can bloom outwards into "unpredictably large intertextual systems."[2]

In Tammi's first example of subtext in Nabokov—comparing a passage from *Lolita* with Turgenev's *Dvorianskoe gnezdo*—he identifies a parallel between a scene from each text, then picks out allusions in preceding and following passages of both texts. He adds that we might then explore these Turgenevian "echoes" elsewhere in Nabokov's works, or view them in light of Nabokov's personal opinion of Turgenev. "Or we might extend the discussion to the narrative functions played by Russian subtexts in Nabokov's English fiction on the whole," Tammi continues. "But at some point we must stop...and start looking for some thematic justification behind the intertextual play."[3]

This is also an issue in Tammi's analysis of Dostoevskian subtexts in *Invitation to a Beheading*, the first time it has been linked to the author towards whom Nabokov harbored a notorious distaste. Many excellent parallels are made: the condemned man of Nabokov's work echoes a similar motif in *Idiot*, and Dostoevsky's own experience of imminent execution; Dostoevsky's oft-invoked theme of crime and punishment and the similarity of the names of Nabokov's antagonists to Raskol'nikov; the motif of the double; spider imagery; and a clever pun of the word "axe" (*topor*) in both English and Russian. But when the allusions stretch to *Alice in Wonderland*, Tammi

---

[1] Tammi, *Subtexts*, 9. See also Kirill Taranovsky, *Essays on Mandelstam* (Cambridge, MA: Harvard University Press, 1976).
[2] Ibid., 12.
[3] Ibid., 15.

acknowledges that the comparison moves toward "a form of insanity," quoting the Nabokov text.[4]

So what is the purpose of this subtextual "game," as Tammi dubs it? Partly, in the latter analysis, it is Nabokov's playful parody of Dostoevskian style, theme and mood, he explains. In addition, Tammi shows how *Invitation to a Beheading* is a study in religious transcendence, suffering of the soul, and the quest for spiritual rebirth; themes which tie in heavily to the world of Dostoevsky, "the quintessential avatar of mysticism in Russian literature."[5] Yet this subtext of Dostoevsky's beliefs is not anchored in mysticism but in the imagination; the creation of art in Nabokov's works — the protagonist Cincinnatus writes a prison diary — brings man closer to the "other world," says Tammi. This refers to the inevitability that the novel will end: seeking to make one last entry in his prison diary, Cincinnatus finds "It has all been written already" — that is, the meaning of his life, the novel itself, is coming to a close and he is off to his execution, to the "other world." Tammi equates Cincinnatus's realization with the closing line of *Dvoinik*,[6] "Alas! He had already known for a long time this would happen" ["*Uvy! On eto davno uzhe predchuvstvoval*"]. This also ties in with fatalism, another common feature of Dostoevsky's works, and rounds out Tammi's Dostoevskian subtext.

In closing his first essay, Tammi writes "An activated subtext is always used by the author for specific thematic ends, and this necessarily affects our interpretation of the primary text." He emphasizes that, in unearthing subtexts, he does not wish to offer a new interpretation but to fill gaps or embolden the text so that it becomes richer, "something has nevertheless been added that was not previously there."[7] This first essay contains the only in-depth analysis of a specific Nabokov text; the remaining three offer further avenues of exploration, possibilities for Tammi's categorizations of Nabokovian subtexts, and examples of their use.

The second chapter examines the typology of subtexts in polygenetic allusions. This expands subtextual interpretation into "three dimensions," in that the roots and branches of Nabokov's "cultural synthesis" are sought. So, allusions come to light in, for example, characters' names, authors' names, and the titles of works; quotations can be compounded from different authors. Previously unlinked writers, works, themes, and passages of text are combined

---

[4] Ibid., 23.
[5] Ibid., 30.
[6] The work by Dostoevsky that Nabokov most respected (rather hollow praise, admittedly).
[7] Ibid., 33.

Jan F. Zeschky

and given new meaning in a Nabokovian subtext—a meaning, of course, that is particular and personal to Nabokov:

> For here a motif originating in the author's own life conjoins a network of subtextual, cross-linguistic, and transcultural echoes... it is no longer possible to trace such compounds of links to a single biographical or textual source, for they are transmitted through the mind of a poet "to whom life and library were one."[8]

Tammi would have us searching for subtexts within subtexts, as well as comparing and contrasting those subtexts that are independently but simultaneously present. Often this bears rich fruit, as in highlighting Nabokov's scathing criticism of Tolstoy's and Dostoevsky's derivativeness by tracing their style and poetic images back to their source, using parody and barbed comment: of *Anna Karenina* in relation to Flaubert's *Madame Bovary*, and Dostoevsky generally in relation to Gogol'. As for *Look at the Harlequins!*, Nabokov's last work, Tammi deems the narrative constructed "from multiple allusions to his own texts," and from his own life.[9] But, in expanding a typology of subtexts into "three dimensions," we also illuminate its core problem: again, when or where do we stop searching for allusions? At what point is the technique stretched so far that it becomes essentially meaningless?

Thankfully, Tammi regains some focus in the third chapter, which concentrates on Nabokov's native city of St. Petersburg as a text and as a mechanism for generating texts and subtexts. Tammi shows how the city looms large in Nabokov's literary imagination, although he is, of course, far from the first writer to exude such an attribute: Pushkin, Gogol', Dostoevsky, Belyi, Blok, Mandel'shtam and Akhmatova are given as other, "basic" examples. The list could go on, but one can argue that the influence of the city refracted through the minds of these particular writers was crucial to Nabokov's own view. Tammi puts Nabokov in their league in an attempt to determine the "textual manifestations of St. Petersburg in Nabokovian writing."[10] He starts by unearthing Nabokov's genuine nostalgia for the city from which he was exiled and then shows how this is manifest in his work: for example, the literary focus on that part of the city around Bol'shaia Morskaia and Nevskii Prospekt, where the family home was located; the fact that Nabokov's Petersburg passages are exclusively set in winter, when he was most often there; and the natural antipathy and linguistic superiority that Peterburzhets feel toward Muscovites.

[8] Ibid., 64.
[9] Ibid., 60.
[10] Ibid., 67.

Tammi asserts that Nabokov most often represents St. Petersburg in an "embedded second-level narrative reality."[11] Similar to those works of the great writers and poets before him, the city becomes the object of reminiscences, dreams, hallucinations, and stories within stories; that is, characters themselves produce new texts about the city. This mode is weaved into the principal text, creating a blend of realities. Tammi traces the source of this method to Nabokov's thwarted dreams of returning to his native city. He points out that characters' physically travel to St. Petersburg only twice in the writer's later works; and even then, it remains foreign to them due to the inevitable changes that have occurred in their absence. This reveals the sad pain of émigré life: "You can dream about it, or dwell on it in your personal memories, or invent fictions about it. But you can never go back—to the past, or to the twice (now thrice) renamed city."[12] Tammi tempers this sadness in an endnote explaining how Nabokov has since returned to Russia in the form of his literary legacy.

The final chapter is a pioneering study on Nabokov's use of fatidic dates, a topic of great fascination for the writer who, in his commentary to *Eugene Onegin*, dwelled on Pushkin's attempts to discern the date of his death. Like the subtexts explored previously, Tammi finds that dates have a thematic and aesthetic function in Nabokov's works, and act metonymically: their seemingly casual use can represent a greater, more significant subtextual background; a simple reference may require further research to fully flesh out its meaning. Here Tammi shows how Nabokov uses dates and their corresponding numerals across his work, across the works of Russian literature, and in the creation of an almost mythical persona of himself—that is to say, facts and dates from his own life assume a "textual status" in his writings, which then shape a different persona of the author in his texts—ultimately, another subtext.[13] This chapter is presented more as reference than a fully fleshed-out essay. Still, Tammi raises some interesting comparisons, including the implications of the difference of twelve or thirteen days between old and new calendars, and how corresponding gaps of time appear as a motif in Nabokov's works. Nabokov's games with dates and numbers also imbue particular texts with a certain sense of fatalism—for example, dates of births, deaths, anniversaries, and notable events often reappear in more banal details such as addresses and phone numbers. This lends a certain binding, cohesive effect.

---

[11] Ibid., 81.
[12] Ibid., 85.
[13] Ibid., 105.

Jan F. Zeschky

Tammi writes clearly and unambiguously throughout this study and seems an objective, trustworthy and modest commentator. He criticizes Nabokov's "banal" earlier poetic verses about St. Petersburg while, admittedly, showing how Nabokov later alluded back to these selfsame verses, in another example of self-referential subtext. Additionally, Tammi makes absolutely no pretence that his study is authoritative or complete, and refers many times to its introductory nature. Much of it is new ground, or patches of old being fertilized in an effort to bring forth new fruit.

Some particularly interesting suggestions for further exploration are raised throughout, not least a comprehensive study of both St. Petersburg and fatidic dates in the Nabokovian imagination. On the latter topic, Tammi hopes to one day see a "full-scale typology of the functions allotted to dates in literature."[14] In the opening chapter, he also hints at how the analysis of one subtext in one work could be reversed, and interpretive light cast back onto the subject of the subtext: that is, Tammi's analysis of Dostoevskian subtexts in *Invitation to a Beheading* could perhaps reveal hitherto unseen aspects of Dostoevsky's canon.

The overriding concern with this study, which Tammi frequently notes, is where do we draw the line in forming allusions? Again, Tammi acknowledges that we can go too far and, by way of addition, says some of his observations on dates "verge on numerological magic."[15] In closing, referencing Umberto Eco, he warns against "unlimited and uncheckable intertextuality."[16] So, does the fact that we can go too far in extrapolation not diminish its interpretive value, apart from our own amusement?

After all, Nabokov's use of subtexts appears to have been, if anything, an intellectual game. His references are rarely illuminated but, rather, left embedded in the text as a "compliment" to those who will understand them. He seemed to delight in catching out those readers "who do not possess the cultural competence presupposed by Nabokov's semiotic and subtextual strategies."[17] Certainly, pinning down the rules and boundaries of this game looks a difficult task, but Tammi lays down some brave and insightful groundwork in these first steps towards a hoped-for "field guide" to Nabokov's intertextuality.

Jan F. Zeschky,
Vancouver, BC

[14] Ibid., 146.
[15] Ibid., 94.
[16] Ibid., 112.
[17] Ibid., 2.

END LINE

BIBLIOGRAPHY

Abrams, M. H. "Introduction" to Alexander Pope, *The Poetry of Pope. A Selection.* Ed. M. H. Abrams. New York: Appleton-Century, 1954.

―――――."The Poem as Heterocosm." *The Mirror and the Lamp.* Oxford: Oxford University Press, 1971.

Agamben, Giorgio. *Homo Sacer: Sovereign Power and Bare Life.* Trans. Daniel Heller-Roazen. Stanford: Stanford University Press, 1995.

Alexandrov, Vladimir E. *Nabokov's Otherworld.* Princeton: Princeton University Press, 1991.

Alter, Robert. "*Invitation to a Beheading*: Nabokov and the Art of Politics." *Nabokov: Criticism, Reminiscences, Translations, and Tributes*, 41-59. Ed. Alfred Appel, Jr. & Charles Newman. Chicago: Northwestern University Press, 1970.

Andersen, Hans Christian. "The Wild Swans." *The Complete Fairy Tales and Stories.* Trans. Erik Christian Haugaard. Garden City, N.Y.: Anchor Press, 1983.

Andersen, Sam. "A Glorious Mess." *New York Magazine,* November 15, 2009, http://nymag.com/arts/books/reviews/62036/

Appel, Alfred. "*Ada*: An Erotic Masterpiece That Explores the Nature of Time." *The New York Times*, May 4, 1969.

Bacou, Roseline. *La donation Ari et Suzanne Redon.* Paris: Editions de la Reunion des musees nationaux, 1984.

Bakhtin, M. *Problems of Dostoevsky's Poetics.* Trans. and ed. C. Emerson. Minneapolis: University of Minneapolis Press, 1984.

Barabtarlo, Gennady. "See Under Sebastian." *The Nabokovian* 24 (Spring 1990): 24-29.

Baring, M. *The Puppet Show of Memory.* London: W. Heinemann, 1922.

Barth, John. "The Literature of Exhaustion." *The Atlantic Monthly* (August 1967): 29-34.

Barthes, Roland. "Myth Today." *Visual Culture: the Reader.* Ed. Jessica Evans and Stuart Hall. London: Sage Publications, 1999.

―――――. "Rhetoric of the Image." *Visual Culture: the Reader.* Ed. Jessica Evans and Stuart Hall. London: Sage Publications, 1999.

―――――. *Camera Lucida: Reflections on Photography.* Trans. Richard Howard. New York: Hill and Wang, 1981.

Bateson, F. W. and N. A. Joukovsky, ed. *Alexander Pope. A Critical Anthology.* Harmondsworth: Penguin Books, 1971.

Bayard, Pierre. *Le plagiat par anticipation*. Paris: Les Éditions de Minuit, 2009. Reviewed by David Coward in *Times Literary Supplement*, May 8, 2009.

Baym, Nina. "*The Marble Faun*: Hawthorne's Elegy for Art." *Nathaniel Hawthorne. Modern Critical Views*, 99-114. Ed. Harold Bloom. New York, Philadelphia: Chelsea House Publishers, 1986.

Beaumont, Cyril. *Vaslav Nijinsky*. London: C. W. Beaumont, 1932.

Bedford, Emmett G. and Robert J. Dilligan, ed. *A Concordance to the Poems of Alexander Pope*, 2 vols. Detroit: Gale Research Co, 1974.

Bell, Michael Davitt. *Culture, Genre, and Literary Vocation: Selected Essays on American Literature*. Chicago: University of Chicago Press, 2000.

Bely, Andrei. *Petersburg*. Trans. Robert A. Maguire and John E. Malmstad. Bloomington: Indiana University Press, 1978.

Bishop, Morris. *Petrarch and his World*. Bloomington: Indiana University Press, 1963.

Bourdieu, P. *The Rules of Art: Genesis and Structure of the Literary Field*. Stanford: Stanford University Press, 1997.

Boyd, Brian. "Handmaid to Genius." Review of Stacey Schiff's *Véra*. The Globe and Mail, Toronto, May 15, 1999, http://www.theglobeandmail.com/

_____. "Nabokov, Literature, Lepidoptera." *Nabokov's Butterflies*. Ed. Boyd, Brian and Robert Michael Pyle. Boston: Beacon Press, 2000.

_____. *Nabokov's Ada: The Place of Consciousness*. Christchurch N.Z.: Cybereditions, 2001.

_____. *Nabokov's Pale Fire: The Magic of Artistic Discovery*. Princeton: Princeton University Press, 1999.

_____. *Vladimir Nabokov: Amerikanskie gody: Biografiya* / Per. s angl. M.: Izdatel'stvo Nezavisimaya Gazeta. St. Petersburg: Symposium, 2004.

_____. *Vladimir Nabokov: The American Years*. Princeton: Princeton University Press, 1991.

_____. *Vladimir Nabokov: The Russian Years*. Princeton: Princeton University Press, 1990.

_____. and Stanislav Shvabrin, ed. *Verses and Versions: Three Centuries of Russian Poetry, selected and translated by Vladimir Nabokov*. New York: Harcourt, 2008.

Brower, Reuben A. *Alexander Pope. The Poetry of Allusion*. Oxford: Oxford University Press, 1986.

Bulfinch, Thomas. *Myths of Greece and Rome*. New York: Penguin Books, 1981.

Carey, John and Alastair Fowler, ed. *The Poems of John Milton*. London: Longmans, 1968.

Carroll, Lewis. Alice's adventures in Wonderland: and, Through the looking-glass and what Alice found there. London: Penguin Classics, 2003.

Chase, Richard. *The American Novel and its Tradition*. Baltimore: The John Hopkins University Press, 1993.

Clark, T. J. *The Sight of Death: An Experiment in Art Writing*. New Haven / London: Yale University Press, 2006.

Clarke Graham. "To Transform and Transfigure: The Aesthetic Play of Hawthorne's *The Marble Faun*." *Nathaniel Hawthorne: New Critical Essays*. Ed. Robert Lee. Totowa, N.J: Barnes and Noble, 1982.

Clegg Christine. *Vladimir Nabokov: Lolita. A Reader's Guide to Essential Criticism*. Duxford, Cambridge: Icon Books, 2000.

Coleridge, S. T. *Biographia Literaria*. London: J. M. Dent & Sons, 1962.

Connolly, Julian W. "Dostoevski and Vladimir Nabokov: The Case of *Despair*." *Dostoevski and the Human Condition after a Century*, 155-62. Ed. Alexej Ugrinsky et al. New York: Greenwood Press, 1986.

─────. "Madness and Doubling: From Dostoevsky's *The Double* to Nabokov's *The Eye*." *Russian Literature Triquarterly* 24 (1991): 129-39.

─────. "Nabokov's Dialogue with Dostoevsky: *Lolita* and 'The Gentle Creature.'" *Nabokov Studies* 4 (1997): 15-36.

─────. *Nabokov's Early Fiction: Patterns of Self and Other*. Cambridge: Cambridge University Press, 1992.

─────. "Nabokov's (re)visions of Dostoevsky." *Nabokov and his Fiction: New Perspectives*, 141-57. Ed. Julian W. Connolly. Cambridge: Cambridge University Press, 1999.

─────., ed. *The Cambridge Companion to Nabokov*. Cambridge: Cambridge University Press, 2005.

Cornwell, Neil. "Secrets, Memories and Lives: Nabokov and Pamuk." *Transitional Nabokov*, 115-33. Ed. Will Norman and Duncan White. Oxford: Peter Lang, 2009.

─────. "Paintings, Governesses and 'Publishing Scoundrels': Nabokov and Henry James," *Nabokov's World. Vol. 2: Reading Nabokov*. Ed. Jane Grayson, Arnold McMillin and Priscilla Meyer. Houndmills, Basingstoke: Palgrave, 2002.

─────. *Vladimir Nabokov*. Plymouth: Northcote House, 1999.

Coustet, Robert. *L'Univers d'Odilon Redon*. Paris: Henri Screpel, 1984.

Couturier, Maurice. "The near-tyranny of the author: Pale Fire." *Nabokov and his Fiction: New Perspectives*, 54-72. Ed. Julian W. Connolly. Cambridge, England: Cambridge University Press, 1999.

Crossman, R. H. S. *Plato Today*. London: George Allen & Unwin, Ltd., 1937.

─────. *Plato Today*. New York: Oxford University Press, 1939.

Daiches, David. "Eighteenth-Century Philosophical, Historical, and Critical Prose, and Miscellaneous Writing." *A Critical History of English Literature*. London: Secker & Warburg, 1960.

Davidson, Dennis. *Dryden*. London: Evans Brothers, 1968.

Davies-Mitchell, Magaret C. "Rimbaud, Arthur." *Encyclopædia Britannica*. 2006. Encyclopædia Britannica Online. 10 May 2006, http://search.eb.com/eb/article-6202.

Davydov, Sergej. "Dostoevsky and Nabokov: The Morality of Structure in *Crime and Punishment* and *Despair*." *Dostoevsky Studies* 3 (1982): 157-70.

─────. "Poshlost." *The Garland Companion to Vladimir Nabokov*, 628-633. Ed. Vladimir E. Alexandrov. New York: Garland, 1995.

de Bellaigue, Christopher. "Portrait in black-and-white." *Times Literary Supplement*, March 21, 2008, 19.

de Man, Paul. "The Concept of Irony." *Aesthetic Ideology*, 163-184. Minneapolis: University of Minnesota Press, 1996.

———. "The Rhetoric of Temporality." Blindness and Insight, 187-228. Minneapolis: University of Minnesota Press, 1983.

DeMoss, John. "An Index to *Strong Opinions*." *Zembla*. Ed. Jeff Edmunds. 10 November 2006. http://www.libraries.psu.edu/nabokov/demossp1.htm.

Derrida, Jacques. "The Other of Democracy, the 'By Turns': Alternative and Alternation." *Rogues: Two Essays on Reason*, 28-41. Trans. Pascale-Anne Bault and Michael Naas. Stanford, CA: Stanford University Press, 2005.

———. "The Last of the Rogue States: The 'Democracy to Come,' Opening in Two Turns": Alternative and Alternation." *Rogues: Two Essays on Reason*, 78-94. Trans. Pascale-Anne Bault and Michael Naas. Stanford: Stanford University Press, 2005.

de Vries, Gerard. "'*Mountain*, not *fountain*,' *Pale Fire*'s Saving Grace." *The Nabokovian* (Fall 2009): 39-52.

———. "'Fanning the Poet's Fire,' Some Remarks on Nabokov's *Pale Fire*." *Russian Literature Triquarterly* 24 (1991): 255-6.

——— and D. Barton Johnson. *Nabokov and the Art of Painting*. Amsterdam: Amsterdam University Press, 2006.

Diment, Gayla. "Strong Opinions." *The Garland Companion to V. Nabokov*. Ed. V. Alexandrov. New York: Garland, 1995.

Dolinin, Alexander. *Istinnaia zhizn' pisatelia Sirina: Raboty o Nabokove* [The Real Life of the Writer Sirin: Works on Nabokov]. St. Petersburg: Akademicheskii proekt, 2004.

Dostoevskii, F. M. *Prestuplenie i nakazanie*. Moscow: Nauka, 1970.

Efimov, M. "Nabokov i Baratynski: Dialog s pamat'u i polemika s sovremennikami" [Nabokov and Baratynsky: Dialogue with the memory and contemporary polemics]. *Nabokov Online Journal* IV (2010).

Elley, Derek. *The Epic Film: Myth and History*. London: Routledge & Kegan Paul, 1984.

Farfan, Penny. "Man as Beast: Nijinsky's Faun." *South Central Review* 25.1 (Spring 2008): 74-92. http://muse.uq.edu.au/journals/south_central_review/v025/25.1farfan02.pdf (accessed August 6, 2009).

Field, Andrew. *Nabokov: His Life in Art*. Boston: Little Brown and Co., 1967.

Fite, Warner. *Platonic Legend*. New York: C. Scribner's Sons, 1934.

Foucault, Michel. *The History of Sexuality*. Trans. Robert Hurley. New York: Random House, Inc., 1990.

Freeman, Elizabeth. "Honeymoon with a Stranger: Pedophiliac Picaresques from Poe to Nabokov." *American Literature* 70.1 (December 1998): 109-154.

Freud, Sigmund. "Medusa's Head." *The Standard Edition of the Complete Psychological Works*, vol. 18. London: Hogarth Press, 1953.

Fuller, Janice M. "Hawthorne as Protomodernist: The Relationship of Flesh and Marble in *The Marble Faun*." *Postscript* 5 (1988): 25-35. http://www.unca.edu/postscript/postscript5/ps5.3.pdf (accessed August 6, 2009).

Gardels, Nathan. "Lunch with the FT: He has seen the future." *Financial Times*, August 18, 2006.

Gass, William. *On Being Blue: A Philosophical Inquiry*. Boston: David R. Godine, 1975.

Genette, Gerard. *Paratexts: Thresholds of Interpretation*. Trans. Jane E. Lewin. Cambridge: Cambridge University Press, 1997.

Godard, Jean Luc. *Week End* (Director, Script: Jean-Luc Godard; Music: Antoine Duhamel), France, 1967.

Gold, Herbert. "The Art of Fiction." Interview with Vladimir Nabokov. *Paris Review* 40.41 (Summer—Fall 1967): 1-19, http://www.theparisreview.org/viewinterview.php/prmMID/4310.

Green, Geoffrey. *Freud and Nabokov*. Lincoln: University of Nebraska Press, 1988.

Green, Hannah. "Mr. Nabokov." *Vladimir Nabokov: A Tribute*. Ed. Peter Quennell. London: Weidenfeld and Nicolson, 1979.

Guerney, Bernard Guilbert. *A Treasury of Russian Literature*. Philadelphia: Blakiston, 1945.

Gumbrecht, Hans Ulrich. *Production of Presence*. Stanford: Stanford University Press, 2004.

Hawthorne, Nathaniel. *The French and Italian Notebooks*. The Centenary Edition, vol. 14. Ed. Thomas Woodson. Columbus: Ohio State University Press, 1980.

———. *The House of the Seven Gables*. Boston, New York: Houghton, Mifflin, 1894.

———. *The Marble Faun*. Ed. Susan Manning. Oxford: Oxford University Press, 2002.

Hazlitt, William. *Lectures on the English Poets*. London: Oxford University Press, 1952.

———. *The English Comic Writers*. London: Oxford University Press, 1920.

Hellman, Eric. "The Scandal of Nijinsky's Faune." *Ballet Review* 22.2 (1994): 18.

Holmyard, E. J. *Alchemy*. Harmondsworth: Penguin Books, 1968.

Hughes, Merry Y., ed. John Milton, *Paradise Regained, The Minor Poems and Samson Agonistes*. New York: The Odyssey Press, 1937.

Huysmans, J. K. *Against the Grain*. New York: Dover Publications, Inc., 1969.

Iglehart, L. T., Jr. "Served By Vladimir Nabokov: A Rich, Slavic Pudding." *St. Louis Globe-Democrat*, June 1-2, 1963.

Ivanov, Georgii. "Konets Adamovicha" ["The End of Adamovich"]. *Vozrozhdenye* 11, 1950, *Sobranie sochinenii v 3 t.* vol. 3. Moscow: Soglasie, 1993.

Jaggi, Maya. "Between two worlds." *The Guardian*, Saturday, December 8, 2007, 11.

Johnson, D. Barton. "Spatial Modeling and Deixis: Nabokov's *Invitation to a Beheading*." *Poetics Today* 3.1 (Winter 1982): 81-96.

———. "The Alpha and Omega of *Invitation to a Beheading.*" *Worlds in Regression: Some Novels of Vladimir Nabokov*, 28-46. Ann Arbor: Ardis Publishers, 1985.

Johnson, Samuel. *Lives of the English Poets*, vol. 2. London: J. M. Dent & Sons, 1954.

Jung, Carl G. *Psychology and Alchemy. The Collected Works*, vol. 12. Trans. R. F. C. Hull. London: Routledge & Kegan Paul, 1953.

Kiely, Robert. "The Reader without a Country: Nathaniel Hawthorne's *The Marble Faun* after Nabokov." *Reverse Tradition: Postmodern Fictions and the Nineteenth Century Novel*, 152-175. Cambridge, Mass., London: Harvard University Press, 1993.

Knapp, Shoshana. "Nabokov and Mirsky." *The Nabokovian* 13 (1984): 35-36.

Kolpakova, N. P. *Lirika russkoj svad'by*. Leningrad: Nauka, 1973.

Kramer, Hilton. "The Strange Case of D. S. Mirsky." *The New Criterion* (January 2002). http://www.thefreelibrary.com/The+strange+case+of+D.+S.+Mirsky.-a082260382.

Kuzmanovich, Zoran and Galya Diment, ed. *Approaches to Teaching Nabokov's Lolita*. New York: The Modern Language Association of America, 2008.

Langen, Timothy. "The Ins and Outs of *Invitation to a Beheading.*" *Nabokov Studies* 8 (2004): 59-70.

Latimer, Bonnie. "Alchemies of Satire: A History of the Sylphs in *The Rape of the Lock.*" *The Review of English Studies* 57.232 (2006): 684-700.

Lerenbaum, Miriam. *Alexander Pope's 'Opus Magnum' 1729-1744*. Oxford: Clarendon Press, 1977.

Lessl, Thomas M. "The Galileo Legend as Scientific Folklore." *Quarterly Journal of Speech* 85 (1999): 146-168.

Levinas, Emmanuel. "Ethics and the Face." *Totality and Infinity: An Essay on Exteriority*, 194-219. Trans. Alphonso Lingis. Pittsburgh, PA: Duquesne University Press, 1969.

Leving, Yuri. V. Nabokov. Sobranie sochinenii russkogo perioda v 5 tt., vol. 2. St. Petersburg: Symposium, 1999.

——— and Evgeniy Soshkin, ed. *Imperia N: Nabokov and Heirs*. Moscow: New Literary Observer, 2006.

Lewis, R. W. B. "The Return into Time: *The Marble Faun.*" *Nathaniel Hawthorne. Modern Critical Views*, 25-31. Ed. Harold Bloom. New York, Philadelphia: Chelsea House Publishers, 1986.

Life Magazine. March 28, 1949, 127.

Lillymans, W. J. "The Blue Sky: A Recurrent Symbol." *Comparative Literature* 21 (1969): 118.

Lodge, David. *Small World*. London: Secker & Warburg, 1984.

Lonyay, Carl. *Rudolph: The Tragedy of Mayerling*. New York: Scribners, 1949.

Lucretius, Titus. *On the Nature of the Universe*. Trans. R. E. Latham. Harmondsworth: Penguin Books, 1976.

Lyons, John O. "*Pale Fire* and the Fine Art of Annotation." *Nabokov, The Man and His Work*. Ed. L. S. Dembo. Madison: The University of Wisconsin Press, 1967.

Lyuksemburg, A. M. V. V. Nabokov, *Sobranie sochinenii amerikanskogo perioda v 5 tomakh*, vol. 1. St. Petersburg: Symposium, 1997.

MacIntyre, C. F., trans. *Stéphane Mallarmé: Selected Poems*. Berkeley, Los Angeles: University of California Press, 1957.

Mack, Maynard. *Alexander Pope. A Life*. New Haven: Yale University Press, 1985.

_____, ed. Alexander Pope, *An Essay on Man*. London: Methuen and Co., 1950.

Malcolm, Donald. "A Retrospect." *New Yorker* XL, April 25, 1964, 198-204.

Mallarmé, Stéphane. *Oeuvres complètes. Poésies*. Ed. C. P. Barbier and C. G. Millan. Paris: Flammarion, 1983.

Mann, Thomas. *Joseph the Provider*. New York: Alfred A. Knopf, 1944.

Manning, Susan. "Explanatory Notes." Nathaniel Hawthorne. *The Marble Faun*. Ed. Susan Manning. Oxford: Oxford University Press, 2002.

Mathieu, Pierre-Louis. *Gustave Moreau, The Watercolors*. New York: Hudson Hills Press, 1985.

_____. *Gustave Moreau: With a Catalogue of the Finished Paintings, Watercolors and Drawings*. Boston: New York Graphic Society, 1976.

McCarthy, Mary. "A Bolt from the Blue." *New Republic* (June 1962), 21-27, reprinted in *The Writing on the Wall and Other Literary Essays*. London: Weidenfeld and Nicolson, 1970, and in Introduction to V. Nabokov, *Pale Fire*. Harmondsworth: Penguin, 1991.

McLean H. "Lectures on Russian Literature." *The Garland Companion to Vladimir Nabokov*, 258-274. Ed. Vladimir E. Alexandrov. New York: Garland, 1995.

McNeill Donahue, Agnes. *Hawthorne: Calvin's Ironic Step-child*. Kent Ohio: The Kent State University Press, 1985.

Merriam-Webster's Collegiate Dictionary Tenth Edition. Springfield, Mass.: Merriam-Webster, Inc., 1993.

Meyer, Priscilla. "Black and Violet Words: *Despair* and *The Real Life of Sebastian Knight* as Doubles." *Nabokov Studies* 4 (1997): 37-60.

_____. *Find What the Sailor Has Hidden: Vladimir Nabokov's Pale Fire*. Middleton, Connecticut: Wesleyan University Press, 1988.

Mirsky D. S. *A History of Russian Literature. From Its beginnings to 1900*. Ed. Francis J. Whitfield. New York: Vintage, 1958.

_____. *Modern Russian Literature*. London: Oxford University Press, 1925.

_____. "The Problem of Pushkin." (D. Mirskii, "Problema Pushkina" [*A. S. Pushkin: Issledovaniya i materialy*]. Moscow: Zhurnal'no-gazetnoe ob'edinenie, 1934: 91-112 (*Literaturnoe nasledstvo*, vol. 16-18).

_____. "Veyanie smerti v predrevoliutsionnoi russkoi literature." *Vyorsty* 2 (1927): 247-254.

_____, ed. *The Life of the Archpriest Avvakum by Himself*. Translated from the Seventeenth Century Russian by Jane Harrison and Hope Mirrlees, with a Preface by Prince D. S. Mirsky. London: Hogarth Press, 1924.

Moore, Edward C. "Ballet Russe Makes Matinee Call at Grand." New York: Manuscripts, Archives and Rare Books Division, New York Public Library.

Nabokov Online Journal, Vol. I (2007); Vol. II (2008); Vol. III (2009); Vol. IV (2010). www.nabokovonline.com

Nabokov, Vladimir. *Ada*. New York: Fawcett Crest, 1970.

——————. *Ada or Ardor: A Family Chronicle*. New York: Vintage International, 1990.

——————. "An Evening of Russian Poetry." *The New Yorker* 21.3, March 3, 1945.

——————. *Ania v strane chudes*. Sobranie sochinenii russkogo perioda v 5 tt. vol. 1. St. Petersburg: Symposium, 1999.

——————. *Bend Sinister*. New York: Vintage International, 1990.

——————. "Chelovek iz SSSR." *Rul'*, January 1, 1927, 2-3.

——————. "Commentary." Alexandr Pushkin, *Eugene Onegin. A Novel in Verse*, 4 vols. Trans. Vladimir Nabokov. Princeton: Princeton University Press, 1975.

——————. *Dear Bunny, Dear Volodya: The Nabokov-Wilson Letters, 1940-1971*, Revised and Expanded Edition. Ed. Simon Karlinsky. Berkeley: University of California Press, 2001.

——————. *Despair*. London: Penguin, 1981 [revised English edition first published 1965; original published as *Otchaianie* 1934].

——————. *Einladung zur Enthauptung*. Trans. and Commentary by Dieter E. Zimmer. Reinbeck be Hamburg: Rohwohlt, 1990.

——————. *Gesammelte Werke: Dramen*, vol. XV/1. Ed. Dieter Zimmer. Hamburg: Rowohlt, 2000.

——————. "Good Readers and Good Writers." *Lectures on Literature*, ed. Fredson Bowers. New York: Harcourt Brace & Company, 1980.

——————. *Invitation to a Beheading*. Trans. Dmitri Nabokov. New York: Vintage International, 1989.

——————. *Istinnaia zhizn' Sevast'yana Naita*. Per. s angl. G. Barabtarlo. St. Petersburg: Azbooka-klassika, 2009.

——————. "Iz perepiski s Edmundom Uilsonom." Per. s angl. S. Taska. Prim. B. Averina i M. Malikovoi. *Zvezda* 11 (1996): 112-132.

——————. *Laughter in the Dark*. Indianapolis: Bobbs-Merrill, 1938.

——————. *Lectures on Don Quixote*. Ed. Fredson Bowers. San Diego; New York; London: Harcourt Brace Jovanovich, 1983.

——————. *Lectures on Literature*. New York: Harcourt Brace Jovanovich/Bruccoli Clark, 1980.

——————. *Lectures on Russian Literature*. Ed. Fredson Bowers. New York: Harcourt Brace Jovanovich/Bruccoli Clark, 1981.

——————. *Lolita*. New York: Vintage, 1991.

——————. "On a Book Entitled *Lolita*." *Lolita*, 311-317. New York: Vintage Books, Random House, 1997.

——————. *Lolita: A Screenplay. Novels 1955-1962*. New York: Library of America, 1996.

———. *Look at the Harlequins!* New York: Vintage International, 1990.

———. *The Nabokov-Wilson Letters. Correspondence between Vladimir Nabokov and Edmund Wilson 1940-1971.* Ed. and Annotated Simon Karlinsky. New York: Harper & Row, 1979.

———. *Nikolai Gogol.* Norfolk: New Directions, 1944.

———. *Pale Fire.* New York: Vintage International, 1989.

———. *P'esy.* Ed. Ivan Tolstoi. Moscow: Iskusstvo, 1990.

———. "Pis'ma V. V. Nabokova k G. P. Struve. Chast' vtoraia (1931-1935)." Publikatsiia E. B. Belodubrovskogo i A. A. Dolinina. Kommentarii A. A. Dolinina. *Zvezda* 4 (2004): 139-163.

———. *Pnin.* New York: Vintage International, 1989.

———. *Poems and Problems.* New York, Toronto: McGraw-Hill, 1970.

———. *Priglashenie na kazn'.* Ann Arbor: Ardis, 1979.

———. Review of Vladislav Khodasevich. *Collected Poems (Sobranie stikhov).* Paris: Vozrozhdenie, 1927. *Rul'* [*Rudder*], December 14, 1927. Reprinted in V. V. Nabokov, *Sobranie sochinenii russkogo perioda v 5 tomakh*, vol. 2, 649-652. St. Petersburg: Symposium, 1999.

———. *Selected Letters 1940-1977.* Ed. Dimitri Nabokov and Mathew J. Bruccoli. San Diego: Harcourt Brace Jovanovich/Bruccoli Clark, 1990.

———. *Speak, Memory: An Autobiography Revisited.* Harmondsworth: Penguin Books, 1987.

———. *Strong Opinions.* New York: McGraw-Hill, 1973.

———. *The Annotated 'Lolita.'* Ed., intro. and annotated Alfred Appel, Jr. New York: Vintage Books, 1991.

———. "The Art of Literature and Commonsense." *Lectures on Literature.* Ed. Fredson Bowers. New York: Harcourt Brace & Company, 1980.

———. *The Defense.* New York: Vintage International, 1990.

———. *The Gift.* New York: Vintage International, 1991.

———. *The Man from the USSR and Other Plays.* Ed. and intro. Dmitri Nabokov. San Diego: Harcourt Brace Jovanovich, 1984.

———. *The Real Life of Sebastian Knight*, New Directions edition. Norfolk, CN.: James Laughlin, 1951.

———. *The Stories of Vladimir Nabokov.* New York: Knopf, 1995.

———. *The Stories of Vladimir Nabokov.* New York: Vintage International, 1997.

———. *The Tragedy of Mr. Morn. Zvezda* 4 (1994): 9-98.

———. *Tragediia gospodina Morna: P'esy, lektsii o drame.* Ed. and intro. Andrei Babikov. St. Petersburg: Azbuka-klassika, 2008.

———. *The Waltz Invention.* Trans. Dmitri Nabokov. New York: Phaedra, 1966.

Nafisi, Azar. *Reading Lolita in Tehran: A Memoir in Books.* New York: Random House, 2003.

Naiman, Eric. "What if Nabokov had written 'Dvoinik'? Reading Literature Preposterously." *Russian Review* 64.4 (October 2005): 575-89.

Nazaroff, Alexander. Internal review of *The Gift* for Bobbs-Merrill, typescript. Washington, D.C.: Vladimir Nabokov Collection, Manuscript Division, Library of Congress.

──────. *The Land of the Russian People*. Philadelphia: J. B. Lippincott, 1944.

──────. *Tolstoy the Inconstant Genius*. New York: Fredrick A. Strokes, 1929.

Nijinska, Bronislava. *Bronislava Nijinska: Early Memoirs*. Ed. and trans. Irina Nijinska and Jean Rawlinson. New York: Holt, Rinehart and Winston, 1981.

Nivat, Georges. "Nabokov and Dostoevsky." *The Garland Companion to Vladimir Nabokov*, 398-402. Ed. Vladimir E. Alexandrov. New York and London: Garland, 1995.

Norfleet, Barbara. *Wedding*. New York: Simon and Schuster, 1979.

Nuttall, A. D. *Pope's "Essay on Man."* London: Allen and Unwin, 1984.

Oakes, Philip. [An Interview with V. Nabokov]. *The Sunday Times*, London, June 22, 1969. Reprinted in *Strong Opinions*, 135-140. New York: McGraw-Hill, 1973.

O'Connor, Katherine Tiernan. "Rereading *Lolita*, Reconsidering Nabokov's Relationship with Dostoevsky." *Slavic and East European Journal* 33.1 (1989): 64-77.

Orlow, Damon. *Red Wedding*. Chicago: Henry Regnery Co., 1952.

Pamuk, Orhan. *The Black Book*. Trans. Maureen Freely. London: Faber, 2006.

──────. *The White Castle*. Trans. Victoria Holbrook. London: Faber, 2001.

──────. "The Collector." Trans. Maureen Freely. *The Guardian Review*, October 18, 2008, 19.

──────. *Istanbul: Memories of a City*. Trans. Maureen Freely. London: Faber, 2006.

──────. *The New Life*. Trans. Güneli Gün. London: Faber, 1998.

──────. *Other Colours: Essays and a Story*. Trans. Maureen Freely. London: Faber, 2007.

──────. *Snow*. Trans. Maureen Freely. London: Faber, 2005.

──────. *The Museum of Innocence: A Novel*. Trans. Maureen Freely. London: Faber, 2010.

Parker, Stephen Jan. "Nabokov's Montreux Books: Part II." Nabokov: Autobiography, Biography and Fiction. *Cycnos* 10.1 (1993). http://revel.unice.fr/cycnos/index.html?id=1307

──────. *Understanding Nabokov*. Columbia: The University of South Carolina Press, 1987.

Pasco, Allan H. The Color-keys to *"A la recherche du temps perdu."* Geneva: Librairie Droz, 1976.

Pera, Pia. *Lo's Diary*. Northwood, Middlesex: Foxrock Books, 1999.

Peterson, Dale. "Knight's Move: Nabokov, Shklovsky and the Afterlife of Sirin." *Nabokov Studies* 11 (2007-08): 25-37.

──────. "Literature as Execution." *Nabokov: Modern Critical Views*. Ed. Harold Bloom. New York: Chelsea House, 1987.

──────. "Nabokov's Invitation: Literature as Execution." *PMLA* 96.5 (October 1981): 824-836.

———. "White [K]nights: Dostoevskian Dreamers in Nabokov's Early Stories." *Nabokov's World. Vol. 2: Reading Nabokov*, 59-72. Ed. Jane Grayson, Arnold McMillin and Priscilla Meyer. Houndmills, Basingstoke: Palgrave, 2002.

Phillips, Angus. "How Books Are Positioned in the Market: Reading the Cover." *Judging a Book by Its Cover: Fans, Publishers, Designers, and the Marketing of Fiction*, 19-30. Eds. Nicole Matthew and Nickianne Moody. Burlington: Ashgate Publishing, 2007.

Plato. *Apology. The Trials of Socrates*. Ed. and trans. C. D. C. Reeve. Indianapolis: Hackett Publishing, 2002.

———. *Crito. The Last Days of Socrates*. Trans. Hugh Tredennick. New York: Penguin, 1993.

———. *Phaedo*. Trans. G. M. A. Grube. Indianapolis: Hackett Publishing, 1977.

———. *Republic*. Trans. G. M. A. Grube. Indianapolis: Hackett Publishing, 1992.

———. *Timaeus. Plato: The Collected Dialogues*, 1151-1211. Trans. Benjamin Jowett. Ed. Edith Hamilton and Huntington Cairns. Princeton: Princeton University Press, 1961.

Plus, Raoul. *Saint Jean-Baptiste dans l'art*. Paris: Editions Alsatia, 1937.

Pope, Alexander. *Alexander Pope. A Critical Anthology*. Ed. F. W. Bateson and N. A. Joukovsky. Harmondsworth: Penguin Books, 1971.

———. *Essay on Man. A Concordance to the Poems of Alexander Pope*, 2 vols. Ed. Emmett G. Bedford and Robert J. Dilligan. Detroit: Gale Research Co, 1974.

———. *The Poems of Alexander Pope*. Ed. John Butt. New Haven: Yale University Press, 1963.

Popper, Karl. *Open Society and Its Enemies*. London: Routledge, 1945.

Porte, Joel. *The Romance in America*. Middletown, Conn.: Wesleyan University Press, 1969.

Probyn, Clive T. "Pope's Bestiary: The Iconography of Defiance." *The Art of Alexander Pope*. Ed. Howard Erskine-Hill and Anne Smith. London: Vision Press, 1979.

Proffer, C. R. *Keys to Lolita*. Bloomington: Indiana University Press, 1968.

Pushkin, Alexandr. *Evgenii Onegin: A Novel in Verse*. Trans. with commentary Vladimir Nabokov, 4 vols. New York: Bollingen, 1964.

———. *Eugene Onegin: A Novel in Verse*. Trans. and commentary Vladimir Nabokov. Princeton: Princeton University Press, 1975.

———. *Eugene Onegin*. Trans. Stanley Mitchell. London: Penguin Classics, 2008.

Pym, Barbara. *Some Tame Gazelle*. London: Pan Books, 1993.

Quennell, Peter. *Alexander Pope*. London: Weidenfeld and Nicolson, 1968.

———. *Hogarth's Progress*. London: Collins, 1955.

Rancour-Laferriere, Daniel. "All the World's a *Vertep*: The Personification/Depersonification Complex in Gogol's *Sorochinskaja jarmarka*." *Harvard Ukrainian Studies* VI.3 (September 1982): 339-71.

———. "Pushkin's Still Unravished Bride: A Psychoanalysis of Tat'jana's Dream." *Russian Literature and Psychoanalysis*. Ed. Daniel Rancour-Laferriere. Amsterdam and Philadelphia: J. Benjamins Publishing Co., 1989.

Reading, Amy. "Vulgarity's Ironist: New Criticism, Midcult, and Nabokov's *Pale Fire.*" *Arizona Quarterly* 62.2 (2006): 77-98.

Redon, Odilon. *To Myself: Notes on Life, Art and Artists.* Trans. Jeanne L. Wasserman. New York: George Braziller, 1996.

Richter, Anne. *Shakespeare and the Idea of the Play.* London: Chatto and Windus, 1962.

Robbe-Grillet, Alain. *Contemporains,* vol. 21. Paris: Editions du Seuil, 1997.

Rogers, Pat. "Faery Lore and The Rape of the Lock." *The Review of English Studies,* New Series 25.97 (1974): 29.

Rosenfeld, Hellmut. *Der mittelalterliche Totentanz: Entstehung-Entwicklung-Bedeutung.* Cologne: Bohlau Verlag, 1968.

Rowe, W. W. "A Note on Nabokov's Erotic Necks." *Russian Literature Triquarterly* 16 (1979): 50-57.

Saintsbury, George. *A Short History of English Literature.* Ed. Bateson and Joukovsky. London: MacMillan and Co., 1908.

⸻. *The Peace of the Augustans.* Oxford: Oxford University Press, 1951.

Schuman, Samuel. "Nabokov and Shakespeare: The Russian Works." *The Garland Companion to Vladimir Nabokov.* Ed. Vladimir E. Alexandrov. New York: Garland, 1995.

Sewell, Elizabeth. *The Orphic Voice: Poetry and Natural History.* New Haven: Yale University Press, 1960.

Shakespeare, William. *Hamlet.* Ed. T. J. B. Spencer. New York: Penguin Books, 1996.

⸻. *King Lear. The Complete Works of William Shakespeare.* Oxford: Oxford University Press, 1955.

⸻. *The Tempest. Twelfth Night. The Complete Signet Classic Shakespeare.* New York: Harcourt Brace Jovanovich, 1972.

Shapiro, Gavriel. "The Salome Motif in Nabokov's *Invitation to a Beheading.*" *Delicate Markers: Subtexts in Vladimir Nabokov's Invitation to a Beheading.* New York: Peter Lang Publishing, 1998.

Shklovsky, Viktor. *The Knight's Move.* Trans. Richard Sheldon. Urbana-Champaign IL: The Dalkey Archive Press, 1995 (Orig. pub. 1923).

⸻. "The connection between devices of syuzhet construction and general stylistic devices." Normal and London: Dalkey Archive Press, 2005 (Orig. pub. 1919).

Shukshin, Vasilii. *Snowball Berry Red.* Ann Arbor, Mich.: Ardis, 1979.

Shute, Jenefer. "Nabokov and Freud: The Play of Power." PhD dissertation. Los Angeles: UCLA, 1983.

⸻. "Nabokov and Freud: The Play of Power." *Modern Fiction Studies* 30 (1984): 637-650.

Sitwell, Edith. *Alexander Pope.* Harmondsworth: Penguin Books, 1948.

Sklyarenko, Alexey. "'Grattez le Tartare...' or Who Were the Parents of *Ada*'s Kim Beauharnais?" *The Nabokovian* 59 (2007): 40-9; 60 (2008): 8-17.

Smeets, Bert. "A Vladimir Nabokov Coverage." 8 Jan. 2009. http://axxc.nl/vn/vn.htm.

Smith G. S. Preface and Introduction. "D. S. Mirsky. Literary Critic and Historian." Mirsky, D. S. *Uncollected Writings on Russian Literature*. Ed. G. S. Smith. Modern Russian Literature and Culture: Studies and Texts, vol. 13. Berkeley: Berkeley Slavic Specialties, 1989.

──────. *D. S. Mirsky: A Russian-English Life, 1890-1939*. Oxford, New York: Oxford University Press, 2000.

Sokolov, Y. M. *Russian Folklore*. Hatboro, Pa.: Folklore Associates, 1966.

Specter, Michael. "The Nobel Syndrome." *The New Yorker*, October 8, 1998, 46-55.

Spenser, Edmund. *The Poetical Works of Edmund Spenser*. London: Oxford University Press, 1932.

Steiner, George. *Extraterritorial: Papers on Literature and the Language Revolution*. London: Faber and Faber, 1972.

Stekhov, A. V. "Strategiia literaturnogo obrazovaniya i taktika chteniia V. Nabokova v knige *Nikolai Gogol*" [The strategy of literary education and the tactics of reading of V. Nabokov in "Nikolai Gogol"]. *Pedagogika iskusstva* 3 (2009), http://art-education.ru/AE-magazine/archive/nomer-3-2009/stechov_06_09_2009.htm

Stephen, Leslie. *Alexander Pope*. New York: Harper, 1880.

Sweeney, Susan Elizabeth. "'Ballet Attitudes': Nabokov's *Lolita* and Petipa's *The Sleeping Beauty*." *Nabokov at the Limits: Redrawing Critical Boundaries*, 111-126. Ed. Lisa Zunshine. New York: Garland Publishing, 1999.

Swift, Jonathan. "Verses on the Death of Dr. Swift." *Selected Poems of Jonathan Swift*. Ed. James Reeves. London: Heinemann, 1967.

Tammi, Pekka. *Russian Subtexts in Nabokov's Fiction, Four Essays*. Tampere: Tampere University Press, 1999.

Taranovsky, Kirill. *Essays on Mandelstam*. Cambridge: Harvard University Press, 1976.

Taylor, Charles. "The Rhetorical Ecology of Science." *Defining Science: A Rhetoric of Demarcation*. Madison: University of Wisconsin Press, 1996.

Taylor, G. *Cultural Selection: Why Some Achievements Survive The Test Of Time And Others Don't*. New York: Basic Books, 1996.

Thulin, Oskar. *Johannes der Taufer im geistlichen Schauspiel des Mittelalters und der Reformationszeit*. Leipzig: Dietrich, 1930.

Tillotson, Geoffrey. *On the Poetry of Pope*. Oxford: Clarendon Press, 1950.

Toker, Leona. "*Invitation to a Beheading*: Nameless Existence, Intangible Substance." *Nabokov: The Mystery of Literary Structures*, 123-141. Ithaca: Cornell University Press, 1989.

──────. "Nabokov and the Hawthorne Tradition." *Scripta Hierosolymitana* 32 (1987): 323-49.

──────. *Nabokov: The Mystery of Literary Structures*. Ithaca: Cornell University Press, 1989.

Tolstoy, Leo. *War and Peace*. Norton Critical Edition, Second Edition. New York: W. W. Norton, 1996.

―――――. *What is Art?* Trans. Aylmer Maude. Indianapolis: Bobbs-Merrill, 1978.

Troyat, Henri. *Pushkin: A Biography*. New York: Pantheon, 1950.

Updike, John. "Books. Back in the U. S. S. R." *New Yorker*, April 15, 1985, 115.

Vickers, Graham. *Chasing Lolita: How Popular Culture Corrupted Nabokov's Little Girl All Over Again*. Chicago: Chicago Review Press, 2008.

Voronina, Olga. "The Tale of Enchanted Hunters: *Lolita* in a Victorian Context." *Nabokov Studies* 10 (2006): 147-174.

Weekes, A. R., ed. *Johnson: Life of Pope*. London: W. B. Clive, 1917.

Weil, Irwin. *Gorky: His Literary Development and Influence on Soviet Intellectual Life*. New York: Random House, 1966.

Wilson, A. N. "Shot at the altar." Review of *Dostoevsky: Language Faith and Fiction*, by Rowan Williams. *Times Literary Supplement*, October 10, 2008, 3-5.

Wilson, Edmund. "Comrade Prince." *Encounter* 5.1 (1955): 10-20.

―――――. "Edmund Wilson on Writers and Writing." *The New York Review of Books*, March 17, 1977). http://www.nybooks.com/articles/8577?email

Wood, Michael. *The Magician's Doubts: Nabokov and the Risks of Fiction*. Princeton, NJ: Princeton University Press, 1994.

―――――. "The Demons of our Pity." *The Magician's Doubts: Nabokov and the Risks of Fiction*, 173-205. Princeton: Princeton University Press, 1994.

Yevtushenko, Yevgeny. *Iagodnye mesta*. Moskva: Sovetskii pisatel', 1982; English translation, *Wild Berries*. New York: W. Morrow, 1984.

Yoder, R. A. *Emerson and the Orphic Poet in America*. Berkeley: University of California Press, 1978.

Young, David, trans. The Poetry of Petrarch. New York: Farrar, Straus and Giroux, 2004.

Zanganeh, Lila Azam. "Interview With Orhan Pamuk." Trans. Sara Sugihara and Lila Azam Zanganeh, from "Orhan Pamuk: Être un artiste libre." *Le Monde*, May 12, 2006. http://www.lazangeneh.com/inside/pamuk.html.

Zimmer, Dieter E. "Covering *Lolita*." 6 Nov. 2008. *The Dieter E. Zimmer Homepage*. 8 Jan. 2009. http://www.d-e-zimmer.de/Covering%20Lolita/LoCov.html.

―――――. Notes to the German edition of *Invitation to a Beheading*. Vladimir Nabokov. *Einladung zur Enthauptung*. Trans. and commentary Dieter E. Zimmer. Reinbeck be Hamburg: Rohwohlt, 1990.

Zunshine, Lisa. "Alexander Pope's *The Rape of the Lock* and Vladimir Nabokov's *Pale Fire*." *Nabokov at the Limits*. Ed. Lisa Zunshine. New York: Garland Publishing, 1999.

INDEX OF NAMES

Abrams, Meyer Howard	104, 123, 297
Adair, Evan	28
Adamovich, Georgii	221, 270, 271
Aeschylus	29
Agamben, Georgio	48-49, 51, 54-57, 59, 297
Alhambra, Maria	269
Aikhenval'd, Iulii	76, 288
Akhmatova, Anna	294
Akikusa, Shun'Ishiro	262, 263
Aldanov, Mark	10, 76, 79
Alexandrov, Vladimir E.	15, 61, 125, 194, 199, 225
Alighirei, Dante	214
Allen, Woody	257
Alter, Robert	4, 50
Amis, Martin	2
Anderson, Hans Christian	70, 71
Anderson, Sam	178
Annenkov, Iurii	290
Annensky, Innokenty	224
Appel, Alfred Jr.	50, 101, 154, 170, 215, 231, 263
Aristotle	119
Ascensius, Badius	XV
Aschenden, Liana	XIX
Assoun, P. L.	270
Averin, Boris	223
Babikov, Andrei	262, 287, 288, 290
Bacou, Roseline	33
Baez, Fernando	179
Bakhtin, Mikhail	271, 278
Bakst, Leon	216
Bakunin, Mikhail	254
Balboa, Vasco Núñez de	180
Ballaigue, Christopher de	20
Barabtarlo, Gennady	11, 12, 193, 194, 229

INDEX OF NAMES

Baratynsky, Yevgeny — 221
Barbier, C. P. — 210
Barbier, George — 216
Bardot, Brigitte — 184
Baring, Maurice — 228, 229
Barnstead, John — XIII, 152-157
Barth, John — 165
Barthelme, Donald — 165
Barthes, Roland — 6, 136-138, 144, 145, 149, 151, 159, 162, 163, 168, 169, 174
Baroll, Lewis — 34
Bashkin, Andrey — X
Bateson, Frederick (Noel) Wilse — 104, 106, 114
Baudelaire, Charles — 60
Bauer, Evgenii — 279
Bault, Pascale-Anne — 49
Bayard, Pierre — 26
Bayly, Thomas Haynes — 111
Baym, Nina — 203
Bazarov, Boris — 226
Beardsley, Aubrey — 216
Beaumont, Cyril W. — 211
Bedford, Emmett G. — 114
Bell, Michael Davitt — 205
Bellow, Saul — 245
Bely, Andrei — 40, 41, 224, 294
Benjamin, Walter — XVI
Berberova, Nina — 76
Berg, Henry W. — 78
Berg, Albert A. — 78
Berlin, Isaiah Sir — 218
Birney, Alice — XIII, 74-77, 79-81, 83-93, 95, 187
Bishop, Morris — 93, 214
Bitov, Andrei — 2-3, 184
Blackwell, Stephen — 271
Blandier, Jean-Bernard — 78
Blok, Alexander — 224, 282, 289, 294
Bloom, Harold — 70, 203
Bobrinsky, Countess — 281
Boethius — 72
Booth, Wayne — 245
Bouchet, Marie — XIV, 263
Bourdieu, Pierre — 79
Bowers, Fredson — 20, 22, 62, 64, 180, 227
Boyd, Brian — XIV, 2, 4-6, 10, 13, 21, 22, 100, 102, 112, 114, 119, 125-127, 131, 139, 161, 168, 179, 185, 264, 266, 270, 281

INDEX OF NAMES

Boyd, Bronwen	266
Braziller, George	28
Brenton, Andrew	29
Brower, Reuben A	107
Browning, Robert	106
Bruccoli, Matthew J.	21, 79, 176, 220
Bulfinch, Thomas	29
Bunin, Ivan	10, 76
Butler, Samuel	106
Butt, John	103, 105, 112
Byron, George Gordon	106
Capote, Truman	V
Carey, John	113
Carson, Johnny	XIII
Carr, Edward Hallett	254
Cartugno, Marianne	280
Cash, Conall	VII, XIV, 124-151
Catherine the Great	218
Celli, Maria	83
Cenci, Beatrice	212
Centerwall, Brandon S.	182, 183
Cervantes, Miguel de	179
Chambers, D. L.	257
Chaplin, Charlie	185, 275
Chase, Richard	204, 205
Chekalin, Dmitri	11
Chekhov, Anton	20, 229
Chernyshevsky, Nikolai	18, 65, 249, 253, 254
Christie, Agatha	XII, 264
Clark, Timothy James	124, 299
Clarke, Graham	207, 212
Clegg, Christine	209
CoConis, Ted	169
Coleridge, Samuel Taylor	107
Connolly, Julian W.	16, 25, 69, 125, 162, 279
Cornwell, Neil	XIV, 15, 25, 26
Cortez, Hernan	180
Cousete, Robert	33, 125
Couturier, Maurice	XI, 236, 263
Coward, David	26
Crone, Lisa	XVIII
Crook, Stephen	187
Crossman, Richard	63
Daleski, Hillel	XIX
Daiches, David	122

INDEX OF NAMES

David, Jacques-Louis	65
Davidson, Dennis	105
Davydov, Sergei	15, 225
Debussy, Claude	210
Derrida, Jacques	48, 49, 51, 52, 55-57, 59
DeMoss, John	161
Denkin, General	219
Dickens, Charles	20, 83, 241, 245
Dilligan, Robert	114
Diment, Galya	XVIII, 231, 277, 279
Dobychin, Leonid	7
Dolinin, Alexander	6, 9, 300
Donohue, Agnes McNeill	204
Dostoevsky, Fyodor	XVI, 15-27, 32, 61, 225, 227, 228, 271, 278, 279, 292-294, 296
Doyle, Arthur Conan	24
Dryden, John	102, 104
Duhamel, Antoine	164
Durrant, Geoffrey	240
Durantaye, Lealand de la	264, 268
Eco, Umberto	296
Edelstein, Marilyn	278
Edmunds, Jeff	XVI, 2, 4-7, 10, 12-14, 161
Efimov, Mikhail	XV, 221
Eliot, Thomas Stearns	26
Elley, Derek	30
Ergaz, Doussia	74
Erskine-Hill, Howard	108
Epicurus	115
Evans, Jessica	159, 162
Falen, James	249
Farfan, Penny	211, 212
Faulkner, William	XVIII
Fecht, Tom	75, 89
Fet, Afanasy	282
Fichte, Johanne	59
Field, Andrew	194, 208
Firbank, Ronald	216
Fisher, Murray	234, 237
Fite, Warner	63
Fitzgerald, F. Scott	257, 258
Flaubert, Gustav	16, 20, 294
Flynn, Errol	275
Foucault, Michel	54, 55
Fowler, Alastair	113

INDEX OF NAMES

France, Rose	281-285
Frank, Siggy	269
Freely, Maureen	16, 19, 27
Freeman, Elizabeth	201-202
Freud, Sigmund	31, 60, 62, 140, 187, 269, 270
Frye, Northrop	58
Fuller, Janice M.	207
Fusso, Susanne	XVII
Gardels, Nathan	231, 301
Gardner, Alexander	137, 138
Garrick, David	108n30
Garrick Mrs. (Veigel, Eva Marie)	108-109n30
Gass, William	33
Genette, Gerard	159
Gerwitz, Isaac	XV, 74, 75, 77, 79, 81, 83-94, 187
Girodias, Maurice	74
Gish, Lilian	274
Glauber, Robert M.	220-222, 228, 229
Godard, Jean Luc	164
Godine, David R	33
Gogol, Nikolai	XVII, 7, 20, 21, 24, 30, 60, 96, 97, 123, 225, 248, 279, 294
Gold, Herbert	179
Goldfarb, Yelizaveta	XV
Gorky, Maxim	XX, 8, 99, 219 227, 228
Grayson, Jane	XVII, 16, 25
Green, Geoffrey	61
Green, Hannah	20
Greene, Graham	263
Griffith, David	275
Grube, George Maximillian Anthony	62
Guerney, Bernard Guilbert	226
Gul, Roman	288
Gumbrecht, Hans Ulrich	13
Gün, Güneli	20
Gur'ev, Konstantin Vasil'evich	154
Hall, Stuart	159, 162
Hamrit, Jacqueline	262
Handler, Dan (a.k.a. Lemony Snicket)	250
Hardy, Oliver	185
Harrison, Jane	226
Haugaard, Erik Christian	71
Hawthorne, Nathaniel	201-205, 207, 211-214, 216, 217
Hazlitt, William	108, 110
Heath, Theresa	XII

INDEX OF NAMES

Hefner, Hugh	235, 237
Heinlein, Robert	XIII
Hellman, Eric	212
Hemingway, Ernest	230, 257, 258, 271
Hensler, Karl Friedrich	153
Hentzner, Paul	103
Hesiod	66
Hoffa, Jimmy	234
Hoffmann Ernst Theodor Wilhelm	26
Hogarth, William	108, 110, 111
Holbrook, Victoria	26
Holmyard, Eric John	120
Horace	119
Horowitz, Glenn	188
Homer	66
Howard, Richard	137
Hughes, Merry	113
Hull, R. C. F.	33, 302
Hurston, Zora	XIII
Hutchins, Robert	96
Huysmans, Joris-Karl	31, 32, 216
Hyman, Stanley Edgar	224
Iakovelev, N. V.	223
Iglehart, L. T. Jr.	257
Il'in, Sergei	11
Ivanov, Georgii	229
Jacobson, Roman	98
Jaggi, Maya	16
James, Henry	XIV, XVII, 25, 203
Jannelli, Altagracia de	255-258
Johnson, Samuel	107, 108, 113, 147
Johnson, Donald Barton	XIX, 49, 53, 84, 196, 202, 189
Joukovsky, N. A.	104, 106, 114, 298, 307, 308
Joyce, James	XIV, 227, 228, 242, 245, 253, 255, 256
Juliar, Michael	5, 76
Jung, Carl G.	33
Kafka, Franz	88
Kahane, Eric H.	78
Kakinuma, Nobuaki	269
Kant, Immanuel	113, 119, 278
Karabchevsky, Nikolai	97, 282, 283
Karlinsky, Simon	21, 61, 223, 224
Karpovich, Michael	98
Kazan, Elia	79

INDEX OF NAMES

Keats, John	180
Kerensky, Alexander	98
Kerouac, Jack	XV, 83
Kharms, Daniil	XIV
Khodasevich, Vladislav	76, 221, 222, 253, 282, 284
Kidd, Chip	158, 178
Kiely, Robert	201, 202
Knapp, Shoshana	227, 228, 302
Knopf, Alfred A.	30
Kolpakova, N. P.	36
Koltsov, Aleksey	282
Konishi, Masataka	271
Konstantin, Grand Duke	153
Korf, Barton M. A.	154
Kramer, Hilton	219
Kubrick, Stanley	165, 175, 185, 262
Küchelbecker, Wilhelm	153
Kulischer, Evgenii	97-99
Kundera, Milan	XV
Kuridenier, Julie	28
Kuzmanovich, Zoran	VIII, XVIII, 277, 302
Lamb, Richard	242
Lahouge, Jean	XV
Lalande, Joseph Jérôme le Français de	115n61
Latham, R. E.	115, 303
Latimer, Bonnie	113
Laurel, Stan	185
Leblanc, Maurice	24
Lee, Robert	207
Leibniz, Gottfried	113, 118, 119
Lerenbaum, Miriam	115, 119
Lermontov, Mikhail	XIV, XVI, 281-284
Lessl, Thomas	159-160
Levinas, Emmanuel	54
Leving, Yuri	XVI, 1-3, 9, 74, 79, 81, 84-88, 90-94, 162, 177, 196, 197, 231-237, 239-250, 265, 271
Lewin, Jane E	159
Lewis, Richard	203
Lichtenstein, Roy	83
Lillymans, W. J.	33, 303
Lingis, Alphonso	54
Lodge, David	26
Logan, Joshua	XIII
Lomonosov, Mikhail	282
Lonyay, Carl	157
Lotman, Iurii	269

317

INDEX OF NAMES

Love, Robert	XIX
Lowell, Robert	282
Loyd, A. L.	88
Luauté, Jean-Pierre	270
Lubin, Peter	12
Lucretius, Titus	115, 117-119, 121
Lyne, Adrian	XIX, 177
Lyon, Sue	165, 166
Lyons, John	123
Lyuksemburg, A. M.	196, 303
MacIntyre, C. F.	210
Mack, Maynard	108, 109, 113, 115, 120
MacLean, Hugh	225-228
Maguire, Robert A.	40
Makovsky, Sergei	79
Malcom, Donald	254
Malenkov, Georgy	130
Malamud, Bernard	XIII
Malikova, Maria	XVI, 2, 4, 6, 7, 9, 10, 14, 223, 267, 270
Mallarme, Stephane	210, 211, 215
Malmstad, John E.	40
Man, Paul de	49, 58, 59
Mandelshtam, Osip	282, 291, 292, 294
Manguel, Alberto	179
Mann, Thomas	16, 30, 35
Manning, Susan	202, 203, 207, 212
Marguez, Humberto	179
Marshak, Samuel	XII, 100
Martinez, Juan	XVI
Marvell, Andrew	106
Matskevich, Lydia	91
Matthew, Nicole	158
Mayakovsky, Vladimir	XIV
McCarthy, Mary	125, 126, 146, 149, 253
McDiarmid, Hugh	229
McMillin, Arnold	XVII, 16, 25
Medlock, Maya	264
Meilah, Mikhail	11
Melville, Herman	XIX, 212
Merezhkovskii, Dmitrii	289
Meyer, Priscilla	XVI, XVII, 16, 25, 121, 196, 197, 199, 214, 239-250, 279
Millan, C. G.	210, 303
Milton, John	106, 113
Minchnic, Helen	224
Mirrlees, Hope	226

INDEX OF NAMES

Mirsky, Prince Dimitri Petrovich Svyatopolk	218-229
Miura, Shoko	XII
Monroe, Marilyn	230, 274, 275
Moody, Nickianne	158, 307
Moore, Edward C.	211
Moreau, Gustave	29-31
Morgan, Joanne	183
Moudrov, Alexander	XVII, 60-73
Mozart, Wolfgang Amadeus	284, 285
Munroe, Alexandra	83
Myers, Terry	76
Nabokov, Dmitri	12, 21, 50, 51, 60, 76, 178, 180-182, 184, 185, 187-189, 191, 220, 233, 235, 265, 273, 282, 288
Nabokov, Elena Ivanovna	88
Nabokov, Evgeni	IX
Nabokov, Hélène (a.k.a. Sikorsky, Elena Vladimirovna)	183
Nabokov, Véra (née Slonim)	XIX, 21, 78, 79, 88, 177, 184-187, 233
Nabokov, Vladimir Vladimirovich (a.k.a. Sirin)	V, IX-XIX, 1-16, 18, 20-27, 30, 32-34, 36-41, 43, 45-58, 60-79, 83-128, 134, 135, 139-141, 143, 147-154, 156-175, 177-189, 191, 193-199, 201-205, 207-217, 219-250, 261-264, 270-272, 274-296
Nabokov, Vladimir Dmitrievich	97, 98, 191
Nafisi, Azar	XIX, 177, 274, 280, 306
Naiman, Eric	26, 306
Nakata, Akiko	264, 266
Nazaroff, Alexander	251-254
Nedbal, Martin	28
Nekrasov, Alexandr	226, 227
Nekrasov, Nikolay	282
Nepomnyashchy, Catharine	XII, 264
Newman, Charles	50
Newton, Arvin	202
Newton, Isaac	122
Nijinska, Bronislava	211, 306
Nijinska, Irina	211, 306
Nijinsky, Vaslav	210-212, 215
Nikolev, Andrei	7
Nivat, Georges	15, 24, 25
Nora, Pierre	88
Norfleet, Barbara	35
Numano, Mityoshui	268-270
Norman, Will	15
Noves, Laura de	214

INDEX OF NAMES

Odoevsky, Vladimir	XIV
Okudzhava, Bulat	282
Opochinin, Fyodor	153
Orlow, Damon	45
Pamuk, Orhan	2, 15-20, 23, 26, 27
Pares, Sir Bernard	228
Parker, Stephen Jan	199, 226
Pasco, Allen H.	33
Pater, Walter	215
Paul, Keegan	30, 33
Payne, Lewis	137, 138, 144
Pellerdi, Marta	XVII
Perkins, Maxwell	258
Pertzoff, Peter	76
Peterson, Dale E.	16, 25, 49, 50, 69, 278
Petipa, Marius	210
Petrarca, Francesco	214
Petrarch	183
Philips, Angus	158
Philips, Rodney	89
Picasso, Pablo	128-134, 144, 147, 130
Pierre-Louis, Mathieu	29-31
Pifer, Ellen	266, 270
Plato	60-73, 278
Plus, Raoul	30, 31
Plimpton, George	79
Podhoretz, Norman	187
Poe, Edgar Allan	26, 60, 202, 208, 262, 278, 279
Polanski, Roman	275
Ponomareva, Tatiana	XVII, 74-77, 79, 81, 83-89, 91-94
Pope, Alexander	102-123
Popper, Karl	63
Porte, Joel	204, 205
Portinari, Beatrice	214
Praxiteles	202, 205, 212
Preminger, Otto	183
Prévost, Abbé	152
Probyn, Clive T.	108
Proffer, Carl R.	181, 215
Proffer, Ellendea	181
Prokofiev, Sergei	X
Proust, Marcel	29, 60, 245
Pushkin, Alexander	2, 6, 7, 10, 16, 20, 36, 60, 77, 99, 100, 106, 120, 152-154, 156, 157, 186, 220, 223, 224, 229, 269, 279, 281-285, 287, 291-296
Putin, Vladimir	181

INDEX OF NAMES

Pyle, Robert Michael	161
Pym, Barbara	111
Pynchon, Thomas	165
Quennell, Peter	20, 108-110, 111
Quincey, Thomas de	114
Rachmaninoff, Sergei	X
Raguet, Christine	XVII, XIV, 239-250
Rampton, David	XVIII, 239-250
Rancour-Laferriere, Daniel	30, 36
Rand, Ayn	XIII, 234
Rawlinson, Jean	211
Reading, Amy	165, 167
Reagan, Katherine	XVIII, 74, 75, 77, 79, 81, 83-94
Redon, Odilon	28-33
Reeve, C. D. C.	66
Reeves, James	105
Reni, Guido	212
Richardson, Samuel	152
Richter, Anne	199
Rimbaud, Arthur	32, 33
Roshchin, Mikhail	229
Robbe-Grillet, Alain	6, 165
Robinson, Spider	XIII
Rogers, Pat	113
Ronen, Omry	235
Rosen, J. H.	31
Rosenbaum, Ron	178, 182-184
Rosenfeld, Hellmut	30
Rosetti, Dante Gabriel	215
Roth, Philip	XIII, 230
Rowe, W. W.	38
Rudolph, Crown Prince	156, 157
Rukavishnikov, Vasily Ivanovich	183
Rurik	218
Sade, Marquis de	54
Saege, Mitsunori	267
Saintsbury, George	105, 106
Salieri, Antonio	284
Schakovskoy, Zinaida	78
Scheiner, Corinne	XVIII
Schiff, Stacy	XIX, 177, 185-187, 239-250
Schiff, Stephen	XIX, 177
Schlegel, Karl	49, 58
Schlesinger, Arthur	234

INDEX OF NAMES

Schuman, Samuel	XVIII, XIX, 266, 271, 278, 280
Sciacca, Franklin	XVIII, 28
Screpel, Henri	33
Scribner, Charles	257
Searle, John	114
Shakespeare, William	IX, XIII, 2, 70, 113, 119, 194, 195, 197-199, 223, 224, 239, 240, 271
Shapiro, Gavriel	30, 69, 87, 191
Shaw, Bernard	289
Sheldon, Richard	197
Shelly, Percy Bysshe	212
Shield, Brooke	274
Shklovsky, Viktor	197
Shrayer, Maxim	XI, XII, 264, 267
Shukshin, Vasilii	36, 309
Shute, Jenefer	61, 309
Shvabrin, Stanislav	281
Simpson, Orenthal James	188
Sitwell, Edith	108
Sklyarenko, Alexey	16
Smeets, Bert	162
Smith, Anne	108
Smith, G. S.	219-221, 225, 226
Smith, Zadie	2
Socrates	62-69, 71-73, 161
Sokolov, Y. M.	36
Somov, Konstantin	289
Soshkin, Evgeny	3, 162
Specter, Michael	167, 309
Spectorsky, Auguste	237
Spencer, Terence	70, 309
Spenser, Edmund	112, 113
Stalin, Joseph	219
Steiner, George	216
Stephen, Leslie	113, 119
Stern, Ernest	XVIII
Sterne, Lawrence	245
Stevenson, Robert Louis	26
Stringer-Hye, Suellen	XIX, 177, 178, 180-182, 184, 185, 187-189, 191
Struve, Gleb	78, 79, 220, 228, 229, 253
Sugihara, Sara	17
Sugimoto, Kazunao	264
Sweeney, Susan Elizabeth	210, 216, 262, 268, 270
Swift, Jonathan	105
Swinburne, Algernon Charles	216

INDEX OF NAMES

Tammi, Pekka	121, 291-296
Taranovsky, Kiril	121, 291, 292
Taylor, Charles	159, 160, 166
Taylor, Gary	88
Thompson, George	XVII
Thulin, Oscar	30
Tiernan O'Connor, Katherine	16
Tilloston, Geoffrey	107, 108
Timenchik, Roman	XVI, 8
Toffler, Alvin	230-238
Toffler, Heidi	231-234, 236
Toffler, Karen	232
Toker, Leona	XIX, 11-13, 49, 201
Tolstoi, Ivan	197
Tolstoy, Leo	XVI, 16, 20, 21, 39, 98, 226, 227, 278, 288, 294
Tredennick, Hugh	62
Troyat, Henri	154
Turgenev, Ivan	16, 20, 23, 228, 292
Tyutchev, Fyodor	224, 225, 281-283
Ugrinsky, Alexej	16
Updike, John	2, 20, 36, 240
Vaginov, Konstantin	7
Veidle, Vladimir	288
Verlaine, Paul	216
Vickers, Graham	273-276
Vigneau, Jean	263
Vonnegut, Kurt	248
Voronina, Olga	208
Vries, Gerard de	XIX, 102-123, 125
Wakashima, Tadashi	263, 266
Weekes, A. R.	105
Weil, Irwin	XX, 99
Wheelock, John Hall	258
White, Duncan	15
White, Edmund	2, 83
Whitfield, Frances J.	218
Whitman, Walt	XIII, XV
Wilde, Oscar	XVII, 215
Williams, Rowan	19
Wilson, Andrew Norman	19
Wilson, Edmund	20, 21, 61, 63, 79, 99, 100, 202, 223, 224
Wilson, John	223
Wilson, Jay	76

INDEX OF NAMES

Wolfe, Thomas	257, 258
Wood, James	242
Wood, Michael	4, 105, 111, 122, 125, 209, 262, 268, 272
Woodson, Thomas	202
Woolf, Virginia	242, 245
Wordsworth, William	240
Xenophon	69
Yevtushenko, Yevgeny	36
Yoder, R. A.	29, 311
Young, David	183
Zanganeh, Lila Azam	17
Zeschky, Jan	291-296
Zhdanov, Ivan	153
Zhukovsky, Vasily	282, 283
Zimmer, Dieter	XV, 4, 162
Zunshine, Lisa	102, 110, 210

www.ingramcontent.com/pod-product-compliance
Lightning Source LLC
Chambersburg PA
CBHW071359300426
44114CB00016B/2123